Politics and History in Central Asia

Series Editor
Timur Dadabaev, University of Tsukuba, Tsukuba, Japan

In the past few decades, Central Asia has drawn the attention of academic and business communities as well as policy professionals because of its geostrategic importance (being located between Russia and China and in close proximity to Afghanistan, Pakistan, Iran, Turkey, and India), its international stability, and its rich energy resources. The region also faces challenges, such as post-conflict peacebuilding, impacts of the Afghan conflict, a number of recent inter-ethnic conflicts, and post-Socialist development paradigms. Approaching the problems and issues related to this region requires a multi-disciplinary perspective that takes into account political science, international relations, political economy, anthropology, geography, and security studies. The Politics and History in Central Asia series serves as a platform for emerging scholarship on this understudied region.

Susanne Fehlings

Traders, Informal Trade and Markets between the Caucasus and China

palgrave
macmillan

Susanne Fehlings
Frobenius-Institut
Frankfurt am Main, Germany

Politics and History in Central Asia
ISBN 978-981-19-5204-3 ISBN 978-981-19-5205-0 (eBook)
https://doi.org/10.1007/978-981-19-5205-0

This Palgrave Macmillan imprint is published by the registered company Springer Nature Singapore Pte Ltd.
The registered company address is: 152 Beach Road, #21-01/04 Gateway East, Singapore 189721, Singapore

Praise for *Traders, Informal Trade and Markets between the Caucasus and China*

"Dr. Fehlings' book is an important step towards a historical economic anthropology of everyday economic action, because she succeeds excellently in making this everyday action transparent in its diversity and its historical plasticity."

—Werner Plumpe, *Professor of Economic History, Goethe University, Germany*

"Why and how do Georgian and Chinese traders travel across Eurasia without any formal institutional support and what consequences are there of such 'globalization from below' for economy, markets, sociality and materiality?

Susanne Fehlings' ethnography skilfully explores the structural conditions, background and everyday lives of such traders and businessmen, scrutinizes their activities, narratives and logics of action and offers a rich anthropological discussion embedded in historical, legal and political contexts. "

—Lale Yalçın-Heckmann, *Docent for Social Anthropology, University of Pardubice, Czech Republic*

Contents

Note on Language

For the different languages I used different systems for transliteration.

- For Cyrillic into Latin characters the ISO 9 (1995) system, except for established writings of names (e.g., Cherkisovsky Rynok) and the term "chelnoki".
- For Georgian into Latin characters, with the help of Zakharia Pourt-skhvanidze, the ISO 9984 system, except for established writings of names and places.
- For Armenian into Latin characters the ISO 9985 system.
- The Chinese characters are copied from the characters used in literature.

List of Figures

List of Tables

CHAPTER 1

Introduction: Markets, Trade, and the Study of the Post-Soviet Economy

> I have not come here to see big buildings. I have not come here to breathe this air. I have come here to do business. This is why we are all here. This is what we do, and we work well. May our business be successful.
>
> —A Georgian trader's drinking toast

In a broad sense, this is book is a study of long-distance traders who travel throughout Eurasia, focusing on businesspeople from the Caucasus and China who work in local bazaars in Tbilisi, Georgia, and Beijing. Their activities, their motivations, their backgrounds, the environments, and their interactions with one another constitute its subject.

I got interested in this topic when I first encountered traders in the trains traveling through Russia, Ukraine, Central Asia, and the Caucasus. Traveling days and nights together in a shared train compartment creates intimacy. After the train leaves the station, one puts on one's pajamas, taps boiled water from the compartment's public samovar, shares chicken and cake, and naturally integrates into a community of destiny, sharing anxieties and hopes about border controls and everything else. On these trips, space and time melted away for me, swamped by boredom, fatigue, and the rhythm of the rails. The journey may be limited and relationships fleeting, but the person sitting and sleeping alongside one feels close. It feels as though they will sit and sleep there forever.

S. Fehlings, *Traders, Informal Trade and Markets between the Caucasus and China*, Politics and History in Central Asia,
https://doi.org/10.1007/978-981-19-5205-0_1

It was in this context of fleeting landscapes and the smell of travelers' food, squeezed between luggage and trade goods, that I became fascinated by traders' stories and adventures, as well as intrigued by the confidence with which they managed their business—sometimes for little more than survival. I was impressed by their flexibility, their readiness to risk everything they had, and their mutual cooperativeness. The idea of doing research while traveling, spending days and nights with people who could not escape my questions—anthropological fieldwork made easy—was appealing. I realized soon enough how foolish this romantic methodological fantasy was, but I remained fascinated by the topic that had inspired it.

The research on which this study is based was conducted in the context of a project funded by the Volkswagen Foundation entitled "Informal Markets and Trade in Central Asia and the Caucasus." This book is thus the outcome of individual research and analysis within that framework, and at the same time the product of an on-going engagement with the research results of all members of the overall project, including both young and senior researchers from Armenia, Georgia, Germany, Kazakhstan, Kyrgyzstan, Pakistan, and Switzerland, with backgrounds in social and cultural anthropology, history, area studies, and/or economics.[1] The focus of our joint research was on commercial activities and exchanges by individual entrepreneurs—sometimes described as micro-entrepreneurs (Maloney, 2004)—which are not underground and (at least partly) unregulated by state institutions. We were thus interested in what Hart (1973, 1992), Sassen (2001, 2006) and others have described as "informal economic activity," which on the global level has been conceptualized as "globalization from below" (Mathews et al., 2012; Portes, 1997).

In *Globalization from Below: The World's Other Economy* (2012), Gordon Mathews, Gustavo Lins Ribeiro, and Carlos Alba Vega take issue with the idea that globalization is usually initiated and managed by powerful actors, arguing that empirical evidence shows that much international trade and exchange starts "from below." They describe "globalization from below" as an anti-hegemonial world system and reject the categorical condemnation of "informal practices" as illegal.

[1] Project members: Yulia Antonyan, Meiirzhan Baitas, Susanne Fehlings, Hasan H. Karrar, Ketevan Khutsishvili, Hamlet Melkumyan, Zviad Mirtskhulava, Arman Mussin, Ana Ramazashvili, Philippe Rudaz, Aigerim Sarsenbayeva, John Schoeberlein, and Gulniza Taalaibekova.

The traders described in this book can be perceived as typical agents of "globalization from below". They profit from so-called globalization from above—from trade agreements and established infrastructures—but use personal networks and individual (so-called informal) strategies to cross borders and to run their businesses.

In post-Soviet studies the topic of "informality" was in fashion when our research group started our research. The most popular readings have been *Russia's Economy of Favours* (1998), *How Russia Really Works* (2006) and *Can Russia Modernise?* (2013) by Alena Ledeneva, *Informality in Eastern Europe* edited by Hayoz and Giordano (2013) and *Informal Economics in Post-Socialist Spaces* by Morris and Polese (2014). In 2018 Ledeneva published two volumes of a "Global Encyclopaedia of Informality," which contain a whole section devoted to "informal entrepreneurship". Indeed, the link between "entrepreneurship", "small-scale trade" and "informality" has been a major concern of many studies of development and transition in national economies (Williams & Round, 2007; Williams et al., 2009, 2012).

Globalization from below and the notion of informality coined by Keith Hart in 1973 apply to a wide variety of practices, associated with diverging contexts and circumstances, but there are benefits to using these broad notions and contrasting them with their opposites, the "formal" sphere and "globalization from above," because they provide a vocabulary that is understood beyond the discipline of anthropology. As argued by Ngo and Hung "commonly used concepts such as this allow easier access for a broader audience and create space for new vocabularies to develop as inquiry progresses" (Ngo & Hung, 2018: 179; Ngo, 2015: 47).

Contrasting formality and informality is useful in discussing at least three major themes: first (1), the relationship between state regulation and anarchic individual non-state structures; second (2), moral evaluations; and third (3), the opposition between formality and culture.

First, (1) the state is usually imagined as an ideal entity corresponding to Max Weber's (1985 [1921]) definition of "rational-legal government" and its legal bureaucracy. In this sense, the state is interpreted as an impersonal, whereas "informality" refers to behavior, practices, and ideas that are not part of this supposedly neutral mechanism. The "formal economy" is thus state-regulated, while "informal economy" is not. This assumption inevitably leads to contradictions: In a widespread post–Cold War understanding, state economies usually fall under the rubric of "market economy." This assumption is quite astonishing if one thinks of the market as a regulatory mechanism (the invisible hand) in contrast to government interference, as was originally argued by Adam Smith (2002 [1776]), the father of neoclassical economics. But market economies usually appear in the guise of national (state) economies (Hart, 1986, 1992), which is why states and formality are identified with the "market principle."[2] This nexus, which does not receive much attention in Western discourse, is very present in post-Soviet societies, where the state, state ideology, and the economic system are perceived as the same thing. In the past, the state apparatus was communist; today, it is neoliberal, which for many people does not seem to make any difference. The state is still the state.

However, in this post-Soviet context, informality is frequently presented as a relic of the sick Soviet system or as a transitional phenomenon that must be overcome to catch up with modernity. It is simultaneously presented as a last resort of the poor and identified as the reason why economies fail to develop and grow (see Chapter 2). By contrast, in line with the so-called Mandeville paradox[3] (Mandeville, 1989 [1714]; see Dumont, 1977), *formal* market economy is praised for its potential for development, economic growth, and fairness. If a national economy is not working as it should, politicians and economists consequently hold the people "sticking to their personal networks and traditions" responsible, as is happens frequently in Georgia.

The second theme is (2) the moral evaluation of the above-mentioned oppositions. Practices, behavior, motivations, institutions, and relations are judged, by academics as well as by policy makers and local people, as moral or immoral, fair or unfair, legal or illegal, good or bad, and effective or ineffective. In the academic realm, one can find many discussions of the link between formality, informality, and moral economy (in economic history research, see, e.g., Fontaine, 1996, 2014: 95–127; Palomera/Vetta, 2016). Citing Karl Polanyi's *The Great Transformation* (1944) and Paul Bohannan and George Dalton's *Markets in Africa* (1962), researchers in the substantivist-formalist debate of the 1960s

[2] As shown by Polanyi in *The Great Transformation* (1944) and as summarized by Gudeman and Hann "the heyday of liberalism in the nineteenth century was made possible only through the interventions of states [...]" (2015: 15).

[3] Mandeville's paradox is named after Bernard de Mandeville, who argued that vicious actions of individuals may turn out to be good for society as a whole.

discussed the role of moral obligations in economic behavior, but in academia and beyond, the formality-informality dichotomy has become a dispute over what is moral and immoral in ethical terms. This has implications for the understanding of "moral economy". "[T]he idea of moral economy has been increasingly popular in the social sciences ... given a confusing variety of meanings and [is] sometimes invoked as an empty symbol" (Carrier, 2018: 18; cf. Hahn, 2018). In the tradition of the historian Thompson (1971) and the anthropologist C. Scott (1977), "moral economy" was earlier perceived as an economic activity rooted "in the mutual obligations that arise when people transact with each other over the course of time," distinguishing "between the moral values that are the context of economic activity and those that arise from the activity itself" (Carrier, 2018: 18), but nowadays, "moral economy" is often associated with a moral critique of neoliberal capitalism.

The state is usually mistrusted in the Caucasus (see Chapter 4). However, in the context of the formality-informality debate and economic success and failure, the formal state remains an imaginary ideal linked to modernity and progress. Consequently, even though informal practices are a contemporary phenomenon that seems to be expanding, informality is often treated as backward (or, less negatively, "traditional") in official or public discussion of the nation-state and the market economy (as an idea).

The consequent next step from equating informality with tradition is to equate tradition with "local culture," and thus culture with informality. This concludes in the third theme: (3) the opposition of formality and culture, which sometimes leads to a negative assessment of culture. This happens if culture is perceived as the opposite of modern behavior and civilization, contrasting global with local standards, rationality with social behavior, neutrality and professionalism with kinship, and the explicable with the inexplicable. Thus, for example, the Kyrgyz custom of bringing gifts of expensive carpets to funeral ceremonies having been identified as the cause of the indebtedness of many Kyrgyz households, the Kyrgyz government promulgated a law prohibiting it, leading to further debate about the dangers and benefits of cultural traditions (Beyer, 2016). Similarly, in Georgia, my interlocutors themselves often claimed that their and their compatriots' "sociocultural attitude" was detrimental to "welfare and happiness." The feasting ritual called the *supra*, which follows strict rules and involves the lavish consumption of food and wine (Mühlfried, 2006, 2007), was thus sometimes said to exemplify a Georgian mentality that prefers feasting to working. Some Georgians are even convinced that "traditional practices" like these hinder progress and are an obstacle to something they call civil society (Mühlfried, 2014).[4]

Descriptions of everyday manifestations of the state, like those by Gupta (1995, 2012), Fuller and Harris (2001) or Luong (2004) exemplify the fact that the Weberian state is an illusion. Studies of state institutions (public schools) in Central Asia, such as that by DeYoung, Reeves, and Valyayeva (2006), show that many so-called formal procedures would not work absent agency or interpretation. There certainly is a line between effective and ineffective and socially beneficial and harmful informal practices. Kandiyoti (2003) and Rasanayagam (2011), who studied social relations in Uzbekistan, and Iskandaryan (2014), Stefes (2008), Christophe (2005), and Di Puppo (2004), who analyze political structures in the Caucasus, argue that some states or governments were/are entirely constructed around informal networks that they call "mafia-like," which my interlocutors also did when talking about criminal networks in Georgia under Eduard Shevardnadze (1995–2003).

To grasp these complexities, all investigators of the research group parsed their studies into three interrelated fields of inquiry: (1) economic practice, (2) interaction with institutional frameworks, and (3) the importance of social and cultural value dynamics in the economy. Besides sharing hypotheses concerning these research fields and their interrelation, the methodology of the individual researchers converged at three points, enabling comparison between the different subprojects: (a) the research sites, (b) the sources, and (c) the methods of investigation were similar. Data on small and medium entrepreneurs in Central Asia, the Caucasus, and across Eurasia more broadly, on trade routes, as well as in border markets, flea markets, and bazaars, were analyzed as a rule according to classical methods in social and cultural anthropology (see Fig. 1.1).[5]

We met regularly to discuss the research data and to consult with the Ph.D. and M.A. students who got funding from the project. Between

[4] In Georgian folklore, when God was distributing the land, the Georgians, who had been drinking and feasting, came too late, and no land was left. The Georgians told God that they had been feasting in his honor, however, and He rewarded them with a piece of his personal garden. Thus, in the end, the *supra* mentality proved beneficial, which raises issues in economic anthropology such as gift exchange, reciprocity, and moral economy.

[5] For a detailed description of the project see Fehlings and Karrar (2016).

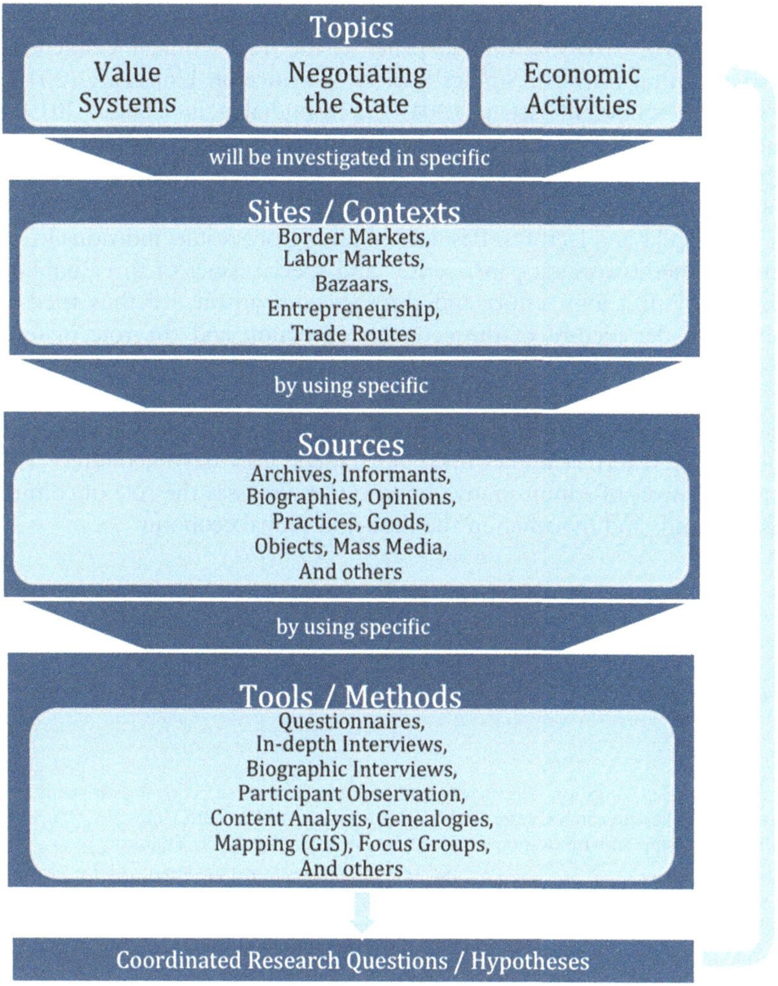

Fig. 1.1 Schematic overview of the overall project

2016 and 2019, we organized three workshops in Germany and Georgia (2014, 2016, 2018), a double panel at the 17th Annual Conference of the Central Eurasian Studies Society at Princeton University (2016), a summer school in Astana (2017), a roundtable in Tbilisi (2019),[6] and participated in an event funded by the Volkswagen Foundation in Almaty (2018).[7] We visited one another's research fields, did research together, organized a photo exhibition (2019),[8] and presented our results in public talks and lectures. Besides publishing our results individually, we put together a working paper series[9] and special issues of three publications.[10] With a joint effort and through comparison, we thus tried to get a broader picture of the economic situation and the role of local marketplaces and trade in the post-Soviet periphery. This book is only one attempt to contribute to this endeavor. It aims at describing the traders' practices as an example of globalization from below, discusses the relationship between formal frameworks and traders' everyday encounters with representatives of administrative bodies, and discusses the role of cultural backgrounds and dynamics in the local and global economy.

[6] Roundtable/Workshop organized by Philippe Rudaz in cooperation with the Economic Policy Research Centre, Fribourg University and Ilia State University: "Survival, Entrepreneurship and Innovation in the Caucasus," 23 May 2019, Tbilisi.

[7] Status Symposium organized by the Volkswagen Foundation: "Between Europe and the Orient—A Focus on Research and Higher Education in/on Central Asia and the Caucasus," 16–17 April 2018, Almaty, Kazakhstan.

[8] Photo Exposition in cooperation with Tbilisi Photo Festival and Fabrika: "Entrepreneurs on the New Silk Road: Photographs of Small Businesses in the Caucasus and Central Asia," Tbilisi.

[9] The "Informal Markets and Trade Working Paper Series" is produced by the project on "Informal Markets and Trade" with the support of a grant from the Volkswagen Foundation's funding initiative "Between Europe and the Orient—A Focus on Research and Higher Education in/on Central Asia and the Caucasus." ISSN: 2510–2826; Goethe University (UB) "Working Paper Series on Informal Markets and Trade," http://publikationen.ub.uni-frankfurt.de/solrsearch/index/search/searchtype/series/id/16223.

[10] *Caucasus Analytical Digest* (2017), *Anthropological Research* (Tbilisi, 2018), and *Central Asian Survey* (2020).

Marketplaces and Long-Distance Trade in Anthropology

The Caucasus, Central Asia, and China are traditionally links in the Silk Road and long-distance Eurasian trade. In popular accounts, contemporary traders are frequently presented as the successors of traders who in past centuries travelled across the region on foot or camelback, loaded with valuable cloth, gems, perfumes, spices, and other precious goods. But much more than the ancient or medieval past, recent history visibly impacts the present economic, social, and political situation—and the traders' lives. Soviet domination and influence have altered the landscape, reshaped the economic system, and impacted the make-up of societies. It has left its footprints in the convictions and attitudes of the people, who lived under Soviet rule and with Soviet ideology for more than seventy years. This rule and ideology, among other things, put an end to many, although by no means all, of the commercial practices that used to be associated with Silk Road trade.

However, within the Soviet Union, Caucasians retained their reputation as skilled traders. Like Jews, they were known for maintaining informal (and also illegal) trade links and for providing Moscow with agricultural produce (Sik & Wallace, 1999). Nevertheless, even though "under the Soviet command economy, trading was one of the most important activities" (Skvirskaja, 2019), it was only after the end of the Cold War, the dissolution of the Soviet Union, and the reform era in China that the bazaar trade fully re-emerged and expanded throughout the region. Made possible by the introduction of a liberal market economy and the opening of borders, this became an acceptable way to make a living in the troubled early 1990s. In the Caucasus, those years were marked by conflict and war (e.g., the Russian-Georgian conflict, the Chechenian and the Karabakh wars) and the negotiation of new power relations in which the United States, the European Union, Iran, Turkey, the Russian Federation, and the People's Republic of China have either remained or become important players.

These days, petty traders selling their goods—and sometimes their personal belongings—were part of the picture on streets, in bazaars, and at almost any bus or railway station, airport, or border crossing in post-Soviet Eurasia. This has led to a proliferation of open-air markets and bazaars in Russia, the post-Soviet periphery and neighboring countries. These bazaars became pivotal and still predominate in the circulation of goods, although challenged in recent years by modernization campaigns and new shopping malls (Fehlings & Karrar, 2016). Such marketplaces can teach anthropologists a lot, not only about economics, but also about political, social, and other aspects of everyday life in local and global Eurasian settings.

In economies, "a market is not a place, but a situation in which a good is supplied by some (sellers), demand by others (buyers), and the value (price) of that good is determined by decisions of all buyers and sellers" (Plattner, 1989: 102). "A market" or "the market" is an abstraction, whereas a "marketplace" is "an actual physical meeting place" with, "social, economic, cultural, political and other referents" (Belshaw, 1965: 8; see Bohannan & Dalton, 1962). Anthropologists, given their theoretical leanings and methodological practices, have predominantly explored the latter in their fieldwork (Endres, 2018). Most of these studies have been conducted in peasant or agrarian societies, such as those of Redfield in Mintz in Haiti (1961), and Firth in Polynesia (1939).

Studies of marketplaces have foregrounded different aspects. For Bohannon and Dalton (1962), they were places of social interaction—for meetings, feasts, rituals, political control, juridical activities, and communication. Thus, markets are often studied as public spaces and spaces of—sometimes unexpected—encounters (see, e.g., Black, 2012; Dines, 2007; La Pradelle, 2006; Watson, 2009). Mintz (1957, 1961) was interested in gender, stocking functions, and the long-term exchange relations of integration (*pratik*) of marketplaces in Haiti. Herskovits (1938) explored the relation between marketplaces, state organization (kingdoms), and bureaucracy (taxation) in Dahomey in West Africa. Bourdieu (2001 [1998]) describes the Moroccan souk as a locus of masculinity. Geertz (1978) refers to the bazaar in Sefrou in Morocco as a "bazaar economy." Gell (1982) interprets the marketplace as a site of symbolic representations mirroring the sociocultural order of society, reflecting local cosmology.

These studies, based on dense ethnographic descriptions, usually link the economic activities of individual actors to specific sociocultural settings structured by local rules of conduct, social relationships (networks), and economic aspirations. This is true even of those anthropological studies that focus on the bastions of liberal market economy and high finance, like Hertz's (1998) ethnography of the Shanghai stock market or Zaloom's (2006) study of the trading floors of the London and Chicago financial futures markets. This interest in social and cultural aspects results from the recognition that "capitalists must have not only knowledge and skills, but sentiments and desires that enable and incite them to engage in particular kinds of productive activities" (Yanagisako, 2002: 13).[11]

Yet marketplaces are not just influenced by their environment. They equally shape and change it. As noted by Hahn, "the appearance of new goods on the market", for example "often marks the beginning of new social relationships and may even be regarded as an expression of radical cultural change" (2018: 3). Keeping this dialectic in mind, in this book, I explore both the individual biographies of traders in marketplaces viewed as sociocultural systems and the linkages between marketplaces, traders, and broader economic, political, and social contexts. I look at the marketplace as a *fait social total,* as defined by Mauss (1968, 2015) and use it as a tool to discuss a wide range of questions related to post-Soviet and other societal contexts.

How markets can give access to the study of society is exemplified in Alfred Gell's (1982) research, which shows how the materiality and spatial outline of a marketplace in India can be interpreted as a map of the local hierarchies and the relationships between different tribes in a district. Gell thereby also points to the importance of temporal aspects of markets. The periodicity of a marketplace, for example, can be revealing of its position in a broader territorial, political and social constellation.[12] Yet temporality, as I approach it in this book, is less a matter of the periodicity of markets than of the developments of local contexts and the often turbulent trajectories of individual marketplaces. The markets I studied reflect and shape the societies in which they are embedded. At the same time, they are linked to other wholesale and resale markets in China and in post-Soviet Eurasia. They are integrated into global commodity and supply chains, which connect different people from across the globe, such as those for tuna and matsutake mushrooms described by Bestor (2001) and Tsing (2015). Like the markets, these chains, dependencies, and links change over time, which impacts the traders' practices and travel routes.

I classify the traders travelling and trading goods between marketplaces in Eurasia as long-distance traders. Long-distance trade, as a concept, is

[11] See Marsden (2016: 2).

[12] Compare, e.g., Davis (1977) on Mediterranean market, Hahn (2019) on West African markets, Mikesell (1958) and Benet (1957) on North African markets, or Gregory (1997) on Indian markets.

usually associated with ethnographic examples from West Africa, especially with the Hausa and their trading networks as described by Cohen (2004 [1969]). Scholarship on African markets contrasts "long-distance trade markets" with "local markets." While local markets are linked to villages and cities, according to Saul (2018), long-distance trading markets do not have such links and emerge a considerable distance from settlements. They are related to itinerant traders who move between these markets according to a market calendar that couples specific market days with specific locations. According to Hahn (2019), long-distance trading markets and local markets differ in their spatial organization, their position within market networks, their catchment area, their gender composition, trading activity, the daily routines, the merchandise, the clients, clients' demands, and the use of money. In this book, I look at different types of markets and their characteristics. However, for me, long-distance trade is not defined through distinguished forms of markets, but rather through specific trading activities of specific groups of traders. These activities and groups of traders can be found among other practices and groups in one and the same marketplace. In Eurasia, long-distance trade is a question of mobility. The traders from China and the Caucasus with whom I did research usually went on business trips for two or more weeks, crossed one or more borders, experienced alien places, and had to interact with strangers. This is not about itinerant trading and traders going from marketplace to marketplace according to some market calendar, but about journeys to more or less alien terrain, to places thousands of kilometers away, and about a branch of trade that has emerged and changed since the early 1990s.

Generally speaking, marketplaces are associated with social and ethnic heterogeneity (Sprenger, 2017). In intertribal or so-called border markets all over the world, goods are exchanged between different social groupings, ecological regions (mountains and lowlands), and rural and urban dwellers. Trade "operates by making a profit from the differences between the state of affairs in one place and that of another and this means that traders, almost by definition will infringe boundaries between regionally defined units" (Humphrey, 2002: 96–97). Because it is in marketplaces that individuals of different backgrounds come together, it is there that conflicts are judged and settled. This is true of the Caucasus, Central Asia, and China's Eurasian borderlands, historic regions "comparable to one another not least because of the ways in which they are defined by internal heterogeneity, political fluidity, and forms of mobility and trade that bind their diverse populations together" (Marsden, 2016: 22). Indeed, the investigation of the balance of intersecting oppositions being part of local polity (Davis, 1977) is an interesting endeavor for anthropologists when it comes to the description of grassroots interactions between traders, middlemen, consumers, officials, and other market actors in these regions. In long-distance trade, however, these interactions occur in a different environment. Here, traders work beyond their local settings. They are literally away and interact with people, who are not their neighbors, but "real strangers". Although traders are used to mobility and are familiar with most of the trade routes and practices along these routes, long-distance trade in Eurasia thus, despite all technological innovations, has maintained some of the adventurous aspect associated with the trading expeditions along the medieval Silk Road. Long-distance trade carries with it risks and hardship, but also a hope that one will come across Ali Baba's cave.

Post-Soviet Markets and Their Background

This study looks at many different marketplaces and their interconnections, but three are central to it: Yabaolu Market (Ябаолу, 雅宝路) in Beijing (Chapter 2); Lilo Bazroba (ლილოს ბაზრობა) on the outskirts of Tbilisi (Chapter 3); and the Chinese Hualing Sea Plaza Market (Hualingi Tbilisis Zġvis Plaza, ჰუალინგი თბილისის ზღვის პლაზა) in a new Chinese-built quarter in Tbilisi (Chapter 5).

Lilo Bazroba has a common history with many other bazaars that emerged across the territory of the former Soviet Union in the early 1990s. Over time, these bazaars have developed into transnational wholesale and retail trading points (Dyatlov & Grigorichev, 2015; Fehlings & Karrar, 2016; Humphrey & Skvirskaja, 2009). Having an ambivalent standing within the societies in which they materialized, they are often criticized for not meeting modern standards and for representing the dark side of capitalism, namely, poverty. Quite frequently, bazaars in post-Soviet Eurasia are associated with crises. At the same time, capitalism, the "modern economy" in many post-socialist countries, was first experienced in the form of bazaars merchandise. Even today, much of the merchandise available across the Caucasus and in Central Asia is sold in bazaars. They believe that they are setting trends and are aware of the fact that they are the ones through whom their clients access not just goods but global lifestyles.

The emergence and expansion of Yabaolu Market in Beijing is tightly linked to the development and the fate of bazaars in post-Soviet territories. Yabaolu (among other marketplaces in China) is a place where post-Soviet bazaar traders—including Lilo Bazroba's traders—buy their merchandise. It lies at the opposite pole of the trade route, within the segment of the commodity chain I discuss here.

Hualing Sea Plaza Market, the new Chinese-run market in Tbilisi, by contrast, is the outcome of massive Chinese foreign investment in recent years, promoted as "The New Silk Road Initiative," which has been altering market structure, the flow of goods, and the dependencies and power relations within existing networks and global commodity chains (cf. Gereffi et al., 2003). Although Hualing Sea Plaza Market has a completely different background, it shares a lot of commonalities with, and links to, markets such as Lilo Bazroba and Yabaolu.

What is unique about these markets, and why did bazaars like Lilo Bazroba, Yabaolu Market, and Hualing Sea Plaza Market emerge in these post-socialist locations? Why have they not emerged (or at least not to such an extent) in developed (Western) capitalist economies? "Medieval trade fairs developed to link trade across politically divided regions and borders, and they seem to have flourished best at places where caravan routes intersected and a nearby city provided protection," Humphrey and Skvirskaja (2009: 66) note, drawing an analogy between them and post-Soviet bazaars. This corresponds with the ethnographic and historical data from Africa mentioned above and with current Silk Road narratives (Karrar, 2018), as well as with historical evidence from the region:

> Markets and bazaars were always very important not only for economic reasons, but also as important meeting places in the system of peaceful coexistence in the Caucasus. They were established in certain places that were more appropriate for the representatives of various groups to meet for exchange (of goods, information, knowledge, etc.). These kinds of places were situated near crossroads or main trade routes. Traditionally, marketplaces were parts of settlements, but some of them (larger ones) were also situated a certain distance from settlements but on connecting routes. (Khutsishvili, 2018: 41)

Usually, the introduction of Soviet planned economy put an end to such market structures.

In Europe, most bazaars perished even earlier, "in the nineteenth century with the development of regularized international trading, banking, insurance, and reliable communication, all of which reduced the popularity of face to face transactions" (Humphrey & Skvirskaja, 2009: 66, citing Allix, 1922; Braudel, 1979). This development in Europe could be read as a consequence of a gradual "formalization" of different realms of life. In times of crisis and of political instability, however, trade fairs re-emerged. This happened, for example, after the breakup of the East and Central European empires and in the context of political instability in the wake of World War I.

Generally, it is a lack of state control and crisis that are seen as factors promoting the development of bazaars and the social structures they are associated with. This is why the informal aspects of such markets and trading are so prominent in the academic debate on post-Soviet economies:

> The literature on commodity fairs suggests that they flourished when, on the one hand, free trade across borders was not made impossible by warfare and when transaction costs where not prohibitively raised by the need for protection, and, on the other hand, when political conditions created barriers and hampered the smooth generalized operation of banking and insurance, when travel was still relatively insecure (necessitating caravans or their equivalents), and people of different cultures were mutually mistrustful, even though they wanted to trade with one another. (Humphrey & Skvirskaja, 2009: 66)

These assumptions have a certain compelling logic, but my observations suggest that the causes are more complex. Although many of the reasons and preconditions for the emergence of bazaars described above seem to fit the post-Soviet case well, it is difficult to say how much regulation prevents the existence of bazaar trade. Is there a limit? What does political division mean in a globalized world? How much risk are traders ready to take on before perceiving it as insecurity? How much trust is needed? And at what point does mistrust become a limiting factor? As my findings in this book reflect, although there is a general trend toward formalizing economic exchange in almost all post-Soviet republics, bazaars seem to be resilient. Political division, even in a globalized world, structures traders' logistics and pathways, as this book shows. Equally, economic activities in so-called informal markets are highly dependent on choices that are based on assessments about how much a relationship can be trusted.

Throughout my fieldwork, I noted conditions that either enabled trade or hindered it, with bazaars themselves changing over time. Today's bazaars, although they are still called and recognized as bazaars, are not the same as those of the 1990s. For example, while today's markets may be less chaotic or informal, they may be perceived as chaotic or informal in comparison to, for example, new shopping malls. How can one measure them if one has no yardstick? The descriptions in this book try to capture these dynamics. The main question stimulating the analysis it therefore, not why things happen, but how.

Markets and Trade in Post-Soviet Economies

The dynamics one can observe in marketplaces in post-Soviet Eurasia are often explained as a response to the Soviet heritage, the transition period,[13] and the responses and developments of post-Soviet regimes. Indeed, the Soviet era has left a deep imprint on Eurasian societies and has created a space, which is commonly referred to as post-Soviet. Academics, dealing with this space, including anthropologists are, accordingly, often assigned to post-Soviet studies and sometimes—like myself—fail to engage with current concepts and theories that are being developed and used in other parts of the world and are discussed in social and cultural anthropology or the social sciences more broadly. In some respects, post-Soviet studies seem often to lag the latest developments and are accused for not generating new theories or not contributing to current debates. To some degree this is surprising, because many findings could provide new impulses and raise new questions in, for instance, the study and understanding of economic processes.

Several topics that have extensively been investigated by anthropologists working in post-Soviet Eurasia and China (and Vietnam), and which might be of general interest to economic anthropologists and other specialists, have been listed by Hann (2005). These include social inequalities, residential segregation, property relations, continuity and change in the informal economy, gift exchange, gender relations, the ritual economy, the role of elites and the significance of kin and friendship

[13] Which is a highly contested notion.

networks and "trust" in everyday life. Furthermore, Hann foregrounds studies of the moral dilemmas of entrepreneurship, and the changing patterns of money use, markets, and consumption. For Hann, postsocialism is "an instructive setting in which to revisit classical issues in economic anthropology, to open up some new ones and to reflect on the relationship between the disciplines." This is so, because "neoliberal orientations grounded in rational choice models that assume utility-maximizing individuals as agents have failed to provide adequate predictions and descriptions of this so-called 'transition.'" As a consequence, there is a need for anthropological research offering "more realistic analyses which engage with the embeddedness of the economy, recognise the complexity of decision taking, and the impossibility of changing values and assumptions overnight" (Hann, 2005: 555). Meanwhile, there is a growing body of literature focusing on exactly this research agenda. Among the first and most popular ethnographic works on post-Soviet economies were those by Verdery (1996), Humphrey (1983, 2002) and Hann. This research in part explicitly focuses on Soviet and post-Soviet markets and trade, the volume edited by Mandel and Humphrey (2002) being probably the best-known publication.

Researchers specializing in the study of Soviet and post-Soviet markets have explored (a) border markets and cross-border trade, often subsumed under the label of so-called border studies. Recent such works have been authored by Dabaghyan and Gabrielyan (2011, 2014), Holzlehner (2014), Humphrey (2017, 2018), Karrar (2020; Karrar & Mostowlansky, 2018), Khutsishvili (2016), Lehti and Romashov (2021), Rippa (2019) and Yalçın-Heckmann and Aivazishvili (2012). Other anthropologists investigated (b) open-air markets, spontaneous forms of commercial activity like street vending, and local bazaars, discussing, for example, retail or wholesale markets, container markets, flea markets, or so-called ethnic markets. Geographically, these studies often concentrate on Siberia (Дятлов & Григоричев, 2015; Григоричев & Дятлов, 2017; Григоричев & Тимошкин, 2019; Grigorichev et al., 2019), Central Asia (Alff, 2015, 2016; Karrar, 2017, 2018, 2020; Nasritdinov, 2006; Spector, 2017), Eastern Europe and Russia (Venkov, 2022; Wielecki, 2015), and the Caucasus (Amiryan & Kalantaryan, 2019; Melkumyan, 2017; Rekhviashvili, 2015).

While one part of the ethnography spotlights the actual marketplace, the other part is interested in (c) the people working in or linked to these commercial areas: similarly to classical anthropological studies by, for example, Geertz (1963) and Stewart (1992), or new works by Harris (2013a, 2013b) and Marsden (2016), this analysis focuses on the merchants and traders, their activities, their sociocultural backgrounds and motivations, their networks, trade routes and mobility patterns. For example, they describe specific forms of trade, like the shuttle trade (Holzlehner, 2014; Konstantinov, 1996; Nyíri, 2007), or social networks linking producers, traders, and consumers (Marsden, 2016, 2018; Steenberg, 2016, 2018; Yalçın-Heckmann, 2014).

Long-distance trade as defined above (d), has been given little attention in post-Soviet studies. There is some literature on the shuttle trade and trade tourism, which mainly is about cross-border trade, including only little and nearby mobility. The works on Afghan and Tajik traders' networks by Marsden and Ibañez-Tirado (2020), on Kyrgyz traders' activity in Siberia and China by Schröder (2020), and on Tajik traders coming to Dubai by Stephan-Emmrich (not yet published) figure among the exceptions. Yet long-distance trade not only offers new insights into so-called transition and post-transition, in my opinion, but also engages with questions relevant and debated beyond post-Soviet studies. Besides economic topics, it touches, for example, on the topic of mobility discussed in migrant and diaspora studies. Relatedly, it speaks to concerns about transnationalism, translocality, and globalization, mirrored in, among other things, infrastructure, and trading routes and networks. It enables one to recognize the enmeshment of narratives and infrastructures of globalization and global interconnectedness, which, in the region, are commonly bundled together under the Silk Road imaginaries (Karrar, 2018; Rippa, 2018) as the idea of interconnectedness between East and West through ancient caravan trails. China's twenty-first-century reinterpretation of globalization processes, which I discuss in Chapter 5, explicitly refers to this idea. Discussing my ethnographic materials, I try to relate to big questions, although I approach these questions from below/from the point of view of actors. I focus on everyday practices, personal relationships, and local concepts that shape the bazaar trade and small entrepreneurship.

Fieldwork and Data Collection

My research on markets and trade was done in the framework of the aforementioned research project funded by the Volkswagen Foundation between 2014 and 2019. My fieldwork conducted in this context took place over a bit more than six months in all and was split into several research periods, ranging from three weeks to up to two and a half months. I was thus able to build upon previous long-term fieldwork in the region. Since 2003, I have variously studied, lived, and conducted research in Bishkek (Kyrgyzstan), Moscow (Russia), Simferopol (Crimea), Baku (Azerbaijan), Yerevan (Armenia) and Tbilisi (Georgia) for periods ranging from several months to more than a year. I was thus able to contextualize my new data and to paste it into a broader picture. At the same time, as part of a bigger project, I also had use of the data and insights of my team colleagues for comparative analysis. Together, we were able to cover thirty years of bazaar and trade history by comparing data from a range of bazaars and marketplaces in Central Asia and the Caucasus.

Studying markets and trade requires flexibility and mobility. I adopted a mixed approach. To get an overview of local bazaars, I visited them regularly, observed the activity there, talked to traders and consumers, and started to describe and map the locations. It is in the bazaar where everything comes together in one place—goods, people, and stories. It is here that thick description reveals thick materials, which point into many directions, and which took me to other places and topics related to trade, such as relevant formal institutions and related activities. Starting from here I traced back the traders' travel routes, which took me to Beijing. Business is a field with an atmosphere that is sometimes hostile. In my previous research, I had experienced the enthusiasm of my local interlocutors, who seemed happy to share their practices, knowledge, and opinions. The traders who are central to this book, in contrast, were not at all eager to talk about what they do and did not like to be observed. Traders distrusted one another and equally distrusted me as an outsider.[14] People would rather talk about their deepest religious beliefs or sexual troubles

[14] Since I had told my interlocutors that the study was being paid for by the Volkswagen Foundation, I was suspected of working for Volkswagen. Perceptions of me as a researcher—my growing up, getting married, and becoming a mother—have doubtless also changed over the years. Furthermore, I did not fit their concept of an anthropologist. Few laypeople see "something as ordinary as trade" as an interesting aspect of culture and worthy of being investigated. In the post-Soviet understanding, ethnographers are supposed to write about "traditions" and to collect drinking toasts and information on costumes and customs like the ethnographer Shurik, a well-known character in the 1967 Soviet film *Kidnapping, Caucasian Style* (Кавказская пленница), who embodies this stereotype.

than about how much their merchandise had cost. Building a relationship of trust with a small group of traders whom I met regularly over the years was thus a major, time-consuming challenge. Thanks to the networks and assistance in Georgia of my colleague and Ph.D. student Zviad Mirtskhulava', I was able to join a group of Georgian traders on a business trip to China that was a key experience for me. It was the basis of a close relationship to people through whom I entered the world of long-distance trade, and through whose perceptions, assessments, explanations, and opinions I was able to make sense of information I got from other traders in the bazaar.

Still, I must admit that I was never totally at home in this male domain. The business activity and the marketplaces I observed never really appealed to me, either in Georgia or in China. I was shocked by the masses of plastic goods I saw in Beijing and the mindless consumption in the Caucasus. Think of what this does to our world and environment sickened me. Unlike many of my colleagues, I had trouble empathizing with many of my interlocutors and what they did. Still, I must say that I deeply respect the Georgian and Chinese businesspeople, who struggle to feed their families. Their labor may be more honest than that of an anthropologist.

Much of the traders' business activity takes place outside of the bazaar. Goods are produced, ordered, transported, declared, registered, and so on. Traders travel, choose merchandise, keep accounts, maintain business contacts abroad, deal with institutional frameworks, and organize their lives. To get an overall understanding of the local trading business I visited places like customs terminals and other administrative buildings and talked to people, whose work and activities were directly or indirectly linked to the business of traders. My interlocutors can be clustered into four groups: (1) my local friends, acquaintances and colleagues, from whom I got random information, (2) traders working in local bazaars in Tbilisi—some of whom travel to China—and their Chinese counterparts in Beijing, (3) Georgians who work for formal or semi-formal institutions and/or mediate between formal institutions and traders (market administrations, credits experts, bank employees, customs officials, lawyers), and (4) Georgians working for Chinese in Georgia. Most of my interviews were conducted in Russian, the lingua franca of Georgian-Chinese business. Some conversations, especially with bank and credit experts, took place in English, while my colleague Zviad translated others from Georgian to Russian or English.

Although we had developed a kind of topic guide and defined some core questions with the research team, most of my interviews were open conversations. Since recording, in this context, was inappropriate, I took notes on a traditional notepad or typed some keywords into my cell phone, which helped me remember what had happened and been discussed. It is difficult to say how many interviews I did. Spending a day together, people say a lot of interesting things, and much of my material is the fruit of long work days. Other data are not directly related to the bazaar or traders but to everyday life as I witnessed it by simply being there, interacting with other social beings and managing my own living in this societal context. Of course, there were also some more formal situations, such as the roughly thirty meetings in which I "interviewed" an official, a representative of a cargo company, or a bank manager. There were many conversations, too, in which I started by introducing myself as an anthropologist. My fieldwork thus involved a variety of different situations and contexts, to which I adapted my methods and which I used to approach the topic of markets and trading from different angles.

Every evening, I wrote down my observations and recapped the conversations I had had during the day. As aide-mémoires, I also used photographs and short videos taken with my phone. Later, I discussed some of these materials with the traders or with my local friends, with students to whom I read lectures at the Ivane Javakhishvili State University in Tbilisi, and with colleagues, who would give me their interpretations and add to the data. An extremely close, and for me beneficial, cooperation developed with my Armenian colleague Hamlet Melkumyan and my Georgian colleague Ketevan Khutsishvili. Both probably know my materials much better than I do myself. Equally, Hasan H. Karrar was a close and reliable companion throughout the whole project in many respects. My interpretations are thus the result of continual reflection on and conversations about the data and an on-going writing process. When absent, I kept in touch with my friends and partners through WhatsApp, Facebook, and email and followed the local news. During the on-going project, all our research team members including myself published some of their findings. Reactions to public talks, our photo exhibition, and our first written texts provided me with some valuable feedback from within and beyond the region. An extremely nice experience in this process was the positive reaction of the traders to whom I showed our first results published in a blog. In the texts, names of almost all individual actors are anonymized for obvious reasons.

A small set of quantitative data, which is now open access,[15] was collected in the course of our project in four surveys by Philippe Rudaz and Philippe Rudaz, Ana Ramazashvili, and Zviad. The first survey, on Dordoi Bazaar in Bishkek (Kyrgyzstan), was conducted in summer 2017; the second survey, on Lilo Bazroba in Tbilisi (Georgia), in winter 2016/17, the third and fourth survey, on Kara-Suu in Osh (Kyrgyzstan) and on Barakholka in Almaty (Kazakhstan), in summer 2018. Each included three hundred respondents, who answered to short questionnaires on entrepreneurial activity in the bazaar. The questionnaire included the core questions we had developed as a research team. To guarantee the authenticity of the answers, the questions were asked orally and inserted into the questionnaires by the researchers using the "Google form app." Excel tables were then created from the data, prepared and published for statistical analysis using software called "R." This analysis led me to check and compare some of my qualitative data and to carve out differences between the situation in the Caucasus and Central Asia.

Structure and Argument of the Book

The book is divided into five chapters, each of which focuses on a specific aspect of trade. The chapters complement each other and together provide a description and analysis of the local economic environment in the Caucasus and of so-called Chinese-Georgian business. The "fundamental interconnectedness of all things" (Adams, 1987) structures the book, which as a result includes a series sub-sections, cross-references, and some overlapping. However, I hope to propitiate the reader with clear ethnographic descriptions, which, I believe, are amusing, sometimes confusing, and seemingly contradictory, but at the same time express serious matters. In each chapter I discuss the relevant theories and literature and try to suggest models reflecting my methodological and theoretical conclusions.

The second chapter after this introduction (first chapter) is ethnographic. It gives insights into the development of small-scale long-distance trade between post-Soviet countries, the Caucasus, and China. It starts with a description of the activity of the so-called *chelnoki* (челноки) (suitcase-traders, or trade tourists), who pioneered the market economy

[15] The raw data is available at Havard Dataverse: https://dataverse.harvard.edu/dataverse/entrepreneurship_eurasia (accessed 20 March 2022).

and international trade in Eurasia in the early 1990s. The *chelnoki* and their situation are then compared with the new generation of traders, who are referred to as *biznesmeny* (бизнесмены; ბიზნესმენი). The term *biznesmen* encompasses a whole spectrum of entrepreneurs, including some very poor and some very rich, who started to do business in the post-Soviet sphere. Here, I focus on bazaar traders dealing in Chinese merchandise, some of whom travel to Beijing regularly.

After having portrayed the evolution of bazaar trade since the 1990s, I turn to the current situation and describe a business trip of contemporary bazaar traders to China. This account is based on my aforementioned trip with a group of traders from Lilo Bazroba to Yabaolu Market in Beijing. The case study describes the Chinese marketplace and reflects the perspectives of four individuals, three Georgians and a Russian, three men and one woman. Three of them started their businesses in the 1990s, one of whom belongs to the younger generation.

Analyzing the data, I come to several conclusions that concern the practices, motivations, and networks of Georgian traders: (a) traders' motivations are linked to family and kinship obligations, and profits are usually put into housing; but (b) these traders usually base their business on contacts other than those linked to kin networks. These other relationships develop while doing business—on the one hand between other travellers and fellow post-Soviet traders within and outside the own ethnic group, on the other, between post-Soviet and Chinese businesspeople. These relationships, even though they are conceptualized in local terminologies, have a very specific content and context. Long-distance trade creates a reality, a "culture" of its own, which encompasses complex social contexts, relations and interactions, codes of conduct, and moral judgments—and an ideology that partially contradicts local sociocultural paradigms and formal institutional frameworks.

Chapter 3 discusses why local bazaar traders do not formalize their businesses according to official and Western standards. It describes the broader local economic field in the Caucasus and explains different aspects of Caucasian *biznes* (бизнес), providing an overview of activities subsumed under that rubric and suggesting parameters that help classify economic activities and forms of small entrepreneurship. These parameters include (a) the location where business is done (ranging from public pavements to bazaars, shopping malls, and private spaces); (b) personal background (e.g., age, gender, education, personal skills, and ethnic and religious affiliation); (c) social networks along which business is organized (which may originate in the criminal sphere, in local networks conceptualized as friendship, brotherhood, ethnic community and kinship, or in the interaction within business activities); (d) the mobility of traders, (e) the goods that are traded, and, finally, (f) the amounts of goods and capital, means of transportation, and the frequency of the activity.

Ideology is another parameter that must be considered, embracing ideas, beliefs, and values. Ideology, parameter (g), is an integral part of the sociocultural setting, and, among other things, provides the framework within which economic activity is assessed. I suggest considering three overlapping value systems, which together constitute a set of ideas. These value systems respectively relate to (1) local society, culture, and cosmology, (2) Soviet ideology, and (3) the neoliberal market economy. Which of these value systems is taken as the point of reference depends on the context, situation, and the actors involved.

By giving detailed descriptions of all these parameters and their combinations, I depict the variety of the local businesses' environment, or ecology. I define the place of long-distance and bazaar trade within the local social hierarchy and socioeconomic context, which, again, results from a specific entanglement of the aforementioned parameters. I visualize this entanglement by adapting Alexander von Humboldt's *Naturgemälde*, an attempt to reflect on the organic causalities between different factors composing an environment. These causalities create specific niches, which constitute the ecosystems of specific kinds of trade. Forms of trade and entrepreneurship linked to these niches can be viewed as sophisticated adaptations, which do not work in other niches or contexts. Normative definitions of entrepreneurship thus do not capture local realities, especially those of bazaar traders. This is also why these traders do not formalize and/or meet the expectations linked to the Western definition of entrepreneurship associated with innovation and the discovery and exploitation of opportunities, described as "one of the primary drivers of industrial dynamism, economic development, and growth" (Carlsson et al., 2013: 913). Chapter 3 thus reviews a variety of themes related to the economic activity of the traders studied and of the Caucasus in general. Above all, it describes the position of bazaar and long-distance traders within a broader local economic system.

The picture of the economic environment is of course incomplete, if one ignores the formal institutional framework, described in Chapter 4. In my experience, traders in general interact with the state only (a) when they have to deal with banks or credit institutions, (b) when they cross borders at border posts and customs posts, (c) when paying taxes, and (d) when legal problems arise.

The local institutional frameworks significantly transformed after Georgia's independence, especially after the 2003 "Rose Revolution" and Mikheil Saakashvili's reforms. These changes, which were initiated in the sphere of politics, resulted in formalization processes, which in Georgia have been accompanied and accelerated by the digitalization of many formal procedures. My examples show how traders cope with and assess the current situation. Petty and bazaar trade are economic spheres, which, in the Caucasus, as elsewhere, are associated with informal practices. As described in Chapters 2 and 3 of this book, the latter are to a high degree based on personal relationships, oral contracts, and face-to-face interactions. They take place in locations that are at the margins of formal control, and involve trading volumes that are considered irrelevant by the state. However, the Georgian government has taken measures to regulate the activity of traders classified as Small and Medium/Mid-sized Enterprises/Entrepreneurs (SMEs). In cooperation with national and international microfinance institutions, it has undertaken reforms to provide assistance to develop the SME sector, subject to clear formal requirements. Traders are reluctant to adjust to these requirements, however, and do not properly comply with them as officially mandated. There are different reasons for this, one being that traders do not have sufficient capacity and resources to meet official standards of creditworthiness, for example. Another reason is that many SMEs have difficulties filling out the complicated administrative paperwork. To overcome these obstacles, traders often turn to intermediaries or brokers (such as private credit agencies, lawyers, or cargo companies), who bridge the gap between the formal administrative sphere and the informal sphere of the bazaar and bazaar trade.

In comparison to traders in other post-Soviet countries, Georgian traders comply quite well with state regulations. But they do so through interim solutions, which usually create buffer zones between the impersonal machine of the formal state apparatus and personalized and negotiable interactions with individuals. The relationship between traders and state institutions is characterized by expectations and mistrust on both sides. Discussing the attitudes of Georgian citizens to the state, bureaucracy, and legislation in general, and of Georgian traders, in particular, I in conclusion assess the state from an SME perspective.

Chapter 5 draws attention to a very new development and presence in the Caucasian market environment. After having introduced post-Soviet Caucasian long-distance traders who travel to China and described the so-called Russian Market in Beijing and the local business environment in Georgia in detail, in this chapter, I now turn to Chinese entrepreneurs, who have started to come to Georgia to do business in the Caucasus. Given my background, I approach Chinese from the "Georgian perspective". This thus might say more about the perception of Chinese than about real Chinese activities.

Unlike in other parts of the world, Chinese presence is a relatively new phenomenon in the Black Sea region. Here, three groups of people represent Chinese interests: First, individual, relatively poor Chinese traders, who have begun to work in Georgian marketplaces; second, big investors, the most important one being embodied in the Xinjiang-based Hualing Group, which implements giant projects in Georgia, including the construction of housing areas, infrastructure, and marketplaces; and, third, representatives of Chinese state- owned companies, who come to the region as constructors of the so-called New Silk Road, the Belt Road Initiative (BRI) proclaimed by the PRC's president, Xi Jinping.

China-Georgia cooperation is promoted by both governments. Given its historic role as a trading hub, and centrally located at the crossroads between Asia and Europe, Georgia is an important infrastructural node on the China–Central Asia–West Asia Corridor of the PRC's New Silk Road. I describe the recent encounters between Chinese entrepreneurs and Georgian citizens on the ground and the impact of Chinese activity on local bazaar traders' business, discussing tensions and conflicts, but also partnerships and mutual understanding on different levels of social interaction. Functioning as cultural brokers, Georgian middlemen play an important role in this, helping Chinese businessmen from Xinjiang—Muslim Uyghurs—navigate the local business environment and mediating between Chinese and Georgian institutions and bureaucracies, communicating local codes of behavior in the fine line between formality and informality.

Since they have seemingly similar honor codes, Georgians and Chinese Uyghurs favor similar types of relationships, linked to comparable values. Georgian notions of friendship, which are used in or transferred to business contexts, for example, are compatible with Han Chinese and Uyghur equivalents, such as those captured by the Chinese concept of *guanxi* (关系; 關係). However, Chinese do not yet seem to be successful in acquiring clients, which is why local traders do not perceive them as a threat. Chinese-built and Chinese-run marketplaces in Georgia are still empty. How Chinese presence in the Caucasus will impact local business in the future remains an open question. Adopting C. K. Lee's concept of "encompassing accumulation", I suggest that Chinese (of different groups) create space for "achieving other types of return" (Lee, 2014) than direct profit from trade. These other types of return have to be analyzed from the perspective of Chinese economic and political ambitions on a global level, but can be observed in this specific local context.

In the book's Epilogue I briefly summarize my findings and offer a model of the culture-economy-state nexus of Georgian and Chinese traders' business environments as a complex and dynamic system of mutual dependencies, interrelations, influences, linking mechanisms, and distinctions. The two business cultures are presented as separate systems that are compatible when they are linked through exchanges in the Yabaolu Market or in Georgia. Traders in these two settings share a common interest in economic exchange and profit-seeking and are equally shaped by the global market, institutional frameworks, international agreements, state policies (e.g., like China's Silk Road Initiative), and by concepts originating in their respective local cultures. The model furthermore includes the different strategies of dealing with state institutions, thereby considering the role of mediators. Finally, I conclude with some general remarks and offer suggestions for future research.

References

Adams, D. (1987). *Dirk Gently's Holistic Detective Agency*. William Heinemann.

Alff, H. (2015). Profiteers or Moral Entrepreneurs? Bazaars, Traders and Development Discourses in Almaty, Kazakhstan. *International Development Planning Review, 37*(3), 249–267.

Alff, H. (2016). Markt unter Druck: Der Dordoi-Basar in Kirgistan unter dem Einfluss von Eurasischer Wirtschaftsunion und Wirtschaftskrise. *Zentralasien Analysen, 105*, 2–6.

Allix, A. (1922). The Geography of Fairs: Illustrationed by Old-World Examples. *Geographical Review, 12*(4), 532–569.

Amiryan, T., & Kalantaryan, S. (Eds.). (2019). *Firdus: The Memory of a Place*. CSN Lab.

Belshaw, C. S. (1965). *Traditional Exchange and Modern Markets*. Prentice-Hall Inc.

Benet, F. (1957). Explosive Markets: The Berber Highlands. In K. Polanyi, C. M. Arensberg & H. W. Pearson (Eds.), *Trade and Markets in the Early Empires*. Free Press.

Bestor, T. C. (2001). Supply-Side Sushi: Commodity, Market, and the Global City. *American Anthropologist, 103*(1), 76–95. https://doi.org/10.2307/683923

Beyer, J. (2016). *The Force of Custom. Law and the Ordering of Everyday Life in Kyrgyzstan*. University of Pittsburgh Press.

Black, R. E. (2012). *Porta Palazzo: The Anthropology of an Italian Market*. University of Pennsylvania Press.

Bohannan, P., & Dalton, G. (1962). *Markets in Africa*. Northwest University Press.

Bourdieu, P. (2001 [1998]). *Masculine Domination*. Stanford University Press.

Braudel, F. (1979). *Les jeux de l'échange (Vol. 2: Civilisation materielle, économie et capitalisme, XVe–XVIIIe siècle*. Livre Poche.

Carlsson, B., Braunerhjelm, P., McKelvey, M., Olofsson, C., Persson, L., & Ylinenpää, H. (2013). The Evolving Domain of Entrepreneurship Research. *Small Business Economics, 41*(4), 913–930.

Carrier, J. G. (2018). Moral Economy: What's in a Name. *Anthropological Theory, 18*(1), 18–35. https://doi.org/10.1177/1463499617735259

Christophe, B. (2005). Kultur der Korruption? Anmerkungen zur politischen Ordnung in Georgien. In B. Schröder (Ed.), *Georgien: Gesellschaft und Religion an der Schwelle Europas* (pp. 33–46). Röhrig Universitätsverlag.

Cohen, A. (2004 [1969]). *Custom and Politics in Urban Africa: A Study of Hausa Migrant in Yoruba Towns*. Routledge.

Dabaghyan, A., & Gabrielyan, M. (2011). Rural Transcaucasian Trade Before and After National Border. *Acta Ethnographica Hungarica, 56*(2), 333–357.

Dabaghyan, A., & Gabrielyan, M. (2014). On a Village Market at a South Caucasian Border. In A. Bobokhyan, L. Abrahamian & K. Franklin (Eds.), *Market Beyond Economy* (pp. 37–53). NAS RA "Gitutyun" Publishing.

Davis, J. (1977). Economic Anthropology of Mediterranean Societies. In J. Davis (Ed.), *People of the Mediterranean: An Essay in Comparative Social Anthropology* (pp. 17–72). Routledge.

DeYoung, A. J., Reeves, M., & Valyayeva, G. K. (2006). *Surviving the Transition? Case Studies of Schools and Schooling in the Kyrgyz Republic since Independence*. Information Age.

Di Puppo, L. (2004). Corruption as an Instrument of State Control in Georgia. *Berliner Osteuropa-Info, 21*, 47–54.

Dines, N. (2007). *The Experience of Diversity in an Era of Urban Regeneration: The Case of Queens Market, East London*. Fondazione Eni Enrico Mattei (FEEM).

Dumont, L. (1977). *From Mandeville to Marx: Genesis and Triumph of Economic Ideology*. University of Chicago Press.
Dyatlov, V., & Grigorichev, K. (2015). *Ethnic Markets in Russia: Space of Bargaining and Place of Meeting*. Publishing House of ISU.
Endres, K. W. (2018). Markets. In H. Callan (Ed.), *International Encyclopedia of Anthropology*. Wiley Blackwell.
Fehlings, S., & Karrar, H. (2016). Informal Markets and Trade in the Caucasus and Central Asia: A Preliminary Framework for Field Research. *Informal Markets and Trade Working Paper Series, 1*.
Firth, R. (1939). *Primitive Polynesian Economy*. Routledge.
Fontaine, L. (1996). *A History of Pedlars in Europe*. Duke University Press.
Fontaine, L. (2014). *The Moral Economy: Poverty, Credit, and Trust in Early Modern Europe*. Cambridge University Press.
Fuller, C., & Harriss, J. (2001). For an Anthropology of the Modern Indian State. In C. Fuller & V. Bénéi (Eds.), *The Everyday State and Society in Modern India* (pp. 1–30). Social Science Press.
Gaonkar, D. P. (2001). *Alternative Modernities*. Duke University Press.
Geertz, C. (1963). *Peddlers and Princes: Social Developments and Economic Change in two Indonesian Towns*. Chicago University Press.
Geertz, C. (1978). The Bazaar Economy: Information and Search in Peasant Marketing. *The American Economic Review, 68*(2), 28–32.
Gell, A. (1982). The Market Wheel: Symbolic Aspects of an Indian Tribal Market. *Man, 17*(3), 470–491. https://doi.org/10.2307/2801710
Gereffi, G., Humphrey, J., & Sturgeon, T. (2003). The Governance of Global Value Chains. *Review of International Political Economy, 12*(1), 78–104.
Gregory, C. (1997). *Savage Money: The Anthropology and Politics of Commodity Exchange*. Harwood Academic Publishers.
Grigorichev, K., Dyatlov, V., Timoshkin, D., & Bryazgina, D. (Eds.). (2019). *Bazaar and the City: People, Spaces, Images (Базар и город: люди, пространства, образы)*. Ottisk.
Gudeman, S. F., & Hann, C. (2015). Introduction; Ritual, Economy, and the Institutions of the Base. In S. F. Gudeman & C. Hann (Eds.), *Economy and Ritual: Studies of Postsocialist Transformations* (pp. 1–30). Berghahn.
Gupta, A. (1995). Blurred Boundaries: The Discourse of Corruption, the Culture of Politics, and the Imagined State. *American Ethnologist, 22*(2), 375–402. https://doi.org/10.2307/646708
Gupta, A. (2012). *Red Tape: Bureaucracy, Structural Violence, and Poverty in India*. Duke University Press.
Hahn, H. P. (2018). Introduction: Markets as Places: Actors, Structures and Ideologies. In H. P. Hahn & G. Schmitz (Eds.), *Market as Place & Space of Economic Exchange: Perspectives from Archaeology & Anthropology* (pp. 1–18). Oxbow.

Hahn, H. P. (2019). Rural Markets in West Afrika: What Criteria are Required for an Appropriate Description. *Weight and Value, 1*, 367–378.
Hann, C. (2005). Postsocialist Societies. In J. G. Carrier (Ed.), *A Handbook of Economic Anthropology* (pp. 547–557). Edward Elgar.
Harris, T. (2013a). *Geographical Diversions: Tibetan Trade, Global Transactions*. Universityof Georgia Press.
Harris, T. (2013b). Trading Places: New Economic Geographies across Himalayan Borderlands. *Political Geography, 35*, 60–68. https://doi.org/10.1016/j.polgeo.2012.12.002
Hart, K. (1973). Informal Income Opportunities and Urban Employment in Ghana. *Journal of Modern African Studies, 11*(1), 61–89.
Hart, K. (1986). Heads or Tails? Two Sides of the Coin. *Man, 21*(4), 637–656. https://doi.org/10.2307/2802901
Hart, K. (1992). Market and State after the Cold War: The Informal Economy Reconsidered. In R. Dilley (Ed.), *Contesting Markets: Analyses of Ideology, Discourse and Practice*. Edinburgh University Press.
Hayoz, N., & Giordano, C. (2013). *Informality in Eastern Europe: Structures, Political Culture, and Social Practices*. Peter Lang.
Herskovits, M. J. (1938). *Dahomey*. J.J. Augustin Inc.
Hertz, E. (1998). *The Trading Crowd: An Ethnography of the Shanghai Stock Market*. Cambridge University Press.
Holzlehner, T. (2014). *Shadow Networks: Border Economics, Informal Markets and Organized Crime in the Russian Far East*. LIT Verlag.
Humphrey, C. (1983). *Karl Marx Collective: Economy, Society and Religion in a Siberian Collective Farm*. Cambridge University Press.
Humphrey, C. (2002). *The Unmaking of Soviet Life: Everyday Economics after Socialism*. Cornell University Press.
Humphrey, C. (2017). Loyalty and Disloyalty along the Russian-Chinese Border. *History and Anthropology, 28*(4), 399–405. https://doi.org/10.1080/02757206.2017.1351356
Humphrey, C. (Ed.). (2018). *Trust and Mistrust in the Economy of the China-Russia Borderlands*. Amsterdam University Press.
Humphrey, C., & Skvirskaja, V. (2009). Trading Places: Post-Socialist Container Markets and the City. *Focaal: European Journal of Anthropology, 55*. https://doi.org/10.3167/fcl.2009.550105.
Iskandaryan, A. (2014). Formalization of the Informal: Statebuilding in Armenia. In C. Giordano & N. Hayoz (Eds.), *Informality in Eastern Europe: Structures, Political Cultures and Social Practices*, (pp. 451–484). Bern: Peter Lang.
Kandiyoti, D. (2003). The Cry for Land: Agrarian Reform, Gender and Land Rights in Uzbekistan. *Journal of Agrarian Change, 3*(1–2), 225–256.
Karrar, H. (2017). Do Bazaars Die? Notes on Failure in the Central Asian Bazaar. *Informal Markets and Trade Working Paper Series, 4*.

Karrar, H. (2018). The Silk Road Versus the Central Asian Bazaar: Two Thousand Years or Twenty-Five Years of Exchange and Mobility? *Anthropological Researches, IV*, 13–22.

Karrar, H. (2020). The Bazaar in Ruins: Rent and Fire in the Barakholka, Almaty. *Central Asian Survey, electronic preprint.*

Karrar, H., & Mostowlansky, T. (2018). Assembling Marginality in Northern Pakistan. *Political Geography, 63*, 65–74.

Khutsishvili, K. (2016). Across the Enguri Border: Lives Connected and Separated by the Borderland Between Georgia and Abkhazia. In T. Bringa & H. Toje (Eds.), *Eurasian Borderlands: Spatializing Borders in the Aftermath of State Collapse* (pp. 107–131). Palgrave Macmillan.

Khutsishvili, K. (2018). Market Infrastructure: Past and Present Transformations. *Anthropological Researches, IV*, 40–47.

Konstantinov, Y. (1996). Patterns of Reinterpretation: Trader-Tourism in the Balkans (Bulgaria) as a Picaresque Metaphorical Enactment of Post-Totalitarianism. *American Ethnologist, 23*(4), 762–782.

La Pradelle, M., & d. (2006). *Market Day in Provence.* University of Chicago Press.

Ledeneva, A. (1998). *Russia's Economy of Favours: Blat, Networking and Informal Exchange.* Cambridge University Press.

Ledeneva, A. (2006). *How Russia Really Works: The Informal Practices That Shaped Post-Soviet Politics and Business.* Cornell University Press.

Ledeneva, A. (2013). *Can Russia Modernise? Sistema, Power Networks and Informal Governance.* Cambridge University Press.

Lee, C. K. (2014). The Spectre of Global China. *New Left Review, 89*, 29–65.

Lehti, M., & Romashov, V. (2021). Suspending the Antagonism: Situated Agonistic Peace in a Border Bazaar. *Third World Quartely.* https://doi.org/10.1080/01436597.2021.1962274

Luong, P. J. (2004). *The Transformation of Central Asia: States and Societies from Soviet Rule to Independence.* Cornell University Press.

Maloney, W. F. (2004). Informality Revisited. *World Development, 32*(7), 1159–1178.

Mandeville, B. (1989 [1714]). *The Fable of the Bees.* Penguin Group.

Marsden, M. (2016). *Trading Worlds: Afghan Merchants Across Modern Frontiers.* Hurst & Company.

Marsden, M. (2018). Islamic Cosmopolitanism Out of Muslim Asia: Hindu-Muslim Business Co-Operation Between Odessa and Yiwu. *History and Anthropology, 29*(1), 121–139.

Mathews, G., Ribeiro, G. L., & Vega, C. A. (2012). *Globalization from Below: The World's Other Economy.* Routledge.

Mauss, M. (1968). *Die Gabe: Form und Funktion des Austausches in archaischen Gesellschaften.* Suhrkamp Verlag.

Mauss, M. (2015). *Schriften zum Geld* (H. P. Hahn, M. Schmidt, & E. Seitz, Eds.). Suhrkamp Verlag.
Melkumyan, H. (2017). Informality, Politics and Mutual Support in Flea Markets in Post-Soviet Armenia. *Informal Markets and Trade Working Paper Series, 5.*
Mikesell, M. W. (1958). The Role of Tribal Markets in Morocco: Examples from the "Northern Zone." *Geographical Review, 48*(4), 494–511.
Mintz, S. (1961). *Pratik: Haitian Personal Economic Relations.* Paper Presented at the 1961 Annual Spring Meeting of the American Ethnological Society, Seattle & Washington.
Mintz, S. W. (1957). Aspects of the Internal Distribution System in a Caribbean Peasant Economy. *Human Organization, XV, 2*, 18–23.
Morris, J., & Polese, A. (2014). *The Informal Post-Socialist Economy: Embedded Practices and Livelihoods.* Routledge.
Mühlfried, F. (2006). *Postsowjetische Feiern: Das Georgische Bankett im Wandel.* ibidem-Verlag.
Mühlfried, F. (2007). Celebrating Identities in Post-Soviet Georgia. In T. Darieva & W. Kaschuba (Eds.), *Representations on the Margins of Europe: Politics and Identities in the Baltic and South Caucasus States* (pp. 283–300). Campus Verlag.
Mühlfried, F. (2014). A Taste of Mistrust. *Ab Imperio, 4*, 63–68.
Nasritdinov, E. (2006). *Regional Change in Kyrgyzstan: Bazaars, Open-Air Markets and Social Networks.* Univeristy of Melbourne.
Ngo, T.-W. (2015). Asia and the Historicity of the Market Economy. *Verge: Studies in Global Asias, 1*(1), 44–50.
Ngo, T.-W., & Hung, E. P. W. (2018). The Political Economy of Border Checkpoints in Shadow Exchanges. *Journal of Contemporary Asia, 49*(2), 1–15. https://doi.org/10.1080/00472336.2018.1555273
Nyíri, P. (2007). *Chinese in Eastern Europe: A Middleman Minority in a Transnational Era.* Routledge.
Palomera, J., & Theodora, V. (2016). Moral Economy: Rethinking a Radical Concept. *Anthropological Theory, 16*, 413–432. https://doi.org/10.1177/1463499616678097
Plattner, S. (1989). *Economic Anthropology.* Stanford University Press.
Polanyi, K. (1944). *The Great Transformation: The Political and Economic Origins of Our Time.* Beacon Press.
Portes, A. (1997). Globalization from Below: The Rise of Transnational Communities. *WPTC-98-1.*
Rasanayagam, J. (2011). Informal Economy, Informal State: The Case of Uzbekistan. *International Journal of Sociology and Social Policy, 31*(11/12), 681–696. https://doi.org/10.1108/01443331111177878

Rekhviashvili, L. (2015). Marketization and the Public-Private Divide: Contestations Between the State and Petty Traders Over the Access to Public Space in Tbilisi. *International Journal of Sociology and Social Policy, 35*(7/8), 478–496.

Rippa, A. (2018). *Which Silk Road, and for Whom? Economic Corridors and the End of Proximity at China's Borders* [Unpublished manuscript].

Rippa, A. (2019). Cross-Border Trade and "the Market" Between Xinjiang (China) and Pakistan. *Journal of Contemporary Asia, 49*(2), 254–271.

Sassen, S. (2001). *Global Cities: New York, London, Tokyo*. Princeton University Press.

Sassen, S. (2006). *Territory, Authority, Rights: From Medieval to Global Assemblages*. Princeton University Press.

Saul, M. (2018). Markets in West Africa: Karl Polanyi, Or What Sort of Social Formation. In H. P. Hahn & G. Schmitz (Eds.), *Market as Place and Space of Economic Exchange: Perspectives from Archaeology and Anthropology*. Oxbow.

Schröder, P. (2020). Business 2.0: Kyrgyz Middlemen in Guangzhou. *Central Asian Survey, electronic preprint*. https://doi.org/10.1080/02634937.2019.1711023.

Scott, J. C. (1977). *The Moral Economy of the Peasant: Rebellion and Subsistence in South East Asia*. Yale University Press.

Sik, E., & Wallace, C. (1999). The Development of Open-Air Markets in East-Central Europe. *International Journal of Urban and Regional Research, 23*(4), 697–714.

Skvirskaja, V. (2019). New Trade Formations: Precarity, Pragmatic Cosmopolitanism and Long-Distance Trade in the Caucasus. *Global Networks, electronic preprint*, 1–17. https://doi.org/10.1111/glob.12267

Smith, A. (2002 [1776]). *An Inquiry into the Nature and Causes of the Wealth of Nations*. Chicago University Press.

Spector, R. A. (2017). *Order at the Bazaar: Power and Trade in Central Asia*. Cornell University Press.

Sprenger, G. (2017). Goods and Ethnicity: Trade and Bazaars in Laos from a Gift Perspective: A Discussion. *Heidelberg Ethnology, 6*, 1–31.

Steenberg, R. (2016). Embedded Rubber Sandals: Trade and Gifts Across the Sino-Kyrgyz Border. *Central Asian Survey, 35*(3), 405–420.

Steenberg, R. (2018). Accumulating Trust: Uyghur Traders in the Sino-Kyrgyz Border Trade After 1991. In A. Horstmann, M. Saxer, & A. Rippa (Eds.), *Routledge Handbook of Asian Borderlands* (pp. 294–303). Routledge.

Stefes, C. H. (2008). Governance, the State and Systematic Corruption: Armenia and Georgia in Comparison. *Caucasian Review of International Affairs, 2*(2), 73–83.

Stewart, M. (1992). Gypsies at the Horse Fair: A Non Market Model of Trade. In R. Dilley (Ed.), *Contesting Markets: An Analysis of Ideology, Discourse and Practice* (pp. 79–96). Edinburgh University Press.

Thompson, E. T. (1971). The Moral Economy of the English Crowd in the Eighteenth Century. *Past & Present, 50*, 76–136. https://doi.org/10.1093/past/50.1.76
Tsing, A. L. (2015). *The Mushroom at the End of the World: On the Possibility of Life in Capitalist Ruins*. Princeton University Press.
Venkov, N. A. (2022). Marketplace Decline Heads East: Neoliberal Reform, Socio-Spatial Sorting and Patterns of Decline at Sofia's Public Markets. In C. S. Sezer & R. v. Melik (Eds.), *Marketplaces: Movement, Representations and Practices*. Routledge.
Verdery, K. (1996). *What Was Socialism and What Comes Next?* Princeton University Press.
Watson, S. (2009). The Magic of the Marketplace: Sociality in a Neglected Public Space. *Urban Studies, 46*, 1577–1597.
Weber, M. (1985). Wirtschaft und Gesellschaft: Grundriss der verstehenden Soziologie. Tübingen: LCB Mohr.
Wielecki, K. M. (2015). *Coping with Uncertainty: Petty Traders in Post-Soviet Russia*. Peter Lang.
Williams, C. C., Nadin, S., & Rodgers, P. (2012). Evaluating Competing Theories of Informal Entrepreneurship: Some Lessons from Ukraine. *International Journal of Entrepreneurial Behaviour & Research, 18*(5), 528–543.
Williams, C. C., & Round, J. (2007). Entrepreneurship and the Informal Economy: A Study of Ukraine's Hidden Enterprise Culture. *Journal of Development Studies, 12*(1).
Williams, C. C., Round, J., & Rodgers, P. (2009). Evaluationg the Motives of Informal Entrepreneurs: Some Lessons from Ukraine. *Journal of Development Studies, 14*(1), 59–71.
Yalçın-Heckmann, L. (2012). Re-thinking Citizenship in the South Caucasus. *Europe Asia Studies, 64*(9), 1724–1738.
Yalçın-Heckmann, L. (2014). Informal Economy Writ Large and Small: From Azerbaijani Herb Traders to Moscow Shop Owners. In J. Morris & A. Polese (Eds.), *The Informal Post-Socialist Economy: Embedded Practices and Liveliyhoods* (pp. 165–186). Routledge.
Yanagisako, S. J. (2002). *Producing Culture and Capital: Family Firms in Italy*. Princeton University Press.
Zaloom, C. (2006). *Out of the Pits: Traders and Technology from Chicago to London*. University of Chicago Press.
Григоричев, К. В., & Дятлов, В. И. (2017). «Китайские» рынки России: Роль в постсоциалистической трансформации (случай Иркутска). *Вестник Томского Государственного Университета, 419*, 121–132. https://doi.org/10.17223/15617793/419/16

Григоричев, К. В., & Тимошкин, ДО. (2019). Базар в движении: Иркутский открытый рынок как точка концентрации мобильностей. *Регионалистика*, *6*(1), 26–39. https://doi.org/10.14530/reg.2019.1.26

Дятлов, В. И., & Григоричев, К. В. (2015). *Этнические рынки в России: пространство торга и место встречи*. Иркутск: Изд-во ИГУ.

CHAPTER 2

From *Chelnoki* (Shuttle Traders) to *Biznesmeny*

> Now look here. I'm a trader out there—out toward the rim of the Galaxy. I've located some old maps, and I'm out to open new markets.
>
> —Isaac Asimov, *Foundation I*

In as much as the activity I am looking at started in the early 1990s, I first trace back its development since these early years. The dissolution of the Soviet Union, the easing of restrictions on individual commerce in the context of the transition to market economy, and the new accessibility of foreign markets impacted economies in former Soviet territories. In Armenia and Georgia, as in other post-Soviet countries, individuals acting on their own, so-called "suitcase traders" or *chelnoki* (челноки), started to travel abroad—some of them to China—to make some "easy" cash through trade. This first generation of the 1990s was followed by a new generation of so-called *biznesmeny* (бизнесмены; ბიზნესმენი). These *biznesmeny* became a huge and heterogeneous group within Georgian and Armenian society. Some of them, who are classified as "small" or "micro entrepreneurs," fill the bazaars of Tbilisi and Yerevan today.

As mentioned in the introduction, the emergence of petty trading concluded in a proliferation of bazaar-marketplaces, including Lilo Bazroba (ლილოს ბაზრობა) in Georgia, founded in 1991, which consists of some five thousand trading booth on the outskirts of Tbilisi. It covers twenty-two hectares, is the working place of approximately four

S. Fehlings, *Traders, Informal Trade and Markets between the Caucasus and China*, Politics and History in Central Asia,
https://doi.org/10.1007/978-981-19-5205-0_2

thousand traders, and has become the biggest trading hub in the South Caucasus (a detailed description of Lilo follows in Chapter 3). According to the information supplied to our research team by its administration in 2017, 41 percent of the imported merchandise sold in Lilo originated in China. Another 46 percent of imports came from Turkey, 6 percent from the Arab Emirates, 4 percent from Azerbaijan, and 2 percent from Iran. Furthermore, our survey of three hundred respondents conducted by Ana Ramazashvili, Zviad Mirtskhulava, and Philippe Rudaz in the marketplace in 2017 revealed that 19.5 percent of the respondents regularly or sporadically travelled to China.

In March 2017, Zviad and I travelled with a group of Georgian traders to Beijing, a perfect opportunity to get insight into the whole process of the contemporary long-distance trade. The material presented in this chapter fleshes out the theoretical skeleton and the theories and hypotheses discussed in the coming sections, where I argue (1) that the traders of my target group do not fit the classical definitions of entrepreneurs, (2) that they view the world from the perspective of their specific businesses, with the result that the dichotomies of formality and informality become irrelevant, since they belong to another "value system," and finally, (3) that the traders' experiences of business in China strengthen their different perspective and create a culture apart, shaped by its own rationality, values, codes of honor, and social relationships.

Chelnoki

The years of the dissolution of the Soviet Union were experienced as a time of chaos and suffering in both Armenia and Georgia. In Armenia, these years are remembered as the "dark years" (*c'owrt tariner*, ցուրտ տարիներ), when there were food, heating, and electricity shortages. This period was perceived as the "nation's metaphorical dark end" (Platz, 2000: 114). The state was experienced as absent or corrupt, and groups of criminals and racketeers controlled street life and the many new marketplaces that emerged in public spaces (Melkumyan, 2017). The situation in Georgia was similar. In those days, the majority of people in Armenia and Georgia lost their jobs and had to seek new ways to make a living. This was the beginning of the time of the so-called *chelnoki* (челноки).

The term *chelnoki* derives from the Russian term for the "shuttle" (*chelnok*, челнок) used in weaving. The shuttle carries the weft by moving back and forth, and because of this motion, it is associated with the commuting travel activity of (shuttle) traders. Unlike the English term "shuttle traders,"[1] the Russian term *chelnoki* is used only for post-Soviet suitcase traders in this particular historical context.[2] Although the term is used all over the former Soviet territory, it is not very common in Georgia, and many of my Georgian interlocutors did not even recognize it. They would use the Georgian terms, *gadamq̇idevli* ("reseller," გადამყიდველი) or *šemomṭani* ("importer," შემომტანი), or talk about *vaç̌ari* (ვაჭარი) or *movaç̌re* (მოვაჭრე), which simply mean "trader." In Armenia, the term *chelnoki* is currently used. The checkered, zip-up tote bag used to carry merchandise became the symbol of the *chelnoki*.

According to a Russian law that went into effect on 1 August 1996, merchandise weighing up to fifty kilograms, or having a value of U.S.$1000, could be imported duty-free into the Russian Federation. In 2003, this law was adjusted. Henceforth, the goods had to be accompanied by a person officially treated as a "tourist" (*turist*, турист), who was allowed to claim the weight allowance only once a week (Holzlehner, 2014: 91; Zuev & Habeck, 2019).[3] Similar regulations were put into place in all the former Soviet republics. Petty trading thus continued under the guise of tourism, which is why the Georgian businesspeople currently travelling to Beijing are still called *turisty* ("tourists," туристы) (Mukhina, 2009). In the early 1990s, groups of people lugging bags or resting in a corner surrounded by their merchandise suddenly appeared in airports and on public transportation all over Eurasia. An Indian colleague of mine told me, for example, about the "Russian and Ukrainian trade tourists" she saw in the Karol Bagh and Janpath neighborhoods in Delhi.

To my knowledge, there is only a limited amount of in-depth literature about the phenomenon of *chelnoki*. There are a few articles concerned with shuttle traders in post-Soviet Eurasia,[4] but shuttle trade with China,

[1] In its handbook on the "non-observed economy" the OECD (Organization for Economic Co-operation and Development) offers the following definition: "Shuttle trade refers to the activity in which individual entrepreneurs buy goods abroad and import them for resale in street markets or small shops. Often the goods are imported without full declaration in order to avoid import duties (OECD, 2002)."

[2] Some of the *chelnoki* had already started their activity during the perestroika period in the 1980s.

[3] The weight limit changed from time to time (Humphrey, 2018a).

[4] In Russia (Mukhina, 2009; Zabyelina, 2012), in Bulgaria (Konstantinov, 1996; Konstantinov, Kressel, & Thuen, 1998), between Belarus and Lithuania (Sasunkevich,

in particular, has rarely been described. Some of this research is about Central Asian traders from Kyrgyzstan and Kazakhstan and ethnic Chinese minorities in Chinese border regions (Alff, 2016a; Cieślewska, 2014; Niyozov & Shamatov, 2007; Schröder & Stephan-Emmrich, 2016; Steenberg, 2016b; Лыкова, 1995), who still maintain trading links to China. Another three exceptions are Natalia Ryzhova's (2008) research on the informal economy in the twin cities of Blagoveshchensk and Heihe, Fedorova's (2012) analysis of interethnic communication in the context of trading at the Russian-Chinese border, and Holzlehner's (2014) work on border economics, informal markets, and organized crime in the Russian Far East. The latest publications on the topic are collected in Humphrey's (2018b) edited volume on trust and mistrust in the economy of the Chinese-Russian borderlands.

Holzlehner, who discusses the *chelnoki* crossing the Russian-Chinese border between Primorsky Kray and Heilongjang Province, distinguishes two different types of *chelnoki*: first, *naemnye čelnočniki* ("hired shuttle traders," наемные челночники), also referred to as *pomogajki* ("helpers," помогайки) or *kemely* ("camels," кемели), who are hired by wholesalers through so-called *turističeskie firmy* ("tourist companies," туристические фирмы) that arrange transport, accommodation, and border formalities; and second, *svobodnye čelnoki* ("independent shuttle traders," свободные челноки), who invest their own capital, organize everything themselves, and work at their own risk. In Primorsky Kray in the 1990s, both groups of *chelnoki*, the hired and the independent traders, took advantage of the weakness or absence of state control and their physical proximity to China.

In contrast to Central Asians, Siberians and other Asian people, who have lived (and traded) with their Chinese neighbors for centuries (see Nyíri, 2007; Zhang & Saxer, 2017b; Zuev & Habeck, 2019), the people of the Caucasus and others living far from the Chinese borderlands experienced trade trips to China as adventurous journeys. Shushan's father, for example, who lives in Yerevan, sold the family's jewelry to reach Suifenhe. He took an airplane to Vladivostok and crossed the Chinese border, like the shuttle traders described by Holzlehner, at Pogranitshny, which he reached by public transportation. On the way back, he travelled through Khabarovsk, where he took a cargo plane to Kuybyshev. There, he waited

2014), between Ukraine and Poland (Polese, 2012), from Uzbekistan (Turaeva, 2014), and at the Finnish-Russian border (Stammler-Gossman, 2011).

another whole week for a connecting flight to Armenia. In the 1990s, this was a common trade route.

People like Shushan's father, who had worked as an engineer in his previous life, were not necessarily "good traders." They had problems choosing merchandise, bargaining, and playing the game called capitalism, which, especially in these years, was experienced, as "wild" (*dikij*, дикий), "uncivilized" and "anti-social." Thus people used to talk in Russian about "wild capitalism" (*dikij kapitalizm*, дикий капитализм) and in Armenian about "village/rural capitalism" (*gyowġakan kapitalizm*, գյուղական կապիտալիզմ), meaning primitive and rude forms of competition and profit-seeking (cf. Fehlings, 2014, 2016).

Being a good trader meant you had to be predatory and "slightly insane", and consequently it was not perceived as particularly shameful to fail at this business, but even interpreted as a positive character trait. Still, many people made good money in the *chelnoki* business. Even though it was ugly, according to his daughter, the merchandise Shushan's father brought from China was sold for a good profit in the little "bazaar" the family organized at home, simply because there was a shortage of everything at that time. Yet Shushan's father travelled to China only once. After this experience, he decided that this was "not the business for him." This was true of many *chelnoki*, for whom trade was a temporary economic strategy. As soon as the national economies of the post-Soviet republics recovered, they went back to their former professions or tried to find other, more prestigious jobs.

According to Tea, a Georgian friend of mine who was a teenager in the 1990s, some of the former *chelnoki* do not even want to remember that they once had to work as traders, "the experience was too painful for them." Aside from the fact that the 1990s were hard years, trading was often experienced as an embarrassing occupation. One reason for this embarrassment was that in Soviet times, even though trading small quantities of local products—agricultural produce, for example—was allowed, trade was perceived as "speculation" (*spekuljacija*, спекуляция), which was condemned and forbidden as anti-social and considered selfish and unworthy, because immoral (Humphrey & Skvirskaja, 2009; Mandel & Humphrey, 2002).

Trade and profit-seeking seem to be a problem in many cultures and are often condemned as immoral, or, at least, a contested virtue. Not surprisingly, in many societies, "a special position or often even a degree of separation went along with the attribute 'trader'" (Hahn, 2018: 6), as was, for example, the case with Jewish tradesmen in medieval Europe, Arab traders in West Africa (Van der Laan, 1992), Indian populations in East and Central Africa, and Indian, Jewish, and Armenian merchants in Central Asia (Kalandarova, 2005). Money is the ultimate signifier of the dark side of the economy. According to Graeber, by creating a new logic and pseudo-morality, the monetization of obligations overcomes moral scruples (Graeber, 2011; cf. Chapter 4).[5] Pseudo- or im-morality is usually put on a level with antisocial behavior, which takes one to the question about the relationship of economy and social conduct, and economy and community and/or society.

For Aristotle, a city's economy naturally had to be at the service of the community (*koinonia*) and the goodwill (*philia*) binding community should lead to fair and determined prices (Dilley, 1992). Communists were less optimistic about fair trade and found positive social behaviors in societies in which trade was absent or less developed. According to this reasoning, hunter-gatherer societies are said to be based on egalitarian social relations and common ownership, so-called "primitive communism" (Engels, 1975 [1884]).[6] Trade was defined as the opposite of

[5] Thomas Aquinas regarded the desire for money as a sin, and Karl Marx contended that it alienates producers from their products, conceals the value of labor, and leads to commodity fetishism, the origin of social inequality and the immiseration of the working class (Dilley 1992).

[6] The relationship between social contexts/societal institutions and economic patterns is also central to the works of Polanyi. In *The Great Transformation* (1944) he distinguishes three types of economy, which he explicitly links to historio-cultural frameworks and social organization: First, "reciprocity," found in acephalous societies like that of the Trobriands described by Malinowski, who practice gift exchange; Second, "distribution" found in hierarchical societies like the ancient kingdoms in Syria, Greece, Mexico, Western Africa, India, and Babylonia, where surpluses were accumulated and administered by bureaucracies; and third, "market exchange," found in modern societies like those in western Europe, which are governed by the market principle. Bohannon and Dalton (1962) seized on Polanyi's distinction of these three causal relations between social organization and economy, but focused on different kinds of markets and marketplaces. Making these types of markets and marketplaces the major features for the classification of societies, they distinguished, first, "societies without marketplaces" such as hunter-gatherer societies; second, "societies with peripheral markets," like ancient Babylon, where neither buyers nor sellers entirely depended on trade; and, third, so-called "market societies," shaped by market economy, like modern Western societies. Observing the current changes in African societies, Bohannon and Dalton came to the conclusion that the first and second type transform into the last type as soon as "all purpose money" is introduced.

"real work" (*trud*, труд; *rabota*, работа) (Humphrey, 2002).[7] *Spekuljant* ("speculator," спекулянт) was, according to one of my interlocutors, a "term you used for someone you really hated or whom you did not respect at all."

Thus people whose self-esteem was based on their identity as "good workers" (schoolteachers, engineers, or industrial workers) really had to overcome moral scruples and felt that their social and moral status declined when they turned to shuttle trade (cf. Humphrey & Skvirskaja, 2009; Kaneff, 2002; Mandel & Humphrey, 2002; Niyozov & Shamatov, 2007; Taalaibekova, 2018). For some people, especially from the intellectual elite (*inteligencija*, интелигенция), this could be traumatic, as I was able to witness during many of my discussions with representatives of that group.[8] But the *chelnoki* did not only face moral, ideological, and psychological obstacles. Their travel routes were exhausting, they moved through unknown terrain, racketeering was commonplace, and there was always a risk of failure. Women in particular had to fear sexual abuse and loss of reputation.

But although some memories might still hurt, I also encountered nostalgia for the shuttle trade. Narratives from both Georgia and Armenia describe a positive influence of the catastrophic economic situation on sociability. Thus many accounts describe an intense social life during the period of economic crisis in the 1990s: Social hierarchies were neglected, people sat and laughed together, shared the little they had, and helped one another whenever possible (Fehlings, 2012).[9] As my friend Marianna explained to me:

> We cooked with the neighbors, we told each other anecdotes, and all the neighbors watched TV together. We connected a car battery with the television for two hours and everyone was there. I remember these times, and

[7] Gulniza Taalaibekova has investigated the meaning of the concept of "real work" in the context of Armenia. Her research was conducted at the Vernissage Flea and Souvenir Market in Yerevan.

[8] Whether trade can be considered "real work" is a question discussed in many different cultural contexts. However, as Marsden notes, "traders are largely absent from scholarly debates about 'work'. More popularly, indeed, they are said to lack basic human capacities, sentiments and modes of feeling, and even of demonstrating animalistic behaviour" (Marsden, 2016: 34).

[9] Nikolotov speaks about a "nostalgic Golden Age of lost futures" that is remembered as a time of solidarity (2019: 901).

> I liked it. For my parents, it was different, of course. But back then neighbors helped one another. After the crisis, the situation changed. Perhaps that is how it must be. Animals help one another during bush fires, and then they are on their own again. Perhaps we are animals. Perhaps it is natural.

Inasmuch as everything—even public transportation—had ceased to function, citizens went out for walks to exchange information and strolled public streets, in parks, or at flea markets, where they met neighbors and fellow citizens (Melkumyan, 2017). People who otherwise would not have engaged in a relationship started to meet, talk, and cooperate. The *chelnoki* experience is part of these memories. On their journeys, people got to know new people, learned to trust strangers, and sometimes made new friendships that became very close and have been maintained until today. At a minimum, the *chelnoki* experience is remembered as an adventurous intermezzo that unified post-Soviet people.

Biznesmeny and the Bazaar

It is difficult to say how many *chelnoki* remained in trade and made it their permanent and "real" profession. Despite the fact that many locals perceived trading (*torgovlja*, торговля) as a temporary occupation and stopped trading (*torgovat'*, торговать) as soon as there were other opportunities to make a living, marketplaces (*rynki*, рынки) and bazaars (*bazary*, базары) in the Caucasus and Central Asia have grown constantly since 1991. According to the National Statistics Office of Georgia, "Geostat," on 1 July 2016, in the year I started my research, 65 percent of Georgian businesses were registered with the legal status of "individual entrepreneurs,"[10] and 20 percent of economic activity was in "trade, repair of motor vehicles and personal and household goods" (unknown activity accounted for 57.9 percent), which gives an idea of the importance of the trading sector in Georgia.[11] Apparently, there are a lot of young people among these entrepreneurs. However, 56 percent of the traders participating in our survey in Lilo Bazroba belonged to the older

[10] National Statistics Office of Georgia: http://geostat.ge/index.php?action=page&p_id=239&lang=eng.

[11] National Statistics Office of Georgia: http://geostat.ge/index.php?action=page&p_id=233&lang=eng.

generation (aged over 41), most of whom had started trading in the 1990s.[12]

Levan (aged about 60), is a good example of this group of people. Before the breakdown of the Soviet Union, he worked as a miner (*šahtër*, шахтёр). When he started to trade, he felt uncomfortable. First, like his friend and age mate Ramaz, he resold goods he got (in the form of a credit) from an already established Azeri trader. Usually, this merchandise came in two bags. Standing in the marketplace, he says, "I was ashamed [*ja stesnjalsja*, я стеснялся]. But then I became used to it. Now I do business and that's it [*no potom ja privyk i sejčas u menja est' biznes i vse*, но потом я привык и сейчас у меня есть бизнес и все]."

Today, Levan is a successful and respected businessman who owns several shops in Lilo Bazroba and travels to China regularly. As he explained, "bringing the stuff [from China] means I am the boss." He is not just a reseller (*gadamq̇idevli*; russ.: *perekupŝik*, перекупщик), but has become an importer (*šemomṭani*), one who brings the goods into the country. He is an expert in what he is doing, and other people ask him for advice. Our project colleagues Gulniza Taalaibekova and Hamlet Melkumyan, who did research among traders at the Vernissage Market in Yerevan, collected several such accounts. They usually talk about inner conflicts concerning prejudices and long-held beliefs about the morality of trade, which had to be overcome for the traders to become self-confident entrepreneurs (Melkumyan, 2020; Taalaibekova, 2018). Some people, especially those who work as traders out of necessity and rank among the poor, still live with this conflict, mourning the Soviet past. The younger generation, which grew up with capitalism, does not, however, struggle with these kinds of nostalgia or conflicts. They perceive trading as something very natural. For them, commercial success is the sine qua non of a good life and social prestige. Trade, at least the kind of trade they call *biznes* (бизнес), is a promise of a better life, as lived by the rich.

Much has changed since the time of the *chelnoki*. The economic and political situation has calmed down and become more stable. Even though many people still struggle with poverty, the overall situation has improved. Racketeering has been banned from the streets, the state has regained control, and even though corruption and other illegal practices are still an issue in both Armenia and Georgia the legal system constitutes

[12] The situation at Dordoi Bazaar is slightly different.

an officially binding framework, which is generally respected (Di Puppo, 2013).

At the same time, the attitudes to trading have changed. Of course, this depends on what kind of trade one is talking about. First, there is the activity designated in Chapter 3 as highly informal, for example, street vending and individual shuttle trading. In public discourse (in both Georgia and Armenia), this kind of activity is linked with chaos and failure. As a marker of poverty, it is perceived as an obstacle to Western-style modernization and so-called Europeanization, which became a state-promoted agenda after the Rose Revolution of 2003 in Georgia, as well as in post-Soviet Armenia. Such trading was judged backward and "unsanitary." As a result, formal regulation of street vending was introduced in Armenia (Antonyan, 2018; Melkumyan, 2017; Taalaibekova, 2018; Taalaibekova & Melkumyan, 2018), and it was prohibited in Tbilisi in 2006 (Rekhviashvili, 2015). This naturally caused a lot of problems for the vendors, who occupied the lower end of the social spectrum, many of whom were elderly and had no alternative source of income.

As part of the same movement, Armenian marketplaces like Pak Shuka[13] in Yerevan and Tbilisi's bazaars like Sakolmeurneo (Kolkhozni), the Central (Deserters') Bazaar, and Saburtalo Bazaar were transformed or closed, followed by a debate about the government's rights over and public access to public land (Khutsishvili, 2006). Laws prohibiting street vending have subsequently been relaxed again, but the discussion goes on. Natia (aged around 55), who is a documentary filmmaker and can be taken as a representative of the post-Soviet artistic avant-garde, explained her point of view to me as follows: "If these people in the bazaars do not sell anything, this is a good omen for the country. This means that people do not have to buy this 'cheap quality' anymore. Nowadays, we have all these boutiques selling better-quality goods. There is often a 'sale,' and even students can afford it."

The fact that shopping malls and boutiques have popped up like mushrooms in the Caucasian capitals is often taken as an indicator of national wealth. The main avenues and pedestrian underpasses in Yerevan and Tbilisi are lined with shops selling brand-name merchandise, giving their modernized city centers a glamorous touch, as is the case, too, in Azerbaijan (Kocha & Valiyev, 2015) and Central Asia (Alff, 2014, 2015).

[13] Hetq, "Yerevan's Supermarkets & Big Box Stores: Squeezing Out the Little Guy", 16.05.2016.

Whether this really says anything about the population's affluence and well-being is another question. My neighbors in Yerevan avoided going to the central avenues, for example, because they did not want to expose their children to a world of consumption they could not afford. As they put it, that was not "for their pockets" (*ne po karmanu*, не по карману). This second kind of "fancy" trading activity is promoted and supported by state institutions, however, because it fits the image of a European-style market economy to which Armenia and Georgia aspire.

Bazaars like Lilo Bazroba bridge the large gap between the two aforementioned types of trade, informal trade and Western-style shopping malls, and between luxury and the financial means of the majority of customers and of traders who depend on the bazaar's trade and taxation norms (cf. Humphrey & Skvirskaja, 2009). As I learned from Dato, a trader in Lilo Bazroba in his fifties, Lilo supplies many so-called brand-name shops, shopping malls, and upscale outlets like Carrefour, as well as street vendors and inexpensive small shops. As I was able to verify for myself, customers are thus in many cases not choosing different merchandise, but a simply different place to buy it—a lifestyle choice, whether forced or voluntary.

Although bazaars have a lower status in terms of prestige than upscale shops, traders in prosperous bazaars like Lilo Bazroba are very self-confident. Trade and making a profit have lost their negative moral connotations, and traders who perceive themselves as entrepreneurs, or *biznesmeny*, are proud of being successful. Dato, for example, loves to talk about his innovative business ideas, his business relations with partners in China and Turkey, and his customers, who range from contractual partners like Carrefour to individual "designers who buy things to decorate the houses of rich people." He considers himself wealthy, lucky, and respected, which enables him to support his relatives and play a central role in his social surroundings. Many traders in Lilo make a good living in this way.

The major bazaars obviously continue to play an important role as import and trading hubs in the region, so state institutions accept them. But what exactly does this mean for individual bazaar traders? Can one get rich in the bazaar? Or is it, as politicians and economists usually say, a place just to "get by"? Is the state supporting bazaar traders or not? These questions are hard to answer. Our survey revealed that 26.5 percent of respondents in Lilo were able to grow their businesses, 55.1 percent of respondents' businesses remained the same, and 2.9 percent of the traders recorded losses (those who left the marketplace are not included, of course). There are stories of success as well as about disappointment and failure.

The financial crisis of 2008 led to many businesspeople going bankrupt, who were thus unable to repay their loans. Failure in bazaars is difficult to investigate, because those who fail simply disappear from the marketplace (Karrar, 2017). At the same time, many businesspeople hide their success. In general, people in the Caucasus are reluctant to reveal their exact sales and incomes, which was a challenge for my research. Levan, who finally took my colleague and myself to China, was wary of our questions and confessed that he did not want to share this information. "You wanted to know things I would not even tell my wife," he said. Such prudence, which has been identified as an obstacle to the development of innovative entrepreneurship by stakeholders,[14] seeks to prevent jealous competitors taking advantage of the information. Another factor is caution about state institutions. According to my colleague Zviad, especially in the Shevardnadze era,

> [...] people from the government would have approached you in an informal way. They would have forced you to invest your money in governmental projects like infrastructure and housing. Even if you did not want to, they forced you. They threatened you with fake or real accusations, and this would have affected your business, or even worse, they would take you to court based on false evidence. And then they would fine you and put you in jail.

We might conclude from this that the state comes across as a threaten to business in general. But things are not so simple. Unlike Soviet bureaucrats, post-Soviet government officials are not perceived as alien invaders. In general, they are considered to support business both formally and informally, inasmuch as they are part of it. In the Caucasus, as shown in the next chapter, political and religious elites overlap with business elites. At the same time, they represent an official legal system that advocates private ownership and economic exchange. This is important, and the "foundation for subsequent productive enterprise," according to

[14] This topic was extensively discussed during a roundtable with stakeholders organized by ASCN in 2014 to present the survey data from the "Emergence and Evolution of Entrepreneurship in Georgia and Armenia" Project, coordinated by Philippe Rudaz.

Belshaw, who cites the history of capitalist development in North America (Belshaw, 1965: 115). People expect the state to function as a guarantor of private ownership and social order in general, which is sometimes in conflict with the elites' own economic interests.

Elites abusing these rights for their own profit usually results in a scandal (Fehlings, 2015). Such accusations fueled the Rose Revolution in Georgia in 2003 (and protests against the leader of the Georgian Dream Party, Ivan Ivanishvili, in 2018) and the Velvet Revolution of 2018 in Armenia. Officials turning a blind eye to informal economic practices that are the basis of people's economic survival—such as semi-legal street vending and the officially restricted importation of Japanese cars, for example—is also common knowledge and even expected.

Opinions about the state's support of bazaar trading differ. Local economists like Irinia Guruli are of the opinion that entrepreneurship (including small business) "is fostered through a number of support initiatives by the current Georgian government,"[15] but 74.6 percent of our survey respondents told us the opposite (14.2 percent were unable to answer the question, and 11.2 percent said that the state was helping them).

As further discussed in Chapter 4, the state is not today the negligable factor for businesspeople in Armenia and Georgia that it was in the early 1990s. Unlike the *chelnoki*, today's "businesspeople" operate within a much more "official" framework and on a more "visible" level. Traders, at least those who have stalls and shops in marketplaces like Lilo Bazroba, must register their businesses, report their accounts, declare the importation of merchandise to customs, and pay taxes, and they usually do so.

Nevertheless, indicated in Zviad comment, quoted above, officials make use of the law in very "informal" ways. Post-Soviet elites are famous for knowing all the (informal!) rules of the game called capitalism, which Zviad calls *formal'nyj obman* ("formal fraud," формальный обман). All businesspeople, successful and less successful, of course, have to adapt to this formal-informal environment, which means, for example, that they

[15] In the 1990s and early 2000s, unfavorable tax regimes and high levels of corruption hindered entrepreneurial activity. This changed after 2006, when the Georgian government implemented radical reforms. Taxes and bureaucratic procedures were simplified and corruption reduced (Di Puppo, 2004, 2013).

may hide their success and "cook their books." Some forms of adaptation are illicit; many are not. There are various legal but informal ways to cope with the situation. Traders like Dato, for example, may do everything according to the law but draw on informal resources like their social networks, in the process. Unwritten obligations and favors from friends and kin that are neither illegal nor conspicuous may benefit such traders, avoiding official control.

Making a profit is no longer seen as objectionable in itself—ideologically, morally, or legally. In fact, wealth, regardless of where it comes from, often leads to social recognition and admiration. In Georgia and Armenia, the representatives of the state and of the Orthodox Church, who adorn themselves with the trappings of prosperity and are included among business elites, serve as role models (Antonyan, 2016). Nevertheless, trading is perceived as a stressful, risky occupation. In Lilo Bazroba, 36.1 percent of respondents said that they did business because they saw no alternative. Half of them (50.7 percent) admitted that they would stop doing what they did if they could earn the same income as employees. As one can see from a comparison of our data sets from Central Asia and the Caucasus, business is much less profitable in the Caucasus than in Kyrgyzstan or Kazakhstan (Rudaz, 2020). The many reasons why Caucasians are less likely to make a profit and be able to invest in growing their businesses are further discussed in Chapter 3.

Biznes in "Russian Beijing"

Unlike Shushan's father, whose business ventures were haphazard, contemporary traders from Lilo Bazroba travel to China regularly and have established business relations there with Chinese partners they trust, with whom they have been working for years. Dato's wife's Chinese counterpart, for example, informs her regularly about sales opportunities; Levan usually orders shoes, which are especially produced for him; and Irma, a female trader in Lilo in her fourties, goes to China once a month, knowing exactly where to go and what to buy. The business trips of traders of the new generation are more predictable than those of the *chelnoki*, and risk and uncertainty are merely economic factors for them.

The destinations Georgian traders favor today are Beijing and Guangzhou. Usually, they stay for about ten to fourteen days and visit Chinese marketplaces, shops, and factories, buying wholesale. In my description of traders' activities, their social environment, relationships with Chinese business partners, and behavior on one such journey, my information is derived from just the single group of traders I accompanied, but I believe that my findings can to a great extent be generalized. According to the literature, my team members' research, and my own materials, collected over many years, the practices and experiences I describe below are common not only to Georgian or Caucasian traders but to the vast group of post-Soviet entrepreneurs as a whole.

From the beginning of my research, I planned to travel with "shuttle traders" to gain insight into long-distance trade in post-Soviet Eurasia. But Georgian traders, as I experienced many times, are not eager to share their business secrets. It was very difficult to explain why I was interested in their activity, and I was generally met with caution. The fact that the Volkswagen Foundation funded the project was another problem. Traders immediately linked my research to the German automobile company and suspected a business interest in "secret knowledge."

In September 2016, my colleague Zviad and I approached a businesswoman in Lilo Bazroba who seemed very open to the idea of collaboration and promised to take us to Turkey. However, after a month of constant calling and asking, she finally left without us. When we met her again, she told us that she had decided on her trip spontaneously overnight, and that "this is how business works." I thus believe that we were lucky to get access to a trader through Zviad's friend Bacho, who asked his father to take us to Beijing. Bacho's father, Levan, whom I have introduced above, is a successful trader who owns several stalls in Lilo. He was also very suspicious about our research. Again and again Zviad and I had to explain what we do, why we do it, and who wants to know about all this. These questions never stopped. However, Levan called us when he started planning his business trip. We bought tickets with him and were finally in the privileged position of sharing his adventures.

Visa formalities did not cause any problems. I applied for a tourist visa at the Chinese embassy in Germany, while the traders did the same in Georgia. They asked a friend to take their passports to the embassy and paid 100 GEL for a tourist visa and 60 GEL for taking a passport to the embassy and picking it up again. A three-month tourist visa was issued within three days (it may take up to a week).

Our flight connection to Beijing was through Baku and Doha. We agreed to meet at the gate in the Tbilisi airport. Levan did not come alone, which came as a surprise. Besides twelve liters of Georgian wine, which he was planning to consume during our trip, he brought two friends, Giorgi and Ramaz, each of whom was carrying another five liters of homemade wine[16] and a ten-day supply of Georgian bread and cake. Levan was in a good mood. At the time of our trip, he was in his sixties and weighed almost 234 pounds (106 kg).[17] Before becoming a trader in the 1990s, he had worked as a miner. He now specialized in athletic shoes and supplied many traders in Lilo, where he worked as a wholesale (*optovik*, оптовик) and retail trader (*rozničnyj torgovec*, розничный торговец).

Giorgi, who was about thirty—the youngest trader in the group, as I learned later—lived in Batumi, where he had a shop selling women's clothes. He asked a lot of questions and seemed to be worried, since it was his first trip to China. Levan and Giorgi had never met before. Ramaz had introduced Giorgi to Levan a few minutes before our departure. Giorgi's mother and Ramaz's wife were friends. They had asked Ramaz to take Giorgi to China and show him how to do business there. Ramaz, a calm person, has been travelling with Levan to China since 1998 and specialized in women's and children's clothes. Levan was the leader and chief entertainer of the group without any doubt.

Levan and Ramaz had previously flown via Moscow, but going via Qatar was now cheaper and less complicated. Boarding the plane, someone called Levan's name, and he chatted briefly with three women on a business trip to Guangzhou, who also worked in Lilo Bazroba. Later, dismbarking, we met another of Levan's and Ramaz's acquaintances, a young woman called Diana, who stayed with us until Beijing. In Doha, Giorgi was drunk. He had had some drinks during the flight and now was hugging airport staff and starting a Russian conversation—even though he was the only one who did not speak good Russian—with everyone who crossed his path. In Doha as well as in Beijing, the traders extensively used the help of others. Every step was accompanied by a lot of discussion within the group, with other Georgians in the same queue, or

[16] Some of my colleagues and students who read the manuscript of this chapter were irritated by the fact that I mentioned the lavish consumption of alcohol in the trading context. They felt it would put the traders in a negative light. I personally think that it is important to mention the consumption of wine because it has a social and ritual meaning in this context. In Georgia, wine consumption is linked to masculinity and other positive values.

[17] Levan and I had a small competition about who would lose more weight during the China exhibition.

with airport and security staff members. Filling in the migration card, for example, might involve a quarter of an hour's lively conversation.

In Beijing, Levan and Ramaz immediately linked to wi-fi, essential to doing business there, and Levan called a Chinese partner, who sent a driver to pick us up. The men invited Diana to share our ride to the traders' hotel, which took about an hour. On the way, I curiously tried to get a first impression of the surroundings. Ramaz told me that in summer, everything was blooming and looked "even more beautiful." Giorgi was not impressed. Looking at the skyscrapers, he commented, "We have the same in Batumi." He had sobered up and was struggling with a headache.

We stayed at the Sinczinshan hotel (*gostinica*) in the middle of Beijing, a popular base for post-Soviet traders, which looked nice from the outside but was squalid, with big bags of merchandise always stacked in the foyer. In the elevator, I met a lot of trade tourists from the Baltics, the Caucasus, Ukraine, Central Asia, and Siberia. The charge for a room was U.S.$51 a night, and no one cared how many individuals shared it. Apparently, Chinese middlemen subcontract with the building's administration for rooms that they manage and rent. Levan's contact had promised him four rooms. We got three, and since I was the only woman, I got one and the four men shared the other two. Levan was expecting a guest, and so Giorgi, Ramaz, and Zviad took one room the next day, while Levan stayed in the other. We registered at the main desk, paying 30 renminbi, and then went up to the eighth floor. The rooms were like small apartments. It seemed as though the previous occupants had left them just a moment ago. Each one had a small kitchenette, a bathroom with a washing machine, an enormous TV, a small sofa and table, a huge bed, an extra mattress, and plastic curtains. In my room, there were old slippers under the table, a mountain of Russian DVDs, and some food left behind in the cupboards. A cockroach sitting on an old bar of soap welcomed me. To my regret, another night, I stepped on one of his siblings. I was fascinated by how fast my fellow travellers settled in, while I was just trying to touch as little as possible. The next day, at least after Lena's arrival, I felt as if I was visiting my friends' living rooms: Russian soap operas in the background and the tables overflowing with Georgian and Russian food. Levan even bought some beautiful bedclothes.

A few minutes after moving into the rooms, we all met at the elevator to go to the market, which was literally around the corner, just a five-minute walk away. I had expected a bazaar like Lilo, but the shopping area consisted of several tall warehouse buildings along a huge avenue and its side roads. The whole place is called Yabaolu Rynok (Yabaolu Market, Ябаолу рынок, 雅宝路) and first emerged in 1988, after perestroika and the reform era in China. It developed from a street market on Yabao Street into a covered market in 1999, and finally into a shopping center covering an area of more than 220,000 square meters adjacent to Ritan Park (Guzei, 2015; Гузей, 2015). Guzei, who, together with Sun (Сунь, 2002), provides one of the few ethnographic sources on Yabaolu, states that the development of Yabaolu Market was tightly linked to the development of the Cherkizovsky market (Черкизовский рынок) in Moscow, which in the 1990s became a hub for the redistribution of Chinese merchandise all over the former Soviet Union. Several other marketplaces are also linked to Yabaolu's evolution, including Lilo Bazroba in Georgia (Fig. 2.1).

Yabaolu, also known as the "Russian Market" (*Russkij Rynok*, русский рынок), is a meeting place, not only for traders, but, according to Guzei, also for Russian permanent residents of Beijing (Guzei, 2015). Cyrillic signs on the façades of the small shops that line the sidewalks, as well as on those of the huge trading centers, named Goja (Dasha), Zhitan (Dasha), Tjanja (Dasha), Jabao (Dasha), Czili (Dasha), and so on, advertise furs, currency exchanges, and SIM card shops. There is a Russian restaurant

Fig. 2.1 Yabaolu Market, 2017

called Mango, and everywhere there are Russian-speaking traders carrying bags, who cluster in groups to chat.

Ramaz told me how he had come to this place for the first time. A friend had brought him, and after half a day there, he was confident enough to do business without further help. He had also gone to Guangzhou for a day, "but," he says, "I can't do business there. It is too hot. I arrived there and immediately felt sick. I had a jacket on, while everyone else was wearing a T-shirt and shorts. I just can't be there. Beijing is on the same latitude as Tbilisi. It is the same climate as ours."

Levan took the lead and navigated us along some sidewalks. There were a lot of small shop. The shop owner of our first destination, a grumpy Chinese man called Sasha by his clients, sold SIM cards, repaired cell phones, and exchanged money. Like almost all Chinese individuals we met during our ten-day journey, he spoke Russian and introduced himself with his Russian nickname. Levan, Ramaz, and Lena seemed to have known him for a long time, and on the following days I saw him again and again, as there were constant problems with the businessmen's cell phones and wi-fi connections.

After having exchanged money and resolved the wi-fi issues for the time being, we went to the first trade center, Czili Dasha. The building looked like an old-fashioned Soviet hotel. The upper floors were labyrinths of somber corridors with curtained entrances leading off them. Levan seemed to know exactly which of these he wanted. Each entrance usually opened onto another corridor, lined with trade goods. The effect was rather like entering Ali Baba's cave. A shop's address consists of the name of the trade center, the floor number, and the stall number. This address, the shop's name, the owner's contact data, and the bank account number are the information the Chinese traders print on their business cards. The traders collected these business cards and easily found their way back. Later, I discovered that there are also much fancier trading centers (Fig. 2.2).

That evening, we visited three shoe shops and one sportswear shop. The owner of the first destination was a Chinese businesswoman named Sofia. Levan had a look at the latest styles of sneakers and tried on every pair himself, loudly sighing with pleasure when the shoes were soft and comfortable. I had the job of trying on the women's shoes. Levan and Sofia talked to each other like old friends, teasing each other:

Fig. 2.2 Inside Yabaolu, 2017

"Why haven't you lost weight?"
"Because I have to eat! Why don't you ditch the old merchandise?"
"I can't. It's all money. Just order this one without asking questions …"

A few clients came in from time to time, but the whole building otherwise seemed almost empty. Levan told us that the place had once been a vibrant trading center: "You had to give way to people. You could hardly walk without pushing past someone.... [Things have changed] because of the crisis." Lena told me the next day: "In the past, there were a lot of people from all over the former Soviet Union. We had a lot of fun. We went dancing and there was always a lot of laughter... Now, we have the crisis. People don't come anymore. Our business is finished."

The term *krizis* ("crisis," кризис) was on everyone's lips, and as soon as two traders met—no matter where they came from—they started to talk about it. Given that the development of Yabaolu Market and marketplaces like Cherkizovsky in Moscow (Guzei, 2015), Lilo Bazroba near Tbilisi, and places like Sed'moi near Odessa (see Marsden, 2018) were and are tightly linked, the markets share their ups and downs. Consequently, if the profitability of local bazaars in the Caucasus and in other post-Soviet countries declines, as happened because of the crisis, this affects their sister markets in China.

However, there are obviously still many people profiting from long-distance trade, not least the Chinese, who have created a whole service sector for post-Soviet trade tourism. Every day I got fliers advertising medical care (including plastic surgery or dental care), massage and spa treatments, beauty salons, hairdressers, etc. Levan, for example, used his business trips for facelifts and tattoo removal. This time he had a second treatment, and his tattoo almost disappeared. Several times I was asked in the guesthouse elevator on which floor to find a barber named Dima. The shops in the district sold Russian chocolate, and Mango Restaurant, bordering Ritan Park in the center of the area, offered many Russian dishes like Olivier salad (*salat Oliv'e*, салат Оливье), which according to the science fiction writer Dmitry Glukhovsky (2007) is a cultural symbol freighted with a chain of associations longer than the Kremlin Wall. Rickshaws take Russian tourists from one place to another, and taxi drivers and travel agencies offer trips to the Great Wall or other tourist attractions with Russian-speaking guides. Even in times of crisis, this place has remained a Russian quarter, a so-called "little Moscow" in Beijing, a counterpart to "Chinatowns"[18] all over the world.

Levan's Biznes

The next morning Zviad knocked on my door to tell me that the men were having tea. They all sat around one table with mountains of Georgian bread, homemade *gat'a* (cakes գաթա), and sweets (*konfety* конфеты) in front of them and discussed the quality of the tea leaves that someone had left in the cupboard. Giorgi invited me to help myself: "we are all friends, and you are my sister." I wondered whether he was still drunk. Apparently, I had missed a party the previous night. Levan had offered some toasts, they had drunk some wine, and at one point, Zviad reported, they had had a guest, a Georgian man who organized cargo transport for Georgian traders. The morning tea was not a lengthy event. The men talked about the possibility of going to Guangzhou after finishing their business in Beijing. Tickets can be changed on the spot, and the men were now discussing the pros and cons ("People say that

[18] Of course, Chinatowns have a completely different history and structure. An African counterpart in Guangzhou is the so-called Boahan Street (Pelican, 2014; Pelican & Dong, 2017).

prices are lower there. There, factories are closer to the shopping malls. You do not pay for transport"). After a few minutes, everything was put aside, and everyone got down to business. Zviad and I went with Levan to see Sofia first. Giorgi and Ramaz had left a little earlier.

Levan brought Sofia a little gift, a bag of sweets. (A few days later, he added five liters of wine.) Sofia, who in the mornings usually does sports in Ritan Park, had come to work earlier because of Levan, who had said that he would come to see her at 10 a.m. We arrived late, and Sofia made some snappy cracks about it. Levan again started to inspect the merchandise. When Sofia's husband entered the shop, Levan welcomed him with hugs. Sofia's husband did not speak Russian. He stayed in the background and prepared tea, coffee, and small sweet tomatoes. After a while, Levan made a move. He had shown some of the shoes to his nephew via WhatsApp, and after some discussion, he chose some styles. I am not sure what the nephew was able to see on his screen, yet it was apparently enough to make a final decision. In the next step, Sofia checked via phone and computer to find out which colors and sizes were available at the factory. Then the discussion started again.

Cell phones were essential for such shuttle traders, who used them to connect with Chinese middlemen, traders, and translators. They were also used to show photographs of products one was looking for and to take photos of the goods available, which were sent back home to relatives (acting as business partners) or to potential clients, who could have a look and text back whether they would like the trader to bring this special shoe or item of clothing or not. Such special orders also brought in a little money, Levan said (*èto tože malen'kie den'gi*, это тоже маленькие деньги). He had potential commissions of this kind in mind when he took pictures of the latest sportswear dresses. Cell phones were used by the Chinese traders, too, who got photos from their Georgian clients that they could then compare with offers from the producing factories. Goods that were not available in the shops but could be ordered through the Chinese shopkeepers, as well as the latest fashions, were presented to the clients on smartphones, iPads, or notebooks. Georgian traders (and traders from other post-Soviet countries), in China as well as back home, are permanently in touch with their Chinese partners via WhatsApp or Skype. Sofia, whom I saw almost every day during our stay, was always chatting with someone online discussing business. However, I never observed phones being used to transfer money. This is uncommon among Georgian traders—unlike among Kyrgyz or African businessmen (Schröder, 2020).

Sofia wrote down Levan's first order that day: he took eleven styles of shoe in different sizes, for a total of 600 pairs. Sofia said this was not a lot for him. In the past, he had sometimes bought more than 1,000 pairs. He usually spent about U.S.$50.000 on such a trip, he told me and Zviad. But Sofia gave him the shoes for a good price, and Levan seemed happy. He never buys the cheapest merchandise, trying to find a balance between price and quality, something he proudly mentioned when comparing himself to another Georgian trader. This other trader regularly came to Levan's stall in Lilo in Tbilisi to check the prices and then sold his lower-quality goods for a little less, which made him a dangerous competitor. This man got his merchandise from a shop next to Sofia's stall, and Sofia agreed: "competition is big" (*konkurencija bol'šaja*, конкуренция большая)—in the local marketplaces, where the tourist traders sell the Chinese merchandise, as well as between Chinese traders, who work in the same places in Beijing and compete for the same foreign clients (Fig. 2.3).

Ordering the goods took about three hours. Sophia ordered everything from the factory and informed Levan that the styles that were immediately available would be sent directly to the cargo terminal by the factory.

Fig. 2.3 Trader choosing his merchandise, 2017

The rest would leave Beijing in trucks on March 16 or later on March 23 or 28. After having concluded the business with Sofia, we visited several other shops. But no one worked as well with Levan as Sofia did. Because of her good Russian, but also because of her way of communicating, business with her went smoothly. She comes from northern China, near the Russian border. She has never been to Russia, but there, Russia was always close, and she learned Russian in school.

In the other shops, Levan wanted to buy some sportswear. But in the end, he was not satisfied with the prices, the colors, or the quality. All the sellers spoke good Russian. The tone in this environment was direct, almost harsh. Levan tried to bargain, but most of the Chinese vendors (except Sofia) were unwilling to reduce their prices. When Levan asked for special rucksacks and sweaters, everyone just told him, "There aren't any" (*Èto netu!* Это нету!). As we went from shop to shop until the evening, everything looked pretty much the same. A big froglike statue, covered with coins, could be found on almost every shopkeeper's desk. It is supposed to bring good luck in business and to attract money. Another odd-looking statue represents a cauliflower, which has a similar meaning.[19] Sometimes, the shopkeepers had a tea set and offered green tea. The entry halls and staircases of the buildings were usually impressive and faced with marble. But the corridors with the little shops where we went with Levan were shabby. There were some more people around on this day: Russians, Armenians, a man from Siberia, and other Russian-speakers. In one shop we crossed paths with Ramaz, who said that he works much more slowlier than Levan. At one point, Levan spent about U.S.$850 in a shop to buy a shoe style that Sofia did not have. In other shops, he placed orders and promised to come back.

For lunch, Levan invited Zviad and me to McDonald's. Then we visited Levan's cargo company, which was hidden in the lower part of a huge trade-center building and included terminals for cargo to Bishkek, Astana, and Tbilisi. It had numerous employees. After the merchandise is sent to the terminal by the factories, the goods have to be unpacked. The traders come themselves to count the items to make sure everything has been done correctly. According to Levan and Ramaz, the Chinese factories always try to cheat, which means one must be careful. A few

[19] The Chinese terms for cauliflower and money sound similar, which is why the cauliflower is a symbol of money. It is an amusing coincidence that the Russian term for cauliflower (***kapusta***, капуста) is slang for money.

Fig. 2.4 Levan's cargo terminal, 2017

days later, Levan sat there until midnight. After being counted, the goods are put into boxes one by one. This is done by Chinese workers, but as Levan told us, the process must be monitored, as everything has to be placed correctly to save space, because space is money. Finally, the goods are packed, weighed, and measured. The shipping costs are calculated according to a table that take into account weight and size (Fig. 2.4).

The Georgian middleman, who organized cargo, made Levan a "gift" (*podarok*, подарок): He only calculated the size of the packages and only mentioned half of the merchandise in the official documents. As the last step, a personal number (and sometimes the name of the trader) is written on each box. Until the goods are loaded on trucks, they are piled in the terminal warehouse. The trucks start from Beijing regularly. They first go to Urumqi, then through Astana to the Caspian Sea, Baku, and Tbilisi.[20] The terminal workers welcomed Levan and showed him some of his merchandise. Levan announced that many more goods would be coming, and after having dropped into the terminal boss's office, we left for another tour through shops and malls. The last stop of the day was a supermarket, where we bought some food for dinner before going back

[20] Such routes are responsive to the political situation and border regimes, and they may change at any moment (Marsden, 2016; J. Zhang & Saxer, 2017a).

to the hotel. I was exhausted. Levan, who does not look like an athlete, proved to have amazing stamina, which, according to him, is needed to conduct this kind of business.

Lena's Biznes

The next day, Lena arrived. Lena is a blond woman in her fifties, who immediately transformed her room into a Russian apartment. From now on, the television was switched on twenty-four hours a day showing non-stop Russian music-video clips with barely dressed sexy women and Russian gangsters with hard shells and soft hearts. Lena and I easily became friends. In the following days, we cooked for the men and went through all the dramatic ups and downs of the soap opera *Uznaj menja esli smožeš'* ("Recognize me if you can", Узнай меня если сможешь).

Lena has known Levan and Giorgi for about seven years. They met in China during a business trip and now coordinated their journeys to meet regularly. Lena was a "real Russian woman": she welcomed everyone in her satin pajamas and was very hospitable and communicative. She owned a shop for men's fashions in Blagoveshchensk on the Amur River. When her husband died, she was, as she told me, "left behind with nothing" and had two children to feed. This was the beginning of her business career. Meanwhile, Lena had a grandchild. She had been trading since the 1990s and was nostalgic about the past. Repeatedly, she said things like "our kind of business is dying," "our business is a remnant of the past," "our business is in decay," and "our time is over." Over lunch at the Russian restaurant, she remembered, "In the past, there were a lot of people here. It was so crowded and funny. We chatted and we had fun. But now: crisis! You should have come in the nineties. Now all this is gone."

I persuaded Lena to take me with her on her shopping tour, which was not easy. In the beginning, she was suspicious and argued that I would be bored. Lena started her workday the same way as Levan. First, she went to Sasha, to buy a SIM card. Then, she visited Sofia, whom she knew well. The rest of the day, we went from shop to shop to view the merchandise together. Lena's shopping tours took us to much more luxurious places than those I saw with Levan (Fig. 2.5). We went through large shopping malls with many levels, opening onto beautiful balconies and courts, and in one of these courts, there was even a replica of St. Basil's Church on Moscow's Red Square.

As already mentioned, Lena owned a boutique for men's wear in Blagoveshchensk. By its nature, such merchandise (*tovar*, товар) is more

Fig. 2.5 Shopping mall in Yabaolu, 2017

expensive than Levan's sneakers, and it therefore demands more capital investment. In the morning, Lena showed me a nice picture of her shop. In the following days, we went to some places to buy showcase lighting and other items like hangers. In Beijing's Russki Market, everything to set up a Russian shop is available, even Russian price and sale tags.

Like Levan, Lena knew the different sellers and shop owners who sell the kind of merchandise she was interested in. Even before we entered one of the trading centers, a Chinese shopkeeper recognized her on the street. Lena told him she was looking for winter clothes. As she explained to me later, she always orders merchandise six months in advance for the next season. The Chinese shopkeeper answered that he only had spring clothes but that she should come back, because winter clothes would arrive the next day—or the day after the next day (something we got to hear in many shops). Lena wanted him to make a deal with her. She asked him to come to an agreement not to sell to any other trader from Blagoveshchensk. The trader did not agree, and Lena left him in an angry mood. "I don't work this way," she told him, explaining to me, "It doesn't make sense if he sells the same goods to everyone. Blagoveshchensk is a small city. Everyone will have the same thing, and consequently nobody will buy this fashion."

Some of the shops I saw with Lena really had the atmosphere of designer boutiques. In one of her favorite shops, winter coats and jackets were nicely presented along the walls. In the middle of the room, there was a huge wooden table with a beautiful tea set. The shop was managed by a tough Chinese woman, Lina, who had studied in Ukraine and spoke perfect Russian. Lena and Lina had a good relationship. Lena had brought Lina a present and praised her for giving her good advice. She said that she had sold the goods Lina had recommended to her last time "very well and even for very good money." Lina reaffirmed, "Without putting it on sale? That's good" (*Ne nado bylo delat' skidki? Kak horošo!*, Не надо было делать скидки? Как хорошо!), and underlined her sentences with facial expressions and gestures that could not have been more "Russian". I was astonished.

When we started to talk to Lina, another trader, a Ukrainian man in his forties, had just finished placing his order. He had bought a lot of goods and was putting all his documents into a folder. Like Lena, he had a notebook with addresses of shops, and like Lena, he took notes. The man seemed shy but was eager to talk. He made a joke about the Ukrainian-Russian war (he said he was not sure whether he would go back home to Ukraine or to Russia) and showed us the list of the goods he had just ordered. He and Lena exchanged stories about their business experiences. They both mentioned the crisis but nevertheless admitted that their businesses were doing well—even though they were selling only half of what they sold before 2008. Both were excited about the new collection and started a typical conversation about quality, design, and taste, for which the highest standard was Europe:

> Lena on winter coats: "These are just wonderful. They really look like they are from Europe."
> Man from Ukraine: "Yes, that is what I said before! They are really great. Really like European merchandise."
> Lena: "Who designed them?"
> Lina: "Here, this is the designer" (she pointed to a very young Chinese woman).
> Lena: "Good girl [*molodec*, молодец]. But she studied in Europe, right?"
> Lina: "No. In China. The most important thing is that she has some experience."

Lena then had a closer look at the display. She immediately chose some of the clothes (about 150 pieces) that she wanted to be written on her account, meaning that she would order them later. She chose the pieces that in my opinion looked most Russian in style. There was a detail that disturbed her about one coat that attracted her special attention. The inner lining, in her opinion, did not go with the fur trim of the hood. There were other details like this, and Lina took some notes. She then said that she could order all the coats with the desired changes. The factory would produce the ordered pieces with the desired materials, colors, and extras (like extra pockets or zippers) within two days.

A lot of discussion circled around the question of which goods, styles, and quality sell well. Lena discussed this question with her Ukrainian colleague, but also with all the Chinese traders we visited on this and the following days. As I learned, it is crucial to know about the latest trends. This issue was a constant concern, not only for Lena but also for Levan, Ramaz, and Giorgi, who all told me that this was the major challenge and the reason why you needed a lot of experience, a lot of time to view the products, and luck. "This is why we have to think so much," said Levan. Ideally, a trader should be able to predict the next season's trends. "You have to feel the trend before the others do," Lina said. "You have to buy it before everyone else. Otherwise, you will have the same goods as everyone else. And then, after a while, people realize that there is a new trend and buy new stuff. But then it is too late. Again, everyone will have it." Levan had said something similar the day before, noting: "Clients are very aware of the latest trends, because they see the displays in brand-name shops and check clothes and styles on the Internet."

Lena had two types of customers: young men who bought cheaper clothes and men who had already settled down and went to work. For both, she tried to find the right fashions. Like Levan, Lena went from shop to shop the whole week. I often accompanied her and understood that her approach differed from Levan's. She was less rude and much gentler, took notes, from time to time stopped to look at clothes for herself, her daughter, or her grandchild, and always said "thank you" and "goodbye". However, Lena asked the same questions as Levan, Ramaz, and Giorgi. Every potential deal started with the same inquiries:

> "What is the *optom* [оптом] price?" Meaning, "What is the wholesale price?"
> "How much is a package [*pačka*, пачка]?" Meaning, "How many pieces are in one packet, and what is the minimum quantity required in order to get the wholesale price?"

> "How soon can you order it?" Meaning, "Are the goods available within the next few days, and will the trader be able to inspect the goods before they are ordered and sent to the cargo terminal?"

In the case of the things Lena asked about, the answers to the first question ranged between 28 and 45 renminbi for a shirt, 50 renminbi for a tie, and 150 to 300 renminbi for a coat. There were different packages of 4, 8, 12, and 24 pieces. Usually, the delivery of the goods could be expected within two to four days. After this was clarified, the traders turned to questions concerning the available sizes, colors, and qualities.

Lena called every Chinese saleswoman *kuniška*, which is a Russian diminutive form of the Chinese term *kunja* ("woman"). Lena explained this invented term as the equivalent of Russian *devuška* (девушка), which, it seemed to me, set the tone of the relationship between Chinese seller and Russian buyer right from the start.

Like Levan, Lena used WhatsApp to consult with knowledgeable people back home, in her case, the women who worked in her shop, her best friend, who knew everything about fashion trends, and her daughter. The rule was to leave a text or voice message, which would be answered within a short time by a similar message. In the trendier shops I visited with Lena, which put a lot of work into decor and presentation, taking photographs was forbidden, because the Chinese traders were afraid that their designs would be copied by business rivals. Lena was thus only exceptionally allowed to send pictures to her partners.

When Lena entered one of these shops, she was usually asked by the salespeople whether she had ordered/bought goods in the shop before. Usually, her answer was yes. Then, if the shopkeepers did not recognize her, they checked how much and how often Lena had bought previously on their computers. The Chinese traders kept records. They kept track of their clients' names, addresses, and past orders, and they assigned their clients numbers. Classified as a reliable client (who buys a lot and does so every year), Lena got discounts. The Chinese traders were also able to check in their client registers whether they had other clients from Lena's catchment area, Blagoveshchensk and its Chinese twin city, Heihe: "If a Chinese trader in Heihe has the same goods, it makes no sense. I will make no profit, because people will go there then." In a designer shop called Clasno, where Lena had been a customer for years, another woman from Blagoveshchensk had started to buy goods. Lena got angry. The Chinese trader told her which styles the other woman had taken, and she decided to take different styles, for which she left a deposit of 1000 renminbi. Leaving a deposit was a common practice. After having checked all the other shops and producers, the traders came back, finalized their orders, and paid the rest of the amount when the deal was completed. This was why they visited the same shops many times during their trips.

In addition to her regular business, Lena did some extra shopping for acquaintances and friends. In some cases, this brought in some extra money. Thus, we bought, for example, eight pairs of glasses, Chanel and Gucci knockoffs, which Lena had ordered in advance and which we picked up to bring to the cargo terminal. In such cases, it is important to get the goods in boxes covered with the right brand logo. A nice box lets the seller mark up the price (which was also true for Levan's sneakers). We also bought a bundle of fake brand-name belts for men. Unlike the "big orders", which are sent from the factory to the cargo terminal, we took these small quantities from the shops and lugged them in plastic bags to the next rickshaw. We sat in the cargo space next to the merchandise and were brought to Lena's storage unit by the rickshaw driver.

Lena rented a small storage unit in a shabby facility. There, we consolidated everything into a kind of gunnysack. A worker then checked the weight, sewed the gunnysack shut, and wrote the address (Lena's name and telephone number and cargo terminal number) on it.

When I asked Lena how much money she spent on a trip for one season, she told me that she usually spends U.S.$30,000 (Fig. 2.6). Like Levan, Lena paid in cash. Most of the time, we walked around with a plastic bag containing thousands of dollars.

Last year, the cargo company lost Lena's merchandise (*bagaž poterjali*, багаж потеряли) on the way to Blagoveshchensk. The company covered the loss of the goods, but insurance took a long time to pay the money. Lena was finally left without goods for the season. This was a very difficult time. The business is hard, as I learned from Lena, and she had to adapt to it: "When my husband passed away, I was left without a kopek. That's why I am like this. That's why I do this business and why I work hard and fast." Talking to Lina earlier the same day, Lena said that for business, "You need to show masculine qualities. But if you are with a man, you have to show your feminine side." All in all, Lena believed that men were better at doing business. But unlike many traders who participated in our survey, Lena really wanted to work as a trader. It was her choice: "I like it. It's better you do something you like, right? I could have started

Fig. 2.6 Rickshaw cargo, 2017

something different a long time ago. But I have been doing this for so many years now, and so much money has gone into this."

Giorgi's Biznes

Giorgi was the youngest and the least experienced trader of the group. As mentioned earlier, this was his first trip to China, and unlike Levan, Ramaz, and Lena, he had not yet established relationships with Chinese partners. Until our trip together, he had been buying merchandise in Turkey, especially in Istanbul. His aim thus was to explore the Chinese market and new business opportunities. Whereas Levan, Ramaz, and Lena headed for specific shops and traders that they knew, Giorgi was in search of business partners, so he was frenetically visiting as many places as possible to get an overview of the possibilities. Giorgi could rely on the help and contacts of Ramaz and Levan, but in the end he had to make his own decisions, which, of course, he discussed with his mother and his wife, who ran his shop at home. In pursuit of the best deal, he talked to everyone who crossed his path and tried to learn about secret business opportunities. The whole group participated in one of his flirtations with a Russian woman named Sabina. As Giorgi was not fluent in Russian, the other men helped him to write her messages, and everyone rejoiced together when she texted back and gave Giorgi a rendezvous in a "secret marketplace, which only Chinese people know". Giorgi appreciated her help and concluded that she was a "good girl" (***horošaja devuška***, хорошая девушка).

One day, Zviad and I accompanied Giorgi on one of his excursions to a shopping mall outside of the "Russian district." Giorgi had heard about a place close to Beijing's zoo where the goods were less expensive, because "it is a place for the Chinese." To get there, we met up with Meghab, a Georgian in his seventies. The only thing he asked me was whether I was Georgian. Since the answer was no, he lost interest. Meghabi lived and owned a house in Beijing. He did not speak Chinese or Russian, but he organized cargo transport from Beijing to Tbilisi. Zviad suspected he lived in a Georgian community. To get to the shopping mall, we followed Meghabi into a hotel. There, Meghabi used a few Russian imperatives to ask a hotel bellboy to call a taxi to Beijing's zoo. The bellboy ordered a car and asked us to wait on the street, but Meghabi and Giorgi simply ignored him and took comfortable seats in the hotel lobby.

The shopping mall next to Beijing's zoo was a huge building with many floors. We easily found the floors for women's fashions, and Giorgi immediately started to inspect the merchandise. Meghabi had some business of his own to do, so we split up. Giorgi literally ran from shop to shop. His gaze quickly slid along the displays, he touched a few pieces, and then he asked the core questions. As the Chinese sellers (most of them women) did not speak Russian in this place—and Giorgi did not either—the communication was reduced to gestures seeking to elicit details of the cost, availablity, and quantity (***opta***) of the goods. The numbers were typed into their cell phones, which were handed back and forth between Giorgi and the salespeople. From time to time, Giorgi showed the Chinese sellers photographs of the styles he was looking for: black dresses, sporty sweaters, and leather items.

Giorgi called his mother, his sister, and his wife for advice. He angrily shared news that he got from them about protests in Batumi against police fining people for illegal parking and other minor violations of the law with us, explaining that this unfairly threatened their livelihoods: "If you get a pension of 150 lari, 50 lari is already significant money," he said, adding that the police did similar things in the marketplace. A friend of his had had to pay a large sum for falsifying his accounts: "They check you and then you get a fine [*štraf*, штраф], which is very bad for a small stall keeper."

At the end of our morning's excursion, Girogi was not satisfied. He concluded that the merchandise in the "zoo mall" was of bad quality and worse than in the Russian quarter. But this was not his only problem. In general, he was disappointed in Beijing as a marketplace for wholesale shopping. "The good pieces are as expensive as in Turkey, and the cheap ones are of very bad quality," he said. That evening, after he had gotten drunk, he told me, "Just write in your book, 'Giorgi cried every day. He didn't buy any merchandise.'" Indeed, Giorgi bought only about fifteen furs in Beijing. In the end, he decided to travel to Guangzhou with Ramaz. Both were hoping for better business opportunities there. Zviad told me that the men talked about Guangzhou before going to sleep one night. Apparently, he said, "Guangzhou is more popular today" (*Guančžou [sej]čas bolee populjarno*, Гуанчжоу [сей]час более популярно). Many factories had opened near Guangzhou, and prices were said to be low. All four traders decided to make an exploratory trip there after having finished their business in Beijing. Giorgi and Ramaz planned to travel by train. They left one morning and travelled two days and a night.

Before they left, Giorgi organized the transport of his merchandise. As noted, he had bought about fifteen furs over the previous week and did not intend to pay duty on them. He thus asked each of us (Levan, Ramaz, Zviad, and me) to take two, three, or four pieces in our personal luggage. Crossing the border, we would not have to declare them, since travelers were allowed to import a few items "for personal use." "There is no problem, I guarantee it" [*ja garant*, я гарант], if you take two different ones and tell the customs they are for yourself," he assured me. In Tbilisi, Zviad and I, who were returning separately, would have to hand the furs over to Giorgi's mother. When Giorgi gave me his enormous, hairy bundle, he added, "I trust in you" (*Ja tebja doverjaju*, я тебя доверяю). Giorgi's furs filled everyone's bags, and no one was happy about it. We all wanted to take our own stuff, which now had become impossible. Giorgi did not give us a choice, and the day after his departure, Zviad and I found the bill for the furs under a piece of chewing gum that he had left on the table.

The Social Life of Biznes

Lena and Levan recommended that Zviad and I visit the Great Wall, the Forbidden City, and Beijing's Food Street. They had been to all these places themselves, and Zviad and I also encountered many Russians at the Great Wall. Mango, a Russian restaurant, hosts dance performances, and many "tourists" are among its customers. Lena had a VIP card there and invited Zviad and me to dinner, where the food we ordered cost about 150 renminbi, more than the price of a man's winter coat, and three times more than I spent on a (fake) Louis Vuitton tie. Lena and Levan sometimes also took the two of us to fancy shopping malls where we were among the few non-Chinese. These malls had little in common with the places where they bought their trade goods. We walked from brand-name shop to brand-name shop, looked at all the displays, and visited art exhibits and food courts. Lena wanted to see the latest Zara and Vero Moda fashions, and Levan was interested in Adidas and Puma sneakers. The few items they bought for themselves and for family members, they bought there: expensive shampoo, shoes, and handbags. But usually, after work, the traders sat together, ate, and drank. Lena cooked nutritious hot dishes with a lot of meat, beans, and potatoes, and Georgian bread, cake, honey, and bottles of wine covered the table. On such occasion, Levan proposed this toast: "I have not come here to see big buildings, I have not come here to breathe this air, I have come here to do business. This is why we are all here. This is what we do, and we work well. May our business be successful." It is obviously true that the primary purpose of the traders' trips was trade. Everything else was viewed from that perspective. However, business consisted of more than buying and selling goods and travelling back and forth. Traders live, eat, drink, have fun, grieve, and make friends.

Georgians are experts in feasting, and there is a special Georgian style of doing so, the so-called *supra* (სუფრა), which involves the lavish consumption of food and wine and follows strict rules (Mühlfried, 2006, 2007). Even though the *supra* is often viewed as backward and an obstacle to development in Georgia,[21] it is regarded as a source of prosperity in folklore, where it is associated with themes like gift exchange, reciprocity, piety, and morality. A *supra* always needs a master of ceremonies, called a *tamada*, who is responsible for seeing that the toasts are offered in the right ritual order. *Supras* may take place in any situation

[21] The *supra* is sometimes portrayed as an example of the Georgian mentality that is said to choose feasting over work. A good brief overview of the different attempts to analyze the Georgian *supra* as a cultural, historical, and poetic phenomenon is provided by Ram (2014).

and do not always follow all formal rules. However, a *tamada* must be chosen, and toasting is obligatory.

When we had a spontaneous *supra* on our fourth evening in Beijing, Levan took on the role of the *tamada*. This was the beginning of a long evening with endless toasts, a huge tin of caviar from Blagoveshchensk (Lena always brings caviar as a present), and a lot of drinking. When Lena mentioned that she got the impression that Georgians drink wine like water, Ramaz said:

> No. We have known each other so many years. How can you say something like that? Sometimes one has to relax. But then, for many months, I do not drink a single drop of wine. Every day, we do the same thing. We go to work. We go to the bazaar, and we go back home. Every day, all the time. Sometimes, you need to drink and to have fun. We only drink when there is this special opportunity and if it's needed. Sometimes you simply must drink [*inogda prosto nado*, иногда просто надо]!

The very emotional toasts that evening revealed some of the businessmen's thoughts. Much was said about love and respect. Some talked about their experiences in China. There was also singing ("Georgia, you are beautiful, there is only one Georgia") and dancing. As mentioned earlier, Levan had brought twelve liters of wine. Ramaz and Zviad had brought another five large bottles each. All of these had to be tasted, because "there are no bad wines, but only different ones. The higher the alcohol percentage [*gradusov*, градусов], the better." Lena looked a little bit annoyed. She sat next to Levan in her pajamas and kept one eye on the Russian television serial that was the background of the whole scene. The toasts seem to me to illustrate significant sides of the traders' mind-set. The ones I can recall were as follows:

(1) A Toast about Business

Levan: "This toast is about traders and our businesses. May both always prosper! When Zviad and Susanne asked me whether they could come with me, I asked my son, 'Why do they want to come with us? I do not even tell my wife how much money I spend! Why should I show them everything, why should I tell them? What kind of people are they?' Now you have this kind of business. You are writing this book. Now you have seen my business, later I want to see your business. I want to see your book. We'll all be there with our names."

Ramaz: "Oh, no! My name should not be there. On the other hand... everyone knows that I am here. There are no secrets!"

(2) **A Toast to Children**

Levan: "All of us have children, and they are what is most important to us. May they always be healthy and happy!" We showed each other photographs of our children, and Lena was specially honored, as she already had a grandchild.

(3) **A Toast to Giorgi's Departed Child**

This toast was offered by Ramaz, since he had the closest relationship with Giorgi. Ramaz explained that Girogi had lost a son at the age of eight months. Lena was shocked and asked that we not remember this now: "This is not the place for sadness." Giorgi replied that there was nothing bad about it, and that he thought of his son as an angel every day. The other men agreed and stood up for the ritual toast. Ramaz then dipped his fingers into his wine glass and sprinkled some drops of wine onto a piece of bread, a gesture for remembering the dead.

(4) **A Toast to Families**

Levan: "Because family is the most important thing in life, and because we all do the business we do for our families. We travel far for this reason. We suffer. But this is the way it is, and we do this for our families."

(5) **A Toast to Levan's Friend Gogi and to Friendship**

Levan: "This is for Gogi, who is in Guangzhou right now and who has travelled many, many years with me. We have been doing this business together. We are more than just friends now. We are already family. We have met here. When you are far away from home, you realize who is who. We helped each other. When I felt bad, he was with me, and the other way around. This is the way we are. This is the way things work here. When I had a fever and had to stay in bed, he was running around for me. This is friendship. This is important. This is how we can do all this."

(6) A Toast to Men's Love

All the men pointed out that this was not about homosexuality, but about one of the most important things in life, because men need each other. The Georgian term used in this context was *ʒmaḳacebi* (ძმაკაცები). *ʒma* (ძმა) is the term for "brother," and *ḳaci* (კაცი) means "man" (plural *ḳacebi*, კაცები). The *ʒmaḳacoba* (ძმაკაცობა) is the "brotherhood," and people who get to know each other through close friends consider each other *čerez ʒmaḳaci* (ჩერეზ ძმაკაცი), which is a compound of the Russian *cherez* ("through") and the Georgian *ʒmaḳaci* ("close friend," ძმაკაცი) (see Chapter 3).

(7) A Toast to Levan (the *tamada*) and Group Members

Ramaz said a lot of good things about Levan, describing him as an open-minded person: "If I feel without energy, I talk to Levan and get this energy. Levan gives energy to everyone. He is such a person." Then Levan answered with a toast to Ramaz, followed by short speeches describing each one of the group. Special attention was paid to Levans's distinct feelings toward each person and the relationship that he maintains with each. Everyone responded with a similar speech, describing the qualities of the others and the established ties between them. All this was very emotional, even though some of the group members had met for the first time only a few days before.

(8) A Toast to Peace

Ramaz then launched into a long speech about Hitler and Stalin and told us that he had lost two grandfathers in World War II. I think that this toast was directed at me. It ended with the following sentence: "May we all forget about this and may our children—mine and yours—live peacefully together!"

(9) A Toast to God the Father

"May God the Father always protect us!" summarizes this toast, but it was related to the Georgian Orthodox Church, an important institution for Georgian self-identification, and the patriarch was mentioned. Being Georgian is often equated with being Georgian Orthodox.

(10) A Toast to Georgia and Other Countries

First, the toast was about Georgia, then Russia, and finally Germany. Each country was lauded and wished a bright future.

In my judgment, the toasts referenced the following major values shared by the traders and their communities:

- First (1), the toasts address trading, a shared experience. The traders share the troubles and hopes linked to their activities. The aim is to make a profit and become wealthy.
- But second (2), making a profit and becoming wealthy is not a goal on its own. Every burden is taken on in the name of the most important thing in life: family or children.
- Nevertheless, third (3), business (and life in general) is difficult without social relations beyond the family. In this regard, friendship and especially friendship among men were mentioned as a core value in life, essential for survival. I think this is why much energy is put into the expression (and sometimes exaggeration) of the emotions one feels for others.

In sum, social relations are essential to business, and in all business relationships "trust" (*doverie*, доверие) or "to trust" (doverjat, доверять),[22] the traders expressed it, is one of the most significant factors.

[22] In Russian, "the religious root of trust—*do-verie* ('before faith')—is unmistakable, whereas the economic-commercial applications of the term seem opaque"; furthermore, "ethnography in Russia suggests that when taking practical decisions religion-infused *doverie* can often be an inappropriate word, and people will reach for a range of other ideas that suit the economic situation, such as *nadezhnyi* ('reliable', 'promising', 'hopeful') or even *avos'* ('taking a chance')" (Humphrey, 2018b: 30). Russian is not the mother tongue of Georgian traders, of course, and they used the term in a much more pragmatic way, probably not thinking of any religious link.

As the toasts reveal, relationships are rooted in different contexts. There are ties that origin in the traders' local, Georgian environment (toasts 2, 3, 9, and 10). These ties (some of them rooted in ideas about kinship) were linked to local cultural values associated with Georgian traditions, the Georgian state as an abstract entity, the Georgian Church and religion, and so on. Other relations resulted from the traders' business and travel activity. There were relationships with fellow countrymen who, over the course of a joint experience, became close or even closest friends. Gogi and Ramaz were such friends for Levan. Back home in Georgia, they kept in touch and treated one another like family members, although they would never have met outside of business (toasts 5, 6, and 7). In China, again, these business friends and people from other countries formed a community, which was united though the joint experience of being and doing business abroad (toasts 5, 6, 7, 8). Thus, national/ethnic and international (post-Soviet) trader communities have developed in Beijing and Istanbul. Some traders just greeted one another on the street, while others formed tight-knit groups. The only social relationships not mentioned in a toast were the relationships traders maintained with Chinese business partners and middlemen. Some of the relationships mentioned and the values attached to them are discussed below.

Family and Kin

Ethnographic works on the Caucasus very often mention the importance of the nuclear (and extended) family not only as a basic social unit in Caucasian societies but as an ideal concept associated with major social values and ideas about how to live a "proper" Armenian, Georgian, or Azerbaijani life. These ethnographic descriptions usually mention the house as the ultimate symbol of the family (and kin in general) and family values, which are reflected and represented in its construction. Individuals act as representatives of their house and are inseparably linked to its reputation, which is the reputation of the social unit it embodies.[23]

It thus makes sense, and confirms the ethnographic evidence from the region, that Georgian traders, like their fellow countrymen, do what they

[23] Armenia (Abrahamian, 2007a; Fehlings, 2014, 2015); Georgia (Dragadze, 2016; Grigolia, 1939; Mars & Altman, 1983); Azerbaijan (Pfluger-Schindlbeck, 2005; Roth, 2013, 2016). Similar evidence is reflected in data from Central Asia. See, e.g., Steenberg on Uyghur households (Steenberg, 2016b: 413).

do for their families and put most of their profits into housing.[24] In our survey conducted in Lilo Bazroba in 2017, 37.8 percent of respondents told us that if they won the lottery, they would put the money into an apartment. Another 11.3 percent would buy land, and only 27.8 percent would invest in their businesses. When I told Levan that many people in Germany live in rented houses and apartments, he was surprised: "We put everything into the house. For us, this is important [*U nas vse kladujut v dom. U nas èto važno*, У нас все кладуют в дом. У нас это важно]," he said. "I have just finished building a house, and now I am starting to buy a second one."

In this study, I do not discuss the topic of family and kin and the importance of the house in depth, because I have done so previously (Fehlings, 2014, 2015). I am convinced that this triumvirate represents major social values in Armenian and Georgian society, which are directly linked to local cosmologies and interpretations of the world. This society/kin/family-cosmology-house nexus has been widely discussed in anthropology (Carsten & Hugh-Jones, 1995; Hardenberg, 2007), and the Caucasian case can be taken as an interesting example. Here, I focus on the role of the family and kin *within the trading business*.

Literature on petty trading in general—and the businesses of Caucasian and Central Asian traders in particular—often mentions the vital role of family and kin as a principle of organization and solidarity (Humphrey, 2018b; Steenberg, 2016b; Yalçın-Heckmann, 2014). Especially in the context of long-distance trade, Central Asian and Caucasian kinship networks and diaspora communities are described as providing the basic infrastructure for a successful enterprise. In some exceptional cases, trading is even portrayed as a tool—a kind of pretext—for establishing or deepening social ties among relatives and community members (Steenberg, 2016b, 2018). Authors like Bram (2017), Holzlehner (2014) and Yalçın-Heckmann (2014) thus use or at least mention the concept of "ethnic entrepreneurship" (for a discussion of this term, see Chapter 3), which relies on networks linking local communities with marketplaces in Russia and China, including producers (of herbs, dried fruit, spices, etc.), drivers (transporting goods from Central Asia or the Caucasus to Russia or China), and traders (owning stalls in foreign marketplaces) from a single family or at least from a single ethnic group, imagined in terms

[24] Cf. Hart 1970.

of kinship. The advantage of such networks, as argued in these examples, is that they provide social trust and control in a sphere of uncertainty where the state is absent or perceived as an enemy.

Brednikova and Pachenkov (1999) criticize such emphasis on kin and ethnicity in trading networks, arguing that cooperation among members of the same ethnic group cannot be explained in terms of a shared sociocultural identity, but is merely pragmatic. According to them, ethnic entrepreneurship is based on rationality and a choice in favor of simplicity. Thus, traders of the same ethnic group cooperate because they can communicate in the same language, move, and live in the same space, and are equiped for social control.

My findings point in yet a different direction, contradicting both arguments. In our survey in Lilo Bazroba, 62.9 percent of respondents stated that they worked alone. Only 18.9 percent got help from family members living in Georgia, and even fewer, only 3.4 percent, could count on family members living and working abroad. The survey is far from being representative, but it aligns with my observations. Levan, back home, ran his stalls in Lilo Bazroba with his nephew; Giorgi with his mother, sister, and wife. This is not surprising. As noted by Bechhofer and Elliott (1981), dependence on family labor is a feature of petty bourgeoisies everywhere. The same is true of "personalistic and familistic ties, which are part of business operation in all capitalist societies" (Aldrich & Waldinger, 1990: 126; cf. Zimmer & Aldrich, 1987).[25] But neither Levan nor Ramaz relied on extensive (kin) networks—either in Georgia or abroad.

Of course, the business I describe is different from the businesses described by the aforementioned authors, who report on traders who work permanently in marketplaces abroad. The traders from Lilo who deal in Chinese merchandise just go to China to shop. They use infrastructure and need contacts, but instead of building on existing networks to do business, they make contacts *in the course of doing business*. As described in the section above on the *chelnoki*, the first traders from the Caucasus who went to China in the 1990s were real adventurers, stepping out into terra incognita. Information was scarce, and according to some of my interlocutors, it was not shared, because of mistrust, envy, and rivalry. All they had to build on were the experiences reported by others, rumors, and

[25] The fact that researchers have not compared their findings on ethnic entrepreneurship to non-ethnic business operations may have resulted in an overemphasis on the ethnic aspect (Aldrich & Waldinger, 1990).

gossip. As noted earlier, a "friend" who had been to Beijing before had introduced Ramaz to trading. Thereafter, Ramaz made his own friends.

The people who are important for traders in Beijing are not family. They are friends and acquaintances from the same ethnic group or from other post-Soviet countries whom they have met in the context of "doing business in China," hence, people from the international post-Soviet trading community, Georgians and other Russian speakers working in the service sector linked to trade in Beijing's Russian Market, and Chinese trade partners and middlemen. Thus, the question of social control, trust, and the nature of relationships in this context leads to completely different conclusions, discussed in the following section and explored further in Chapter 3.

Business Partners and Friendship

Observing the activity and interactions of my fellow travellers, I got the impression that this was their everyday life. They knew the place like the backs of their hands, they lived as if they were in their own homes, there were many of their acquaintances around (we were always running into such acquaintances on shopping expeditions and in the hostel elevator, and sometimes traders arranged to meet). There was a routine. "We've been meeting here like this for seven years, and we live like old couples," Lena said. Such trading expeditions seem to have become a second life for them, very different from everyday life back home.

Obviously, it takes some time to establish such a second life. Ramaz, Levan, and Lena all remembered stories about sickness, about feeling lost and lonely, and about getting help from people who only later became close friends. Ramaz and Levan once helped an Azerbaijani trader "just because there was nobody else to help him." "We are all abroad," Ramaz explained. "It doesn't matter who you are and where you come from. Here, we need and help each other." Lena had once got food poisoning in a restaurant. Levan had to take her to a hospital and thought she would die: "It's horrible, if you know nobody and you don't understand a word." Such memories, more than a common ethnic background, are the foundation of the intense relationships between traders who have worked, suffered, and spent a lot of time together. At the same time, besides sympathy, there is trust.

Sympathy and trust, again, are not bound to ethnicity, and they have also been established among Chinese and Georgian or Chinese and other tourist traders. This observation surprised my colleagues who work among African traders. Apparently, mistrust of the Chinese is very strong among Africans. According to my colleague Mamadou Diawara, African traders would never ally or engage in a deeper relationship with their Chinese counterparts (either in Africa or in China).[26] The situation is different in the context I have described above. Many traders from Lilo, for example, Dato, who was introduced earlier, talked about their Chinese partners in a very positive manner. Levan, Lena, and Ramaz emphasized that they have worked with their Chinese partners for many years. Their relationships with Chinese partners are first of all business relationships with people who have proved to be more reliable than others.

"The conduct of trade through personal understanding and without insurance is generally the norm in China," Humphrey and Skvirskaja (2009: 72) say.

Apparently, it is not easy to find such reliable people, which is why time and experience are needed. Ramaz explained, "We know good people there. But there are also people you should not even talk to." There has also thus historically been prejudice and a lot of mistrust of Chinese traders (and the Chinese in general) (cf. Humphrey, 2018b). "You have to check everything, because the Chinese always try to cheat you," Lena warned me. "Where they find a way to cheat you, they will cheat you. They give you bad quality, they send you a color different from the one you ordered, sometimes something is wrong with the numbers." Levan spends hours at the cargo terminal counting his merchandise. When we went there a second time, the terminal was crowded with different groups of traders observing how the cargo workers packed their goods for transport. Like Levan, a Georgian woman counted her merchandise before it was put into boxes. Levan got help from Sofia. That day he worked until late in the evening. "Sometimes, I sit until 2 o'clock in the morning to count all this," he said. "Ramaz once got the wrong goods. That's why one has to check all this."

On the other hand, there is a great deal of trust in Chinese traders one has been working with for a long time. Sofia, as far as I could observe, has even become a friend. Lena and Levan joked with her, and they talked about personal topics like family and holidays. When Levan planned to

[26] This mistrust of African traders towards Chinese is currently described in academic literature. See, e.g. Mathews (2015). Marriages between Africans and Chinese seem to be much more common than marriages between Chinese and Georgians or Armenians, however, presumably because ordinary Chinese encounter the latter more seldom.

travel to Guangzhou, Sofia booked the flights[27] for him and stored his luggage until he came back. Lena maintains a similar relationship with Alicia, one based on long-term cooperation, trust, and sympathy.

Apparently, such relationships can also be understood as alliances against competitors who work in the same marketplace and compete for the same clients. For Lena, these are Russian and Chinese traders who work in Heihe and Blagoveshchensk; for Levan, Georgians who buy similar merchandise in China and sell it in Lilo Bazroba in Georgia; and for the Chinese sellers working in the Russian district, other Chinese sellers from nearby shops. Mixed groups of Chinese sellers and tourist traders therefore team up to oppose fellow countrymen and members of their own ethnic groups. If it is forbidden to take photographs, it is because the Chinese are afraid other Chinese might copy designs. Alicia once asked Lena questions about Clasno, the other Chinese shop selling winter coats, for example, saying confidentially that she would like to come with us to have a look at the merchandise there. But then she said, "Better I don't come with you. Perhaps they will recognize me, and then this will be bad for you. For me, it is just interesting to see what they have."

Even though the cooperation described is business-oriented, I think that it would be wrong to define it as purely opportunistic. There must be some affinity, too. Lena, for example, told Alicia that she would not order much from Clasno because they had changed their staff and she did not want to work with different people. "You go there and there are only strange faces. No one wants to work like that." Alicia, in contrast, personally introduced her new partner to Lena, creating a personal contact for the future. Personal contacts and communication are based on some Chinese sellers' ability to speak perfect Russian and to set the right tone. I asked every Chinese person I met where he or she had learned Russian. Many had lived in Russia or Ukraine or were from the Chinese-Russian border region. At a minimum, they have been working with Russians and people from post-Soviet countries for a long time.

There are also a few foreigners who own shops in the Russian district or work as salespeople in Chinese-owned shops, but they are rather the exception. One salesman working at Clasno was from Turkmenistan. He had finished his education in China and spoke perfect Chinese. A Russian

[27] Apparently, it was not the first time she had done this, because Sofia already had scans of Levan's passport on her computer.

couple managed another shop. Interethnic marriage seems unusual. We only met one foreigner who had a Chinese spouse, a woman from Ufa Bashkortostan who lived in Beijing, worked in one of the shops, and had a two-year-old child. Lena was curious about this exceptional liaison and asked her whether "the Chinese are good men." The woman replied at some length, which in the end led to the conclusion that women face the same problems everywhere, last but not least with mothers-in-law. "Some are good, some are less good—like Russian men," she said. "Perhaps they are more reliable, in general. But they have a very strong relationship with their parents. We live with my husband's parents." Lena immediately expressed some sympathy (I did too), and then they went on doing business.

Trust as manifested in the kind of long-term cooperation described in this section—in practices of exchange, such as, for example, "working without money," in easy communication, in mutual help over and above business, and in readiness to listen and to consider advice—is thus not bound to ethnicity and social control through relatives. Rather, it is established in the context of business. Magnus Marsden noted the same thing observing traders from Afghanistan—Hindu or Muslim Afghans with different ethno-linguistic backgrounds—working in or between Odessa in Ukraine and Yiwu in China. Cooperation there, too, "arises from the pragmatic concerns of hard-nosed traders whose lives are caught at the cusps of multiple forms of co-dependencies" (Marsden, 2018: 136).

Biznes Culture and Its Rules

The literature on informal economy, but also the anthropological literature cited in the coming chapters, has much to say about the importance of trust (and mistrust), which according to this literature, has to replace written contracts and law enforcement in spheres that are not regulated by state institutions (Gellner, 1988). But trust, like legislated law, needs guarantors and instruments of enforcement. Usually, it is argued that social control within a tight-knit community (linked through kinship or cohabitation) serves as such an instrument. However, I would argue that in the context described above, it is not social control and so-called moral obligations alone that create trust.

To participate in this kind of long-distance trade requires that entrepreneurs—at least at the beginning of a trading relationship—take the risk to trust people (trade partners, fellow traders) with whom they do not have any relationship other than an economic one. Without a minimum of credit of trust, this kind of economic activity simply does not work. Trust thus means "an intention to accept uncertainty and risk based on a positive expectation of others" (Humphrey, 2018a: 10) and only later becomes "a product of experience and ... is constantly updated on accordance with calculations about probability of default or satisfactory completion of a given partner" (ibid., 12).[28]

As I was able to observe in my interviews with individuals whose daily lives take place in a sphere that is framed, on the one hand, by the legal system and state institutions and, on the other, by social networks and close relationships with family, kin, neighbors, peers, and friends, trusting strangers is quite a difficult and unusual challenge.[29] As Marsden (2016: 40, 133), Carey (2017), and Mühlfried (2019) argue, mistrust can in fact be a good strategy in this context, since low expectations of the trustworthiness of others can result in positive relationships that can be trusted for their predictability (see also Broch-Due & Ystanes, 2016; Carey, 2017; Hart, 1988).

Still, there are moments when one must take the leap. Thus many traders—I remember, for example, the accounts of Armenian and Georgian female traders who talked about their first business trips to Turkey—recall the very emotional, hence frightening, moment when they had to hand over the money for the goods they had chosen in a foreign bazaar (in Istanbul, New Delhi, or elsewhere) to a foreigner, how they returned home with nothing but a receipt, and their astonishment when, a few weeks later, they really received the goods they had paid for, without having been cheated: "I got my goods," one female trader exclaimed. "They hadn't tricked me, and absolutely nothing was missing!"

Notwithstanding such astonishment, the fact that businesspeople do not cheat one another, at least not in an obvious way, is unsurprising if one takes a close look at the mechanisms of the kind of economic activity described above.[30] The so-called "Yabaolu Rynok" or Russian Market in Beijing, like many other bazaar sections and marketplaces in China,

[28] Humphrey refers to Dasgupta (1988).

[29] According to the World Values Survey (WVS) of 1997 and the Caucasus Barometer (CB) of 2010, the level of social trust in the South Caucasus is extremely low (Paturyan, 2011).

[30] For comparison, Humphrey and Skvirskaya (2009) also talk about how traders have to overcome mistrust and briefly mention Odessa traders' business relationships

Turkey, India, and elsewhere, specializes in individual entrepreneurs coming from post-Soviet territories. These post-Soviet entrepreneurs form a kind of "imagined community" (bounded by the idea of sharing a common past, future goals and a similar idea of capitalism) within which they exchange information and rumors. This information and these rumors are crucial for the traders' decisions about where to go and where to invest their money. If a marketplace and its business community or local traders acquire a bad reputation, the so-called tourist traders simply avoid them. Cheating a client thus affects one's future relationship, not only with that person, but with the whole business community, and business itself.

This might have been different in the time of the ***chelnoki***, when business culture was not yet established. Then, as mentioned earlier, traders, or small groups of traders, were like pioneers, just relying on themselves. They did not feel that they belonged to a broader community, and they were not even sure that they would make another business trip themselves. The system they had been living in for decades had just crumbled and been replaced by chaos. Uncertainty, bad experiences, and an atmosphere of "wild capitalism" (***dikij kapitalizm***) led them to perceive their environment as dangerous.

According to Levon Abrahamian, two jokes capture the very essence of the fears of the ***chelnoki*** of the 1990s. One of these jokes is about sexual harassment, the other about mistrust. The latter describes the situation of a trader who has bought a lot of merchandise, which he is carrying with him in big bags:

> The trader, an Armenian from Yerevan, is in Istanbul. There he asks a Turkish man, "What do you think about the genocide?" The Turk answers, "It was horrible, and I am so sorry about it." The Armenian asks another Turkish man, "What do you think about the genocide?" Again, the answer is the same. But the third time, the Armenian approaches a different person and gets an angry answer, "There was no genocide, and we should have slaughtered all of you." "Thank you," says the Armenian, "you are an honest man. Please keep an eye on my goods for a minute. I really have to go to the toilet."

with Chinese partners. As in my example, these interethnic relationships are based on long-standing cooperation and trust.

The joke thus alludes to traders' need never to lose sight of their merchandise, and the difficulty of trusting anyone.

Today, the situation is different. During our stay in Beijing, there was an incident that reflected the "business culture" there. Zviad and I were with Levan, who was involved in noisy bargaining, when a Chinese man from a neighboring stall approached him. This man, who sold gloves, remembered that he had seen Levan a few years before with another Georgian trader, who had left without paying a debt of U.S.$1000. When the Chinese trader showed Levan a photograph of this Georgian trader on his cell phone, Levan recognized him. He expressed his deep regret and emphasized that the person was not a friend of his, just an acquaintance. He called him on the spot, but the man did not answer the phone. However, the Chinese trader was very grateful. Both he and Levan agreed that things like that should not happen. I asked Levan whether he believed that a phone call from him would resolve the situation, he replied that the Georgian had not been lucky with his business in recent years, but that he should not have left without settling his bill: "It is shameful not to pay one's debt. Sometimes people pay if you pressure them, because they do not want to lose their good reputation. It is important that your name is clean. Otherwise, you can't do business." The local traders from Georgia probably apply the pressure Levan is talking about. However, this anecdote is not about mutual trust within a specific ethnic community but about an honor code that guarantees smooth and effective transactions between traders of any ethnic, social, or religious origin for the sake of everyone's business.

Traders naturally establish long-term relationships with specific business partners, whom they trust more than others. Within these kinds of relationships, trust is even greater, enabling more flexibility. Kazakh traders he interviewed frequently spoke of the "moral accountability, flexibility and adaptability" of their Chinese partners as being "conductive to societal improvement and entrepreneurial success alike," Henryk Alff writes. Chinese "flexible capitalism" calls "for trustful and enduring interpersonal connections," he notes (Alff, 2014, 8). Sometimes, as discussed in Chapter 5, the Chinese notion of *guanxi* (关系, 關係) is said to explain this Chinese quality of being able to establish reciprocal business relationships (Lee, 2014). If Levan wanted styles that he had seen in some shop or other, he first asked Sofia whether she could somehow find these styles and order them for him. This was good for both of them. Levan preferred to do business with Sofia, because "they work without money" (*bez deneg*, без денег), meaning that Levan did not have to pay immediately, but could send the money later. Levan and Sofia trusted each other, exchanged presents, and called each other friends, but their relationship was built on a good working business partnership.

Business clearly defines and structures much of the traders' social lives and, at the same time, influences their perception of the world. Knowing—at least a bit—the local Armenian and Georgian contexts, it was a challenge for me to accept that much of my knowledge did not necessarily apply to local traders. Even though they are part of the local cultures they live in, their daily lives, behavior and moral attitudes are strongly shaped by business. A conversation with Lena was very revealing in this respect. Apropos of Russia's annexation of the Crimea, she concluded that America is everyone's enemy, and that Europe should be friends with Russia. She was very angry that doing business with Europe had now become impossible. She had formerly bought and sold German dresses. "The quality is very high. You also have very good shoes in Germany. You can wear them for years, and they will still look good." Now, all these business opportunities have vanished. A friend of hers had gone bankrupt as a result, she said.

> Who needs this [*komu èto nužno*, кому это нужно]?! Can you imagine how many people lost their jobs in Russia as well as in Germany because of this politics!? Europe will lose all its individuality. In a few years, they will only have goods from America. I have a friend in America. Americans have to work until the age of 65. At the age of 50, you already can't work as hard as before. Then they fire you. You won't get any money. The health-care system is very expensive. They will help you, but then you will have to take out horrible loans. They do this simply to make old people die, so as not to have to pay for them. Europe is very stupid to cooperate with America. We live on one continent, and we should be friends.

Overwhelmed by her talk, I did not really know what to answer and told her that I believed that Europe might have some problems with Russian ideology (I don't actually know myself what I meant by this). As a result, Lena became even more exited. It came out that she had a very pragmatic approach that started from the perspective of her business activity. "Have you seen what has happened in Turkey? Now women [there] have to wear these chadors and so on. But this does not harm business. Business runs as usual. They earn money, we earn money. That's good. What is bad about it? We ordinary people have to live. Why can't it be the same with

Europe?" Lena did not care about national, ethnic, religious, or moral differences. Like Marsden's Afghan traders, she relied on her "capacity to interact with people who are different" (2016: 24). For her, as for many other traders, the world revolved around business, which colored their perceptions of interactions of all kinds, of the state, and of life in general.

The Chinese state did not seem to play any role in the Georgian traders' business. Levan and Ramaz both confirmed that "the Chinese government doesn't care," and that "this is good." The Georgian state, on the contrary, was perceived as a problem. Ramaz, who was slightly drunk at the time, tried to explain to me how absurd it was to have to pay taxes and customs duties to the government for nothing: "This just doesn't make sense. I sell you [something]... That's business... then you have to pay ten lari to the state. This is wrong... The state has nothing to do with it."[31]

In Chapter 4, I discuss the role of taxation, customs, and state institutions in traders' business. Here, it suffices to emphasize that business in the context of long-distance trade creates a reality, a culture of its own, that encompasses complex social contexts, relationships, and interactions, codes of conduct and moral assessments, and an ideology that partially contradicts local sociocultural paradigms and formal institutional frameworks. This business culture is sensitive to external influences. Since the early 1990, political and institutional changes have had a deep impact on long-distance trade. The global economic crisis of 2008 reduced overall trading activity and led to the market "slowing" (Marsden, 2018). Profit margins declined, as did the number of traders. Wholesalers replaced "tourist" shuttle entrepreneurs. Lena and many others were convinced that their kind of business had seen its best days.

Levan's son Bacho is not planning to follow in his father's footsteps. He wanted to be independent and have his own business, he told me one day, giving me a ride from Lilo Bazroba back to the city center. He had started a business growing mushrooms in Rustavi in Georgia, accepting some money from his father to that end. But this first experiment failed, because the mushrooms did not turn out well (Bacho had no idea why the mushrooms did not grow as they should have. The mushroom spawn was

[31] Writing about Kazakh traders, Alff reports a similar contrast being drawn between the Chinese and Kazakh states. China is praised for "representing a linear development path resulting from effective state intervention," while the Kazakh state is criticized for corruption (2014: 8).

from Russia, and he suspected that it was bad). Bacho now wanted to go to America or Canada: "Because I want to have my own business and my own money. I want to do something for myself." He had some relatives there who would probably help him. "There are a lot of ways to make money," he told me, for example, as a driver or by working in a candy factory, "In a few months, you have enough money to start a business." He had previously failed to get a visa. "It was my father's fault. He said we would go there for business. Then they rejected us. Now, I will go alone and tell them I am a tourist." In the past, Bacho had been to Israel. There he also worked as a driver and made some "good money." But then he was caught by the police and arrested. "Just because they did not trust me. No other explanation." He had been in prison for five days, getting food only once a day. Then he was sent back to Georgia. However, he was still optimistic about America. Whatever he did, he would not continue to do what his father did. He did not want to go to China or Europe. "There is nothing in Europe, and in China you only get *kopejki* [small change, копейки]."

Some members of the younger generation may perceive long-distance trade with China as unprofitable, but Chinese traders who have started to come to the Caucasus may also influence the fate of Caucasian long-distance trade with Asia (see Chapter 5).

Conclusion

In this chapter I have traced the development of long-distance trading by local traders from the Caucasus (Armenia and Georgia) who travel to China to conduct their business. The sporadic trading of the *chelnoki* in the 1990s, undertaken by default, assessed as shameful and not "real work," has been replaced by the *biznes* of self-confident entrepreneurs who are proud of what they do. As Table 2.1 shows, not only the business environment but business itself has changed.

My analysis to some degree contradicts the standard discourses concerning the social setting and culture of local communities in the Caucasus (and post-Soviet territory in general). Business itself creates the traders' living conditions and environment in the first place. It shapes their behavior, their social relationships, their rules of moral conduct, and their understanding of the world.

The argument that the nature of business lies at the origin of human decision-making behavior is highly reminiscent of neoclassical theory in

Table 2.1 Comparison of *chelnoki* and *biznesmeny*

	Chelnoki *(shuttle traders)*	Biznesmeny *(entrepreneurs engaged in long-distance trade)*
Historical background, economic situation	• Dissolution of the Soviet Union • Transition period (“dark years”) • Transition to market economy	• Stabilizing the nation-state • Stabilizing the market economy
Institutional framework	• Weak state/government • Chaos, anarchy, criminal milieu • Missing infrastructure • Individual initiative (“wild capitalism”)	• Consolidation of state institutions and state control • Calming down of the situation • Legal framework • Institutional framework (market economy) (registered businesses, taxation…)
Motivation for doing business	• Survival	• Making a profit/having a good life
Economic activity	• Shuttle trade • Temporary activity	• Trade • Permanent activity
Assessment of trading and self-esteem	• Low prestige/embarrassing • Not “real work” • Moral inferiority • Status decline	• High prestige • Real profession/experts • Proud; part of moral lifestyle/self-confident entrepreneurs • Economic success is linked to prestige and status (elites)
Circumstances/travelling	• Dangerous/adventurous • Scarce information/based on gossip • No established contacts • No sales facilities/informal vending	• Predictable • Experience/technological aid (phone, internet) • Established contacts and infrastructure • Marketplaces: bazaars, shops
Destinations	• Chinese cities bordering Russia	• Beijing • Guangzhou
Sales volume and profit margins	• Very small (survival level)	• Small (making a living, goal of growing the business)

economics. However, in my understanding, the notion that individual human behavior is ruled by supply, demand, and the rational decisions of buyers and sellers is not confirmed by the data. Even though the traders described above make very pragmatic decisions, not everything they do, feel, and think can be explained in terms of the market. *Biznes* and the "market principle" are not equivalent concepts. The concept of *biznes*, as I understand it, and as I have described it above, includes social dimensions, and creates a sociocultural milieu both parallel to and in between local cultures and global trends. Traders working in this specific sphere of post-Soviet trade tourism all jointly contribute to the creation of this culture.

The following chapters seek to describe and define post-Soviet *biznes* in more depth and connect my findings to major debates in economic anthropology.

References

Abrahamian, L. (2007a). Armenia and Armenians between East and West. *21st Century, 1*, 72–76.

Aldrich, H. E., & Waldinger, R. (1990). Ethnicity and Entrepreneurship. *Annual Review of Sociology, 16*, 111–135.

Alff, H. (2014). Embracing Chinese Modernity? Articulation and Positioning in China-Kazakhstan Trade and Exchange Processes. *Crossroads Asia Working Paper Series, 21.*

Alff, H. (2015). Profiteers or Moral Entrepreneurs? Bazaars, Traders and Development Discourses in Almaty, Kazakhstan. *International Development Planning Review, 37*(3), 249–267.

Alff, H. (2016). Introduction. *Central Asian Survey, 35*(3), 327–333.

Antonyan, Y. (2016). *Elites and "Elites": Transformations of Social Structures in Post-Soviet Armenia and Georgia*. ASCN.

Antonyan, Y. (2018). Interplay between the Formal and the Informal: Marketing Religious Festivals in Contemporary Armenia. *Anthropological Researches, IV*, 65–77.

Bohannan, P., & Dalton, G. (1962). *Markets in Africa*. Northwest University Press.

Belshaw, C. S. (1965). *Traditional Exchange and Modern Markets*. Prentice-Hall Inc.

Bram, C. (2017). Moscow Azerbaijani-Juhuro "Oligarchs" and the Eurasian Trade Networks. *Caucasus Analytical Digest, 96*, 5–8.

Brednikova, O., & Pachenkov, O. (1999). Ethnicity of "Ethnic Economy": Economic Immigrants to St. Petersburg. In O. Brednikova, V. Voronkov &

E. Chikadze (Eds.), *Ethnicity and Economy: Proceedings of the Seminar Held in St. Petersburg (9—12 September 1999)* (Vol. 8, pp. 108–115). CISR.
Broch-Due, V., & Ystanes, M. (Eds.). (2016). *Trusting and Its Tribulations: Interdisciplinary Engagements with Intimacy*. Berghahn Books.
Carsten, J., & Hugh-Jones, S. (1995). Introduction: About the House—Lévi-Strauss and Beyond. In J. Carsten & S. Hugh-Jones (Eds.), *About the House: Lévi-Strauss and Beyond* (pp. 1–46). Cambridge University Press.
Carey, M. (2017). *Mistrust: An Ethnographic Theory*. HAU Books.
Cieślewska, A. (2014). From Shuttle Trader to Businesswomen: The Informal Bazaar Econommy in Kyrgyzstan. In J. Morris & A. Polese (Eds.), *The Informal Post-Socialist Economy* (pp. 121–134). Routledge.
Dasgupta, P. (1988). Trust as a Commodity. In D. Gambetta (Ed.), *Trust: Making and Breaking Cooperative Relations* (pp. 49–73). Wiley-Blackwell.
Di Puppo, L. (2004). Corruption as an Instrument of State Control in Georgia. *Berliner Osteuropa-Info, 21*, 47–54.
Di Puppo, L. (2013). The Construction of Success in Anticorruption Activity in Georgia. *East European Politics, 30*, 105–122.
Dilley, R. (1992). *Contesting Markets: Analyses of Ideology, Discourse and Practice*. Edinburgh University Press.
Dragadze, T. (2016). *Rural Families in Soviet Georgia: A Case Study in Ratcha Province*. Routledge.
Engels, F. (1975 [1884]). Der Ursprung der Familie, des Privateigentums und des Staats. In K. Marx & F. Engels (Eds.), *Werke* (Vol. 21). Dietz.
Fedorova, K. (2012). Transborder Trade on the Russian-Chinese Border: Problems of Interethnic Communication. In B. Bruns & J. Miggelbrink (Eds.), *Subverting Borders: Doing Research on Smuggling and Small-Scale Trade* (pp. 107–128). Verlag für Sozialwissenschaften.
Fehlings, S. (2012). Auf der Suche nach der verlorenen Zeit. In W. Kaschuba, M. Krebs, & M. Pilz (Eds.), *Die Postsowjetische Stadt: Aushandlungsprozesse im Südkaukasus* (pp. 150–167). Panama Verlag.
Fehlings, S. (2014). *Jerewan: Urbanes Chaos und soziale Ordnung*. LIT Verlag.
Fehlings, S. (2016). The Ignoble Savage in Urban Yerevan. *Central Asian Survey, 35*(2), 195–217. https://doi.org/10.1080/02634937.2015.1134142
Gellner, E. (1988). Trust, Cohesion and the Social Order. In D. Gambetta (Ed.), *Trust: Making and Breaking Cooperative Relations* (pp. 143–157). Wiley-Blackwell.
Glukhovsky, D. (2007). *Sumerki—Dämmerung*. Heyne.
Guzei, I. (2015). The "Russian" Market in the Center of Beijing. In V. Dyatlov & K. Grigorichev (Eds.), *Ethnic Markets in Russia: Space of Bargaining and Place of Meeting* (pp. 159–170). Publishing House of ISU.
Graeber. (2011). *Dept: The First 5.000 Years*. Melville House Publishing.

Grigolia, A. (1939). *Custom and Justice in the Caucasus: The Georgian Highlanders*. AMS Press.
Hardenberg, R. (2007). Das "einschließende Haus": Wertehierarchien und das Konzept der "Hausgesellschaft" im interkulturellen Vergleich. *Anthropos, 102*, 157–168.
Hahn, H. P. (2018). Introduction: Markets as Places: Actors, Structures and Ideologies. In H. P. Hahn & G. Schmitz (Eds.), *Market as Place & Space of Economic Exchange: Perspectives from Archaeology & Anthropology* (pp. 1–18). Oxbow.
Hart, K. (1970). Small-Scale Entrepreneurs in Ghana and Development Planning. *Journal of Development Studies, 6*(4), 104–120.
Hart, K. (1988). Kinship, Contract and Trust: The Economic Organization of Migrants in an African City Slum. In D. Gambetta (Ed.), *Trust: Making and Breaking Cooperative Relations* (pp. 176–193). Blackwell.
Holzlehner, T. (2014). *Shadow Networks: Border Economics, Informal Markets and Organized Crime in the Russian Far East*. LIT.
Humphrey, C. (2002). *The Unmaking of Soviet Life: Everyday Economics after Socialism*. Cornell University Press.
Humphrey, C. (2018a). Introduction: Trusting and Mistrusting Across Borders. In C. Humphrey (Ed.), *Trust and Mistrust in the Economy of the China-Russia Borderlands* (pp. 9–35). Amsterdam University Press.
Humphrey, C. (Ed.). (2018b). *Trust and Mistrust in the Economy of the China-Russia Borderlands*. Amsterdam University Press.
Humphrey, C., & Skvirskaja, V. (2009). Trading Places: Post-socialist Container Markets and the City. *Focaal: European Journal of Anthropology, 55*. https://doi.org/10.3167/fcl.2009.550105
Kalandarova, M. (2005). Indian Merchants in Nineteenth-Century Bukhara: Trade Network and Socio-Cultural Role. In M. Gervers (Ed.), *Traders and Trade Routes of Central and Inner Asia: The "Silk Road", Then and Now* (pp. 93–162). Asian Institute, University of Toronto.
Kaneff, D. (2002). The Shame and Pride of Market Activity: Morality, Identity and Trading in Postsocialist Rural Bulgaraia. In R. Mandel & C. Humphrey (Eds.), *Markets and Moralities: Ethnographies of Postsocialism* (pp. 33–51). Berg.
Karrar, H. (2017). Do Bazaars Die? Notes on Failure in the Central Asian Bazaar. *Informal Markets and Trade Working Paper Series, 4*.
Khutsishvili, K. (2006). Bazaar Culture in Georgia: The Case of Tbilisi. *Berliner Blätter, 59*, 41–52.
Kocha, N., & Valiyev, A. (2015). Urban Boosterism in Closed Contexts: Spectacular Urbanization and Second-tier Mega-events in Three Caspian Capitals. *Eurasian Geography and Economics, 56*(5), 575–598.

Konstantinov, Y. (1996). Patterns of Reinterpretation: Trader-Tourism in the Balkans (Bulgaria) as a Picaresque Metaphorical Enactment of Post-Totalitarianism. *American Ethnologist, 23*(4), 762–782.

Konstantinov, Y., Kressel, G. M., & Thuen, T. (1998). Outclassed by Former Outcasts: Petty Trading in Varna. *American Ethnologist, 25*(4), 729–745.

Lee, C. K. (2014). The Spectre of Global China. *New Left Review, 89*, 29–65.

Mandel, R., & Humphrey, C. (2002). *Markets and Moralities: Ethnographies of Postsocialism*. Berg.

Mars, G., & Altman, Y. (1983). The Cultural Bases of Soviet Georgia's Second Economy. *Soviet Studies, XXXV* (4), 546–560.

Marsden, M. (2016). *Trading Worlds: Afghan Merchants Across Modern Frontiers*. Hurst & Company.

Marsden, M. (2018). Islamic Cosmopolitanism out of Muslim Asia: Hindu-Muslim Business Co-operation between Odessa and Yiwu. *History and Anthropology, 29*(1), 121–139.

Mathews, G. (2015). African Logistics Agents and Middlemen as Cultural Brokers in Guangzhou. *Journal of Current Chinese Affairs, 44*(4), 117–144.

Melkumyan, H. (2017). Informality, Politics and Mutual Support in Flea Markets in Post-Soviet Armenia. *Informal Markets and Trade Working Paper Series, 5.*

Melkumyan, H. (2020). From Economic Survival to Lifestyle Choice: Flea Markets in Georgia and Armenia. *Central Asian Survey, electronic preprint.*

Mühlfried, F. (2006). *Postsowjetische Feiern: Das Georgische Bankett im Wandel.* ibidem-Verlag.

Mühlfried, F. (2007). Celebrating Identities in Post-Soviet Georgia. In T. Darieva & W. Kaschuba (Eds.), *Representations on the Margins of Europe: Politics and Identities in the Baltic and South Caucasus States* (pp. 283–300). Campus Verlag.

Mühlfried, F. (2019). *Misstrauen: Vom Wert eines Unwertes*. Philipp Reclam jun. Verlag GmbH.

Mukhina, I. (2009). New Losses, New Opportunities: (Soviet) Women in the Shuttle Trade, 1987–1998. *Journal of Social History, 43*(2), 341–359.

Nikolotov, A. (2019). Volatile Conviviality: Joking Relations in Moscow's Marginal Marketplace. *Modern Asian Studies, 53*(3), 874–903.

Niyozov, S., & Shamatov, D. (2007). Teaching and Trading: Local Voices and Global Issues from Central Asia. *Toronto Studies in Central and Inner Asia, 8*, 281–300.

Nyíri, P. (2007). *Chinese in Eastern Europe: A Middleman Minority in a Transnational Era*. Routledge.

OECD. (2002). *Measuring the Non-Observed Economy: A Handbook.* OECD Publications Service.

Paturyan, Y. (2011). (Dis)Trusting People and Political Institutions in Armenia. *Caucasus Analytical Digest, 31.*

Pfluger-Schindlbeck, I. (2005). *Verwandtschaft, Religion und Geschlecht in Aserbaidschan*. Reichert Verlag.
Pelican, M. (Ed.). (2014). *Baohan Street: An African Community in Guangzhou: Documentary Photographs by Li Dong*. Department of Cultural and Social Anthropology, University of Cologne.
Pelican, M., & Dong, L. (2017). Baohan Street: An African Community in Guangzhou. In D. L. Hodgson & J. Byfield (Eds.), *Global Africa*. University of California Press.
Polese, A. (2012). Who has the Right to Forbid and Who to Trade? Making Sense of Illegality on the Polish-Ukrainian Border. In B. Bruns & J. Miggelbrink (Eds.), *Subverting Borders: Doing Research on Smuggling and Small-Scale Trade* (pp. 21–38). Verlag für Sozialwissenschaften.
Platz, S. (2000). The Shape of National Time: Daily Life, History and Identity during Armenia's Transition to Independence, 1991. In D. Berdahl, M. Bunzl, & M. Lampland (Eds.), *Altering States: Ethnographies of Transition in Eastern Europe and the Former Soviet Union* (pp. 114–138). University of Michigan Press.
Ram, H. (2014). A Feast for Thoughts. *Ab Imperio, 4*, 85–92. https://doi.org/10.1353/imp.2014.0108
Rekhviashvili, L. (2015). Marketization and the Public-Private Divide: Contestations Between the State and Petty Traders over the Access to Public Space in Tbilisi. *International Journal of Sociology and Social Policy, 35*(7/8), 478–496.
Roth, S. (2013). The Making of Home, the Making of Nation: Cultural Notions of Conflict and Displacement in Post-Soviet Azerbaijan. In S. Voell & K. Khutsishvili (Eds.), *Caucasus Conflict Culture: Anthropological Perspectives on Times of Crisis* (pp. 169–194). Curupira.
Roth, S. (2016). *Making a Home in Baku: Dynamics of Housing, Family and State in Azerbaijan*. (PhD), University of Halle.
Rudaz, P. (2020). Trading in the Bazaars of Dordoi and Lilo at the Frontier of Formality, Entrepreneurship and Globalization. *Central Asian Survey, electronic preprint*.
Ryzhova, N. (2008). Informal Economy of Translocations: The Case of the Twin City of Blagoveshensk-Heihe. *Inner Asia, 10*(2), 323–351.
Sasunkevich, O. (2014). "Business as Casual": Shuttle Trade on the Belarus-Lithuania Border In J. Morris & A. Polese (Eds.), *The Informal Post-Socialist Economy*. Routledge.
Schröder, P., & Stephan-Emmrich, M. (2016). The Institutionalization of Mobility: Well-being and Social Hierarchies in Central Asian Translocal Livelihoods. *Mobilities, 11*(3), 420–443. https://doi.org/10.1080/17450101.2014.984939
Stammler-Gossman, A. (2011). "Winter-Tyres-for-a-Flower-Bed": Shuttle Trade on the Finish-Russian Border. In B. Bruns & J. Miggelbrink (Eds.),

Subverting Borders: Doing Research on Smuggling and Small-Scale Trade (pp. 233–256). VS Verlag.

Steenberg, R. (2016a). The Art of Not Seeing Like a State. On the Ideology of "Informality". *Journal of Contemporary Central and Eastern Europe, 24*(3), 293–306.

Steenberg, R. (2016b). Embedded Rubber Sandals: Trade and Gifts Across the Sino-Kyrgyz Border. *Central Asian Survey, 35*(3), 405–420.

Taalaibekova, G. (2018). The Changing Perception of Trade as "Real" Work: The Unmaking of Soviet Workers at the Vernissage in Armenia. *Informal Markets and Trade Working Paper Series, 8.*

Taalaibekova, G., & Melkumyan, H. (2018). Public Space Comercialised and Comodified: A Case Study od the Vernissage in Yerevan. *Anthropological Researches, IV*, 48–64.

Turaeva, R. (2014). Mobile Entrepreneurs in Post-Soviet Central Asia: Micro-Orders of Tirikchilik. *Communist and Post-Communist Studies, 47*(1), 105–114. https://doi.org/10.1016/j.postcomstud.2014.02.001

Van der Laan, L. H. (1992). Migration, Mobility and Settlement of the Lebanese in West Africa. In A. Hourani & N. Shehadi (Eds.), *The Lebanese in the World: A Century of Emigration* (pp. 531–547). Tauris.

Yalçın-Heckmann, L. (2014). Informal Economy Writ Large and Small: From Azerbaijani Herb Traders to Moscow Shop Owners. In J. Morris & A. Polese (Eds.), *The Informal Post-Socialist Economy: Embedded Practices and Liveliyhoods* (pp. 165–186). Routledge.

Zabyelina, Y. (2012). Costs and Benefits of Informal Economy: Shuttle Trade and Crime at Cherkizovsky Market. *Global Crime, 13*(2), 95–108.

Zimmer, C., & Aldrich, H. E. (1987). Resource Mobilization through Ethnic Networks: Kinship and Friendship ties of Shopkeepers in England. *Sociological Perspectives, 30*(4), 422–445.

Zuev, D., & Habeck, J. O. (2019). Implications of Infrastructure and Technological Change for Lifestyles in Siberia. In J. O. Habeck (Ed.), *Lifestyle in Siberia and the Russian North.* OpenBooks Publishers.

Zhang, J., & Saxer, M. (Eds.). (2017). *The Art of Neighbouring: Making Relations Across China's Borders.* Amsterdam University Press.

Гузей, Я. (2015). «Русский» рынок в центре Пекина. In В. И. Дятлов & К. В. Григоричев (Eds.), *Этнические рынки в России: пространство торга и место встречи* (pp. 159–171). Иркутск: Изд-во ИГУ.

Лыкова, М. (1995). Время «челноков» на исходе. *Вечерний Иркутск.*

Сунь, Х. (2002). Китайско-российская народная торговля на примере рынка Ябаолу (The Sino-Russian People's Trade on the Example of theYabaolu Market). *Проблемы Даль-Него Востока, 1*, 92–106.

CHAPTER 3

Caucasian *Biznes*, Local Trade, and Entrepreneurship

> The goals for which I strove were to depict nature in its prime traits, to find proof of the interworking of [natural] forces, and to achieve a sense of enjoyment which the immediate view gives to sensitive man.
>
> —Alexander von Humboldt, *Views of Nature*

In official statistics and public discussions, the traders described in the previous chapter are usually classified as small and medium/mid-sized or even micro-entrepreneurs (SMEs).[1] Such classifications are based on Western categories and linked to particular expectations. According to the awards committee for the 2011–2012 Global Award for Entrepreneurship

[1] The Georgian Ministry of Finance recognizes three categories of entrepreneurship or business: micro-business, small business, and big business. Micro-businesses are those with an annual sales volume below GEL 30,000 (ca. U.S.$18,000), small businesses are those with an annual sales volume below GEL 100,000 (ca. U.S.$60,000), and big businesses are those with over GEL 100,000. GeoStat, the national statistical office, differentiates between small firms (with fewer than twenty employees and an annual sales volume of less than GEL 500,000 [U.S.$300,000]) and medium-sized enterprises (fewer than a hundred employees and an annual sales volume of less than GEL 1,500,000 [U.S.$900,000]) (Rudaz, 2018: 80–81).

S. Fehlings, *Traders, Informal Trade and Markets between the Caucasus and China*, Politics and History in Central Asia,
https://doi.org/10.1007/978-981-19-5205-0_3

Research,[2] "entrepreneurial activity is one of the primary drivers of industrial dynamism, economic development, and growth" (Carlsson et al., 2013: 913). The entrepreneur, according to this understanding, is one who perceives, discovers, creates, and exploits opportunities (Shane & Venkataraman, 2000), an innovator making decisions and taking risks (Hébert & Link, 1989), and thus the prime agent of economic change (see Schumpeter, 1942).

A question currently debated in the post-Soviet context is how SMEs can unfold their full potential in a so-called transition economy. In this respect, SME studies focus on the relationship between SMEs, informality and formalization, and economic development (Williams & Round, 2007; Williams et al., 2009, 2012). Economists, in particular, have come to the assumption that, as says Philippe Rudaz "the integration of informal economic activities into the formal economy is an important part of the 'transition' process of former communist countries and one of the biggest challenges of building a market economy from scratch"(Rudaz, 2018). Usually, formality in this context is put on a level with keeping accounting records, using bank accounts, and operating with written contracts, which indicate cooperation with formal institutions like banks, tax authorities, and the law. The aim of current research thus usually is to understand under what conditions and at what point entrepreneurs transform their businesses from informal to formal and how this development is brought about—or could be accelerated (by training, for example). In short, how can these people be transformed into reliable taxpayers?[3]

Rudaz's analysis of a survey in Georgia in the course of our joint project revealed that the self-employed individuals and micro entrepreneurs of our target group did not usually meet economists' expectations by growing and formalizing their businesses; in Georgia, "the informal sector does not seem to be a building block for formal private sector development" but remains "unproductive and stagnant" (Rudaz, 2018: 88; cf. Karrar & Rudaz, 2022). From an economist's point of

[2] "The Global Award is a direct continuation of the International Award for Entrepreneurship and Small Business Research first launched in 1996 by the Swedish Entrepreneurship Forum (then the Foundation for Small Business Research, FSF) and the Swedish Agency for Economic and Regional Growth" (Carlsson et al., 2013: 914).

[3] Most of these studies come to the conclusion that local entrepreneurs need training and could be supported by reducing bureaucratic burdens (Sass et al., 2015).

view, this conclusion makes perfect sense. However, as an anthropologist, I would like to challenge the meaning of "entrepreneurial spirit" in this context and try to explain why traders are not interested in formalizing their businesses. I argue that the classification of *biznesmeny* (бизнесмены) as entrepreneurs obscures the local reality, inasmuch as the term "entrepreneur" is not representative of the local group of *biznesmeny* and traders, who are embedded in the local economic environment and occupy specific niches in this local setting.

If you ask a young Georgian or Armenian man about his job, you often will get the same answer, "I am a businessman" (*Ja biznesmen*, Я бизнесмен). The definite meaning of such a self-description is rather obscure. I was never sure how my Caucasian friends, neighbors, and interlocutors earned their livings. Obviously, they were very flexible and changed their jobs quite often. Unlike their parents, who had worked in permanent professions and workers' collectives, members of the younger generation surf the wave of capitalism, where business opportunities are rarely long-lasting or certain. Most of these business opportunities arise in the context of trading (*torgovlja*, торговля).

A young man (in his late twenties) I interviewed[4] during my fieldwork in Yerevan back in 2010 told me:

> I won't become a lawyer. That's 100 percent certain. Because I only went to the university twice after the fourth class. ... I had a computer shop for a long time. ... It wasn't going well anymore, and I shut it down. ... I bought ten computers from. ... [someone who] had no documents or anything. ... Two days later, the police came and told me the computers were stolen. ... I had to go to court, and this guy told them that I knew that the computers were stolen. For six or seven months, I had to go to court every day. But then I was 100 percent acquitted. Well, but then, how shall I explain? It wasn't going well anymore, and I shut it down. [...] There were some big problems. I bought ten computers from ... well ...there was a guy, and he told me he had an Internet cafe, and he would sell me the computers [...]. He had no documents or anything ... but I bought them. Two days later, the police came and told me the computers were stolen. [...] Then I had to go to court, and this guy told them that I knew that the computers were stolen. For six or seven months I had to go to court every day. But then I was 100% acquitted.

[4] Interview conducted in Russian and recorded.

This experience did not prevent this young man from engaging in further business activity. He found a job as manager of a supermarket and worked as a real-estate broker, because

> In Armenia, you make money if you buy and sell something. There is no such thing as a monthly salary. If there were a fixed monthly salary for a certain job, that would be great. In our country, it's different. You do a job and you get percentages; if you don't, you don't. You can't feed a family like that, right?! One month, it goes well, and you make money for a year in advance. Another month, you don't make enough for a normal living. You never know how much you will get in a month.

Hence, my interlocutor was enthusiastic about trade opportunities:

> Whatever you want to sell in Armenia, you will always find a customer. Prices are not important. There are people who tell me that they would like to have a shop or a flat in this or that building. When I ask them how much they are ready to spend, they tell me that it doesn't matter. "I want it, and that's it." We go there, and if I tell them, "It's $1,500 a square meter," then they'll say, "I'll pay $2,000. Just find me a place." Every year, everything is getting more and more expensive. That's why they buy. You can be 100 percent sure that you won't lose money. They will always profit.

These quotations are very typical. Many people in the Caucasus work as occasional traders and trade in everything, and sometimes in everything at the same time, while also pursuing other work opportunities (cf. Skvirskaja, 2019). Such "entrepreneurial eclecticism" (Hart, 1970) is common worldwide and has, for example, been noted by ethnographers in the Mediterranean region (Davis, 1977), where it has been called a *combinazioni*, using a Sicilian term (Schneider, 1969).

The Russian term *biznes* (бизнес) encompasses many activities, including both those of powerful business elites and the much less successful endeavors of individual petty, shuttle, and bazaar traders. While the first type of *biznes* has led to the complete rebuilding of post-Soviet cities, with the construction of commercial centers and shopping malls, hotels, and so-called elite housing (Fehlings, 2015), the second type has led to the proliferation of petty trade and bazaars. These have been developing and growing since the early 1990s and are often perceived by governments and elites as an obstacle to modernization (*modernizacija*, модернизация) and the adoption of a Western lifestyle (Alff, 2015, 2016; Fehlings, 2018; Karrar, 2020).

The people involved in the second type of *biznes* constitute a very heterogeneous group. They usually have little capital and rely on personal networks and their individual abilities. Since their economic impact as individuals seems unimportant, their activity is often overlooked and unregulated by state officials and thus does not figure in official statistics. In what follows, I focus on bazaar traders, albeit taking into account the fact that business elites' image and success, and perceptions of these, impact such small businesses. Treating informal practices as rational strategies of adaptation to specific niches, and showing how groups of traders adjust their economic activity to these niches within the broader system, I seek to provide an overview of local understandings of biznes (бизнес) and biznesmeny (бизнесмены).

Business Parameters

As noted above, Keith Hart uses the term "entrepreneurial eclecticism." Contrasting the "truly capitalistic entrepreneur" in the Western sense, who exploits a particular niche, with Ghanaian entrepreneurs who do not restrict themselves to one field, but, like Armenian businessmen, flexibly adapt to a variety of possibilities, Hart defines "anyone who controls the management of capital which he has invested in some enterprise in order to realize profit" as a "small-scale entrepreneur." Diversification in this context might be one particular "entrepreneurial strategy", used in "economies of uncertainty" to handle risk. Hart argues that the rigid categorization of activities (e.g., working as a cattle merchant, corn dealer, transport operator, property speculator, landlord, moneylender, or casual retailer) is of "limited sociological validity" in this context, because it obscures a reality in which diversification/eclecticism is a coherent economic approach (Hart, 1970: 107–108).

Although this view fits well with the evidence from the Caucasus, I believe that a preliminary categorization—at least of different aspects—of entrepreneurial activity is useful to get a better understanding of the many facets and the local meaning of *biznes*, which includes more than the management of capital, investment, and profit-seeking. A preliminary classification can provide a vocabulary with which to talk about and understand the complexity of the aforementioned entrepreneurial eclecticism. At the same time, it helps to understand the eclectic nature of the trading sector itself.

I argue that it may help to describe the practices one observes on the ground by thinking of them as a combination of (a) the locations where economic activity takes place, (b) the personal backgrounds of the people involved, (c) their networks, (d) their mobility, (e) the types of goods that are traded, and (f) the exchange volume and frequency of activity. Of course, in the next step, the parts must be put back together again. The parameters are linked to and determine one another, and they adapt to historical, political, and sociocultural dynamics. Employing Alexander von Humboldt's concept of the *Naturgemälde*, or "portrait of nature"),[5] I treat these parameters' combinations and interrelations as integrated into a broader ecosystem, seeking to determine the nature of each *biznes*, consisting in adaptations to various economic niches. In what follows I thus cluster my data accordingly, starting with the location where economic activity takes place.

Location and Types of Commerce

Anthropologists have studied "marketplaces" to learn more about economic activity, but also to learn something about social dynamics and culture in general. As mentioned in the Introduction, Alfred Gell (1982), for example, treated a marketplace in Dhorai as a symbolic map of Madhya Pradesh in Central India, showing how the outline of the market mirrors social hierarchy and how the booths are arranged according to the social status of market people.

In Tbilisi, in my experience, the quest for such spatial organization and coherence comes to almost nothing. The city is cluttered with street vendors, boutiques, bazaars, markets, small shops, and shopping malls. They coexist in close proximity, and often it is almost impossible to distinguish between them. Neither the people working in a given area nor the various types of businesses located there clearly delimit specific commercial areas. However, some physical and spatial characteristics do exist that point to contestable but possible classifications, corresponding to local terms such as *supermarketi* (Western-style "supermarket," შუპერმარკეტი), *maġazia* ("shop," მაღაზია), *bazari* ("bazaar" [an old-fashioned term, usually used for fruit and vegetable markets], ბაზარი), *bazroba* ("open air market" or "bazaar" [usually

[5] Broadly speaking here, a picture of different informal economic practices as rational coping strategies and perfect adaptations to specific conditions and niches in a system.

for huge places with a wide range of merchandise], ბაზრობა), *buṭiḳi* (Western-style "boutiques" or "brand shops", ბუტიკი), and *budḳa* (ბუდკა) in Georgian, for example, and *sowpermarket* (սուպերմարկետ), *xanowt'* ("shop," խանութ), *šowka* ("bazaar," շուկա), *krpak* (կրպակ), and so on, in Armenian.

The locations of economic exchange in Tbilisi (and in the Caucasus and Central Asia in general) can, in a first step, be classified as more or less formal or informal. In this context I use the adjectives "formal" and "informal" to describe the level of solidity and durability of the sales facilities, their ability to meet official sanitary standards, and their legal status. The sales facilities that I describe with these terms range from a piece of cloth spread on the ground in front of the vendor to pushcarts, booths, and stalls, small shops and kiosks (*kioski*, киоски), permanent boutiques and supermarkets, shopping malls and department stores, and roofed and unroofed bazaars of different sizes and levels of importance.

Public Space (Street Vending)

The less formal structures can be found in public spaces like streets, around bus and metro stations, or in parks. As Hamlet Melkumyan (2017) observed, proximity to central traffic junctions is typical of informal marketplace structures in Yerevan, as well as in Tbilisi. He argues that such structures appear in periods of instability and are removed when the state regains control. Rekhviashvili describes the same process and reports how in Georgia, street vendors who had populated public space in Tbilisi since the early 1990s were expelled from it starting in 2004 for two reasons: first, because "they did not fit into the government's political project of emphasizing Georgia's Europeanness, as they were a reminder of poverty, misery and disorder" (2015: 487), and second, because

> for the Georgian government, control of public space was necessary in order to pursue neoliberal marketisation policies. These policies required the removal of street vendors from public spaces, first because some of the sites previously occupied by petty traders were subjected to privatisation and second, and more importantly, because the state needed to restrict access to public space as a free/unlimited productive resource and limit its commercial use to delineate public and private property and allow commodification of urban land and property. (Rekhviashvili, 2015: 490)

The question of the legitimacy of street vending and its role in the city landscape is widely discussed in many post-Soviet countries. Street vendors' displays of goods are usually perceived as an obstacle to formal urban order and a modern city lifestyle, and the poor hygienic conditions are a main argument for critics (Dyatlov & Grigorichev, 2015; Pachenkov, 2011; Polese et al., 2016; Stephan-Emmrich & Mirzoev, 2016).

On the other hand, it is also generally admitted that street vending is a financial last resort for the urban poor and, moreover, a social meeting place, where elderly people, especially, come to talk and spend their leisure time (Melkumyan, 2017; Pachenkov, 2011). As a rule it is here that the poor vendor meets the poor costumer. But buying something from a street vendor may also have a charitable aspect (Antonyan, 2018). Quite often I heard that my acquaintances bought goods from street vendors to give them support. Prohibition of street vending in the Caucasus is therefore often interpreted as an inhumane act, which is why many state officials turn a blind eye to it. In Georgia, measures to ban street vending were relaxed with the change of government in 2012. It had never really disappeared, but after 2012, it was practiced openly again. It is currently part of the picture described above, even though there have been new attempts to restrict it.[6] Metro stations and the sidewalks of major streets like Rustaveli Street in the center of Tbilisi are lined with vendors who sell books, jewelry, souvenirs, religious objects, baby animals, flowers, fruit, and vegetables (Fig. 3.1).

But there are also places where vendors cluster as though in a marketplace. Some of these unofficial marketplaces, over time, can turn into official markets, which means that state institutions officially recognize them. This has been the case with the Suhoi Most (сухой мост, also called "Mshrali Khidi" in Georgian) flea market in Tbilisi and its Armenian equivalent, the Vernissage in Yerevan. As described by Melkumyan (2017) and Taalaibekova (2018; Taalaibekova & Melkumyan, 2018), both marketplaces came into being in the early 1990s and were unofficial trading places for spare parts and everyday household goods until, in recent years, they developed into tourist attractions and art and souvenir markets.[7]

[6] See *Legislative Herald of Georgia*: https://www.matsne.gov.ge/ka/document/view/2669376?publication=0&fbclid=IwAR3yBfn8Gzr2QZFMobk-ELK_NEsJBN2poCdyZr_RhaBrUlC5zMLdffMrTuU.

[7] Similar developments took place in other post-Soviet cities. Pachenkov's (2011) account of Udelnaja Flea Market in St. Petersburg, for example, reflects a similar history, a comparable background, and the same post-Soviet discourses.

Fig. 3.1 Open air market/street vending in Tbilisi, 2014

Bazaars (ლილოს ბაზრობა , Lilos Bazroba)

In 2004, the Georgian government, as mentioned, restricted street vending, calling on street vendors to move to privately owned marketplaces. This was difficult for many traders, who could not afford the rent of a stall in such a place. But those traders who managed to pay the bill automatically got an official license to sell their merchandise in their allocated location.

Marketplaces in Tbilisi vary widely in appearance. Some look like chaotic bazaars; others are orderly places that resemble shopping malls. Some specialize in food (e.g., the Deserter's Bazaar), others in spare parts and building materials (e.g., the Eliava Market, ელიავას ბაზრობა) or second-hand cars (e.g., the Rustavi Car Market, რუსთავის ავტობაზრობა), and still others in clothes, furniture, or everyday household goods (e.g., the Sadguri Bazaar, სადგურის ბაზრობა, and parts of Lilo Bazroba). Usually, there is a market administration, which collects rent from the traders and takes care of security measures. When I asked the manager of a privately owned market in Tbilisi's center how the market was organized, the conversation quickly came to an end: "People pay, they get a stall with a certain number of square meters, and then everything is fine. I do not know how they manage for the rest. That is none of my business."

The most important legal bazaar in Georgia is Lilo Malli (ლილო მოლი) or Lilo Bazroba (ლილოს ბაზრობა) (formerly called Elsavako) next to Tbilisi's airport. It is the largest bazaar in the Caucasus and Levan's and Ramaz's working base. Like many other bazaars of its type, it is located outside the city. According to Humphrey and Skvirskaja, "in relation to the city, which is also commercialized, such a market is like a bad boy alter ego" (2009: 62). Yet such markets "exert a huge influence on the city's regional clout, income, employment, immigration, and transport links" (2009: 62). This is true inter alia of the Central Bazaar in Astana, which was moved from the city center to the outskirts after 2008 (Baitas, 2017, 2019), of Dordoi in Bishkek (Alff, 2016; Karrar, 2017; Spector, 2017), Sed'moi in Odessa (Humphrey & Skvirskaja, 2009; Marsden, 2018), and Barakholka in Yerevan (Melkumyan, 2017) and Lilo Bazroba is not an exception. "Attempts to contain the market and its influences from seeping into urban life also reflect aspects of Russian orientalism: the bazaar was one of the key images of exotic yet dangerous Central Asia," Marsden writes (2016: 35).

In front of Lilo Bazroba, there is a parking area for private cars, taxis, and minibuses. Public transportation connects Lilo to the Varketili metro station, which is the final station on one of Tbilisi's metro lines and connects to the city center. Lilo Bazroba was the first commercial center in Georgia established with the government's official permission. Like most similar bazaars in Central Asia and other post-Soviet countries, including Cherkizovsky (Черкизовский рынок) in Moscow (Guzei, 2015) and the bazaars mentioned in the previous paragraph, it was founded in 1991.

In an interview in September 2018, the marketing manager of Lilo told me that the founders and the current owners of the marketplace were "seven individuals—seven friends—who bought the site of the bazaar very cheaply in the 1990s, when it was considered wasteland." These seven individuals (who have since become millionaires, I was told) did not have a background in commerce. One of them was a school director. In photographs displayed in the market's administration building, they look like ordinary people—a group of friends. As far as I know, they were not associated with crime or violence—unlike the Central Asian key figures who wield power in bazaars in Kyrgyzstan and Kazakhstan as described by Karrar (2019) and Spector (2017). Still, the 1990s were opaque times, and there are jokes about businesses that emerged in that period. Nino, one of my friends, who worked as a psychologist, said: "These rich people always tell you the same story: 'At that time it was really very cheap.' Or 'Ah, you know, I got it as a present... from someone.' We make fun of them saying: 'Don't ask me about my first million! About the second million, please, go right ahead and ask—it's clean!'" Still, the image of Lilo's owners is relatively neutral.

Lilo Bazroba covers a territory of about 22 hectares and includes more than 5000 trading units.[8] In September 2018, the administration had registered 4000 traders. An official map at the bazaar entrance announces a tidy structure of clustered sectors, which are assigned to specific groups of goods like furniture, clothes, and kitchen- and tableware. In reality, the picture is much more confusing. The market consists of a labyrinth of narrow corridors, which have names like "Italian Corridor," "French Corridor," or "European Corridor" and are lined by thousands of stalls chockful of cheap merchandise from Turkey, Iran, and China. There are corridors for specific goods, but usually, this order does not correspond to the official map (or to the corridors' names), and advice from market people is necessary to find a specific outlet (Fig. 3.2). While some parts of the bazaar are terribly crowded on busy days, other parts are literally deserted. There are areas for wholesale *optovaja torgovlja* (оптовая торговля) and retail sale (*rozničnaja torgovlja*, розничная торговля), for Chinese goods, and for Turkish goods. In some sectors the majority of vendors come from Azerbaijan, and there are also some Chinese businesspeople and representatives of other ethnic minorities. But unlike in other trading hubs in Eurasia (cf., e.g., Humphrey & Skvirskaja, 2009; Marsden, 2016, 2018; Steenberg, 2016), the space is not organized according to ethnic merchant groups, perhaps because it is relatively homogeneous ethnically and most of the traders are Georgian.

However, in the corridors, clients from all over the Caucasus and further abroad walk from stall to stall to compare the quality and prices of the merchandise. "Lilo is always crowded, and people come here to buy things, because they get them cheaper here than anywhere else," my interlocutors claimed. The marketplace was constantly growing, according

[8] Tbilisee: http://tbilisee.com/en/place/is/882-Lilo-Mall.

to the market's marketing manager, who proudly told me that a recent inquiry showed that every citizen of Georgia had visited Lilo Bazroba at least three times in his or her life. Sales are highest in the month before school starts. Irma said her clients came from Azerbaijan, western Georgia, and even Israel; whereas Azeris and western Georgians were big spenders, easy to please, Tbilisi residents and foreign Jews loved to bargain:

> They are always bargaining, take the cheapest clothes, and pay the lowest prices. This is different with Georgian clients coming from western Georgia (from Guruli), who like to spend more money, because they like to show off. These people live close to the Turkish border. ... The Turkish cities along the Georgian border are small, and thus one can find a bigger assortment of Turkish goods (coming from Istanbul) at the Lilo market than in those places.

Prices in the bazaar are negotiable but do not differ too much from the initial, written prices, although bargaining is an art characteristic of the "bazaar economy" in the Caucasus and expected at Lilo. Zviad told me that his father was an expert bargainer, who teased his son and wife about it, saying, "You'd pay more than the trader asks!" He himself was unskilled at it, Zviad confessed. "Once we tried with some of my friends, and the traders got really angry. You have to know how to talk, how to joke, how to behave." Zviad's father spent a lot of time going around the whole marketplace, checking all the prices, comparing them, and criticizing the quality of the goods, all in a gentle, joking manner. Whether it was "about cucumbers or something important and valuable" made no difference to him.

Traders and shopkeepers usually sit inside or in front of their stalls. They might own one or more stalls, which they run with the help of close family members or an employee. Sometimes they visit other traders and shopkeepers in their stalls for a chat or to help out if one of them has to leave for a while. Men sometimes play backgammon (***nardy***) or chess on an improvised table in a corner of the corridor, and from time to time someone comes by with a pushcart selling hot drinks, bread, boiled corn, or pastries.

Next to the bazaar, there is the administration building, where traders can register their businesses and buy or rent stalls. Four hundred people

Fig. 3.2 Inside a Tbilisi bazaar, 2014

were employed to run the market, to organize documentation, registration, selling of stalls, insurance, infrastructure, and so on, the market manager told me in 2018. There were firemen, a medical center, and even a market TV channel. Not long before, the market's management had funded "Lilo Capital," a bank offering microcredits exclusively to Lilo Bazroba's traders.

Around the market, there are other bank branches, currency exchange offices, coffee shops and fast-food outlets, and a little further away, huge warehouses, whose facilities were sometimes shared by several traders. Zviad told me that, as a microcredit expert, he had visited some of these to check conditions there and the merchandise. In Zviad's opinion, the security measures were poor: "Sometimes, there is just a dog, which serves as a guard for a huge quantity of goods." Some traders told him that goods had been stolen, and that they had not realized it immediately, but only at the end of the month, when something was missing in the inventory. Goods are usually brought to the warehouses after having cleared customs. Tbilisi's customs area is not far off. Lilo Bazroba also has its own terminal, but it is too small for the incoming goods. When Zviad and I talked to a security man, he told us that all warehouses of the market's terminal were full. Sometimes goods are stored in the customs area while the import duties on them are being paid in instalments (see also Chapter 4 on this). After duties have been paid on it, merchandise is brought to Lilo Bazroba on small trucks by the post office. Irma once told me that she did not have enough money to pay the import duties on all the dresses she had bought in Turkey on her latest trip. She first had to sell some of the merchandise to be able to pay the duties on the rest, withheld by the customs officials. This seems to be a common situation. The usual period for paying the amount due is five to thirty days after clearance. But goods can be stored in the customs warehouse for up to five years.[9]

The prices traders pay for spaces in Lilo seem to vary. A market woman told me in 2016 that she paid an initial price of 10,000 lari (U.S.$5,882)[10] to get her space, which means, she paid for the right to use it. Two years later, prices had gone down. She had heard that a neighboring stall was sold for 5,000 lari (U.S.$1,850).[11] Additionally, traders payed a monthly fee or rent of 200 lari (U.S.$74). According to the bazaar administration, the minimum rent in spring 2017 was 10 lari (U.S.$4)[12] per square meter and the maximum rent 20 lari (U.S.$8) per square meter. Rents were usually slightly more expensive in the retail sector than in the wholesale one.[13]

It is very difficult to estimate the average monthly sales volume and profit of a Lilo trader. The administration told me that they have no information about it, and in our survey, 44% of respondents refused to

[9] Revenue Service "What do you know about the clearance of goods": http://www.rs.ge/en/5380.

[10] Exchange rate from September 2014.

[11] Exchange rate from September 2016.

[12] Exchange rate from September 2017.

[13] The marketing manager of Lilo Bazroba told me in 2018 that the market owners were about to change the regulations and would start to really sell the land to the traders, which would make traders owners of their allocated spots. Then, they would only have to pay a monthly fee for security and cleaning. Zviad tried to find out about the prices but was told that he would have to write an official inquiry and that the market administration would then decide individually about the price of a possible place based on its location.

answer questions about their earnings or said they didn't know. About 25%, however, said they earned less than U.S.$2,400 annually, about 22% of them said they earned between U.S.$2,400 and U.S.$6,000, and about 10% said they earned more than U.S.$6,000 (Rudaz, 2019). Profit margins were definitely small. 62% of the respondents stated that they were not able to reinvest in their businesses. According to their answers, about 26% of traders, apparently just managed to survive, while about 42% of them could afford only a very simple living standard. Just 2.4% of traders stated that they lived comfortably on their incomes (Rudaz, 2019). The cohort of traders in a position to grow their businesses is thus rather small.

Irma is a good example. She told us that she had a monthly sales volume of about 10,000 lari (U.S.$5,882).[14] She travelled to Turkey once a month and usually imported fifteen to twenty dresses, each of which she sold for about 180 lari (U.S.$79). The ticket to Istanbul and back to Georgia costed between 300 and 700 lari (U.S.$130–300), usually, about 500 lari (U.S.$220). Besides the ticket, she had to pay for accommodation during her travels, import duties (18%), and taxes. We got to know Irma through one of Zviad's friends working for BIG, a private micro-credit agency, which had given her a loan. Her working routine is typical for many traders working in Lilo and other Caucasian bazaars. When we arrived at her stall, she was usually busy with customers. Usually, some woman was trying on a dress and looking at herself in the mirror while Irma gave her cheerful comments. There was a small, enclosed area in the back of the stall where customers could change clothes and where Irma could rest and drink a cup of coffee. Irma was 45 years old and attractive, with a stylish hairstyle, bright eyes, and an athletic figure. Her daughter was a philologist and taught English at a school in Tbilisi, and Irma had a five-year-old granddaughter. As Irma lived on the other side of the city, she had to bike to the market every day. On a usual working day, she started work about nine in the morning and stayed in her stall until four or five in the afternoon. Irma specialized in evening gowns and cocktail dresses. In the beginning, she told me, she had travelled to Baku. Starting in 2000, she bought winter clothes from China there. In 2005, she started to travel to Istanbul. Even though similar merchandise was produced in Georgia, importing was profitable. Irma kept all

[14] Exchange rate from September 2014.

her stock—about a hundred dresses—in her stall. She had no storage and only one of each dress. As she told us, her strategy was not to buy things just because they sold well. Unlike Levan or other traders in Lilo, she did not buy in bulk but just because there was demand. She always tried to have something new in stock and had to travel two or three times a month to achieve this.[15] Customers continually stopped to have a look at her goods while we sat with her. In about an hour, she sold two dresses. Most customers did not take a long time over their decisions. Maybe they had already compared the dresses to other dresses in other stalls. Irma had some clients who came back to her regularly. Most of these bought dresses to wear themselves. She had only a few clients from western Georgia who bought larger quantities to resell. Irma would prefer to buy merchandise of higher quality, because, as she said, there was a demand, and because few traders stocked clothes of superior quality. However, she did not yet have enough capital to do so.

The term "bazaar" (Georgian *bazroba*) covers the structures, practices, and strategies described for Lilo Bazroba. Since they are officially recognized, bazaars in Georgia differ from street vending. Having a bazaar stall requires the capital to pay fees and comply with tax regulations, but bazaars are very chaotic, especially in their physical appearance. As in Kazakhstan, bazaars in the Caucasus are "frequently represented in public as shady leftovers of post-Soviet transition. They are associated in political and public discourse with Chinese-made contraband goods, illegal appropriation of land as well as anti-sanitary conditions and are envisaged [as eventually] to be transformed, through state intervention, into 'modern' or 'civilized' shopping centres" (Alff, 2014: 1). In Georgia, the semi-legal outskirts of the Sadguri Bazaar (სადგურის ბაზრობა) were cleared by the Georgian police in 2011[16] (Polese et al., 2016). The same thing happened in Armenia, and in Kazakhstan and Bishkek, parts of major bazaars have burned down under obscure circumstances (Karrar, 2020).

Upper-class shoppers (the upper middle class and the local elites) therefore prefer to avoid bazaars, seen as places of low prestige. They have the smell of backwardness, associated with a negative image of "the Orient"

[15] In September, she travelled only once. The reason—apparently—was that she did not have enough money for more travel.

[16] Radio Tavisupleba, 21 October 2011: https://www.radiotavisupleba.ge/a/24366836.html?fbclid=IwAR0GXcYKQEG6KMwkhLQWjdTFTq20wmC1dKoao4LKsTP3p_OTsE2j0x-9M.

and their own "oriental" past (Humphrey & Skvirskaja, 2009; Karrar, 2017). Lilo Bazroba is, however, the most important trading hub in the region, a business worth millions, and, like other bazaars in the Caucasus, it is expanding.

Boutiques and Shopping Malls

Natia, with whom I lived regularly when I stayed in Tbilisi, told me that she was happy that "fewer and fewer Georgians shop at bazaars." In her opinion, this was a marker of positive change and a sign of the recovery of Georgia's national economy:

> If these women[17] don't sell anything in the bazaars, this is a good sign for our country. It means that people don't have to buy this cheap stuff anymore. Now we have little boutiques, where one can buy better quality. They often have sale opportunities. Students are already able to shop there. ... Before, everyone was walking around in the same clothes. It was so sad. There was no individuality. All women had the same skirts, and all men looked the same. They had these black leather jackets. The term "black leather jacket" became a synonym for "Georgian man" because of that.

As we can see from Natia's remarks, fancy boutiques (*buṭiḳebi*, ბუტიკები), malls (*molebi*, მოლები), and supermarkets (*supermarḳeṭebi*, შუპერმარკეტები) are not merely places to buy utilitarian objects but represent a lifestyle. They are where people spend their leisure time. Tbilisi has five Carrefours, and a new shopping mall called East Point opened recently, with brand-name shops, an attractive pedestrian area, restaurants, a playground for children, and slot machines, bowling, and other attractions for adults. People like to go there with their friends in the evenings or on weekends. The mall is also an evening destination for day-trippers from neighboring Azerbaijan. It is easy to access, since it is located on the main route between Tbilisi and the airport. As I could see for myself, the mall was a world apart, and everyone who came there looked stylish and wealthy.

I often heard that the things sold in boutiques in the city center and in Carrefour hypermarkets did not really differ from those sold in Lilo Bazroba. There was a huge discussion about fake brands and authentic

[17] Natia was talking about women because we had previously had a conversation about female shuttle traders.

goods. Goods sold in bazaars were usually suspected of being fake. But apparently boutiques and malls often obtained their merchandise from Lilo's traders and resold it for a much higher price. One of my interlocutors, Dato, who sold garden furniture and plastic items from Turkey and China, was just about to sign a contract with Carrefour when I visited him in his shop. This trader fully understood that some people simply did not want to come to Lilo. Even Zviad admitted that he preferred to go to a boutique instead of "taking crowded public transportation to Lilo and strolling around the bazaar corridors, where the amount of goods is overwhelming, it is necessary to compare prices and bargain, and it takes a lot of time just to buy a few items." Lilo Bazroba's traders like Dato or Levan did not mind. Both reported that the new shopping malls did not affect their business.

Other Commercial Facilities and General Remarks

Boutiques, malls, and supermarkets take many forms and do not, of course, constitute the full spectrum of sales outlets in the Caucasus. Economic exchange also occurs at other locations, including kiosks (***kioski***, киоски), small shops, and brand-name outlets. All these places, even the more permanent structures, are constantly undergoing changes in appearance.

Shopping malls, bazaars, and street vendors coexist side by side and sometimes compete for the same territory. Shops, goods, merchants, and consumers come and go, and one can probably classify all the places mentioned above as "non-places" as defined by Marc Augé (2008), which is to say, places characterized by the transit of large numbers of people who do not have strong ties to the location, such as airports and train, bus, or metro stations. This is certainly true of many commercial spaces, independent of their importance or central location. However, such places are "humanized" by people's "disagreements and confusions," making them "very much *places*," Caroline Humphrey and Vera Skvirskaja insist. "Along with face-to-face encounters with traders and purchasers," they include several types of "networks" and "clusters of trust, cooperation, and hostility" (Humphrey & Skvirskaja, 2009: 62).

Importance and centrality are two important features that have to be considered in order to understand marketplaces' position within the local and global geographical, political, and economic landscape, and within trade/commodity chains and the web of marketplaces and trade routes within and beyond the Caucasus (Dannhaeuser, 1989; Gereffi et al.,

2003; Hahn, 2018; Humphrey & Skvirskaja, 2009). Lilo Bazroba plays a major role in this web, as we have seen. Before opening his stall in Lilo, Levan had a shop in the Voksali/Sadgori Bazaar in the city center of Tbilisi's city center. He told me that he could sell shoes he sells for 60 lari in Lilo for 300 lari there. But whereas he might sell one pair of shoes per day in the city center, he sold 50–100 pairs in Lilo, he claimed. Even though these numbers appear highly exaggerated, they reflect a certain logic.

But let me come back to the topic of sales facilities and space. Not all the economic activities in the Caucasus or Central Asia have a proper and defined space. This is true in several senses. Some activities are simply invisible, in the sense that they are not apparent in public spaces, marketplaces, or commercial buildings. Some traders, for example, trade from their private homes. Customers have to know where to find them, and in their own neighborhoods, they usually do. Then there are traders and vendors who go from house to house. The Georgian *mac̣oni* (მაწონი) and the Armenian *t'an* (թան) vendors (curd vendors) are typical examples. Like the *chelnoki* mentioned in the previous chapter, many shuttle traders who bring goods from other countries do not sell them publicly, but collect orders from neighbors, relatives, friends, and acquaintances and deliver the goods directly to these clients, or they organize a little bazaar, as Shushan's family did in the 1990s.

Finally, young people, especially, use virtual space for selling and shopping. Amazon does not operate in Georgia, but Amazon and other online shops can be accessed through intermediaries. A friend of mine regularly bought toys and clothes for her two-year-old daughter in Canada using the services of an intermediary with an American address. After the ordered items had been sent to this address, they were forwarded to Georgia, where they had to pass through customs. Then Tamta simply picked up her package at an address in Tbilisi. A colleague of mine used a similar service (USA2Georgia) to buy clothes and shoes from the United States and was very satisfied: "As amounts are small, there is no customs fee. But of course, you have to be honest and declare everything the right way. Otherwise, you are going to be fined." I asked her why not everybody takes advantage of this option. She was sure that it was a matter of education: "People just don't know about it and don't know how to use the Internet." But there might be other reasons, too. Zviad had two friends who each wanted to sell a car. One advertised his car on the Internet; the other regularly went to the Rustavi Car Market. Zviad explained that it was a question of time. In his opinion, it takes time to sell something on the Internet. In Zviad's words:

> People come to the marketplace because they really want to buy a car. There are many potential buyers, and these buyers want to see and touch the car. They want to drive a little bit to check whether everything is fine. You cannot check these things by looking at a photograph on the net. And then, not all people use the Internet. There are a lot of buyers from abroad, for example, from Iran or from Azerbaijan. They may not know the Georgian websites.

When my roommate Natia bought her car, she adopted a mixed strategy. She went to Rustavi to check the prices and to get an idea of how much she should pay. Then she bought a car that she found on a website. She thought it was cheaper than it would have been in Rustavi, "because in Rustavi, people have to rent a space. If traders do not manage to sell their cars, they must rent the space for a long time, and therefore the car gets more and more expensive."

I doubt that cheap products from China and Turkey will ever become more easily or cheaply accessible through individual Internet orders. Individual online shopping usually, at least currently, involves luxury goods from Europe or the United States. Thus Internet shopping and Internet advertising are probably not going to affect all branches of trade. However, they may become established in some niches, like real estate, I imagine, which up to now has remained to some extent in the hands of brokers who are in the habit of waiting for clients on the street adjacent to the Suhoj Most ("dry bridge," сухой мост) flea market. Still, Lilo Bazroba's management recently initiated an online service, Liloshop.ge, where one can order a selection of goods sold by traders in the bazaar. The administration takes the goods from the traders and then delivers them to the costumers, even to those living in outlying regions.

Personal Background

As is obvious in the case of Internet shopping, there is often a relation between the type of economic activity and the personal backgrounds of the people who choose to engage in it. Age, gender, family, class or social status, education, ethnicity, religion, and urban or rural origins may all influence economic practice.

Age
Elderly people practicing strategies of survival are commonly found at the lower end of the trading spectrum. When I gave a talk in Tübingen about my initial idea of doing research on "elderly women involved in the petty and shuttle trade," my colleague Shahnaz Nadjmabadi asked ironically how old these "elderly women" were to be. There is a comforting answer: this question cannot be answered with a precise number. To some degree, the saying that a person is always as old as she feels is very true in this context. People who feel and are perceived as old in post-Soviet economies are usually people who have had difficulties in adapting to new post-Soviet circumstances. They feel like victims of historical events—of the dissolution of the Soviet Union and the transition. Aged from fifty upward, they made their work careers and professional lives under socialism. Many of them worked as skilled workers in factories, engineers, school or university teachers, or state officials. When Soviet factories and institutions closed, they were left with nothing but a small pension and an education that had lost its importance. In the 1990s, this was the recruitment group of the so-called *chelnoki*, whose story is told in the previous chapter.

But the *chelnoki* were a temporary phenomenon, directly linked to the transition crisis of the 1990s. When the national economies recovered, ordinary people stopped engaging in this kind of small-scale trading. Elderly people are in general highly respected in the Caucasus. Their families support them, and their advice is highly valued (Dragadze, 2016). At the same time, since pensions are low, elderly people depend on family and household members economically. If they are obliged to beg or peddle petty goods, social factors—lack of support from relatives, for example—are usually involved. If they get no support from relatives, they find themselves in a precarious and vulnerable situation, which is what pushes them onto the streets. On a night train from Baku to Tbilisi, I once met a woman in her late fifties or early sixties who had just returned from a trading expedition to China. She told me that her son and his wife had died in a car accident, and that she was now alone looking after her grandchild. The life stories that force elderly people into trade are usually as sad as this example and leave their victims without alternatives.

Age, of course, does not per se exclude an individual from becoming an oligarch. Few members of the economic elite are very young. Lilo Bazroba's owners, for example, are approximately in their sixties. As a rule, high social standing is required for oligarch status, which usually means access to a large and important social network. Age is necessary for acquiring this. Let me give an example. During my fieldwork in Yerevan, I met a businessman who was in his sixties. He was a very energetic man and probably did not consider himself old. He had lived in Russia for a while and had worked for the Armenian Economics Ministry after Armenia's independence. He was now buying and selling trains, railway cars, and airplane engines, which he bought from post-Soviet countries and sold in Iran. I once accompanied him to an auction. He bought a train there that was being sold by a friend of his, with whom he reminisced about the army and the Soviet past. This friend had been a kolkhoz head in Soviet times and had obviously profited from privatization. After the breakdown of the Soviet system, "former enterprises did their best to make direct deals, often preferring barter to cash. The leaders of these quasi-feudal 'suzerainties' were of course interested in converting their socialist political credentials into economic capital" (Hann, 2005: 548). Bruce Grant, who published three conversations with Russian entrepreneurs talking about this process and the socioeconomic environment of the 1990s, concludes, "What started as privatization turned into 'grabification'" (1999: 214).

Having friends and being established (both acquired with age), as I deduce from my own conversations and case studies as well as those published by Grant, were essential in this process. On another day, my Armenian acquaintance took me to an informal meeting with two of his friends. One was the head of a huge company (processing tufa granules), the other a young politician, probably "someone's son." They talked about their contacts and discussed business opportunities and the current election campaign. I was not too surprised by this get-together. At least in the first years after independence, Caucasian elites were recruited from among old Soviet cadres and military personnel. Some of them successfully converted their social relations into political or/and economic power.

Subsequently, however, they were gradually replaced by a younger generation of new business elites. This did not mean that the elder generation completely lost its influence (Iskandaryan, 2014). At least in economic terms, the elder elite can still be considered successful and wealthy and maintains contacts to the new league of politician, as shown by the example of my acquaintance, who probably still ranks among the modest representatives of this species. When we travelled to Gumri in his car, the landscape passing by the window transformed into a patchwork of properties that he identified as belonging to the who's who of Armenian society. Locals, in Armenia as well as in Georgia, are interested in their oligarch's property. When I travelled through Georgia, there was always someone around to tell me which oligarch had built which building, restored which city, or bought which lands. Usually, one knows where these people were born, educated and how they made their money. One may regard them with indignation, but also feels awe and admiration.

Although there are few young beggars, being young does not automatically entail economic success either. Unemployment is relatively high[18] among Georgian as well as Armenian[19] (male) youth. Many young men thus cannot meet the expectations of their families and play the traditional role of family providers. They are unable to marry and start their own families or to host guests (or at least have reservations about doing so), since they depend on their parents economically. According to Frederiksen this can be a reason for depression, emasculation, alcoholism, and drug abuse (2012, 2013).

In Georgia as well as in Armenia, many young men find role models among local business elites, who represent the rich segment of *biznesmeny* and whose consumption patterns are imitated (Fehlings, 2014, 2015; Frederiksen, 2012; Humphrey, 2002). Some of these young men do in fact run businesses, perhaps not overwhelmingly successful ones, but ones they can make a living from, and sometimes there are cases of real economic success, even in the bazaar. However, many among this group of young men depend on the small incomes of their parents, who, if they have no other choice, might themselves work in small-scale trade. Sometimes members of the older generation invest almost everything in their offspring's image and put money into cars and clothes that give their sons the appearance of rich businessmen. I observed this among my neighbors in both Yerevan and Tbilisi. Parents hope that this helps their children to become established and gain status, which later may help them to obtain a job and to earn money. Clothes make people.

[18] The youth unemployment rate in Georgia averaged 33.03% from 2007 until 2018, reaching an all time high of 39.87% in 2009 and a record low of 26.60% in 2018 (https://tradingeconomics.com/georgia/youth-unemployment-rate).

[19] The youth unemployment rate in Armenia ranged between 26.96 and 40.71% (in 2009) between 2008 and 2018. It averaged 36.57% between 2016 and 2018 (https://www.statista.com/statistics/811634/youth-unemployment-rate-in-armenia/).

Another solution to the problem of precarious economic status among young people is, of course, labor migration, as shown by the high emigration rates (Dermendzhieva, 2011). Usually, one finds a combination of strategies. The example of the young businessmen from Armenia outlined at the start of this chapter and Bacho's attempts to gain independence from his father are typical of young men in the Caucasus who are "doing *biznes*" in some form or other. As I noted among Georgian students, some of whom I taught at Ivane Javakhishvili University and whom I have known for many years now, young people are still marrying and having kids. They are still making a living, even under difficult circumstances. But young people seek new opportunities outside the bazaar. As our survey shows, the average bazaar trader in Lilo Bazroba is older (around forty-one) than the average trader in Dordoi in Bishkek (around thirty-eight). Since profits are higher in Central Asian bazaars, the bazaar trade might be more attractive to younger people there than it is in the Caucasus.

Gender

Aside from the elderly, many of the poorest traders are women aged from thirty to sixty, who usually work for a very low profit margin. As I learned, this small income is crucial for many family budgets. This was especially true in the early 1990s, the so-called dark or black years (*c'owrt tariner*, ցուրտ տարիներ, *černye gody*, черные годы), when some households literally depended on "women selling cookies in the street." Levon Abrahamian, one of my Armenian colleagues, observed: "In times of crises, like those of the dark years, one falls back on primitive forms of economic behavior: hunting and gathering."

For Abrahamian, trading, especially petty trade, was a form of gathering, which he classified as a natural occupation of women. I am not sure how he came to this conclusion, but it is true that women were pioneers of post-Soviet labor migration and petty trade (Cieślewska, 2014; Mukhina, 2009). When she remembered the women traders of the 1990s, Natia got emotional, saying: "These women saved our country." In times of crisis, they replaced men, who lost their ability to act as breadwinners for their families.

This new role of women resulted in many intrafamilial conflicts. On the one hand, some women, especially young women, acquired unusual status and a respected position within their families because of their contributions to family income, which put them in the new position of competing with male family members (Abrahamian, 2007b). On the other hand, women working as traders, especially young women, were exposed to all kinds of risks, last but not least that of losing their reputations. Petty trade, labor migration, human trafficking, and prostitution are often equated, and there are many stories about women who were sexually abused when travelling abroad (Giragosian, 2009).[20] The temporary or permanent absence of women is thus considered a source of shame for their families—especially for male family members, who could be reproached for their inability to care for their women and their families (Ferry, 2013; Lundkvist-Houndoumadi, 2010). According to traditional role models,

> Whereas the honour of men is achieved by assertion and dominance, the honour of women is passive and mainly associated with sexual modesty. As with manly honour, their passivity reflects also on the wider honour of their family and therefore of their menfolk, and to a lesser extend on that of their associates. Honour, and its corollary shame,[21] are constant preoccupations in Georgia. (Mars & Altman, 1983: 548)

Today, not least the women themselves blame their husbands for exposing them to shameful situations. Thus, a female vegetable trader whom I met on a *maršuṭka* (minibus, маршрутка, მარშრუტკა) ride from Tbilisi to Yerevan told me that she was tired of travelling. "You have to eat, and I have two children," she said in a sarcastic tone, tacitly blaming her husband for not putting bread on the table.

People mention different reasons for why men were more reluctant to start to work as petty traders. Some say that women have better communication skills, which are necessary in this business. At the same time, the low end of petty trade has been regarded up to now as a primitive, low-prestige occupation, sometimes associated with female inferiority (Heyat, 2002; Werner, 2004). There are of course men who work as petty traders, too. But men usually get involved in more institutionalized or at least more respected forms of trade, which are, as mentioned earlier,

[20] There are similar associations and debates in Central Asia (Stephan-Emmrich & Mirzoev, 2016).

[21] In anthropology, especially Mediterranean value systems have been presented as classifications of honor and change. Herzfeld criticizes that honor and shame "are inefficient glosses on a wide variety of indigenous terminological systems." Still, "the various taxonomic systems [...] do nevertheless exhibit a common concern" (Herzfeld, 1980: 339).

distinguished from *chelnoki*-like petty and shuttle trade by calling them *biznes*.[22] *Biznes*—at least as imagined by its practitioners—is less chaotic, less risky, and less dangerous. It promises more profit, more comfort, and more prestige. Above all, it is considered a "real job." Levan and Ramaz, for example, who started their enterprises in the 1990s and had gone through the experience of losing their jobs and becoming *chelnoki* out of necessity, have since managed to establish themselves as *biznesmeny*. In their case, this means that they grew their businesses and turned them into their permanent and respected professions.

According to a Global Entrepreneurship Monitor (GEM)[23] study in Georgia from 2014 (Lezhava et al., 2014), 68.0% of female and 64.6% of male respondents considered starting a new business a desirable career move. More than 70% of both male and female respondents agreed that individuals who are successful in starting a new business enjoy a high level of reputation and respect in society, and 32.8% of women and 38.0% of men believed that they would have an opportunity to start a business in the next six months. While 43.3% of men felt capable of starting a new business, only 26.7% of women felt they had the required skills, knowledge, and experience to do so. Fear of failure, again, was higher among women (42.0%) than among men (31.3%).

Motivations for starting a business point in a similar direction. While 53.3% of women started their businesses because there were no better options (necessity-driven), and 46.7% were opportunity-driven, 41% of men's decisions were necessity-driven, and 58.2% opportunity-driven. According to the data collected by the GEM consortium, "the prevalent opinion is that while it's acceptable for women to start a new business, it's not much encouraged or supported... [although] if they do, there is no discrimination of 'glass ceiling' for them to overcome" (Lezhava et al., 2014: 20). Still, to my experience, the image of the successful "biznesMAN" is associated with male behavior and virtues, which are unlike many of the qualities attributed to Caucasian women.

[22] Compare Heyat (2002) on gender in entrepreneurship in Azerbaijan.

[23] The Global Entrepreneurship Monitor (GEM) was initiated in 1999 as a joint project of Babson College (USA) and London Business School (UK). It is a resource for national and global statistical data and information on entrepreneurship (see Global Entrepreneurship Monitor (GEM) "Mission").

Education, Personal Skills, and Ethnicity

Whether trading can be considered a real job, a question currently raised in the Caucasus, is quite a delicate matter. In an article draft in which I was struggling with classifications in terms of formality and informality, I differentiated between "occasional" and "professional" traders, saying that "many traders who sell their merchandise on streets or in open bazaars do not perceive themselves as (formally) professional traders, as they are usually formally trained in completely different professions." My Georgian colleague Lela Rekhviashvili commented: "Nowhere in the world are all or even a majority of traders and/or entrepreneurs educated in economics." She was right. And even if people are trained in economics as an academic discipline, this does not necessarily imply that they are or become good traders or businessmen, as I learned from a Georgian professor of economics at one of Tbilisi's most prestigious universities.

During one of our conversations, this professor talked about his lectures and his students. He was not very positive about the latter: "In Georgia it's all about a degree. Nothing else matters." Therefore, according to the professor, his students were not really interested in his subject and had no ambitions to learn and to progress. Most of the students, according to him, got their degrees without having acquired any knowledge: "They already have a business and continue as they always did," or "they end up in banks working in the front offices, where one simply has to know some sentences by heart and make some copies." Even though economists like this professor certainly hold a different opinion, the popular conviction is that education is not necessary or at least not essential to becoming a successful trader or businessperson. According to our survey, almost 48% of our respondents had an educational level limited to a primary or secondary school diploma, and 37.5% had a university degree, but not necessarily in economics. These numbers, in comparison to the results of the same survey in Kyrgyzstan, reflect a relatively low educational level among Georgian traders in comparison to their Central Asian counterparts.

In order to become successful, according to the popular perception in the Caucasus, one above all needs specific personal skills: One has to be talented, naturally gifted, and have a certain predisposition. One needs to be able to communicate and to build networks. Language skills (Russian, Chinese, or Turkish) are the only knowledge that might be gained through education and that might be considered beneficial. This was the consensus of most of the traders, friends, and colleagues I talked to.[24]

As noted earlier, in the Caucasus, and perhaps in many parts of the post-Soviet world, talent and predisposition are often associated with gender and ethnic and religious background. Given their attributed virtue of being smart (and sneaky), Jews[25] and Armenians have traditionally been reputed to be talented traders (cf. Skvirskaja, 2019). Especially in Soviet times, when trading was prohibited, Jews were known to be very active *spekuljanty* (traders, спекулянты). According to my colleague Ketevan, "they knew exactly how to do it and could provide everything you needed." Jewish traders even developed a cryptolect, a mixture of Georgian grammar and Georgian and Hebrew terms, which they used as a secret mercantile language (Pourtskhvanidze, 2021). A famous Tbilisian Jew of that era, known as Chashka, worked as a pharmacist: "He never got into trouble" Ketevan said. "Even the government needed him. State officials get ill, too, and they need medecine. He had absolutely everything."

A Soviet story about Jewish traders from the village of Surami is legendary[26]:

> The village people were very famous *spekuljanty*. They traded in everything you could imagine. To do so, they cooperated with the police. One needs these connections. Otherwise, you cannot manage such things. They had these relations. Once, one person had to be arrested. This was an order

[24] "While individual traders may join the trade in a casual and unskilled manner, the entire operation can be highly organised. The success of shadow operations depends on the strategic decisions of experienced traders and brokers about what goods to carry across which checkpoints in what quantity and at which time slot. Such strategic competence derives from experience, co-ordination skills, local knowledge, and network resources." (Ngo & Hung, 2018: 182).

[25] Jews are considered an ethnic group in the Caucasus rather than a religious one.

[26] Kviris Palitra "Operation Black Diamond", 6 July 2015: http://www.kvirispalitra.ge/public/25721-operacia-qshavi-briliantiq-am-tragedisis-tsin-kentcisyra-chatarda-da-tha vgantsirvam-gagulashvils-moutsia.html; Palitra Video, 4 July 2015: http://www.palitravideo.ge/gadacemebi/lurji-vashli/60827-qlurji-vashliq-shavi-brilianti-specoperacia-suramis-ebraeltha-dasakhlebashi-maminacvalis-mier-gaupatiurebuli-sami-tslis-geri-11-tslis-oboli-gogonas-tragedia.html; Ambebi.ge, 13 October 2016: http://www.ambebi.ge/sazogadoeba/118244-vin-iyo-surameli-kaci-visac-sikvdili-kentcisyrith-ergo.html?add=1; GZA, 27 October 2014: http://gza.ambebi.ge/life/413-vin-iyo-surameli-kaci-visac-sikvdili-kentcisyrith-ergo.html.

> from higher authorities. The Jews of Surami found out about it. They got this information from their contacts with the police. What they did was this: they decided by lot who had to take the fall. The one who lost had to do so. This man did not want to, and he committed suicide in prison. With that, the trial came to an end. But the other people in Surami, the other *spekuljanty*, were left in peace because of this sacrifice. Out of gratitude to this man, the people of Surami supported his family. This was a famous story.[27]

Armenians, especially in Georgia and the Middle East, have a similar reputation. Because Georgian self-identity is associated with rootedness in a place (and agriculture), it is often contrasted with the mobility of Armenian merchants—and (less commonly) with the mobility of Azeri shepherds.[28] Armenians themselves, at least those living in Armenia and who grew up in the Soviet system, have ambivalent feelings about trade. Trading, bazaars, and street vending are (as in other places in the former Soviet Union) often perceived as backward and associated with the "Orient" and the Muslim world, especially by Armenians who emphasize their connectedness with Western culture (Fehlings, 2014). On the other hand, trading is proudly mentioned as a "traditional" field of Armenian activity and part of Armenian identity and cosmopolitanism. An Armenian joke, which I heard in Yerevan, says that an Armenian would prefer to die in a gas chamber rather than to make a bad deal. Since the Middle Ages, Armenian traders have travelled the world and along the Silk Road, and they founded Armenian communities and trading posts in the Middle

[27] The police raid this story talks about was called "Black Diamond." It took place on May 19, 1984, in the Jewish district of Surami. The raid did not come as a surprise, since the Jewish population of Surami was famous for being involved in trading and was used to campaigns against *spekulanstvo* by the government. The people of Surami paid a monthly amount to state officials, which was enough to avoid punishment. However, this raid was different. It was related to a burglary that happened in Leningrad. A large number of diamonds—including a very important black diamond—had been stolen from a famous artist, and the trail led to family members of high-ranking apparatchiks. There were two explanations for the raid in Surami: First, the police were searching for the diamonds; second, they wanted to destroy illegal manufacturing enterprises producing clothes with foreign labels. As mentioned above, to protect the others from persecution, the community of Surami decided to sacrifice one man, Namtal Gagulashvili, who committed suicide. The case was closed, the police took in a lot of money that day, and the diamond was not found. Gagulashvili's family later moved to Israel.

[28] Such classifications are quite common. Usually, traders are contrasted to villagers in terms of countervailing moralities (Marsden, 2016: 7).

East, in Russia, and in India (long before the Dutch and British) (Abrahamian, 2007a; Aslanian, 2014; Bhattacharya, 2005; Hopkirk, 1980). Some of these communities still exist and together with the huge Armenian diaspora form a global network facilitating economic exchange. This is not true for the Georgian traders I was working with, who built their businesses from scratch starting in the 1990s and had nothing to rely on but their own initiative.

Perhaps, when talking about ethnicity, most prejudices circulate about the role and techniques of Roma, or so-called *cygany* ("gypsies", цыгане), trading on sidewalks or in flea markets in Tbilisi. Elena Marushiakova and Vesselin Popov (2016) describe different subdivisions among gypsies in different parts of the Caucasus. Generally, gypsies have the reputation for selling the cheapest goods, because, as I was told by a young woman, they "steal what they sell." Gypsies have very low status in Georgian society and are certainly found at the lower end of petty trade. Still, there are also some positive associations with them. In many stalls and small shops of Georgian traders and shopkeepers one can find a picture of a gypsy woman, which, in the style of a small icon or holy image, is believed to bring luck and economic good fortune.

Although ethnicity is often associated with specific trading skills and economic niches, unlike in other Eastern bazaars, Georgian bazaars and marketplaces are not subdivided into ethnic enclaves. Such divisions usually occur "because some types of commodity are allocated their own trading streets, and trade in these commodities has become the preserve of particular nationalities" (Humphrey & Skvirskaja, 2009: 66). But in the Caucasus, bazaars are relatively mono-ethnic, as exemplified by Lilo Bazroba. Minorities do not really figure as trader communities.[29] The only exception are the Chinese, who run their own market sections and are starting to establish new marketplaces, as described in Chapter 5.

[29] Comparing Armenian and Georgian bazaars, Skvirskaja (2019) asserts that Georgian bazaars are multi-ethnic in comparison to Armenian ones. According to her, ethnic Azeris (followed by Armenians) constitute the largest group of traders on Lilo. Furthermore, she argues that Georgians, coming from different regions of Georgia, constitute a heterogeneous group with different sociocultural backgrounds. This is certainly true—although I doubt that Azeris form such a big group in Lilo. Still this diversity is not comparable to the diversity in Central Asian bazaars. There are no sections clearly defined by the ethnicity of the vendors.

Religion

In both Georgia and Armenia, the issue of whether trading can be combined with Christian values is often debated. This discussion is not about professional traders but about local clergy, who are criticized for "doing business" and "profiting from trade." Like Caucasian politicians, the representatives of the Orthodox Church, in Georgia as well as in Armenia, can be considered "business elites." Modest living seems not to figure among their values, which were criticized by many of my local interlocutors. The Georgian Orthodox Church is one of the most powerful and most trusted institutions in the country (Gurchiani, 2017), and 2013, the Caucasus Barometer household survey revealed that 93% of the general public and 95% of those between eighteen and thirty-five years of age regarded religion as important in their daily lives.

The Georgian Orthodox Church is the opposite of Puritanism. Ostentatious rituals, art, and architecture symbolize its grandeur and its accepted importance within the sociocultural and spiritual cosmos. However, the enrichment of individual members of the clergy is perceived negatively. An Armenian friend of mine, for example, once told me that a certain priest was, literally, a "carpet vendor," which she said to underline his moral depravity (Fehlings, 2014). Assessments like this, which oppose trading to purity and spirituality, give an idea of the local moral perception of trade (albeit not of wealth per se).

Money, by contrast, is not emphasized in moral assessments of this kind. Given historical views of money and the findings of anthropologists, this may seem surprising. The negative effects of what is called "all/general-purpose money"[30] have been described and feared since antiquity. In the local context of the Caucasus, however, I never came across any association of money with impurity. *Pecunia non olet.* Money

[30] General-purpose money fulfils the following criteria: fungibility, durability, portability, divisibility, and recognizability (Plattner, 1989: 177). Its opposite, "primitive money" or "special-purpose money," does not have these qualities. It is subject to moral restrictions and bound to specific cultures and specific spheres of exchange within these cultures. Thus, in Tiv society we have three separate spheres of exchange: subsistence, prestige, and supreme. Food can be exchanged for household utensils, but it cannot be exchanged for cattle or brass rods, because these items belong to a different domain. The same is true of the exchange of brass rods for women, which is not possible for the same reason and would be considered immoral. The appearance of "all-purpose money," due to Western influence, according to Bohannan and Dalton (1962), destroys this system of a moral ranking of spheres of exchange, which finally results in daughters being traded away for money.

doesn't stink. It is the activity of trading, not money, that is condemned. Money is not even perceived as very powerful. There is a saying that friends are more valuable than money, which is explained by the fact that networks—not money—are important for success. Unlike money, social obligations and relationships can withstand a crisis. Having good networks means that you can always start a new (social and economic) life, important in a context in which inflation and political instability may potentially leave you with nothing overnight.

Caucasian believers accept without further ado that religious objects and even salvation are exchanged for money. Antonyan (2020), who conducted research on this matter in the course of our project, reports on the trade in religious paraphernalia and services and quotes a representative of the Orthodox Church explaining the Gospel passages that describe how Jesus banishes the merchants from the temple, who said: "Christ was not opposed to trade. He was banishing animals that made the temple impure, but he did not oppose selling ritually pure things such as candles, icons, and other [religious] paraphernalia." The debate is thus about trading, or, more precisely, about the relationship between trading and the Church.

The relationship between traders and religion is usually not a topic of discussion. Some of the traders I met during my research openly showed their piety. Like many other traders, Dato, had a small corner for icons in each of his stalls. When Zviad and I visited him on St. Mary's Day, he told us that he had been to church that morning. During our visit he interrupted our conversation for a few minutes to pray to St. Mary and to light some candles and incense in front of his icon wall. I am not sure whether his religious practices and prayers were directly geared to fostering economic success or whether they were part of a more general attitude. Having little information about this topic, I am not able to comment on this issue (Fig. 3.3).

St. Gabriel, a local Orthodox monk, who had lived between 1929 and 1995 and was canonized in 2012, was disinterred and reburied in Mtskheta in 2014, when I was teaching a course at the Ivane Javakhishvili University. Everyone was talking about this. For several weeks his body lay in state in the Sameba Cathedral in Tbilisi, and everyone I talked to was trying to see him lying there, to touch his body and pray for his intercession. When I went to see St. Gabriel myself, the crowd had to be managed by policemen, and it was necessary to wait a long time for a few seconds in the saint's presence. My Georgian students at the time

Fig. 3.3 A trader's icon wall in a bazaar stall, 2016

joked about believers who went to the church to ask St. Gabriel for a car or a successful business, seeing such requests as profane. Since I felt uncomfortable doing so, however, I never solicited anyone's opinion of St. Gabriel, which is why I am not sure to what extent his patronage is involved in commercial activities. There are indeed saints whose patronage is involved in business. Close to Borjomi (Borjomi-Plato), for example, there is a shrine—donated by a well-known local plutocrat who made his money in Russia—dedicated to Serafim Sarovskij, a saint of Russian origin linked to economic success, whose cult got started in the Russian Orthodox Church. Believers come there to ask St. Serafim to help them get rich.

Identity in the Caucasus is usually linked to ethnicity—and ethnicity is linked to religious affiliation. Sociocultural values that shape local identity are thus associated in the first place with ethnic and only then with religious traditions. In interregional conflicts, it is ethnic difference, not religious difference that is emphasized. The war between the republics of Armenia and Azerbaijan is usually described as a conflict between ethnic Armenians and "Turks," not between Christians and Muslims. The Ingiloi, members of a group of Muslim converts with a Georgian ethnic background who live on Azerbaijani territory, tend to ally with Christian Georgians rather than with Muslim Azeris (Aivazishvili-Gehne, 2015,

2018). Still, as recent studies suggest, religious practices and affiliation seem to be becoming more and more important in the Caucasus. There is a huge debate about who defines right religious practice and behaves like a real believer (Antonyan, 2011; Darieva et al., 2018; Gurchiani, 2017; Körner, 2017).

Still, religion was never emphasized in the context of the trading I witnessed, although it sometimes surfaced in situations like the one, mentioned in the previous chapter, where traders performed a small ritual in honor of Giorgi's dead child. Such situations are rather intimate, and although they may arise in the context of trade, they are not directly related to it. Religious affiliation, for example, is not a major basis for business alliances and cooperation (Fehlings, 2021). This distinguishes Georgian/Caucasian traders from many others, like the Kyrgyz traders described by Varnavskii (2010), for whom identification with Islam seems to be more important than ethnic background and "is an essential part of the moral understanding that underpins their mutual trust" in the context of business (Humphrey, 2018: 25). All my interlocutors, as outlined in the previous chapter, emphasized the importance of sociocultural values, but explicitly linked them neither to religion nor ethnicity. Instead, they usually talked about a "common ground" between Georgians and Chinese, or Georgians and other post-Soviet people of different ethnic and religious backgrounds arguing that "we are all humans" (*my vse ljudi*, мы все люди) and that everyone just wants to earn a living (Fehlings, 2020, 2021).

Social Networks

Economic success, according to the traders and the data my colleagues and I collected in the course of our project, depends in large part on social networks, webs of social relationships connecting individuals directly or through others, enabling (or not enabling) access to resources: to loans, to business opportunities, to information, knowledge, and advantages, to space (see above on location), to documents and permissions, to clients, to power, to protection, and, last but not least, to status, prestige, and the power to define moral values.

In one of our conversations the above-mentioned professor of economics complained that there were very few "real entrepreneurs" in Georgia. According to him, different Georgian governments had had different strategies with regard to trading and small entrepreneurship during recent decades. Informal trading was widespread after the collapse of the Soviet Union, but it was restricted by law in Georgia under Saakashvili. The current government was now promoting small business again, in his view, creating good conditions, not least by relaxing the laws on street vending (see Chapter 4). The professor was not enthusiastic about this. He thought that a good entrepreneur ought to be able to grow his business under any conditions, while a bad businessman never would.

The professor held the opinion that so-called cases of successful businesses should serve as a model and a teaching tool and should aid the develoment of successful business strategies, which could be applied by his students and other young entrepreneurs. Carrefour and Elite Electronics could, for example, serve as such models. But the professor then mentioned something that challenged his hypothesis: "The guy who founded Elite Electronics," he said, "is one of the rare examples of a real Georgian entrepreneur. He started his business in Eliava Market." The professor described his career as a "dishwasher to millionaire"[31] story: "He went to prison because he faked a bankruptcy when, in fact, he was making a lot of money. ... But now he is back out of prison and has become the owner of Electric Boom. ... Probably because he hid some money from officials with the help of his relatives." This, in my opinion, says something about entrepreneurship in the Caucasus and the importance for business there of factors such as one's relatives.

At least according to statistics, success seems limited in the Caucasian SME sector (Karrar & Rudaz, 2022; Rudaz, 2018). Based on my own observations, I would assume that it is the accessibility of certain social networks that is the crucial factor in a business's success or failure, rather than the supposed lack of entrepreneurial spirit cited by economists. The networks in question may be based on criminal structures, friendship, kinship or ethnic belonging, and so on. In the following sections I discuss which networks shaped the economic activity of my target group, and why and how.

[31] This is a common formula.

Criminal Networks
The literature on post-socialist Eurasia is filled with descriptions of networks characterized by the "social glue and lubricant of informal relationships" (Holzlehner, 2014: 129–144) that define them. Some of these networks have their roots in a criminal milieu, like those of the so-called *vory v zakone* ("thieves in law" or "thieves professing the code," воры в законе).

The *vory* (воры), whose major business was the operation of protection rackets, relied on networks that covered, and still may, the whole territory of the former Soviet Union and which rooted in the Soviet penal system (Zakharova, 2017; Захарова, 2010). The estimated ethnic composition of the *vory* in the 1990s was 33.1% Russians, 31.6% Georgians, 8.2% Armenians, 5.2% Azeri, and 21.9% others (Serio & Razinkin, 1995). The Georgian term for *vory v zakone* is *ḳanonieri kurdebi* (kanonieri qurdebi) (Kupatadze, 2009; Light, 2014; Slade, 2009); the Armenian term is *òrenk'ov goġ* (օրենքով գող).

> The qurdebi arbitrate and enforce decisions, protect and extort from legal actors, and act as a vital lubricant for the cogs of organized criminal activity, lowering transaction costs for the actors involved and enabling trust relationships in a naturally volatile underworld. In short, the Georgian qurdebi are not an ordinary organized crime group, the qurdebi are a mafia. (Slade, 2009: 5)

In the 1990s, the *kurdebi* were most parasitic in the area of trade (33% of cases), where this meant protection rackets targeting shops, markets, petrol stations, bakeries, and wine and beverage merchants (Slade, 2009).[32] Many post-Soviet markets were controlled by so-called "roofs" (*kryšy*, крыши), which were associations of *vory*. These mafia-like structures, which sometimes cooperated with the police, were paid protection fees (Fehlings, 2008; Holzlehner, 2014; Humphrey, 2002; Humphrey & Skvirskaja, 2009; Varese, 2001). By extorting protection money from the new class of private entrepreneurs, some of the *kurdebi* got rich and became businessmen themselves. With the dissolution of the

[32] Second came services (28% of cases) (casinos, restaurants, hotels, minibus routes, car mechanics, pool halls, TV stations, and sports teams). Third, the illegal sector (22%) (stealing cars, kidnapping, wholesale and retail drug trafficking). Fourth, the exploitation of natural resources (10%) (trade in timber and scrap metal, petrol distribution). And finally, the financial and construction sectors (7%).

Soviet (penal) system, however, the ***kurdebi*** apparently slowly lost their organizational basis (Slade, 2012). They were replaced by a new generation of criminals, the product of the 1990s, for whom criminal activities had become one of the few available economic options and who were not inclined to honor the ***ḳanonieri kurdebi***'s traditional code or to engage in any restraint when it came to their level of violence (Dudwick, 2003; Frederiksen, 2012; Koehler, 2003; Zakharova, 2017; Захарова, 2010). Beginning in 1994, the situation calmed down, and beginning in 1995, in the Caucasus as in Russia (Holzlehner, 2014), criminals started to cooperate with state regimes, with the result that the boundaries between licit and illicit, and informal and illegal, became blurred (Kupatadze, 2009). At the end of the 1990s, there was a visible consolidation of many criminal groups in the direction of regular enterprises (Holzlehner, 2014: 148).

In Georgia, the Shevardnadze regime took power "in 1992 with a coup led by two figures from a criminal background—Djaba Iosseliani and Tengiz Kitovani" (Di Puppo, 2004: 49), allied with mafias that "managed to accumulate resources through the trade in weapons and drugs, looting and racketeering activities" (49). These groups "developed an interest in a formal restoration of law and order, hoping to stabilize their criminal accumulation and redistribution of resources by means of a semblance of order" (49). Lili Di Puppo concludes that "accumulation and redistribution of resources follows a pattern in Georgia which is different from that normally found in resource-rich developing countries" (49). Soon after Shevardnadze took power, members of the state apparatus got their hands on all kinds of privileges and monopolies and began to use the law to blackmail citizens. This only changed after the Rose Revolution in 2003, when many criminal networks generated by and existing in parallel to state institutions were dismantled by the anti-corruption campaign of Mikheil Saakashvili's government (Corso, 2011; Kupatadze, 2011).

However, according to Alexander Kupatadze, "the key informal institutions which knowingly or unknowingly serve the purposes of crime and rent-seeking, including various forms of clientelism and patrimonialism, have survived and prove to be resilient" (Kupatadze, 2009: 12). The reason, according to Kupatadze, is that "being a 'močaliče' (მოჩალიჩე) (an 'apt, cunning and resilient' person, who 'is able to find an easy path to success and for acquiring material or other goods while circumventing the formal rules') is highly valued in Georgian society," and informal (and criminal) practices are "exacerbated by societal acceptance, for instance rule-breaking is frequently encouraged as a display of 'courage' or 'manhood'" (2009: 12). This statement describes an aspect of youth culture linked to music and lifestyle that I also observed in Armenia, where it is called *ṙabiz* (ռաբիզ) (Fehlings, 2014).

I never personally (at least to my knowledge) encountered criminals or criminal networks like those described in this section, but I heard a lot of rumors about them: relatives (who were always absent) of friends of mine were described as gangsters involved in protection rackets or even human trafficking, and during my research in Crimea, I saw the graves of some of the local mafia bosses (Fehlings, 2008). I was told that relatives of my friends were shot down in the 1990s—but at the time of my research, this was already history. No one ever presented himself to me as a criminal. Yet I regularly came across the concepts of manhood, respect, and honor, which are associated with the world of the criminal code and criminal networks. Young men especially used to talk about these virtues, and it was to this topic that Levan, Ramaz, and Giorgi alluded to in their toasts talking about men's love, which is crucial for many relationships that play a role in local economic exchange and business.

Brotherhoods, Male Bonding, Transnational Experiences, and Friendship

Male bonding is considered an important cultural value in both Georgia and Armenia. In Armenia, besides kin, the so-called brotherhood, or *axperowt'yown* (խպերություն) is a core point of social reference for many young men.[33] The *axperowt'yownner* ("brotherhoods," ախպերություններ) typically originate in neighborhoods. The nucleus of an *axperowt'yown* usually consists of men who grew up around the same courtyard (*bak* [բակ] or *hayat'* [հայաթ]; Georgian equivalent: *ezo* [ეზო]), and who are joined by other men of the same age. According to my interlocutors, the peer group of the *axperowt'yown* is essential for living a good and successful life—not least, for running a successful business, since the *axperners* ("brothers," ախպերներս) will support one another. This support includes financial support, but it also means that the brothers will be (physically) on the spot, if there is a problem, for example, a fight after a car accident (Fehlings, 2014, 2015). I was witness to a friend of mine being called on by one of his *axperner* to help chase out a tenant who

33 Parts of this section have been published in the Central Asian Survey, before.

had not paid his rent, for example. When we arrived at the address, a group of men had already gathered and “solved” the problem. As Gagik, the young man quoted in the introduction of this chapter, put it, “If you have good brothers, you will find a good job. If you have many good brothers... you will have a good life.”

There are two Georgian “equivalents” of the Armenian *axperowt’yown* (ախպերություն)—or at least similar social institutions. One is the *birža*, (ბირჟა), which is considered part of young male street socialization, and the other is the *ʒmaḳacoba* (ძმაკაცობა). *Birža* in Russian means “stock exchange,” but in Georgian slang it indicates identification with the peer group of one’s neighborhood, or *ubani* (უბანი) or *ḳvarṭali* (კვარტალი) (Zakharova, 2010; Захарова, 2010). In contrast to the Armenian *axperowt’yown,* the Georgian *birža,* at least as far as I can deduce from the descriptions of it by Köhler, Zakharova, and Curro, is much more hierarchically structured. This hierarchy and the moral code of the *birža* correspond and are connected to the structure of the criminal world described in the previous section. Understood as an informal group and the initial step in a criminal career (Koehler, 2003), the *birža* was targeted under Saakashvili’s policies and his anti-corruption campaign, but it has reportedly been experiencing a revival in recent years (Curro, 2015). However, nowadays, *birža* is simply used to describe a group of young men who hang around together, and the term is often associated with unemployment and alcohol and drug use (Frederiksen, 2012, 2013).

The moral content of the Armenian notion of *axperowt’yown* is much closer to the Georgian *ʒmaḳacoba* than to the *birža*. Like the *axperowt’yown*, the “brotherhood” (*ʒmaḳacoba*) is related to the trust and loyalty of a very close category of friends (Armen.: *axperers*, “brothers”; Georg.: *ʒmaḳacebi*, a combination of the terms for “brother” and “men”) and to notions of morality, honor, honesty, and masculinity. Trust and honor are particularly emphasized and belong together: “Trust is the basis of honour. A man, who is not trusted has no honour: a man without honour cannot be trusted” (Mars & Altman, 1983: 549). There is another category of friends called *megobari* (მეგობარი). *Megobari* is “a person with whom one eats from the same bowl (*gobi*, გობი)”, including a broader group of people with whom one has good relations. But *ʒmaḳacebi* are the kind of friends you can ask for money, which many young men would not even ask their families for. Such friends look out for one another, providing moral support above all (Fehlings, 2014; Frederiksen, 2012). They are partners in all aspects of life, whether personal or business-related.

As I note in an article published elsewhere:

> The concept of friendship[34] in anthropology has frequently been associated with Western societies and economic transformations connected to the rise of capitalism since the eighteenth century. According to this view, the increasing importance of friendship was a result of a new concept of the person linked to an ideology of individualism and a focus on sentiment. (Fehlings, 2019: 15)[35]

But the local concepts described above clearly demonstrate that notions of friendship are not necessarily bound to Western modernity. Rather, it would make sense to broaden the definition of friendship. Among other dimensions, then, the instrumentality and pragmatism illustrated in the examples above (which are often perceived incompatible with firendship in Western societies) should be considered as legitimate aspects of this relationship (cf. Marsden, 2016: 230; Mains, 2013). In the Caucasus, material benefits are perceived as one of the core advantages of friendship, not excluding affection and good feelings (cf. Killick & Desai, 2010). Another of its emphasized characteristics is equality, reflected, for example, in the fact, that you can ask a friend for money. As has been discussed in the anthropology of friendship, unlike many social relationships that involve "opposed pairs" (father-son, employer-employee, husband-wife), friendship, here, is based on "persons paired in the same role" (Paine, 1969).

Ramaz claimed that his relationship with some of his fellow businessmen was *ʒmaḳacoba*. As described in the previous chapter, one evening during our trip, he dedicated a long toast to *mužskaja ljubov'* ("male love," мужская любовь). He emphasized that this love has nothing to do with homosexuality, and that it is "one of the most important things in life, because men need each other." When I asked him jokingly whether this was about his *birža*, he answered very seriously: "This is not the same. You can take something from the street as well.

[34] See Killick and Desai (2010) and Bell and Coleman (1999).

[35] The focus on sentiment based on unconditional affection and free will, for Carrier (1999), was a reason to reject friendship as a universal category.

At some point in life. But this is different." Thus, *ʒmak̩acoba* comes into being in a new context, one that differs from the traditional local context of the neighborhood or the close circle of people one grows up with. This context is the world of trading and business and the shared experience abroad. Far from home, the fact of coming from the same country, speaking the same language, and engaging in the same business seems enough for building a relationship that, apparently, can become very important in people's lives. Once this relationship is established, as I gathered from conversations with Levan, Ramaz, and other traders, business friends also become incorporated into the local network of more traditionally conceptualized relationships ("we know each other's families").

Social networks are thus not only necessary to start a business but are also created in the process and conceptualized in traditional terms. The traditional terms, in the Caucasus as elsewhere, often allude to kinship relationships. Consequently, classifications like "brotherhood" in anthropology have been conceptualized as pseudo-, fictive, or para-kinship forms of relatedness, founded on a broader understanding of kinship not based on biology (Carsten, 2000, 2004). However, I would be reluctant to frame the Caucasian brotherhoods in any way as kinship. They constitute a distinct category. By "subsuming friendship under a general category of relatedness, we miss what friendship does differently to kinship for the people who practice it, and the different ways in which the two general forms of relationship might be constituted in a particular society" (Killick & Desai, 2010: 5).

The experience abroad is somehow separate from everyday life at home. In Beijing, I observed that when on their journeys, traders temporarily step out of their social environment. They build new relations with people (both Georgians and non-Georgians) they meet regularly during their business trips. These might be business or personal relations or both, like the traders' friendships with Lena and with Chinese partners. Sometimes, as described in the previous chapter, traders form temporary groups. Some groups emerging in such contexts, such as, for instance, the international groupings emerging in Moscow's peripheral markets described by Nikolotov (2019), are rather volatile, and their members disperse quickly. Others can be long-lasting. For Afghan traders, for example, according to Marsden (2016: 192), travelling together tests the possibility of friendship and future economic partnership. Many small, loose ad hoc groups of such close friends can probably be found in hotels near trading hotspots in Turkey, China, and other countries that are popular destinations for post-Soviet traders and businesspeople. The routes and "trading posts" are quite limited and "narrow." Paths cross. On our flight to Doha and later to Beijing, we met some traders who were Levan's and Ramaz's acquaintances from Lilo Bazroba, and during our shopping expeditions in Beijing, we several times ran into Georgian traders whom Giorgi had met before on business tours to Istanbul. With Lena, I met a lot of women traders from all over Russia. All this made me feel that this is a small, closed community.

Of course, not all relationships between traders are without tension. Traders working in the same line of business and in the same marketplace naturally compete for clients and profit. At the same time, I heard about cooperation among traders who own neighboring stalls in Lilo Bazroba. Even though they share no common travel experience or other deep relationship, they visit one another to chat and exchange small services. The very close relationships between fellow travellers conceptualized as *ʒmaḳacoba*, the friendly relationships between colleagues owning neighboring stalls, and the rivalry between others thus structure the networks that emerge within the local marketplaces.

Beyond the local level, economic partnerships with Chinese or Turkish partners abroad are also framed as long-term cooperation and friendship. As discussed in the previous chapter, Georgian and Russian traders exchange little presents with their Chinese counterparts, for example. There is sympathy and trust. Greetings are exchanged on major festivals like Christmas or New Year's, and communication exceeds purely economic contact. It would be too much to describe these social ties in local terms like *ʒmaḳacoba*, but they are conceptualized as "friendship" in a Russian sense (*družba*, дружба), which is already saying a great deal (Fehlings, 2019).

Kin, Ethnic, and Interethnic Networks

"An assumption made in much of the literature on trade diasporas is that the success of a particular trading community depends on the powerful ties of kinship that characterise the social make-up of such communities, and the forms of trust these facilitate," Magnus Marsden writes (2016: 112). The owners of stalls in Lilo or small shops and boutiques in Tbilisi often employ their relatives. Many of our interlocutors run their businesses with the help of their spouses, siblings, children, or other members of their extended families. Giorgi, for example, runs his shop in Batumi with his wife and his mother; Levan employs his two sons and a nephew; and Dato works with his wife, one of her sisters, and his godson. "Dealing with family members is a safeguard against being cheated in an informal economic environment with few judicial safeguards" (Holzlehner, 2014: 81–82), and they provide cheap labor.

But unlike Kyrgyz businesspeople in transnational settings (Humphrey, 2018; Schröder & Stephan-Emmrich, 2016), Uzbek spice dealers in Vladivostok or China (Holzlehner, 2014), Azerbaijani herb traders (Yalçın-Heckmann, 2014), and wealthy Mountain Jews (Juhuro) in Moscow (Bram, 2017), for example, who, according to their ethnographers, rely on extended kin and ethnic networks, the Georgian traders and businessmen of my target group rely on only a small circle of close relatives, friends, and acquaintances (see Chapter 2).

Economic activities based on extended networks linking kin and—in a next step—members of the same ethnic group, conceptualized in terms of shared ancestry, have been termed "ethnic economies" in academic scholarship (Light & Gold, 2000). Research on ethnic entrepreneurship can be traced back to classic works such as those of Max Weber (1993 [1904]), Werner Sombart (2001 [1911]), and Georg Simmel (1992 [1908]). In current definitions (Aldrich & Waldinger, 1990; Volery, 2007; Waldinger, 1994),[36] "ethnic entrepreneurs," are people who use transnational networks of kin and co-ethnics as a strategy for organizing their businesses. The Kyrgyz, Uzbek, Azerbaijani, and Juhuro traders mentioned above, who rely on "geographically dispersed kin networks" that "facilitate international business ties" (Holzlehner, 2014: 82), belong to this group.

But business cooperation does not rest solely on trust among fellow ethnics. As Brednikova and Pachenkov observe, practical considerations may lead to people favoring friends, colleagues, or neighbors rather than

[36] Ethnic entrepreneurship is usually discussed in the framework of migration studies. Usually, it is concerned with migrant entrepreneurs who are self-employed and establish a business in a host country/society. Usually, these migrant entrepreneurs belong to a larger migrant community and respond to a niche demand resulting from this community's consumption habits and specific tastes. External factors in the host environment (like discrimination), cultural predispositions (specific skills, behavior, and traditions) favoring self-employment, and cultural resources (like networks) are the main topics debated in this field (Volery, 2007). A prominent ethnographic example of ethnic entrepreneurship in the trading sector is that of Swasa traders in North Africa (Davis, 1977; Waterbury, 1972, 1973).

kin or individuals of the same ethnic background. According to their research, Central Asian and Caucasian traders in open-air markets in St. Petersburg cooperated with other traders based on a range of factors, including ease (simplicity, lack of problems), economic rationale, trust, outside pressure, and spatial proximity. Azeris did not cooperate with Azeris simply because they shared the same ethnicity, but because it was easier to communicate with others who spoke the same language and had the same sociocultural background. Profit was central to traders' decision-making. They chose cheap labor and worked with people whom they trusted because they shared routines with them. Daily interactions thus led to networks of cooperation—and to complicity, if there was an external threat (Brednikova & Pachenkov, 1999).

Unlike Pachenkov and Brednikova, I think it is difficult to draw a clear line between so-called rational and sociocultural factors. Azeris might cooperate with Azeris because it is more "rational," but perhaps this cooperation is more rational because of the sociocultural factors defining kin and ethnic belonging. Trying to resolve this question involves the debate between formalists and substantivists, so I shall simply summarize what I observed among my target group of Georgian traders.

As I learned from many traders in Lilo, from interviewees who had been travelling to Turkey, Europe or Dubai, and as I could observe during my field trip to China, Georgian traders rely on fellow countrymen when doing business abroad. They probably do so for exactly the reasons mentioned above. The Georgians' networks are possibly less wide-ranging than those of their Armenian, Jewish, or Central Asian colleagues because Georgians have smaller Georgian migrant or diaspora communities to rely on. To put it in a nutshell: they have a less-developed "migrant infrastructure" (access to business opportunities, marketplaces, and meeting points like ethnic cafés and clubs, etc.). At the same time, even though traders told me that they recognized and helped fellow Georgians when doing business abroad owing simply to their common cultural background, the relationships between traders or businesspeople were sometimes very tense. As I realized in Beijing, Georgian traders may perceive one another as competitors. They compete for relationships with Chinese partners, for merchandise, and for clients in their home markets in Georgia. I witnessed alliances between Chinese and Georgian partners in which each partner was acting against his own ethnic and national compatriots.[37] It is "easy to be misled by actors' rhetoric about their wonderfully unbreakable kin ties, while their practice reveals subtle calculations not only about the future behaviour of kin but also about the economy in which everyone has to sink or swim" (Humphrey, 2018: 26).

From my observations I conclude that ethnicity (sociocultural belonging), personal emotions (feeling lonely, homesick, and vulnerable in an alien situation), and business motives (opportunities for increased profit) are held in an equilibrium that determines the traders' behavior, especially in a foreign context (cf. Marsden, 2016: 155). My prior analysis (Fehlings, 2019), led me to conclude that for Georgian businesspeople, especially for those who travel abroad like the group I accompanied to Yabaolu in Beijing, ethnic unity and social control do not by themselves result in trust (cf. Marsden, 2016; Ngo & Hung, 2018). With Hart, I argue that while kinship is about obligations, trust is based on emotions, which stand "in the middle of a continuum of words for belief mixing extremes of blind faith and open-eyed confidence" (Hart, 1988: 188). These emotions and similar mechanisms have been described, among others, by Hart (1988), Marsden (2016) and Nikolotov (2019), who all question the importance attributed to kinship in trading networks, claims that often go uncontested.

As we have seen, Georgian traders create business relationships and trust *while* doing business, and then subsequently legitimize them using kinship-related terminology. This flexibility makes for smoother interactions with Chinese or other business partners from very different cultural backgrounds. Foreign partners are essential, mediating and helping traders navigate an alien culture. A friend who went to Oman to buy some cloth, told me, for example, how hard he had found it to understand the dress codes and behavior towards women there. He had been constantly coached by his local business partner, however, "who became a real friend" and helped him avoid embarrassing and potentially dangerous situations, thus saving his life.

[37] Compare Marsden on Afghan traders (2016: 126).

Mobility

Many vendors and traders who work in bazaars, in malls, in shops, or on the streets in Tbilisi and Yerevan do not travel. They sell goods they buy from wholesalers or through Internet and catalogue orders, leaving their transportation to cargo companies or fellow traders. Badri, an interlocutor of mine who sold Chinese furniture in Sadguris Bazroba (სადგურის ბაზრობა) next to the railway station in Tbilisi's city center, had visited the factory in China that manufactured his goods "a long time ago," but now ordered what he wanted from it online. It was shipped from China in containers, and as soon as the contents of one container had been sold, he ordered the next. Sometimes this took a little more time, sometimes a little less. The process was simple. Payment was made by bank transfer, and cargo companies organized transport and payment of customs duties. There was little risk, and Badri had no need to leave Tbilisi.

The establishment of business relations and the regularity of exchange often result in a structuring, specialization, and division of labor. The outsourcing of cargo transport is a consequence of this process. So one could ask whether the mobility of individual traders is a sign of informality. Indeed, one can observe many different mobility patterns among Caucasian entrepreneurs and traders, which are linked to their social and financial status and their type of business.

Some traders travel very short distances, playing the role of middlemen between nearby markets on two sides of a local border or between central and peripheral markets. Transborder trading is a special case. A very common phenomenon is the establishment of so-called border markets. The evolution of such markets is tightly linked to the daily politics of border regimes, as well as to international relations and conflict situations. Many studies of border markets in the Caucasus and Central Asia and between post-Soviet Eurasia and Turkey, Iran, or China describe the shifting fate of such markets and traders' multiple adaptions to changing circumstances in the border regions. Changes in border trade along the Amur River, have been described by Holzlehner (2014), for example; Dabaghyan and Gabrielyan (2011, 2014) studied marketplaces between Armenia and Georgia; Yalçın-Heckmann and Aivazishvili (2012) focused on economic exchange in the Georgian-Azerbaijani borderlands; and within the framework of our joint research project, Ketevan Khutsishvili and John Schoeberlein investigated border markets and trading relations between Georgia and Abkhazia and between Georgia and Turkey (Khutsishvili, 2006, 2017). Similar studies have been conducted in Central Asia by Turaeva (2014), Reeves (2014) and Ngo and Hung (2018), and along the Chinese-Pakistan border by Karrar and Mostawlansky (Karrar, 2020; Karrar & Mostowlansky, 2018), for example. Two recent publications including materials on border markets and border trade in the Chinese borderlands are Humphrey's edited volume *Trust and Mistrust in the Economy of the China-Russia Borderlands* from 2018 and Zhang's and Saxer's *The Art of Neighbouring: Making Relations Across China's Borders* (2017). Here it suffices to mention that border markets exist and that many people make money in both the Caucasus and Central Asia, by crossing borders once, twice, or even more often per day or week to take goods from one side to the other and to buy and sell them in these specific marketplaces, which are usually interethnic meeting points.

Price differentials, which define profit margins, are linked to the importance, centrality, and size of marketplaces, leading to hierarchical interrelations between them that determine the flow of goods, trade channels, and traders' mobility across and within borders (Dannhaeuser, 1989). Georgians returned from shopping expeditions to Turkey sell their purchases in the early morning to wholesalers at Lilo Bazroba, who then resell the merchandise to middlemen for transportion to places like Yerevan. For example, two women who rented a small space in Sadguri Bazroba, whom I interviewed in 2014, went to Lilo to buy shirts from another female trader, who brought them from Turkey by minibus.

Foodstuffs usually travel along even shorter trade chains. Many traders in agricultural products are themselves farmers (*glexebi*, გლეხები) and produce what they sell, which is thus both fresh and cheap. They set up shop on public streets or near railway or bus stations in cities and are usually quite mobile, traveling to and returning from these points of sale in less than a day. Other peasants, by contrast, stay in Tbilisi for a few weeks or months to try their luck getting more permanently involved in commercial activity. The exchange volume of their transactions is rather modest. For example, they might start with a bag of potatoes that they sell for a few coins. With this money, they then must live and buy some tomatoes, which they sell again in order to buy something else, and so on. With minimal profit margins, individuals trading in this way can afford their daily survival and a dirty room in a shabby hostel next to the railway station.[38] These people's way of life is transient, non-permanent, and chaotic—and can be classified as "translocal."

Mobility is of course a defining aspect of long-distance trade. "Trading routes and the merchants who travel them [...] play a significant role in connecting places that where previously assumed to be rigidly divided by physical barriers and cultural complexity" (Marsden, 2016: 22). There is a long-standing debate about how the mobility of goods and people is linked to globalization. At the same time, especially in the context of labor migration, researchers have been interested in how mobility impacts social and cultural identities. I would like briefly to introduce the term "translocality" to discuss how this concept might shed light on the nature of (Caucasian) traders' mobility and its implications for identity.

Translocality, which is a purely academic notion, is linked in some ways to informality, since both concepts have been developed in the context of the same methodological interest, which Freitag and von Oppen (2010) have characterized as a focus on the grassroots rather than on the "elite level." This focus leads researchers to consider the mobility across marginal zones of actors whose lives take place between local and global connectedness (2010: 7). Thus translocality deals with new and fluid belongings, new identifications, networks, imaginations, livelihoods, and adapted practices that are linked to unconventional definitions of space, which can easily be classified as unregulated by state institutions. In contrast to transnationalism, translocality implies that there are boundaries other than purely political ones (Freitag & von Oppen, 2010; Schetter, 2012; Schröder & Stephan-Emmrich, 2016), which is especially true for the kind of trading networks I have described. Yet, in the aforementioned literature—which often deals with migrants—fluid belongings, networks, imaginations, livelihoods, and adapted practices are usually linked to the formation of "translocal identities" described as a new but permanent mode of being for the actors involved, something that, in my judgment, does not apply to the traders described in the previous chapter.

Long-distance traders, as I have emphasized earlier, build new networks and, to some degree, live a kind of "second life" in the context of their activity abroad. However, I am not sure that this results in new identities. One should not forget that, unlike most migrants, traders only

[38] The Georgian movie director Natia Arabuli-Weg shot a documentary about these traders.

get involved in "translocal lives" for a short period of time: two or three weeks once or twice a year. Even if they do so repeatedly (over many years), being abroad is not a permanent condition but rather an exception for them. Adopting Marsden's term, I would classify them as "sojourners." Thus, even though traders contribute to the creation of what we might call a "translocal" business culture, and may enlarge their networks and slightly change their perception of the world in the process, they usually clearly identify themselves with their original culture and national roots—especially if they experience (cultural) differences in foreign contexts. There is a need to incorporate new business acquaintances met while travelling abroad into already existing, traditional social circles. So, even though travelling is essential for the traders' businesses, it is perhaps not as important for their self-perception as one might think.

The same holds for the *chelnoki,* who, more than any other group of traders, were and are associated with mobility. Both *chelnoki* and the long-distance traders I followed to Beijing are also referred to as "tourist traders," which clearly underlines their temporary identification with the mobile aspect of their occupation. However, especially for the *chelnoki*, mobility was and remains an important experience. Former *chelnoki*'s memories of travelling itself often predominate over their memories of the actual purpose of their travels. In the 1990s travelling was difficult, dangerous, and exhausting in Eurasia. Many *chelnoki* spent more time on the road than selling their goods, and they were reluctant to identify with commerce and perceived their trips as adventures rather that as "work" or a "state of being." "This mode of translocal small trade," according to Alff, "has become unfeasible and [is] largely extinct [in] bazaars. Yet, it gave way to the emergence of sophisticated and flexible cross-border wholesale trade and transport schemes" (2014: 1).

But then, wholesale trade, even when it is based on long-distance trade, is not explicitly or primarily associated with travelling. Mobility (which has become easier) is just one aspect of this economic activity, which predominantly consists in the economic exchange itself and in working in the bazaar. The shuttle trade engaged in by a very poor group of people might perhaps remain the last category of trading activity for which mobility is really the defining characteristic. This might also be true of the activity of modern tourists who combine their holidays with extended shopping tours and for whom the importation of a few items to sell back home is a lucky opportunity to make a little additional money.

Coming back to the question of whether high mobility by individual entrepreneurs is linked to informality, while the outsourcing of travel and transport points to formalization, one must conclude that this correlation might sometimes hold but is not indisputably true. Badri, the trader I mentioned at the beginning of this section, and Levan and Ramaz had quite similar businesses in terms of organization, size, and nature. The only difference was that Levan and Ramaz believed that they had to see, choose, and check their merchandise in person, while placing orders over the Internet satisfied Badri. Our survey revealed that Lilo's successful traders are the 56% who travel for their businesses (Rudaz, 2019). On the other hand, if traders carry their goods in suitcases or other hand luggage, this is obviously an indicator of informal small business, no matter whether they are carrying those goods from Lilo Bazroba to the city center of Tbilisi, from Georgia to Armenia, or from China to Georgia.

Goods

Besides location, personal background, social networks, and mobility, the merchandise, which (besides money) is at the heart of every exchange, is another parameter that helps to classify traders and their activity (cf. Hahn, 2018: 4). For example, traders can be distinguished by the kind, quantity, and quality of goods they sell (cf. Gell, 1982). Usually these are linked to the factors already mentioned and determine, for example, the location of exchange; different locations are frequented by different kinds of customers. A high quantity and quality of goods usually point to more financial capital, more regulated activities, and hence more formalized businesses. Small quantities and poor quality, in contrast, often indicate individual initiative and a weak financial foundation, kept beneath the radar of state control. Small quantities, like Giorgi's furs or the vegetables of itinerant traders crossing regional borders, can pass through customs controls without being declared. If there is only a little money at stake, bureaucrats usually take little interest.

The quality of merchandise is usually associated with its country of origin. In the Caucasus, there are changing trends, which seem to be linked to stereotypes, prejudices, and local consumption patterns, as well as to changing supply and changing access to certain markets and products (cf. Bestor, 2001). For example, although goods from Turkey had a bad reputation in the 1990s, they recently became much more prestigious than goods from China or India. In the early 1990s, goods from Turkey were associated with poverty and the experience of shortage. As I was told by my roommate Natia: "In the nineties, all women wore the same black skirts from Turkey, because they were available and cheap. Today, there are more possibilities for creating an individual look. There is more choice, and people have more money." Turkish goods are of many kinds these days and often preferred to goods from China or elsewhere, since they are easy to access and of comparatively good quality.

As I learned from Lilo's traders, their choices of a piece of goods from a given country are very pragmatic. "We go where good quality is cheap," Lena told me. "If it's China, we go to China; if it's Turkey, we go to Turkey."[39] But of course, there are also personal reasons why a trader will choose a specific destination and therefore specific products. For some traders, like a group of women I talked to in 2016, it was a question of time and distance. They chose the locations in Turkey, which they could reach easily by minibus. Levan and Ramaz avoided Guangzhou because of the climate, and Irakli, who finally ended up in Oman, chose one of the many options he discovered on the worldwide web. Traders talk to each other and compare their experiences. I listened to such conversations frequently on mini-buses and in train compartments, as well as in the bazaars. Irma and a friend of hers, a woman working at a neighboring stall, for example, compared their experiences of working in different places when I was sitting in Irma's stall. Irma was quite positive about the Turkish environment. She said that everything was clean there, and that there were no problems at all. The young woman, by contrast, was less enthusiastic about her experience in Chinese markets. She described the marketplaces in Guangzhou as very dirty and in bad shape, which was why she was thinking of going elsewhere.

Some countries are known to be very good at producing a specific type of goods—or at least keeping a good balance between price and quality. A few years ago most furniture and plastic toys came from Asia, while nowadays many such items are produced in Iran. Electronic equipment, computers, mobile phones, laptops, perfume, and haute couture collections are brought from Dubai, cars from Germany or Japan, and sweets and milk products from Ukraine. The most prestigious products are usually those from western Europe. Even though these goods are available in local brand-name shops, local consumers prefer to buy them

[39] Compare Marsden on Afghan traders (2016: 11).

direct from the source. I was often asked to bring Nivea lotions and other beauty products, because there was a rumor that Nivea and other brands produced lower quality for the "Eastern market" or that local shops diluted the original products. It was the same story with coffee. I sometimes thought I was the only person in Tbilisi who used beans from local shops. My Caucasian friends preferred coffee brought from Germany.

China, as mentioned earlier, has a relatively bad reputation as a producer of cheap and low-quality goods. My friends preferred to buy expensive Legos from Canada and wooden toys from Germany rather than buying plastic ones from China. Some mothers were afraid that Chinese toys would contain toxins. However, traders who travel to China are quite satisfied with the Chinese assortment, which in truth ranges from high-quality to low-end production and covers the whole spectrum of traders' needs and desires. It also covers brand-name and fake brand-name products. As shown in Chapter 4, the importation of such goods is sometimes legal, sometimes illegal, creating mistrust and uncertainty among consumers.

Apparently, traders in Beijing or Delhi are well informed about such fears, needs and desires. As I witnessed in Beijing, the Chinese traders there are familiar with the tastes of their post-Soviet clients. They have mastered not only the Russian language, but the exact wording of arguments significant for and familiar to Russian, Central Asian, or Caucasian consumers. Many discussions among traders were concerned with the latest trends. It is very difficult to say whether something is *modna* (модна) or not, since trends change quickly. It is the task of good businessmen and businesswomen to know and predict trends before their competitors do. And trends are not only temporary but also local. Ana Ramazashvili, one of the project's PhD students, who did research on Laxmi Market in Delhi, reported: "Indian traders understand the specifics of the Georgian market and help Georgian traders select clothing. They say that they have *gruzinskij tovar* ["goods for the Georgian market," грузинский товар] and seemingly effort lessly, they produce the required items from their crowded shops."[40] At the same time, consumers' access to goods depends on the decisions the traders make in Beijing or Istanbul. Thus long-distance traders, at least to some degree, define local supply and thus possible consumption patterns. "This is power," I was told.

Why traders specialize in a certain type of goods, like women's fashions, sneakers, handbags, furs, sunglasses, or furniture, seem rather obscure. Specialization was explained to me as a matter of chance or personal affinity. Of course, goods must sell well. In Lilo, as well as in other bazaars in the Caucasus and Central Asia, traders selling similar goods are grouped in bazaar sections. Consequently, competitors working in the same segment are also working side by side. There are sections for food (e.g., fruits and vegetables), for clothes and shoes, for accessories (e.g., handbags, glasses, jewelry), for plastic and soft toys, for electronics, for spare parts, for furniture and building materials, for antiques (e.g., books, porcelain), and for items of daily use (e.g., kitchen supplies). There are whole areas where one can buy cars, like Rustavi, and specialized bazaars for spare parts and building materials. Even though competition is almost tangible in such places, since there is an obvious oversupply (cf. Steenberg, 2016), sellers seem to profit from this kind of clustering. "Customers go where they are able to compare and choose," I was told by several traders.

Second-hand parts and clothes are obviously less expensive than new merchandise and are usually sold on sidewalks and in open-air and flea markets. Some of these, which have their roots in Soviet times, like the Vernissage in Yerevan or the Sukhoi Most (сухой мост) flea market in Tbilisi, have developed into tourist attractions. These places, as argued by Melkumyan (2019), are nostalgically viewed by customers.[41] As such, they have gained a certain popularity and prestige. Besides silver, porcelain, and other objects that were owned by typical households of the Soviet *intelligencija*, art objects can also now be bought there, designed and produced for tourists by traders who perceive themselves as artistic "masters" (Abrahamian, 2001; Melkumyan, 2017; Taalaibekova,

[40] Informal Markets and Trade in Eurasia (Blog) "From Lilo to Laxmi Market": https://informalmarkets.wordpress.com/from-lilo-to-laxmi-market-%d1%81-%d0%bb%d0%b8%d0%bb%d0%be-%d0%b2-%d0%bb%d0%b0%d1%87%d0%bc%d0%b8-%d0%b1%d0%b0%d0%b7%d0%b0%d1%80-%e1%83%9a%e1%83%98%e1%83%9a%e1%83%9d%e1%83%a1-%e1%83%91/.

[41] Boym (2001) discusses Soviet-made objects as objects of nostalgia symbolizing the Soviet past.

2018; Taalaibekova & Melkumyan, 2018). They put much effort into presenting themselves as such, something that according to my colleague Taalaibekova (2018) is part of an identification game played by the older generation with the goal of justifying one's trading activity and distinguishing oneself from low-prestige *torgovcy* ("traders", торговцы) dealing in ordinary cheap and/or second-hand goods. Individuals who have no other choice, who often belong to the older generation of petty traders and street vendors, described earlier, usually work in the latter segment, which is clearly associated with poverty.

Quantity, Transport, and Frequency

Finally, I would like to mention that the quantity of goods traded, the means of transport used during trade, and the frequency of trading activity are important parameters for gaining a better understanding of economic actors in the Caucasus and their behavior. As mentioned, traders can be classified in terms of the quantity of goods they deal in. Are we talking about a few potatoes or dresses, which a single trader can carry in a bag or suitcase, or about containers of merchandise that need to be shipped to Georgia by cargo companies?

Sales volume is what defines a trader's status in a bureaucratic sense. Statistical services divide traders into micro-, small, and medium entrepreneurs, in addition to large firms. Tax rates are based on these classifications. The Georgian Ministry of Finance[42] recognizes three categories of entrepreneurship or business: micro-business, small business, and big business. Micro-businesses are those with an annual sales volume below GEL 30,000 (ca. U.S.$18,000), small businesses those below GEL 100,000 (ca. U.S.$60,000), and big businesses those over GEL 100,000. GeoStat, the national statistical office, differentiates among small firms (with fewer than 20 employees and an annual sales volume of less than GEL 500,000 [U.S.$300,000]) and medium enterprises (fewer than 100 employees and an annual sales volume of less than GEL 1,500,000 [U.S.$900,000]).[43]

[42] Ministry of Finance of Georgia "Tax Code": https://mof.ge/sagadasaxado_kodeqsi.

[43] Geostat "Classification of Economic Activity": https://www.geostat.ge/en/modules/categories/318/remarks.

Another question is whether trading is a permanent occupation or just a side job. Some people turn to trade only when necessary, engaging in shuttle trading in times of crisis or if they need extra money for special expenses, for New Year's Eve or a wedding, for example. In the first case, the occasional traders work until they get a better job or until other family members can contribute sufficiently to the family's household income. In the second case, the activity is limited to one or two shopping/trade trips per year. Individuals act as members of families or households. Even though husbands and fathers are traditionally perceived as breadwinners, in Georgia, as well as in Armenia, household strategies usually rely on the economic abilities of all household members. Short-term and long-term strategies, salaries, and other income sources are consequently pooled for the good of all. This means that in times of crisis, young women may have to work abroad, and old women may have to sell cookies on the sidewalk to support their families, while in times of stability, a whole household may live on the earnings of the male head of household. Thus in some cases, trading may be a temporary expedient to overcome a crisis or to earn some extra money, while in other cases, it is an integral part of a permanent strategy for household survival or economic success.

Putting the Parts Together

Having described the different parameters that define specific forms of economic activity in the trading sector, especially in the field of small-scale trade, I shall now try to put the parts together again. Location, traders' personal backgrounds, social networks, mobility patterns, and types of merchandise can usually be associated with specific forms of economic activity. But as shown above, the different parameters are so interlinked that it is almost impossible to deal with them separately. One parameter usually determines the combination with others: Traders who have a specific background and rely on a certain type of network work in specific locations. They usually deal in a similar type of merchandise, with similar quality, and in similar quantities. Their mobility patterns overlap, along with their strategies and schedules. Linkages between different parameters are not compulsory or exclusive. But it is at least possible to detect some patterns (see Table 3.1).

Table 3.1 Linkages between parameters

Nr.		*Criteria*	*Street vendors*	*Shuttle traders and* chelnoki*; shopkeepers and vendors in secondhand markets*	*Shopkeepers and market vendors (including long-distance traders)*	*Tourists/moonlighters*	*Elite business*	*Cybershopping*
1	Type of business		Small business	*Chelnoki* and small business	Small business	Small business	Big business	Small and big business
	Location	• Solidity and durability • Sanitary standards • Legal status • Size	**Public space:** central traffic junctions (metro and bus stations, sidewalks), parks, open-air and flea markets; going from house to house **Sales facilities:** pushcarts, a cloth spread on the ground, unregistered	**Small shops or vending without established sales facilities** **Sales facilities:** shop, booth, kiosk, private home, direct delivery to clients	**Bazaars:** roofed or unroofed, specialized in different kinds of merchandise **Sales facilities:** stall, small shop, registered (official license), market administration, security measures	**Vending without established sales facilities** **Sales facilities:** private home, direct delivery to clients/friends	**Boutiques, shops, super-markets, department stores, shopping malls** **Sales facilities:** large, fancy buildings including restaurants and leisure attractions	**Cyberspace:** Internet; local addresses of middlemen **Sales facilities:** local address where you can pick up your ordered goods
			→ perceived as an obstacle to privatization, order, and modernity → accepted as a last resort of the urban poor	→ perceived as personal interaction and as a business of the poor	→ perceived as chaotic, backward, and "Oriental"; low prestige	→ perceived as leisure-time activity	→ perceived as stylish, a marker for lifestyle and wealth	→ perceived as stylish and "modern"

Nr.		*Criteria*	*Street vendors*	*Shuttle traders and* chelnoki; *shopkeepers and vendors in secondhand markets*	*Shopkeepers and market vendors (including long-distance traders)*	*Tourists/moonlighters*	*Elite business*	*Cybershopping*
2	Personal background	• Age • Gender • Education • Personal skills • Urban/rural origin • Status • Ethnicity • Religion	Often women and elderly people who were educated in the Soviet system: the losers of the transition or victims of crisis or tragic circumstances Poor farmers (*glechebi*) may also figure in this group.	People (among them many women) who were educated in the Soviet system: the losers of the transition	People of mixed age, gender, and background. Some of them educated in the Soviet system, others having a low level of education.	Especially young people who do not work in the trade sector	People of mixed age and background, predominantly male. Some of them educated in the Soviet system, others having a low level of education; sometimes with criminal backgrounds.	–
			→ perceive trade as a shameful activity	→ perceive trade as a shameful activity → trade as a reaction to crisis	→ perceive economic success as an important social value	→ perceive their activity as a kind of leisure/supplemental activity	→ associate political, social, and moral power with economic success → role model for local youth	
			Ethnicity and religion are sometimes linked to a "talent" for trade and business. Jews and Armenians, for example, are said to be particularly gifted in this domain. Trade is sometimes associated with Islam, too, but the Christian Orthodox Church in the Caucasus seems to have a positive attitude towards economic success and wealth.					

(continued)

Table 3.1 (continued)

Nr.		*Criteria*	*Street vendors*	*Shuttle traders and* chelnoki*; shopkeepers and vendors in secondhand markets*	*Shopkeepers and market vendors (including long-distance traders)*	*Tourists/moonlighters*	*Elite business*	*Cybershopping*
3	Social networks and rela-tionships with clients	• Size and impor-tance of social networks • Link to legal institu-tions • Relationships and communication with clients	Lack of support from kin; reliance on weak networks	Weak networks; loose relationships	Help from close family members; personal relationships with business partners (suppliers and middlemen, credit agencies) and business friends; ***dzmakatsoba*** (masculine peer group); reluctance to cooperate with state institutions; face-to-face communication with clients; bargaining	–	Rely on large and important social networks grounded in Soviet hierarchies, the military, or local kinship ties. Sometimes links to the criminal world. Sometimes strong links to the Orthodox Church	Anonymous orders over the Internet
4	Mobility	• Distance • Importance of travel experi-ence • Experi-ence of travelling	Usually do not travel or travel short distances, e.g., from rural to urban areas	Usually cross borders; in the case of ***chelnoki***, cover long distances by minibus, train, or airplane	Some businessmen do not travel. Their merchandise is transported by cargo companies. Other businessmen travel long distances by airplane (usually to Turkey or China)	Travelling/having holidays abroad is the main purpose of the trip	May travel but most of the time outsource travelling; use cargo companies etc.	–

Nr.	*Criteria*	*Street vendors*	*Shuttle traders and* chelnoki; *shopkeepers and vendors in secondhand markets*	*Shopkeepers and market vendors (including long-distance traders)*	*Tourists/moonlighters*	*Elite business*	*Cybershopping*
			Travel experience: Exhausting, dangerous, and uncomfortable circumstances	**Travel experience:** Routine, predictable, relatively comfortable	**Travel experience:** Having fun		
5 Goods	• Type of goods • Quality and origin • Value and prestige • Age (new, second-hand, antique)	Food, flowers, clothes, items of daily use, art and religious objects. Secondhand goods, e.g., spare parts, books, silver, porcelain, etc.	Almost any type of merchandise; usually of lower quality	Food, spare parts and building materials, secondhand cars, clothes, furniture, items of daily use; often associated with cheap quality and fake brands from China and Turkey	Latest fashion from Europe, luxury goods, technical devices; usually from Europe, Dubai, United States	Associated with brands but obviously also with merchandise from bazaars	Expensive luxury goods from Europe, the United States, or Canada
6 Amount		Few goods; very low profit margins		Wholesale and retail sale			Individual orders
		Goal: Survival	**Goal:** Survival and/or a small profit	**Goal:** Make a good living; profit	**Goal:** Make extra money	**Goal:** Become rich and powerful	**Goal:**
7 Frequency	• permanent or occasional • trips per year	Trade is usually a permanent occupation. However, the activity might become unnecessary, if a crisis has been overcome.	Associated with crisis (survival strategy); necessity-driven; numbers of trips adjusted to needs	Permanent profession; trips are part of a routine (from once a month to twice a year)	Incidental	Permanent activity	Permanent activity

(continued)

Table 3.1 (continued)

Nr.	*Criteria*	*Street vendors*	*Shuttle traders and* chelnoki; *shopkeepers and vendors in secondhand markets*	*Shopkeepers and market vendors (including long-distance traders)*	*Tourists/moonlighters*	*Elite business*	*Cybershopping*
9	Ideas, beliefs, values, moral perceptions	Often stick to Soviet values, especially if they grew up and were educated in the Soviet system. Assessed as a marker of poverty and as an obstacle to Western-style market liberalization and modernization. Sometimes an object of charity	Often stick to Soviet values, especially if they grew up and were educated in the Soviet system. Assessed as a marker of poverty and as an obstacle to Western-style market liberalization and modernization. Sometimes associated with nostalgia.	Combine Soviet nostalgia with values linked to the market economy and Western-style modernization. Refer to and build on social codes of honor related to kinship, social hierarchies, and peer groups; refer to ideals of masculinity; often present themselves as strong religious believers.	Do not explicitly represent specific values	Link themselves to the market economy and refer to social codes of honor related to kinship, social hierarchies, and peer groups; refer to ideals of masculinity; often present themselves as strong religious believers.	Perceived as a "modern" tool to access a Western lifestyle, which is associated with Western values.

Nr.	*Criteria*	*Street vendors*	*Shuttle traders and* chelnoki; *shopkeepers and vendors in secondhand markets*	*Shopkeepers and market vendors (including long-distance traders)*	*Tourists/moonlighters*	*Elite business*	*Cybershopping*
				Assessed as both pioneers of the market economy and remnants of a transition economy deeply impact by Soviet heritage and local values, which in this context are assessed as backward.		Often associated with "wild capitalism," which is perceived as an extreme and antisocial form of market liberalism. Often associated with corruption. Gain status through economic success and are taken as role models.	

Ideology: Ideas, Beliefs, and Value Systems

At this point I would like to add one more variable, which I have not addressed separately so far, but which has been an integral part of the assessment and description of my interlocutors. This variable is the dimension of ideas, beliefs, and values—in a word, ideology (Dumont, 1980). In the Caucasus, one can identify three core and overlapping value systems that impact economic behavior and its assessment: (1) a local sociocultural and cosmological value system, (2) a value system linked to Soviet ideology, and (3) a value system linked to the sphere of the Western-style liberal market economy.

Put simply, system 1 is grounded on local cosmology, the local perception of social relationships, and core ideas/core principles defining "traditional" local culture (such as ideas about relationships to other individuals, God, and the material world). The concept of "brotherhood" (*ʒmaḳacoba*, ძმაკაცობა), for example, can be seen as related to this system, as well as ideas about kinship, social hierarchies, hospitality, spirituality, masculinity, customary law, informal rules of conduct, and so on. The underlying ideology is characteristic of traditional societies: "The stress is placed on society as a whole [...], it is above all a matter of order, of hierarchy; each particular man in his place must contribute to the global order, and justice consists in ensuring that the proportions between social functions are adapted to the whole" (Dumont, 1980: 9).

This order, justice, and proportion, in my interpretation, are mirrored in the relationships maintained between traders, for example, and in practices like the toasting and feasting (*supra*, სუფრა, sufra) rituals (which follow rules reflecting order, justice, and proportion). The underlying ideas, beliefs, and values are difficult to assign to a specific time period. In the process of post-Soviet nation-building (and even in the context of Soviet national policies) they have often been traced back to pre-Soviet—even ancient—times. Herzfeld (1997) would assign them to what he calls "cultural intimacy." From the point of view of locals, they are what define their specific cultural identity.

System 2 is linked to socialism and the Soviet ideal of modernization (*modernizacija*, модернизация). Socialism, implemented through central planning and collectivization, among many other things, was accompanied by condemnation of commerce, classified as "speculation" (*spekuljacija*, спекуляция) (Humphrey, 2002; Kotkin, 1995: 250: Mandel & Humphrey, 2002). In the Soviet ideology related to economics, "work" (*trud*, труд, *rabota*, работа), physical as well as intellectual, was a core value that defined the individual's place in society—and in the Soviet world: "In the Soviet context work was not simply a material necessity but also a civic obligation. Everyone had the right to work; no one had the right not to work. Failure to work, or to work in a 'socially useful' manner, was a punishable offense, and the chief punishment was forced labor (*prinuditelnaja rabota*). [...] Work served as both the instrument and measure of normality" (Kotkin, 1995: 202).

Trade was conceptualized as work's negative counterpart, the opposite of "real" and productive work." Modernization consequently had a specific meaning. It was tightly linked to industrialization, urbanization, secularization, and the literacy of the working population. The driving force and goal was progress, which was linked to and meant to result in a new kind of society. Thus Soviet modernization differs from the Western understanding of modernity, which, by contrast, is usually related to the ideas of the nation-state, democracy, and capitalism (Bayadyan, 2007: 205–219).

The third set of ideas here (system 3) is linked to a positive assessment of economic success and Western-style modernization. Both are usually associated with Europe (and sometimes the United States). According to Dumont, the two cardinal ideas of this Western system are equality and liberty, both of which assume as their common principle the idea of the human individual. "This individual is quasi sacred, absolute; there is nothing over and above his legitimate demands; his rights are limited only by the identical rights of other individuals" (Dumont, 1980: 4). This, again, fits well with the notion of *homo economicus,* an individual who, at least in theory, interacts with other, equal individuals and makes free decisions that are guided solely by his own rationality.

Of course, ideology is not everything. Dumont admits that "any concrete, localized, whole, when actually observed, is found decisively oriented by its ideology, and also to extend far beyond it" (1980: 37). Furthermore, the context I have described above cannot be perceived as a coherent and isolated system. Historical dynamics—and history has been particularly turbulent in the Caucasus—have resulted in the coexistence of many concepts rooted in different sets of experiences and ideas. The three systems I have presented above are those easily recognized. They sometimes conflict with each other, sometimes complement each other, and sometimes simply coexist. The different relationships between these systems may result in new ideas and values. To some degree, these relations and processes have been discussed in debates on modernity, pointing to the fact that there are many understandings of "modernity" that result from the interrelation of local, transnational, and global ideas (cf. Robbins & Siikala, 2014).[44]

Notions of value (system) and morality have been the subject of lively debate among anthropologists in recent years. Many attempts have been made to explain the relationship between a Durkheimian understanding of these notions, based on or reflected in routine and normative social action, and understandings that emphasize processes of critical reflection and choice making (Robbins, 2007). Scholars then debated whether "critical reflection is a universal feature of human behavior or better conceived of as a product of the Enlightment" (Marsden, 2016: 160). Be that as it may, as the transition from *chelnoki* (челноки) to *biznesmeny* described (бизнесмены) in Chapter 2 shows, values and moral codes become most visible "during periods of social change when societies are called upon to question their moral universes" (Marsden, 2016: 160; cf. Robbins, 2004; Robbins & Siikala, 2014).

I understand the different values systems described above as points of reference and as toolboxes from which people take what they need to make sense of their actions and lives. As my examples have shown, which value system or moral code is given priority and how values from different systems are combined and put into a hierarchical order depends on the social background of different groups within society and on the particular context and situation. As noted, many individuals on the lower rungs of the trading hierarchy (especially older people) are attached to Soviet values, while so-called *biznesmeny* define their status through values linked to the market economy and liberalism. At the same time, both groups combine their convictions with religious beliefs, codes of honor, and ideas about social relationships rooted in local (traditional) values of sociability, religion, and custom. These combinations result in new phenomena and assessments. Thus we have, on the one hand, for example, a new ideology of the so-called "new rich" (an ideology that is neither local in a traditional sense, nor Soviet, nor Western) and, on the other hand, the new moral code of business culture that I have described so far. Traders

[44] See discussions of the interaction of Western modernity and local contexts: "multiple modernities" (Eisenstadt, 2000), "alternative modernities" (Gaonkar, 2001), or the "indigenization of modernity" (Sahlins, 1999). See also Basu (2013) and Englund and Leach (2000).

use traditional terms to define social relationships that are not established in the traditional context. They transfer traditional social values to completely new contexts and linkages that emerge in the context of business—which is, again, influenced by market ideology.

How the values of each social group are assessed depends on the social background of the "valuers." Humphrey, for example, reports on the assessment of local elites:

> The term "New Russian" has acquired a definite and transferable meaning. It refers to an image of people with a new and alien mentality, people who are rapacious, materialist and shockingly economically successful. In short, New Russians are "new" because they do not give precedence to various hoary Soviet values, which are still mostly seen in a rosy hue by everyone else. ... In this mode of talking, New Russians are presumed to be "corrupt." (2002: 177)

But this captures only one side of the coin. As mentioned above, in other contexts, the new elites and their values are taken as role models. A similar change of perspective may show shuttle traders in different lights. Many shuttle traders perceive themselves as "cultured," "masters," and "honest people," a positive assessment in terms of Soviet as well as local values, but they are regarded as indicative of poverty and as obstacles to liberalization and modernization by other people and in other contexts (see Table 3.1).

Entrepreneurs in Local Ecosystems

Local traders and businesspeople are frequently classified as entrepreneurs by official institutions and scientists. This classification, again, is based on ideology—predominantly on Western distinctions. However, the local representatives of this classificatory group regularly do not fulfil the expectations linked to Western definitions of entrepreneurship, which leads to the assumption that something must be wrong with traders who do not want to formalize their businesses, which thus fail to grow.

As noted in the Introduction, one of my aims in this book is to shed light on the activities of traders in the Caucasus in their local environments. These environments are shaped by the factors sketched above, whose entanglement constitutes an ecosystem, and traders perforce adapt their business strategies to specific niches in it.

Defining the Local Entrepreneur
Established definitions present the so-called entrepreneur as the embodiment of agency and the prime agent of economic change (Schumpeter, 1942; Shane & Venkataraman, 2000). Anthropologists like Frederic Barth (1963) and Clifford Geertz (1963) have related entrepreneurship not only to economic development, but also to social change (Firth, 1967).[45] According to Barth, the entrepreneur is imbued with sociocultural values, but at the same time, can change them by introducing new transactions, through which values are shared and integrated. Entrepreneurs who develop new transactions are thus those who create new value consistencies (Barth, 1963; Strathern, 2018). Economic and sociocultural change have been highlighted in studies of the post-Soviet transition. And naturally, the entrepreneur figures as a major agent in this process.

The emerging literature on post-Soviet entrepreneurship focuses in part on nouveau riche "New Russians" (*novye russkie,* новые русские) and their equivalents in other post-Soviet countries, who are usually associated with authoritarian regimes (or plutocracy), criminality, and violence and are seen as agents of social change that treats money as the highest virtue, dividing society into rich and poor, powerful and powerless (Antonyan, 2016; Aslund, 2007; Fehlings, 2018; Grant, 1999; Holzlehner, 2014; Humphrey, 2002). These new post-Soviet economic elites can be divided into two groups, described earlier in this chapter, representing two different forms of capitalism: "capitalism without capitalists" and "capitalists without capitalism" (Eval et al., 2000). In the former, representatives of the old *nomenklatura* became capitalists, since "they were those who had access to [the] privatization of [the] resources of power"; in the latter, the absence of the legal institutions of capitalism and a market economy led to "violent entrepreneurship," in which wealth is accumulated by organized force (Volkov, 2012; Antonyan, 2016). Empirically, the two groups are interconnected, and they are usually studied under the same labels, as "oligarchs" (*oligarhi*, олигархи), "businessmen" (*bizneymeny*, бизнесмены), "new Russians/ Armenians/ Georgians" (*novye russkie/armjane/gruziny* новые русские/армяне/грузины), or simply "elites" (*elita*, элита) (see above).

[45] For an overview over early anthropological studies on entrepreneurship (see Salisbury, 1973).

The role of so-called SMEs (small and medium entrepreneurs) in the transition to a Western-style market economy is the other main focus of scholarly research in this field. Studies usually describe the potential of SMEs for economic growth, linked to modernization and democratization. SMEs, ranging from "craft-based entrepreneurs" in contemporary Kyrgyzstan (Botoeva & Spector, 2013; Krebs, 2011) to producers of *a ǯ̆ iḳa* (აჯიკა) (a local spice mixture) in the Abkhazian-Georgian border region (Khutsishvili, 2017), have thus become not only an object of academic study but also a target of development aid.

In current understandings, the development of SMEs is linked to the formalization of economic procedures (Williams & Round, 2007; Williams et al, 2009, 2012), and this is encouraged to support them. In Georgia, after the Rose Revolution, the country's government embarked on radical reforms to achieve this. Taxes and administrative procedures were reduced and corruption almost banned, creating a business-friendly environment (see also World Bank, 2012; Di Puppo, 2013; Rudaz, 2018). However, despite favorable new conditions, many SMEs in Georgia, did not formalize their businesses. According to Rudaz's research, self-employed entrepreneurs and micro-businesses (with an annual sales volume of less than GEL 30,000 [ca. U.S.$18,000]), have stayed in the informal sector, while so-called small firms (with an annual sales volume of less than GEL 100,000 [ca. U.S.$60,000]) operate in the formal sector. Social and economic mobility has been very limited. Little has changed and much remained the same.

This problem seems to exist in other post-socialist bazaars as well and has become even more evident in recent years: "It is now increasingly difficult for anyone to work his/her way up the social ladder of the Seventh Kilometer[46]—that is, to move from being a mere day-to-day seller, to regular employee, to renter of a container, to owner of a container, and finally to owner of a string of containers" (Humphrey & Skvirskaja, 2009: 68). Many economists (especially neo-institutionalists) suspect that "empirical evidence" for this is explained by the role of institutions and state-building processes in non-Western societies, arguing that entrepreneurs in emerging and transitional countries tend to be dealing with environments characterized by rapid change, extreme uncertainty,

[46] A bazaar in Odessa mentioned earlier in this chapter, also called Sed'moj.

weak market institutions, and many informal and socioculturally determined norms and rules, all making them more likely to fail (Hart 1970; Rudaz, 2018). Even if conditions are favorable, few entrepreneurs are likely to profit under these conditions.

Economists distinguish between entrepreneurship by default and entrepreneurship by choice, or between necessity-driven and opportunity-driven entrepreneurs. Only the latter seem able to profit from good circumstances and to change their situation and make a profit. The gap between self-employed entrepreneurs and micro-firms, including the bazaar traders of my target group, on the one hand, and formalized small enterprises, on the other, between necessity-driven and opportunity-driven entrepreneurs, is said to reflect the entrepreneurial attitude. I have often heard the former group described as less informed, lacking motivation, unwilling to take risks, and having less access to larger markets (see Rudaz, 2018: 86). Most descriptions and explanations stop there.

I think that the materials presented above may contribute to a more detailed analysis. As noted, the problem starts with the fact that common definitions describing the normative entrepreneur do not correspond to local terms. The local term ***biznesman*** covers a social spectrum that ranges from street vendors to bazaar traders and from criminals to plutocrats. It does not necessarily support the idea of the entrepreneur (=***biznesman***) as a driving force in increasing national GDP. "Rather than breaking new ground in products, process, or administrative form," ***biznesmeny*** "simply replicate and reproduce old forms," especially in the retail and services sector, according to Aldrich and Waldinger's study of "ethnic entrepreneurship" (Aldrich & Waldinger, 1990: 112). Can the groups of Georgian traders described above even be called entrepreneurs (Rudaz, 2018)?

One strategy for solving the problem of an adequate definition of entrepreneurship fitting the context seems obvious: develop a new (and more comprehensive) one. Hart did so by saying that the label of "small-scale entrepreneurs" applies "to anyone who controls the management of capital which he has invested in some enterprise in order to realize profit." Belshaw (1965) and Firth (1967) did the same by assessing given definitions and adjusting them, pointing, for example, to the importance of "extensive management" in the function of an entrepreneur: "In one sense an entrepreneur is simply a combiner of resources, that is a production manager whose task it is to decide how much of what kinds of capital, labor, and raw materials are to be combined and in what ways they are to be organized. This is the act of making economizing decisions" (Belshaw, 1965: 115).

In Belshaw's view, "most individuals in modern just as in peasant society flee from the insecurity of fresh decision-making. While some are innovators, and while innovation is praised and rewarded, even innovation is easier when it is patterned." Thus he concludes that "most decision makers are not innovators: They are men who make routine decisions according to precedent" (1965: 113). This is a good description of Caucasian traders, who whether working as street vendors, in bazaars, or travelling to China, usually make decisions with a rather predictable outcome, copying the practices of their peers, following the trade routes established since the time of the *chelnoki,* and usually following a routine first established many years ago. Still, they are businesspeople.

When it comes to so-called entrepreneurial spirit, of course, one must ask, what is meant by this notion? If one looks at keywords like discovery, creation, and exploitation of opportunities and innovation, decision-making, and risk-taking, one can distinguish more and less active entrepreneurs. Dato, for example, who was planning to start a new business with innovative beehives, assured me that he had explored a new market: he had discovered that Europe is not importing honey from Georgia, and he was sure that this was because honey is still produced with traditional methods in the Caucasus.[47] So he wanted to introduce a new technology, which he had found through an advertising video on YouTube. He was in the process of convincing his Turkish business partner to produce these hives, which he hoped to sell for a great profit, inasmuch as he was the first to perceive and create this demand. This example reflects entrepreneurial spirit as defined by Western economists. But Levan, Ramaz, and Giorgi, like any trader, also made decisions and took risks when choosing certain goods, which they then had to sell. Saying that the entrepreneurial spirit is missing in this context, where everything is about business, seems risible to me. Gerald Mars' and Yochanan Altman's *The Cultural Bases of Soviet Georgia's Second Economy* (1983) speaks, conversely, of the pronounced entrepreneurial spirit of Georgians, explained in terms of risk taking as a value linked to masculinity in Georgian society and contrasted to Western equivalents by

[47] After being questioned, he admitted that Georgians also use some chemicals that are not accepted in Europe.

defining Georgians as "gambling entrepreneurs." There are thus contradictory assessments of Georgian entrepreneurship. I think the best that an anthropologist can do in this situation is to take a closer look at the phenomenon of entrepreneurship as embedded in a broader context: to explain it as an adaptation to the local economic ecosystem.

The Embedded Entrepreneur—A "Portrait of Nature"

Treating entrepreneurs from an anthropological perspective as embedded in local ecosystems allows one to address an issue that concerns our colleagues in other disciplines: why do self-employed and micro-firm entrepreneurs not grow and formalize their businesses?

As economists have argued, lack of capital might be a decisive factor. If entrepreneurs are struggling for survival, this will hardly lead to significant reinvestment. As might be deduced from the ethnographic evidence presented, strategies of survival are easy to recognize. Usually in such cases, the volume of traded goods and the sales volume are very small. Hasmik is a good random example. She traded in vegetables to feed her family and considered her work as something one would call subsistence economy. This perception of her activity was why she did not even consider paying taxes or customs duties. Why would she pay the state when she can hardly meet her children's daily needs? The poor, for whom the state fails to care, do not—at least in my experience—care about the state. For them, the state is either culpable or non-existent. The same is true the other way around.

The situation is different for traders like those working in local bazaars, who are expected to make at least some profit, or, to put it briefly, to work for more than mere survival. These traders represent the target group of the state-initiated reforms described above. The formal registration and taxation of successful entrepreneurs, it was hoped, would come as a logical consequence. Traders, as described earlier and as discussed in the next chapter, do not agree with this logic. If one believes our survey data from Lilos Bazroba the reforms did not lead to the expected results. Many traders report that the economic environment has not improved and that formalization is too expensive (see Chapter 4). They claim that if they were to pay the regular tax rates, they would not make any profit at all. In many cases, this might be an exaggeration. It might say more about the traders' assessment of the state and about what they perceive as "fair" than about their profit margins. However, we can—at least to some degree—interpret the traders' reactions and the absent or insignificant formalization and growth of their businesses as an indicator of the failure of state institutions.

I believe that there is another explanation for why the self-employed and micro-firms in the Caucasian small-trade sector do not formalize or grow. The reason is very simple and derives from the particularity of the businesses and business environment described above. This environment is an ecosystem, and the exploitation of niches within this system requires certain assets and skills. Alexander von Humboldt's "portrait of nature" (*Naturgemälde*) can serve as a model to show exactly what I mean by an "economic ecosystem" and the entanglement of the aforementioned parameters.

Unlike scientists who classified flora and fauna according to strict, hierarchical taxonomies, Humboldt aimed to describe individual phenomena in the context of the larger whole (Wulf, 2016). "The great problem of the physical description of the globe is the determination of the form of these types [of stony strata, plants, and animals], the laws of their relations with each other, and the eternal ties which link the phenomena of life, and those of inanimate nature," he observes in his *Personal Narrative* (von Humboldt, 1851: xi).[48] Climbing Chimborazo in the Ecuadorean Andes, a dormant volcano that is one of the highest mountains in the world, in 1802, gave him a fresh perspective.

A. von Humboldt published his ideas in *Ideen zu einer Geographie der Pflanzen* (1807b) and *Essai sur la géographie des plantes* (1807a), which contain his *Naturgemälde,* a huge tableau, measuring 90 by 60 cm, which depicts a cross-section of Chimborazo, showing nature as a web of interconnections between different orders of reality (Fig. 3.4).

In the illustration, different plants are assigned to the altitude at which they grow. Each altitude level is, in turn, assigned to a climate zone. The right and left sides of the illustration are filled by columns with additional information about measurements of the intensity of solar radiation, visibility from sea level, electrical phenomena, zonal locations of cultivated crops, the blueness of the sky (*Luftbläue in Graden des Kyanometers*), humidity, air pressure, and so on (Buttimer, 2012; von Humboldt, 1807b) In Humboldt's *Kosmos: Entwurf einer physischen Weltbeschreibung* (1845–1862), similar representations of other high mountains, which

[48] Translated by Thomasina Ross from *Voyage aux régions équinoxiales* (von Humboldt, 1814).

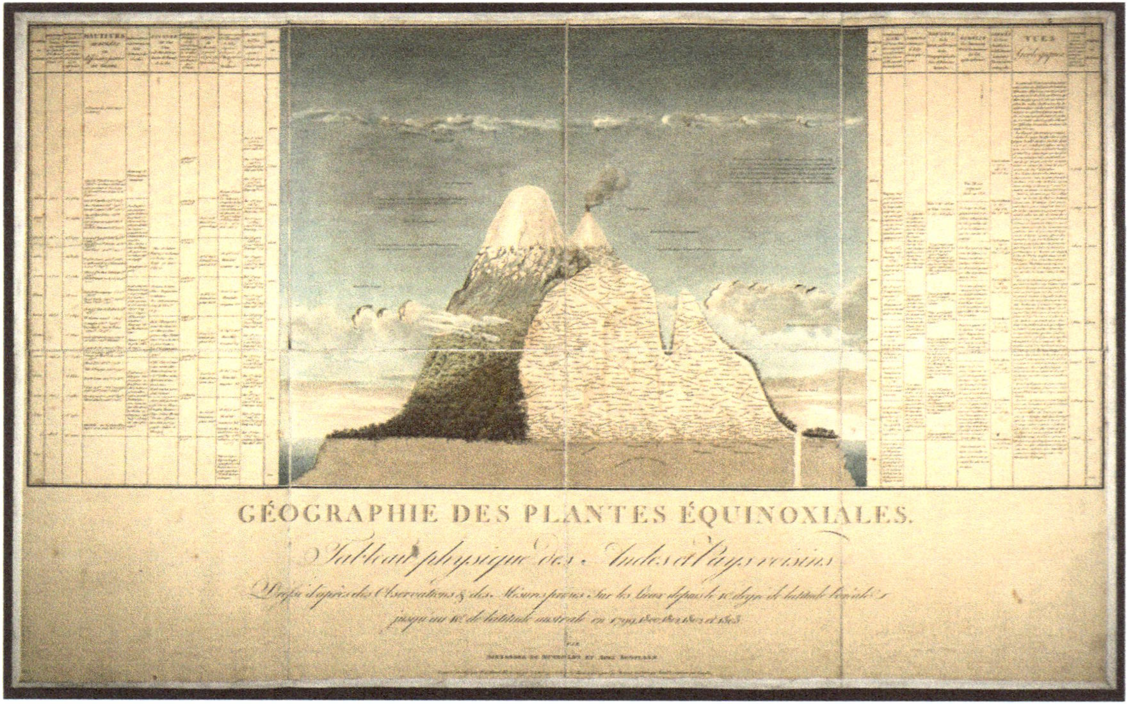

Fig. 3.4 Humboldt's *Naturgemälde* (tableau physique) (Avhumboldt.de "Tableau physique des Andes et pays voisins, Peter H. Raven Library/Missouri Botanical Garden (CC BY-NC-SA 4.0), Biodiversity Heritage Library": https://www.avhumboldt.de/?p=11781)

he added for comparison, flank the data for Chimborazo (Wulf, 2016) (Fig. 3.5).

Representing a complex and interconnected environment in a Humboldt-like visual form is useful for reassembling the elements of the economic environment I describe above and depicting it as a whole. One is not, of course, dealing in this case with measurable quantities like humidity, atmospheric pressure, and the chemical composition of the air, and it is much more difficult to assign "animals" and "plants" to concrete locations. The problems with applying methods from the natural sciences to human behavior are captured in Lord Byron's *Don Juan,* where the poet derives a comical analogy from Humboldt's cyanometer:

> Humboldt "the first of travellers," but not
> The last, if late accounts be accurate,
> Invented, by some name I have forgot,
> As well as the sublime discovery's date,
> An airy instrument, with which he sought
> To ascertain the atmospheric state,
> By measuring "the intensity of blue":
> Oh, Lady Daphne! Let me measure you!

A visual depiction of an economic environment must thus be approached in a much more metaphorical way and needs some additional explanation (although Humboldt also felt his illustration needed explanation, since his whole book was a textual account of what could be seen in his *Naturgemälde* tableau).

Let me take Humboldt's depiction as a model: let Chimborazo be the local economic environment, and let altitude be the approximate position in the social hierarchy (social prestige, political and moral power). Here, however, we need to consider Humboldt's example in light of the painter Henri Matisse's remark that "accuracy is not necessarily truth." Let us then add columns for location, personal background, social networks, mobility, merchandise, quantity of goods, and transport of goods and frequency of activity, which we then may link to different levels of the illustration, as shown in Fig. 3.6.

Time is missing as a factor in Humboldt's *Naturgemälde* tableau, but since the economic environment is dynamic, Fig. 3.6 indicates the temporal dimension as well. Most likely, Humboldt would today take climate change into account. In my case, I presume that historical events and political changes, especially crisis, change the importance of one layer

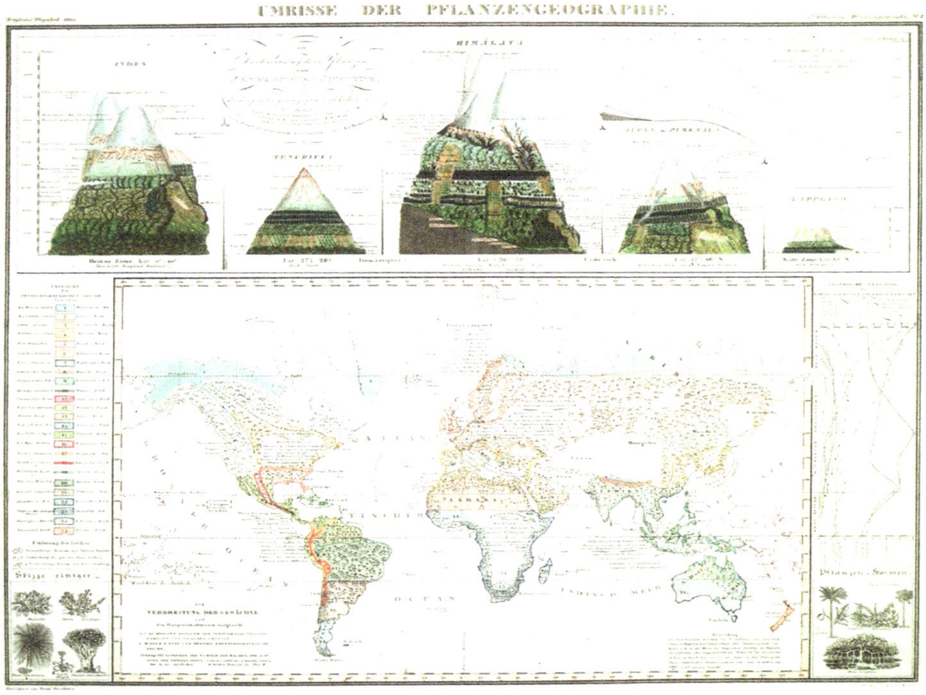

Fig. 3.5 Humboldt's *Naturgemälde* 2 (Cybergeo "Alexander von Humboldt and Planet Earth's Green Mantle", 2012 [by Anne Buttimer]: http://journals.openedition.org/cybergeo/25478; Original Source: H. Berghaus, 1851, Physikalischer Atlas, vol. V, plate No. 1)

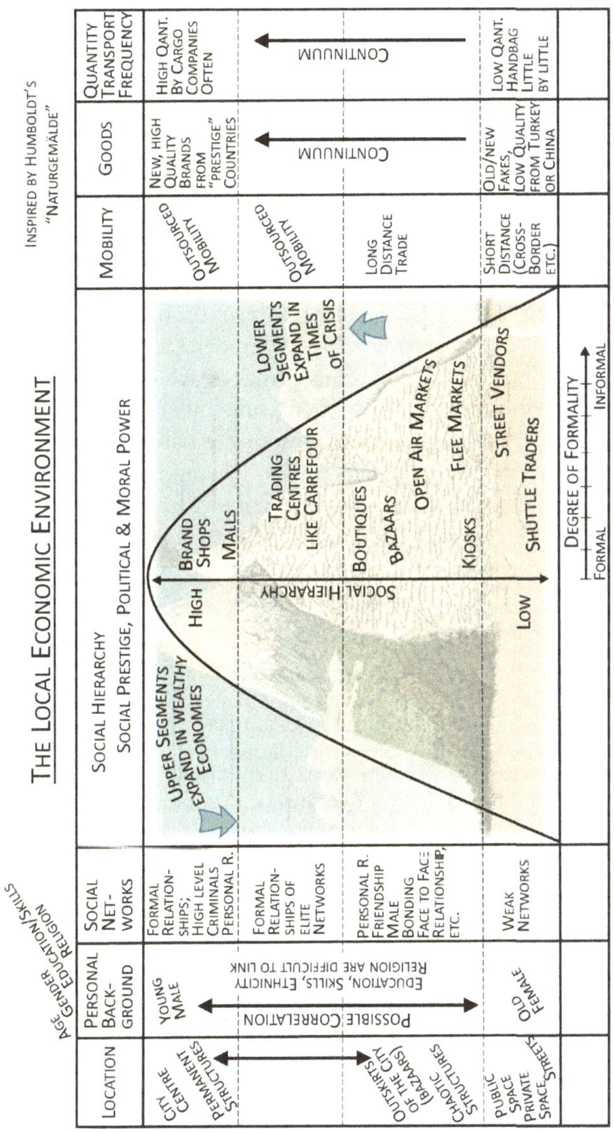

Fig. 3.6 The local economic ecosystem

of the system relative to another. In times of crisis, the lower levels seem to become more important (in numbers and visibility); in times following crisis, the upper levels seems to have the advantage; and in a balanced situation, the middle sections predominate. Of course, the levels are permeable and overlap one another. Since I have used formality and informality to describe the different aspects of business, I also include these abstract, contestable notions in the depiction. By including a medial axis symbolizing formality in the center of the mountain, altitudes on the mountainside can be read as the levels of informality of the respective types of economic activity.

Probably this visual depiction is too ambitious. However, it fulfils the task of a model, which is a generalization of findings meant to provide a helpful tool for clustering material, understanding interdependencies, and comparing evidence.[49] One could create similar depictions of different local economies and put them side by side, as is done in Humboldt's *Kosmos,* to compare the economic environments and the impact of external dynamics on their tectonics. It would be useful to have similar models of the Chinese economy, for example, in order to compare it to the Caucasian model. Probably, one could then also see in what ways these two models and their dynamics depend on one another.

[49] Models are usually associated with structuralism. Claude Lévi-Strauss has much to say about them in his *Structural Anthropology* (1963 [1958]). Much of it is reminiscent of Humboldt's attitude to science. Lévi-Strauss distinguishes (1) empirical evidence, (2) models, which are constructed on the basis of this evidence, and (3) social structure, which is distilled from the models. For Lévi-Strauss, to "observe facts and elaborate methodological devices, which permit the construction of models out of these facts is not at all the same thing as to experiment on the models" (180). Like Humboldt, Lévi-Strauss asserts that he starts his investigation by scrupulously collecting empirical evidence. For him there is a direct relationship between the concreteness of ethnographic description and the validity and generality of the model that is subsequently constructed (180–181). Modelling, in the social sciences, has its problems. Lévi-Strauss contrasts conscious and unconscious models (181–183) and mechanical and statistical models (183–189). As soon as one is dealing with an unlimited number of entities (whether individuals or facts), one has difficulty relating all the parts to one another and understanding their interactions. At this point one has to rely on statistics. The application of statistics, however, is itself a problem: "The objects with which we deal—social roles and human beings—are considerably more numerous than those dealt with in Newtonian mechanics, and at the same time, far less numerous than would be required to allow a satisfactory use of the laws of statistics and probability. Thus we find ourselves in an intermediate zone: too complicated for one treatment and not complicated enough for the other" (314).

First of all, the model helps one to understand the economic niche, in which the traders of my target group work. This niche, in the lower middle part of the mountain, is determined by a specific combination of parameters. Bazaar traders usually work in similar locations, they sell a similar quality and quantity of merchandise, adopt similar practices, and share similar mobility patterns. They have similar social, economic and cultural backgrounds and share similar ideas and values—a similar ideology and attitude to life and work.

The traders of my target group as a rule work in bazaars. They do not belong to either the very poor or the elite segment of society. They are in the most productive periods of their lives (between their thirties and sixties), and they are mostly men. Typically, they have no educational background in economics and perceive themselves as Georgians and Christian Orthodox. To be successful in their specific niche of bazaar trade (and long-distance trade with China), they must possess the ability to establish and to manipulate social relationships with suppliers, middlemen, and other traders and clients. This ability is linked to a culturally determined understanding of what these relationships should look like and what values are attached to them, which is personal and social, irrespective of whether one talks about ***dzamakatsoba*** ("men's love") or trader-client relationships. Dato, Irma, Levan, Ramaz, and Giorgi depend on it for everything. They buy from suppliers, who have become their friends, and cooperate with traders they call their family. Levan has travelled to Almaty and Urumqi to establish a personal relationship with people working along the route of his merchandise takes, and Irma and Giorgi rely on their skills in arguing with customs officials face to face. All the traders of this segment I talked to reported that it is personal networks that give them access to clients. Long-distance traders are always travelling and mobile. They transport their goods with the help of cargo companies and usually operate in a semi-formal sphere, which means that they deal with formal institutions in a specific way (see Chapter 4). They all believe that social relationships and values like honor and trustworthiness are very important, that business is for profit but should be fair, and that trading is hard work. Economic success for them is a basis of status and prestige.

These are the factors that determine specialization in the long-distance bazaar trade, which constitutes an economic niche. It is difficult to say whether traders adapt to this niche or create it. But, and this is my answer to the question of why traders do not formalize or make their businesses grow, fitting one's economic niche determines economic practice and its limits. Growing and formalizing a business means going beyond the scope of this practice—going beyond one's niche. The capital, skills, and strategies that are indispensable to succeeding as a self-employed entrepreneur or as the owner of a micro-firm engaged in informal small-scale trading clash with the capital and skills needed to manage a small or large business operating in the formal sphere. These are different habitats. While the first sphere, at least to some degree, is characterized by the kind of relationships and structures that Émile Durkheim (1969 [1893]) classified as mechanical solidarity, the second sphere is shaped by structures that can be conceptualized as organic. Small and large businesses include more people, which goes along with division of labor and contractual arrangements: the entrepreneur must know the laws and regulations, has to learn how to keep accurate accounts, and needs to cooperate with state institutions. It is not easy for a freshwater fish to adapt to the ocean. In the traders' case, this is also a question of conflicting ideologies. Growth and formalization are linked to cooperation with state institutions, which are not trusted (irrespective of whether represented by Soviet authorities or local elites) and are said to act counter to the sociability and morality of average citizens. For the businesses I have described in these first two chapters, therefore, informality is both a necessity and a choice.

Conclusion

So-called *biznes* is a dominant topic in Caucasian societies. Many people seem always to be on the lookout for a good deal and apparently take advantage of every situation that presents itself in any possible context of economic exchange. However, or perhaps because of this fact, almost all the practices and types of exchange described above are characterized by rather small exchange values. By looking at different aspects of the trading business, I have tried to sketch the local economic environment as a combination of interrelated parameters (location, traders' personal background, social networks, mobility, goods, quantities, transport and frequency of travel, and ideas, beliefs, and values).

These parameters, their combination, and their importance are influenced by permanently changing (historical, political, macroeconomic) conditions. If the national and international political and economic situation shifts, this affects the physical and social environment and challenges ideological and sociocultural value systems. This leaves imprints on local society and markets and influences exchange patterns: old social networks and values are replaced by new ones, economic activities and places of exchange grow or shrink, individuals are forced to leave one kind of business to get involved in another, and people become rich or impoverished.

Travelling to certain countries might suddenly become more complicated and less profitable, on the one hand, while restrictions (conflict situations, visa formalities, taxes, and laws) in the trader's own country might make it more complicated to sell the goods, on the other. Sometimes, a seemingly minor point has the potential to affect an entire segment of the market, in the way that, for example, the introduction of MOT (Ministry of Transport) certificates would impact the second-hand car, scrap, and spare parts trade. By reassembling the parameters identified in my analysis and developing models, I have tried to capture these interdependencies. One goal of this process has been to overcome sharp dichotomies such as formal and informal, globalization from above and globalization from below, and economy and culture.

References

Abrahamian, L. (2001). Afterword: The Artisan: Traditional Figure and Contemporary Functions. In N. Sweezy & L. Abrahamian (Eds.), *Armenian Folk Arts, Culture and Identity* (pp. 261–270). Indiana University Press.

Abrahamian, L. (2007a). Armenia and Armenians Between East and West. *21st Century, 1*, 72–76.

Abrahamian, L. (2007b). *Troubles and Hopes: Armenian Family, Home and Nation*. Campus Verlag.

Aivazishvili-Gehne, N. (2015). *Staatsbürgerschaft an der Grenze: Das Beispiel der georgischsprachigen Ingiloer in Aserbaidschan*. (PhD), Martin-Luther-Universität Halle-Wittenberg, Halle an der Saale.

Aivazishvili-Gehne, N. (2018). "Der Staat ist der Präsident". Ingiloer und öffentliche Zeremonien in Aserbaidschan. *Paideuma, 64*, 27–50.

Aldrich, H. E., & Waldinger, R. (1990). Ethnicity and Entrepreneurship. *Annual Review of Sociology, 16*, 111–135.

Alff, H. (2014). Embracing Chinese Modernity? Articulation and Positioning in China-Kazakhstan Trade and Exchange Processes (*Crossroads Asia Working Paper Series, 21*).

Alff, H. (2015). Profiteers or Moral Entrepreneurs? Bazaars, Traders and Development Discourses in Almaty, Kazakhstan. *International Development Planning Review, 37*(3), 249–267.

Alff, H. (2016). Markt unter Druck: Der Dordoi-Basar in Kirgistan unter dem Einfluss von Eurasischer Wirtschaftsunion und Wirtschaftskrise. *Zentralasien Analysen, 105*, 2–6.

Antonyan, Y. (2011). Religiosity and Religious Identity in Armenia: Some Current Models and Developments. *Acta Ethnographica Hungarica, 56*(2), 315–332.

Antonyan, Y. (2016). *Elites and "Elites": Transformations of Social Structures in Post-Soviet Armenia and Georgia*. ASCN.

Antonyan, Y. (2018). Interplay Between the Formal and the Informal: Marketing Religious Festivals in Contemporary Armenia. *Anthropological Researches, IV*, 65–77.

Antonyan, Y. (2020). Markets at Sacred Sites: The Globalized Mobility and Informality of the Armenian Religious Fairs. *Central Asian Survey, electronic preprint*, 1–17.

Aslanian, S. (2014). *From the Indian Ocean to the Mediterranean: The Global Trade Networks of Armenian Merchants from New Julfa*. University of California Press.

Aslund, A. (2007). *How Capitalism Was Built: The Transformation of Central and Eastern Europe, Russia, and Central Asia*. Cambridge University Press.

Augé, M. (2008). *Non-places: An Introduction to Supermodernity*. Verso.

Baitas, M. (2017). *Traders of the Central Bazaar in Astana: A Perspective on Motives and Social Networks*. (PhD), Nazarbayev University, Astana.

Baitas, M. (2019). The Traders of Central Bazaar, Astana: Motivation and Networks. *Central Asian Survey, electronic preprint*. https://doi.org/10.1080/02634937.2019.1697642

Barth, F. (1963). *The Role of the Entrepreneur of Social Changes in Northern Norway*. Universitetsforlaget.

Basu, H. (2013). Ethnologie und die Vervielfältigung von Modernität. In U. Willems, D. Pollack, H. Basu, T. Gutmann & U. Spohn (Eds.), *Moderne und Religion. Kontroversen um Modernität und Säkularisierung* (pp. 379–414). Transcript.

Bayadyan, H. (2007). Soviet Armenian Identity and Cultural Representation. In T. Darieva & W. Kaschuba (Eds.), *Representations on the Margins of Europe: Politics and Identities in the Baltic and South Caucasus States* (pp. 205–219). Campus Verlag.

Bell, S., & Coleman, S. (Eds.). (1999). *The Anthropology of Friendship*. Berg.

Belshaw, C. S. (1965). *Traditional Exchange and Modern Markets*. Prentice-Hall Inc.

Bestor, T. C. (2001). Supply-Side Sushi: Commodity, Market, and the Global City. *American Anthropologist, 103*(1), 76–95. https://doi.org/10.2307/683923

Bhattacharya, B. (2005). Armenian European Relationship in India, 1500–1800: No Armenian Foundation for European Empire? *Journal of the Economic and Social History of the Orient, 48*(2), 277–322.

Bohannan, P., & Dalton, G. (1962). *Markets in Africa*. Northwest University Press.

Botoeva, A., & Spector, R. A. (2013). Sewing to Satisfaction: Craft-Based Entrepreneurs in Contemporary Kyrgyzstan. *Central Asian Survey, 32*(4), 487–500.

Boym, S. (2001). *The Future of Nostalgia*. Basic Books.

Bram, C. (2017). Moscow Azerbaijani-Juhuro "Oligarchs" and the Eurasian Trade Networks. *Caucasus Analytical Digest, 96*, 5–8.

Brednikova, O., & Pachenkov, O. (1999). Ethnicity of "Ethnic Economy": Economic Immigrants to St. Petersburg. In O. Brednikova, V. Voronkov & E. Chikadze (Eds.), *Ethnicity and Economy: Proceedings of the Seminar Held in St. Petersburg (9–12 September 1999)* (Vol. 8, pp. 108–115). CISR.

Buttimer, A. (2012). Alexander von Humboldt and Planet Earth's Green Mantle. *Cybergeo: European Journal of Geography, Epistémologie, Histoire de la Géographie, Didactique, Document 616*. https://doi.org/10.4000/cybergeo.25478

Carlsson, B., Braunerhjelm, P., McKelvey, M., Olofsson, C., Persson, L., & Ylinenpää, H. (2013). The Evolving Domain of Entrepreneurship Research. *Small Business Economics, 41*(4), 913–930.

Carrier, J. G. (1999). People Who Can Be Friends: Selves and Social Relationships. In S. Bell & S. Coleman (Eds.), *The Anthropology of Friendship* (pp. 21–38). Berg.

Carsten, J. (2004). *After Kindship*. Cambridge University Press.

Carsten, J. (Ed.). (2000). *Cultures of Relatedness: New Approaches to the Study of Kinship*. Cambridge University Press.

Cieślewska, A. (2014). From Shuttle Trader to Businesswomen: The Informal Bazaar Econommy in Kyrgyzstan. In J. Morris & A. Polese (Eds.), *The Informal Post-Socialist Economy* (pp. 121–134). Routledge.

Corso, M. (2011). The Business Climate and Anti-Corruption Measures in Georgia. *Caucasus Analytical Digest, 26*, 10–12.

Curro, C. (2015). Davabirzhaot! Conflicting Claims on Public Space in Tbilisi: Between Transparency and Opaqueness. *International Journal of Sociology and Social Policy, 35*(7/8), 497–512. https://doi.org/10.1108/IJSSP-12-2014-0122

Dabaghyan, A., & Gabrielyan, M. (2011). Rural Transcaucasian Trade Before and After National Border. *Acta Ethnographica Hungarica, 56*(2), 333–357.

Dabaghyan, A., & Gabrielyan, M. (2014). On a Village Market at a South Caucasian Border. In A. Bobokhyan, L. Abrahamian & K. Franklin (Eds.), *Market Beyond Economy* (pp. 37–53). NAS RA "Gitutyun" Publishing.

Dannhaeuser, N. (1989). Marketing in Developing Urban Areas. In S. Plattner (Ed.), *Economic Anthropology* (pp. 222–252). Stanford University Press.

Darieva, T., Mühlfried, F., & Tuite, K. (Eds.). (2018). *Sacred Places, Emerging Spaces: Religious Pluralism in the Post-Soviet Caucasus*. Berghahn.

Davis, J. (1977). Economic Anthropology of Mediterranean Societies. In J. Davis (Ed.), *People of the Mediterranean: An Essay in Comparative Social Anthropology* (pp. 17–72). Routledge.

Dermendzhieva, Z. (2011). Emigration from the South Caucasus: Who Goes Abroad and What Are the Economic Implications? *Post-Communist Economies, 23*(3), 377–398. https://doi.org/10.1080/14631377.2011.595135

Di Puppo, L. (2004). Corruption as an Instrument of State Control in Georgia. *Berliner Osteuropa-Info, 21*, 47–54.

Di Puppo, L. (2013). The Construction of Success in Anticorruption Activity in Georgia. *East European Politics, 30*, 105–122.

Dragadze, T. (2016). *Rural Families in Soviet Georgia: A Case Study in Ratcha Province*. Routledge.

Dudwick, N. (2003). No Guests at Our Table: Social Fragmentation in Georgia. In N. Dudwick, E. Gomart, A. Marc, & K. Kuehnast (Eds.), *When Things Fall Apart: Qualitative Studies of Poverty in the Former Soviet Union*. The World Bank.

Dumont, L. (1980). *Homo Hierarchicus: The Caste System and Its Implications*. The University of Chicago Press.

Durkheim, É. (1969 [1893]). *The Division of Labor in Society*. Free Press. Originally published as *De la division du travail social : étude sur l'organisation des sociétés supérieures* (F. Alcan).

Dyatlov, V., & Grigorichev, K. (2015). *Ethnic Markets in Russia: Space of Bargaining and Place of Meeting*. Publishing House of ISU.

Eisenstadt, S. (2000). Multiple Modernities. *Daedalus, 129*(1), 1–29.

Englund, H., & Leach, J. (2000). Ethnography and the Meta-Narrative of Modernity. *Current Anthropology, 41*(2), 225–248.

Eval, G., Szelenyi, I., & Townsley, E. R. (2000). *Making Capitalism without Capitalists: The New Ruling Elites in Eastern Europe*. Verso.

Fehlings, S. (2008). *Ruhestätten in bester Lage: Räumliche Ordnungen sozialer Werte auf Friedhöfen in Simferopol/Krim*. LIT-Verlag.

Fehlings, S. (2014). *Jerewan: Urbanes Chaos und soziale Ordnung*. LIT-Verlag.

Fehlings, S. (2015). Intimacy and Exposure: Yerevan's Private and Public Space. *International Journal of Sociology and Social Policy, 35*(7/8), 513–532.

Fehlings, S. (2018). Caucasian "Biznes" (Business): Informality, Cultural Embeddedness, and the Global World. *Anthropological Researches, IV*, 23–39.

Fehlings, S. (2019). Encounters at the Grassroots Level: Chinese-Georgian Interactions in the BRI Era. *Caucasus Analytical Digest, 111*, 14–17. https://doi.org/10.3929/ethz-b-000368298

Fehlings, S. (2020). Doing Business in Yabaolu Market, Beijing: (Inter-)Ethnic Entrepreneurship, Trust and Friendship between Caucasian and Chinese Traders. *Central Asian Survey, electronic preprint*, 1–21. https://doi.org/10.1080/02634937.2019.1696281.

Fehlings, S. (2021). „They are like Georgians but bigger“: The Perception of Chinese Businesspeople in Georgia. *New Diversities, 23*(2), 79–92.

Ferry, M. (2013). Female Migration from Georgia: Profiles and Migratory Projects. *Caucasus Analytical Digest, 57*(3), 8–10.

Firth, R. (1967). *Themes in Economic Anthropology*. Tavistock Publications.

Frederiksen, M. D. (2012). Good Hearts or Big Bellies: Dzmakatsoba and Images of Masculinity in the Republic of Georgia. In V. Amit & N. Dyck (Eds.), *Young Men in Uncertain Times* (pp. 165–187). Berghahn Books.

Frederiksen, M. D. (2013). *Young Men, Time, and Boredom in the Republic of Georgia*. Temple University Press.

Freitag, U., & von Oppen, A. (2010). Introduction: "Translocality": An Approach to Connection and Transfer in Area Studies. In U. Freitag & A. von Oppen (Eds.), *Translocality: The Study of Globalising Processes from a Southern Perspective* (pp. 1–24). Brill.

Gaonkar, D. P. (2001). *Alternative Modernities*. Duke University Press.

Geertz, C. (1963). *Peddlers and Princes: Social Developments and Economic Change in Two Indonesian Towns*. Chicago University Press.

Gell, A. (1982). The Market Wheel: Symbolic Aspects of an Indian Tribal Market. *Man, 17*(3), 470–491. https://doi.org/10.2307/2801710

Gereffi, G., Humphrey, J., & Sturgeon, T. (2003). The Governance of Global Value Chains. *Review of International Political Economy, 12*(1), 78–104.

Giragosian, R. (2009). Networks of Crime and Corruption in the South Caucasus. *Caucasus Analytical Digest, 19*, 2–5.

Grant, B. (1999). The Return of the Repressed: Conversations with Three Russian Entrepreneurs. In G. E. Marcus (Ed.), *Paranoia within Reason: A Casebook on Conspiracy as Explanation* (pp. 241–267). The University o Chicago Press.

Gurchiani, K. (2017). How Soviet Is the Religious Revival in Georgia: Tactics in Everyday Religiosity. *Europe-Asia Studies, 69*(3), 508–531.

Guzei, I. (2015). The "Russian" Market in the Center of Beijing. In V. Dyatlov & K. Grigorichev (Eds.), *Ethnic Markets in Russia: Space of Bargaining and Place of Meeting* (pp. 159–170). Publishing House of ISU.

Hahn, H. P. (2018). Introduction: Markets as Places: Actors, Structures and Ideologies. In H. P. Hahn & G. Schmitz (Eds.), *Market as Place & Space of Economic Exchange: Perspectives from Archaeology & Anthropology* (pp. 1–18). Oxbow.

Hann, C. (2005). Postsocialist Societies. In J. G. Carrier (Ed.), *A Handbook of Economic Anthropology* (pp. 547–557). Edward Elgar Publishing.

Hart, K. (1970). Small-Scale Entrepreneurs in Ghana and Development Planning. *Journal of Development Studies, 6*(4), 104–120.

Hart, K. (1988). Kinship, Contract and Trust: The Economic Organization of Migrants in an African City Slum. In D. Gambetta (Ed.), *Trust: Making and Breaking Cooperative Relations* (pp. 176–193). Blackwell.

Hébert, R. F., & Link, A. N. (1989). In Search of the Meaning of Entrepreneurship. *Small Business Economics, 1*(1), 39–49.

Herzfeld, M. (1980). Honour and Shame: Problems in the Comparative Analysis of Moral Systems. *Man, 15*, 339–352.

Herzfeld, M. (1997). *Cultural Intimacy: Social Poetics in the Nation State*. Routledge.

Heyat, F. (2002). Women and the Culture of Entrpreneurship in Soviet and Post-Soviet Azerbaijan. In R. Mandel & C. Humphrey (Eds.), *Markets and Moralities: Ethnographies of Postsocialism* (pp. 19–31). Berg.

Holzlehner, T. (2014). *Shadow Networks: Border Economics, Informal Markets and Organized Crime in the Russian Far East*. LIT-Verlag.

Hopkirk, P. (1980). *Foreign Devils on the Silk Road: The Search for the Lost Treasures of Central Asia*. John Murray.

Humphrey, C. (2002). *The Unmaking of Soviet Life: Everyday Economics After Socialism*. Cornell University Press.

Humphrey, C. (2018). Introduction: Trusting and Mistrusting Across Borders. In C. Humphrey (Ed.), *Trust and Mistrust in the Economy of the China-Russia Borderlands* (pp. 9–35). Amsterdam University Press.

Humphrey, C., & Skvirskaja, V. (2009). Trading Places: Post-socialist Container Markets and the City. *Focaal: European Journal of Anthropology, 55*. https://doi.org/10.3167/fcl.2009.550105

Iskandaryan, A. (2014). Formalization of the Informal: Statebuilding in Armenia. In C. Giordano & N. Hayoz (Eds.), *Informality in Eastern Europe: Structures, Political Cultures and Social Practices* (pp. 451–484). Peter Lang.

Karrar, H. (2017). Do Bazaars Die? Notes on Failure in the Central Asian Bazaar. *Informal Markets and Trade Working Paper Series, 4*.

Karrar, H. (2019). In the Shadow of the Silk Road: Border Regimes and Economic Corridor Development through an Unremarkable Pakistan-China Border Market. *Comparative Studies of South Asia, Africa and the Middle East, 39*(3), 389–406.

Karrar, H. (2020). The Bazaar in Ruins: Rent and Fire in the Barakholka, Almaty. *Central Asian Survey, electronic preprint*.

Karrar, H. H., & Rudaz, P. (2022). A Cautionary Tale: Bazaar Trade and Limitations to Growth in Georgia, Kazakhstan and Kyrgyzstan. *Global Networks*. https://doi.org/10.1111/glob.12367

Karrar, H., & Mostowlansky, T. (2018). Assembling Marginality in Northern Pakistan. *Political Geography, 63*, 65–74.

Khutsishvili, K. (2006). Bazaar Culture in Georgia: The Case of Tbilisi. *Berliner Blätter, 59*, 41–52.

Khutsishvili, K. (2017). Suddenly a Border: Hazelnut Trade Across the De Facto Border Between Abkhazia and the Zugdidi Municipal Region of Georgia. *Caucasus Analytical Digest, 96*, 9–12.

Killick, E., & Desai, A. (2010). Introduction: Valuing Friendship. In E. Killick & A. Desai (Eds.), *The Ways of Friendship: Anthropological Perspectives* (pp. 1–19). Berghahn Books.

Koehler, J. (2003). Die Schule der Straße: Georgische Cliquen zwischen Kämpfen um Ehre und organisierter Kriminalität. In U. Luig & J. Seebode (Eds.), *Ethnologie der Jugend: Soziale Praxis, moralische Diskurse und inszenierte Körperlichkeit* (pp. 43–69). LIT-Verlag.

Körner, A. (2017). Moral Education in Georgian Orthodox Christianity: Striving for a Georgian Modernity. In R. Hardenberg (Ed.), *Approaching Ritual Economy: Socio-Cosmic Fields in Globalised Contexts* (pp. 231–254). RessourcenKulturen Universität Tübingen.

Kotkin, S. (1995). *Magnetic Mountain: Stalinism as a Civilization*. University of California Press.

Krebs, M. (2011). *Zwischen Handwerkstradition und globalem Markt Kunsthandwerker in Usbekistan und Kirgistan*. Klaus Schwarz Verlag.

Kupatadze, A. (2009). Georgia's Fight Against Organized Crime: Success or Failure? *Caucasus Analytical Digest, 19*, 9–12.

Kupatadze, A. (2011). Similar Events, Different Outcomes: Accounting for Diverging Corruption: Patterns in Post-Revolution Georgia and Ukraine. *Caucasus Analytical Digest, 26*, 2–6.

Lévi-Strauss, C. (1963). *Structural Anthropology*. Basic Books.

Lezhava, B., Brekashvili, P., & Melua, I. (2014). Global Entrepreneurship Monitor: Special Topic—Women Entrepreneurship in Georgia. In GEM (Ed.), *GEM* (pp. 1–20). Caucasus University. https://www.gemconsortium.org/index.php/report/women-entrepreneurship-in-georgia

Light, I., & Gold, S. J. (2000). *Ethnic Economies*. Academic Press.

Light, M. (2014). Police Reforms in the Republic of Georgia: The Convergence of Domestic and Foreign Policy in an Anti-Corruption Drive. *An International Journal of Research and Policy, 24*(3), 318–345.

Lundkvist-Houndoumadi, M. (2010). Treading on the Fine Line Between Self-Sacrifice and Immorality: Narratives of Emigrated Georgian Women. *Transcience Journal, 1*(2), 50–71.

Mains, D. (2013). Friends and Money: Balancing Affection and Reciprocity among Young Men in Urban Ethopia. *American Anthropologist, 40*(2), 335–346.

Mandel, R., & Humphrey, C. (2002). *Markets and Moralities: Ethnographies of Postsocialism*. Berg.

Mars, G., & Altman, Y. (1983). The Cultural Bases of Soviet Georgia's Second Economy. *Soviet Studies, XXXV*(4), 546–560.

Marsden, M. (2016). *Trading Worlds: Afghan Merchants Across Modern Frontiers*. Hurst & Company.
Marsden, M. (2018). Islamic Cosmopolitanism Out of Muslim Asia: Hindu-Muslim Business Co-Operation Between Odessa and Yiwu. *History and Anthropology, 29*(1), 121–139.
Marushiakova, E., & Popov, V. (2016). *Gypsies in Central Asia and the Caucasus*. Palgrave Macmillan.
Melkumyan, H. (2017). Informality, Politics and Mutual Support in Flea Markets in Post-Soviet Armenia.
Mukhina, I. (2009). New Losses, New Opportunities: (Soviet) Women in the Shuttle Trade, 1987–1998. *Journal of Social History, 43*(2), 341–359.
Ngo, T.-W., & Hung, E. P. W. (2018). The Political Economy of Border Checkpoints in Shadow Exchanges. *Journal of Contemporary Asia, 49*(2), 1–15. https://doi.org/10.1080/00472336.2018.1555273
Nikolotov, A. (2019). Volatile Conviviality: Joking Relations in Moscow's Marginal Marketplace. *Modern Asian Studies, 53*(3), 874–903.
Pachenkov, O. (2011). Every City Has the Flea Market It Deserves: The Phenomenon of Urban Flea Markets in St. Petersburg. In T. Darieva, W. Kaschuba & M. Krebs (Eds.), *Urban Spaces After Socialism: Ethnographies of Public Spaces in Eurasian Cities* (pp. 181–206). Campus Verlag.
Paine, R. (1969). In Search of Friendship: An Exploratory Analysis in "Middle Class" Culture. *Man, 4*(4), 505–524.
Plattner, S. (1989). *Economic Anthropology*. Stanford University Press.
Polese, A., Rekhviashvili, L., & Morris, J. (2016). Informal Governance in Urban Spaces: Power, Negotiation and Resistance Among Georgian Street Vendors. *Geography Research Forum, 36*, 15–32.
Pourtskhvanidze, Z., & Tskhvediani, N. (2021). Cryptolanguage of Georgian Jewish Merchants. *Working Paper Series on Informal Markets and Trade, 10*.
Reeves, M. (2014). *Border Works: Spatial Lifes of the State in Rural Central Asia*. Cornell University Press.
Rekhviashvili, L. (2015). Marketization and the Public-Private Divide: Contestations Between the State and Petty Traders over the Access to Public Space in Tbilisi. *International Journal of Sociology and Social Policy, 35*(7–8), 478–496.
Robbins, J. (2004). *Becoming Sinners: Christianity and Moral Torment in a Papua New Guinea Society*. University of California Press.
Robbins, J. (2007). Between Reproduction and Freedom: Morality, Value, and Radical Cultural Change. *Ethnos, 72*(3), 293–314.
Robbins, J., & Siikala, J. (Eds.). (2014). Dumont, Values, and Contemporary Cultural Change. *Anthropological Theory, 14*(2).
Rudaz, P. (2018). Informal Entrepreneurship or "Survivalship"? Results of an Empirical Study of Self Employment, Micro-, and Small Businesses in Georgia. *Anthropological Researches, IV*, 79–89.

Rudaz, P. (2019). Trading in the Bazaars of Dordoi and Lilo at the Frontier of Formality, Entrepreneurship and Globalization. *Central Asian Survey, 39*(1), 11–32.

Sahlins, M. (1999). What Is Anthropological Enlightenment? Some Lessons of the Twentieth Century. *Annual Review of Anthropology, 28*, i–xxiii. https://doi.org/10.2307/223385

Salisbury, R. F. (1973). Economic Anthropology. *Annual Review of Anthropology, 2*, 85–94.

Sass, M., Kovacs, O., Jaksa, R. A., & Garbovan, L. (2015). *Transfer of Know-how for Small and Mid-size Businesses in Georgia, Moldova and Ukraine: White Paper Moldova* (SSRN Electronic Journal, CASE Network Reports 122). https://doi.org/10.2139/ssrn.2637286

Schetter, C. (2012). Translocal Lives: Patterns of Migration in Afghanistan. *Crossroads Asia Working Paper Series, 2*, 1–17.

Schneider, J. (1969). Family Patrimonies and Economic Behaviour in Western Sicily. *Anthropological Quarterly, 42*(3), 109–129.

Schröder, P., & Stephan-Emmrich, M. (2016). The Institutionalization of Mobility: Well-Being and Social Hierarchies in Central Asian Translocal Livelihoods. *Mobilities, 11*(3), 420–443. https://doi.org/10.1080/17450101.2014.984939

Schumpeter, J. A. (1942). *Capitalism, Socialism and Democracy*. Harper & Brothers.

Serio, J. D., & Razinkin, V. (1995). Thieves Professing the Code: The Traditional Role of Vory v Zakone in Russia's Criminal World and Adaptations to a New Social Reality. *Low Intensity Conflict & Law Enforcement, 4*(1), 72–88.

Shane, S., & Venkataraman, S. (2000). The Promise of Entrepreneurship as a Field of Research. *Academy of Management Review, 25*, 217–226.

Simmel, G. (1992 [1908]). *Soziologie: Untersuchungen über die Formen der Vergesellschaftung*. Suhrkamp.

Skvirskaja, V. (2019). New Trade Formations: Precarity, Pragmatic Cosmopolitanism and Long-Distance Trade in the Caucasus. *Global Networks, electronic preprint*, 1–17. https://doi.org/10.1111/glob.12267

Slade, G. (2009). The Georgian Mafia. *Caucasus Analytical Digest, 19*, 5–8.

Slade, G. (2012). No Country for Made Men: The Decline of the Mafia in Post-Soviet Georgia. *Law & Society Review, 46*(3), 623–649.

Sombart, W. (2001 [1911]). *Die Juden und das Wirtschaftsleben* (M. Epstein, trans.). *The Jews and Modern Capitalism*. Batoche Books.

Spector, R. A. (2017). *Order at the Bazaar: Power and Trade in Central Asia*. Cornell University Press.

Steenberg, R. (2016). Embedded Rubber Sandals: Trade and Gifts Across the Sino-Kyrgyz Border. *Central Asian Survey, 35*(3), 405–420.

Stephan-Emmrich, M., & Mirzoev, A. (2016). The Manufacturing of Islamic Lifestyles in Tajikistan Through the Prism of Dushanbe's Bazaars. *Central Asian Survey, 35*(2), 157–177. https://doi.org/10.1080/02634937.2016.1152008

Strathern, A. (2018). The Entrepreneurial Model of Social Change: From Norway to New Guinea. *Ethnology, 11*(4), 368–379.

Taalaibekova, G. (2018). The Changing Perception of Trade as "Real" Work: The Unmaking of Soviet Workers at the Vernissage in Armenia. *Informal Markets and Trade Working Paper Series, 8*.

Taalaibekova, G., & Melkumyan, H. (2018). Public Space Comercialised and Comodified: A Case Study od the Vernissage in Yerevan. *Anthropological Researches, IV*, 48–64.

Turaeva, R. (2014). Mobile Entrepreneurs in Post-Soviet Central Asia: Micro-Orders of Tirikchilik. *Communist and Post-Communist Studies, 47*(1), 105–114. https://doi.org/10.1016/j.postcomstud.2014.02.001

Varese, F. (2001). *The Russian Mafia: Private Protection in a New Market Economy*. Oxford University Press.

Varnavskii, P. K. (2010). Nikakikh problem net, yazyk znayu plokho, s dokumentami vse v poryadke': strategii adaptsii migrantov iz Tsentral'noi Azii v Zabaikal'e (na primere goroda Krasnokamensko) ['There Are no Problems at All, I Know the Language Badly, the Documents Are All in Order': Adaption Strategies of Central Asian Migrants in Zabaikalia, the Example of Kransokamensk]. In B. Z. Nanzatov (Ed.), *Transgranichnye migratsii v prostranstve mongol'skogo mira: istoria i sovremenost'* [Transborder Migration in the Mongolian World: History and the Present-Day] (pp. 30–58). BNTs SO RAN.

Volery, T. (2007). Ethnic Entrepreneurship: A Theoretical Framework. In D. Léo-Paul (Ed.), *Handbook of Research on Ethnic Minority Entrepreneurship: A Co-evolutionary View on Resource Management* (pp. 30–41). Edward Elgar.

Volkov, V. (2012). *Silovoje predprinimatelstvo XXI vek (Violent Entrepreneurship, XXi Century)*. European University Saint Peterburg.

von Humboldt, A. (1807a). *Essai sur la géographie des plantes, accompagné d'un tableau physique des régions équinoxiales, fondé sur les mesures exécutées, depuis le dixième degré de latitude boréale jusqu'au dixième degré de latitude australe, pendant les années 1799, 1800, 1801, 1802, et 1903 par A. De Humboldt et A. Bonpland*. Fr Schoelle Librairie.

von Humboldt, A. (1807b). *Ideen zu einer Georgraphie der Pflanzen nebst einem Naturgemälde der Tropenländer: Auf Beobachtungen und Messungen gegründet, welche vom 10ten Grade nördlicher Breite bis zum 10ten Grade südlicher Breite, in den Jahren 1799, 1800, 1801, 1802 und 1803 angestellt worden sind von Al. von Humboldt und A. Bonpland*. Cotta Verlag.

von Humboldt, A. (1814). *Voyage aux régions équinoxiales du Nouveau Continent fait en 1799, 1800, 1801, 1802, 1803 et 1804, fait par A. De Humboldt et A. Bonpland*. Maze.

von Humboldt, A. (1851). *Personal narrative of travels to the Equinoctial Regions of America during the years 1799–1804*. Routledge.

Waldinger, R. (1994). The Making of an Immigrant Niche. *International Migration Review, 28*(1), 3–28.

Waterbury, J. (1972). *North for the Trade: The Life and Times of a Berber Merchant*. University of California Press.

Waterbury, J. (1973). Tribalism, Trade and Politics: The Transformation of the Swasa of Marocco. In E. Gellner & C. A. Micaud (Eds.), *Arabs and Berbers: From Tribe to Nation in North Africa* (pp. 231–158). Gerald Duckworth.

Weber, M. (1993 [1904). *Die protestantische Ethik und der "Geist" des Kapitalismus*. Athenäum Hain Hadenstein.

Werner, C. (2004). Feminizing the New Silk Road: Women Traders in Rural Kazakhstan. In C. Nechemias & K. Kuehnast (Eds.), *Post-Soviet Women Encountering Transition: Nation-Building, Economic Survival, and Civic Activism* (pp. 105–126). Johns Hopkins University Press.

Williams, C. C., Nadin, S., & Rodgers, P. (2012). Evaluating Competing Theories of Informal Entrepreneurship: Some Lessons from Ukraine. *International Journal of Entrepreneurial Behaviour & Research, 18*(5), 528–543.

Williams, C. C., & Round, J. (2007). Entrepreneurship and the Informal Economy: A Study of Ukraine's Hidden Enterprise Culture. *Journal of Development Studies, 12*(1).

Williams, C. C., Round, J., & Rodgers, P. (2009). Evaluationg the Motives of Informal Entrepreneurs: Some Lessons from Ukraine. *Journal of Development Studies, 14*(1), 59–71.

World Bank. (2012). *Fighting Corruption in Public Services: Chronicling Georgia's Reforms*. World Bank.

Wulf, A. (2016). *Alexander von Humboldt und die Erfindung der Natur*. C. Bertelsmann.

Yalçın-Heckmann, L. (2014). Informal Economy Writ Large and Small: From Azerbaijani Herb Traders to Moscow Shop Owners. In J. Morris & A. Polese (Eds.), *The Informal Post-Socialist Economy: Embedded Practices and Liveliyhoods* (pp. 165–186). Routledge.

Yalçın-Heckmann, L., & Aivazishvili, N. (2012). Scales of Trade, Informal Economy and Citizenship at Georgian-Azerbaijani Borderlands. In B. Bruns & J. Miggelbrink (Eds.), *Subverting Borders: Doing Research on Smuggling and Small-scale Trade* (pp. 187–205). VS Verlag für Sozialwissenschaften.

Zakharova, E. (2017). Black Matsoni: The Pragmatics of the Tbilisi Street Code. *Forum for Anthropology and Culture, 13*, 247–279.

Zakharova, E. (2010). Street Life in Tbilisi as a Factor of Male Socialisation. *Laboratorium, 1*, 350–352.
Zhang, J., & Saxer, M. (Eds.). (2017). *The Art of Neighbouring: Making Relations Across China's Borders*. Amsterdam University Press.
Захарова, Е. Ю. (2010). Тбилисская улица как среда мужской социализации. *Laboratorium, 2*, 182–204.

CHAPTER 4

Dealing with Institutional Frameworks

> Intelligence is the ability of a living creature to perform pointless or unnatural acts.
>
> —Arkady and Boris Strugatsky, "Roadside Picnic"

Bazaars, petty trade, street vending, and the forms of economic activity I have portrayed so far are usually classified as belonging to the so-called informal sphere, because, in the Caucasus as elsewhere, they are often not regulated or only partly regulated by state institutions (Fehlings & Karrar, 2016). Still, it would be wrong to expect the state or formal bodies to be totally absent in this economic context. In Georgia, in particular, the Rose Revolution of 2003 and Saakashvili's reforms and anti-corruption campaign put an end to many so-called informal practices on all levels of political, social, and economic life. State officials who were notorious for taking bribes were fired, and many legal institutions took measures to establish and then to implement formal rules (Di Puppo, 2013; Light, 2014; Rekhviashvili, 2015; World Bank, 2012). One of these measures was the digitalization of formal procedures, including taxation, which significantly affected small business.

However, despite these reforms, as mentioned in the previous chapter, according to official statistics on Georgian SMEs, the degree of informality has increased slightly in recent years (Rudaz, 2018, 2019). There

S. Fehlings, *Traders, Informal Trade and Markets between the Caucasus and China*, Politics and History in Central Asia,
https://doi.org/10.1007/978-981-19-5205-0_4

are two explanations for this: first, there is a problem linked to the definition of "informality". Informality is a nebulous term embracing a wide range of behaviors (see Chapter 1, Introduction). Illegal and criminal practices (as defined by Georgian law) have been rigorously combatted in Georgia, and the current state, as a rule enforces its laws. The nature of informality—and this is not reflected in statements about the alleged increase in it—has changed considerably. And second, everything depends on how informality is measured. It is necessary to take a closer look at the sometimes randomly defined standards and classifications scholars have established, which often do not capture the local context and the regulations configuring a specific environment. Standards and classifications must be linked to a larger framework and examined with respect to the local business sphere. Finally, it is necessary to consider how the local state defines regulation and how this definition determines the line between formality and informality from an intrinsic perspective, one that might differ from that of scholars who start from a Weberian understanding of the "legal state."

Still, instead of considering local backgrounds, many studies start with preconceived categories. As mentioned earlier, according to one such view, "the integration of informal economic activities into the formal economy is an important part of the 'transition' process of former communist countries and one of the biggest challenges of building a market economy from scratch" (Freeland, 2000; Rudaz, 2018: 78). So economists, starting from this idea, have established methods to estimate the level of formalization—and development—by checking the level of cooperation with formal bodies like banks, tax authorities, and legally established institutions, asking questions about the keeping of accounting records, the use of bank accounts, and the existence of written contracts (see, e.g., World Bank data[1]). Although answers to these questions give interesting insights, they are only part of the picture and still need further explanation.

According to our survey data from 2017, more than two-thirds of our respondents in Lilo Bazroba recorded their transactions. This, according to the economists' analytical toolbox, points to a rather high level of formalization. On the other hand, only about half of them had bank accounts and used written contracts. This is not illegal, but according

[1] The World Bank "Enterprise Surveys": http://www.enterprisesurveys.org/data/exploretopics/finance; The World Bank "Databank": http://databank.worldbank.org/data/reports.aspx?source=global-financial-inclusion; The World Bank "Global Findex (Georgia)": https://globalfindex.worldbank.org/sites/globalfindex/files/countrybook/Georgia.pdf.

to the established interpretation of such indicators, neither does it indicate a high level of formalization (Rudaz, 2018). It suggests that business is managed face to face and through personal contacts.

The role of social networks based on kinship or other social relationships is often overestimated in current literature on Caucasian and Central Asian local economic practice, as shown by the qualitative data discussed in Chapters 2 and 3. Many authors have written about ritual exchange (Beyer, 2016; Kuehnast & Dudwick, 2004), the mutual obligations that are established through gift exchange between local households (Werner, 1998), and other forms of reciprocal arrangements like *blat* (Ledeneva, 1998), *tapş* (Sayfutdinova, 2018), and rotating saving groups (Gröner, 2010)[2] in the post-Soviet region. These authors have emphasized the importance of such arrangements for economic activity and survival. But do these practices support or enable real businesses? Do they provide enough capital to start an enterprise, run it, and make it grow? Critics of the informality literature argue that there is a unjustified conclusion that the informal sector "is one of the last safe havens in a darkening financial climate" (Barta[3] quoted in Breman, 2009), and that the poor will always find ways to survive, thanks to their safety networks and informal activities (Breman, 2009; Gonzàlez de la Rocha, 2007).

Certainly, one must go deeper into the description of local (gift) exchange practices and reciprocal engagements to understand their effects—and one has to ask whether they belong to the business world. Writing about Kyrgyzstan, Kuehnast and Dudwick (2004), for example, distinguish between the horizontal networks of the poor and the vertical networks of the wealthier segments of society, arguing that horizontal networks provide little or no access to social or monetary benefits, and thus are of little use in economic terms. Different networks have different functions, purviews, and uses, as shown by Baitas in his thesis on Kazakh traders (2017, 2019), Mars and Altman in their 1983 study of the involvement of Georgian Jews in Soviet Georgia's second economy,

[2] Accumulating and rotating savings groups and credit associations exist in Central Asia and the Caucasus. They usually function in the same way as in other places across the world (see Ardener & Burman, 1996; Low, 1999; Schrader, 2006) and are associated with low levels of income—or even poverty. Usually, savings groups consist predominantly of women. But as far as I am aware of, they are used to raise money for personal and social purposes (weddings, school fees, personal purchases), rather than for business.

[3] Wall Street Journal "The Rise of the Underground", 14 March 2009 (by Patrick Barta): https://www.wsj.com/articles/SB123698646833925567.

and Pelkmans and Umetbaeva in their 2018 article on Central Asian moneylenders.

In the contexts I have described in the previous chapters, specific networks proved to be extremely important, but as regards purely financial benefits, they seem to have their limits. Of 300 respondents in Lilo Bazroba, only 66 received financial help from family members, 23 from friends, and 16 from colleagues. Only 3 received financial support from the state in the form of a subsidy, and 183 did not receive any help at all (Rudaz, 2018). At the same time, 156 respondents said that financial resources were the most important element of economic success, while only 29 replied that social networks were the most important.[4] So the question is how most people obtain enough money to start and run an enterprise, which informal, semi-formal, or formal institutions these traders rely on, and how they deal with formal frameworks in the process.

To shed more light on this subject, I will first take a closer look at the acquisition of capital. Loans and credit play an important role, which is why I will focus on the practices of credit agencies and banks that work with traders. When taking out a loan, entrepreneurs must sign legal contracts. But this, again, is only one of many situations in which traders directly or indirectly adjust to legal requirements. Businesspeople have to deal with customs officials, tax authorities, and in general, the formal system of laws, all of which are institutions that have gone through many transformations and reforms since the Georgian Republic's independence. I will therefore discuss the importance and status of these institutions—of bureaucracy and legislation—in their historical context and in comparison to their informal alternatives. The actual importance of state institutions, which becomes obvious by looking at the data, seems—at least partly—contradicted by the assessment of the legitimacy and efficiency of state representatives and state bodies by many Caucasian citizens. Therefore, I will finally discuss how merchants assess the state, the state's role in the economy, and its relationship to small businesses and traders. My materials thus give insight into the relationship between the state, (traditional) local institutions, and small and medium entrepreneurs. They describe the

[4] Mars and Altman (1983) describe how in Soviet times, kinship networks backed up businesses, especially in times of crisis. The case studies presented, however, report discrete personal incidents, when relatives are mobilized to, for example, help another relative to escape the police by paying a fee or bribe. This does not include constant support of a relative's business.

entanglement of formality and informality and add one more perspective for understanding Caucasian business by looking at traders' points of contact with formal institutions and regulations.

Loans

Many traders borrow money to start a business or to keep it going. I heard several times that in the 1990s, people sold their jewelry or other valuable objects—sometimes their flats or houses—to pay for travel and get involved in trade tourism as *chelnoki* (see Chapter 2). Some people engaged in barter, trading Soviet technology like cameras, binoculars, or army equipment for Chinese merchandise (Guzei, 2015). Others borrowed money from relatives, and still others, like Levan and Ramaz, started out by obtaining trade goods on credit from others who were already established, which Levan and Ramaz paid for after they had sold the merchandise.

Business today has a different, more "professional" shape. Georgia having opted for shock therapy, and with the rapid change to neoliberalism in the 1990s, the country became exposed to the effects of external financial linkages. At the same time, microfinance emerged, and international and local financial institutions became established. The microfinance sector has experienced a significant boom since 2008. Traders can fall back on an established infrastructure, and loans (*sesxi*, სესხი) and legal assistance are provided by recognized institutions or agencies. Traders can now choose between different options and strategies for acquiring and saving money.

These strategies range across a wide spectrum. Levan, for example, tried to avoid getting into debt by reinvesting only his own profits. Since his business was prospering, this seemed to be working out well for him. Chinese traders sometimes gave him a loan, which meant that he did not have to pay for the merchandise immediately, but could do so a few months after delivery. Such arrangements are usually not linked to interest rates. Other traders—according to our survey, 22% of our respondents—used money they got from family members. Levan's son Bacho, for example, used his father's money for his various attempts to get started economically. Finally, many traders took out loans, (a) from banks, (b) from private microfinance institutions, or c) from moneylenders. If they did this, they were obliged to sign written contracts.

To borrow money from (a) a bank, one had to show one's creditworthiness and not have been blacklisted by reason of not having repaid a previous loan. If a trader could not meet these requirements, he had to turn to alternatives, meaning, for example, (b) signing a contract with an independent microfinance institution (credit company) or (c) coming to an arrangement with a private moneylender. In the latter two contexts (b and c), signing documents is only the formal part of the interaction. Social relationships are the other part. Here, as in any other social relationship, the link between debt and morality, which has been explored by authors like Gregory (2012) and Graeber (2011),[5] manifests itself in specific interactions between lenders and borrowers, which give insight into how allegedly "formal" and "informal" institutions cooperate and work with traders on a face-to-face level. I tried to get an overview of these interactions by talking to traders and employees of credit agencies and banks.

Lending by Private Credit Agencies (the Example of BIG)

Independent credit agencies were most important for the traders of my target group, so I'll start with them. After presenting a case study, I will discuss the operations of a private microfinance institution or credit agency that has made loans to several traders I interviewed at Lilo Bazroba. As mentioned earlier, my colleague Zviad worked for this microfinance agency before enrolling in a PhD program. Zviad has continued to maintain relationships with traders to whom he made loans and with financial experts who were his friends and who were still working for the agency during my fieldwork, until it was sold to Credo Bank in 2018. Zviad's network of former colleagues and their friends were thus the main source of the data presented here.

The agency Zviad worked for was called BIG (Business Investment Group).[6] It was a joint-stock company and "a Jewish person who lives in the US" owned 51% of the shares, according to Zviad, who told me in 2016: "This man owns the 'control packet,' while the other 49% is

[5] For a comprehensive overview and review of the anthropological literature on credit and debt, see Peebles (2010).

[6] BIG Microfinance Organization "Home": http://www.big.com.ge/.

owned by Georgians. Maybe by three or four individuals. These Georgians are businessmen, who, for example, own a shopping mall or a factory producing jam and products of that kind." Zviad was not sure how the Jewish investor had become rich but told me that he owned similar companies in different countries around the world. As this story closely resembles the urban legends and conspiracy theories that I have heard over the past ten years of my research in the region, I regard it cautiously. But anyhow, perhaps it is not important who owned the company; how it worked is more interesting.

BIG was a successful enterprise, which took out loans from TBC Bank, a leading Georgian bank. This money was used to make loans to clients—usually traders or farmers. Zviad told me from his own experience how this was done. When Zviad started to work for the company, he was introduced to some clients who had previously taken out loans from BIG. Zviad's colleagues had already developed a relationship of trust with these individuals, who were known to be responsible and to pay back their debts. A new client does not just approach the company. Usually, he must be introduced by someone—by another reliable client, for example. As Zviad emphasized several times, it was all about trust, personal relationships, and long-term communication: "If you trust a person, you can trust his friend." The same principle was repeated by all of Zviad's friends working in the financial domain. Vakho, for example, described his relationship with his clients as a very intense one: "These people trust you. This is important. They call you when something is going wrong with their business, and they ask you for personal advice. You are like a friend for them."

When I asked Zviad why traders would prefer to borrow from BIG instead of borrowing from an ordinary bank, he replied that the reason is that banks want a lot of documents and that it is difficult to meet their requirements:

> The process of taking out a loan from a bank takes a long time. It takes about two weeks. BIG works much faster, because they trust their clients and require less proof and fewer documents. This is important, since traders often need money very quickly. There are just a few rules regulating what you are allowed to use the loan for. The main rule is that the money has to go into business and not into private possessions. You can get a loan to buy a car provided the car is used for business. But you can't get a car for personal use, for example, for your family. Actually, you can

> make a loan for private purposes, too. But in this case, you have to know this person very well, and you really have to trust him. You need a good relationship. The person has to tell you the truth about what he is going to do with the money. The credit expert has to know where the money is going. Otherwise he cannot trust this person. Usually, traders use loans to buy merchandise, while farmers borrow to buy seeds, fertilizer, machinery (tractors), and diesel or to pay workers.

Although BIG's requirements differed from the banks' standards, there were obviously some internal rules about when to allow and when not to allow a loan. Zviad drew a relatively positive picture of BIG in 2016, but he was much more critical of the company's methods in 2018. According to the company's principles, loans were only made to businessmen whose businesses already had been running successfully for at least a year. The reason, according to Zviad, was that "too many businesses do not succeed." One type of collateral for a loan was personal property (usually in the form of real estate). Credit experts had to check the client's financial background carefully. One way to do so was to check tax payments and daily income. Government institutions record and will sometimes provide such information.

But credit experts had to dig deeper and try to get any information they could put their hands on. The background checks were intense and touched on very private topics. They were even more intense when other clients or guarantors had not introduced the potential client. Thus the credit agency's employees visited their clients' businesses, including warehouses and so on. Sometimes, I learned from Vakho, traders tried to trick the credit agents and show them their friends' or neighbors' shops or stalls, so the experts tried to take their clients by surprise. They took pictures of the interiors of borrowers' private houses, of the furniture, and of valuable objects. Then they tried to find out what their potential clients spent their money on, "business or having fun?" In the next step, the experts would investigate their clients' social milieu. The expert, according to Vakho, "talks to everyone and tries to find out what is going on in the family." Vakho and Zviad explained that clients were not considered as individuals but as members of their households and networks.

Zviad told me about a case illustrating BIG's usual procedures. The episode was a turning point for him and finally the reason he left the company. There had been several similar cases before, but this one, for Zviad, "was one too many": A *maršuṭḳa* ("minibus", маршрутка, მარშრუტკა) driver needed money because his minibus had broken down. He needed the money quickly, since every day without his bus meant financial losses that could threaten his livelihood. Zviad, who was in charge of the case, had to decide on a loan of 1000 lari. He started to take pictures inside the driver's apartment and checked the credit records of all the family members. As Zviad said: "For BIG the family is like one person. If, for example, one member has no job, this person might take all the money from another and get this person into trouble. Then, the loan is never paid back." In the case of the *maršuṭḳa* driver, it was his wife who had a negative credit record. When Zviad questioned her, she burst into tears and begged him not to tell her husband about it. She had secretly taken out a loan to help her son, who had lost a lot of money gambling. So she had been put on the blacklist. When the situation was discussed inside BIG, Zviad's boss wanted him to tell the husband about his wife's debt. BIG would offer the minibus driver a larger loan to pay back his wife's loan (thus transfer her loan to BIG) and to solve his own problems. Zviad, who had talked to the wife, refused to tell her husband about his wife's secrets and thus did not make the deal. The minibus driver did not understand why he did not get the loan, since he thought he was creditworthy. The whole procedure took a lot of time, so he got into difficulties. He got angry, BIG put pressure on Zviad, and in the end, Zviad quit his job.

Usually, the credit experts write reports. These reports are discussed with the manager and other experts. If a report is positive, the loan is made to the client. The first time, the client only gets a small loan. Later, when he has proven to be reliable, he gets the money faster and in larger amounts. According to Zviad: "One must know how to write a good report. A report is never 'real.' It is just a piece of paper. It is fiction. But it is always like this. You just have to know how it works. The manager knows this too. But if they trust you, they say okay. The credit expert has to trust the client, and the manager has to trust the credit expert."

Still, a risk manager or an auditor always checks the documents. Vakho, who worked for BIG in the past and is now working as a risk manager for another credit agency, is convinced that "every expert is lying." He himself used to do so when he worked for BIG. Now he was more careful. As a risk manager, he got a fixed salary comparable to a credit expert's salary and bonus: about 1,000 lari and a 500 lari monthly bonus, plus additional bonuses totaling about 2,400 lari. Since he was not reliant on having a certain number of clients, he checked all the details of every portfolio and was much more critical than the expert, who needed a certain number of clients to make a living (from bonuses) and therefore took more risks.

If something goes wrong and the client cannot pay, the credit expert has a problem and is forced to pay a fine, which is automatically deducted from his salary, and he also loses his bonus. I asked Zviad what else happened if someone was not able to pay. According to Zviad's boss, clients pay back the first, second, third, fourth, and perhaps the fifth loan. But then "there always comes the point at which they take out a loan that they cannot repay in time." According to Zviad:

> This is usual. Sometimes the reason is that people really go bankrupt. For example, in the past few months, when the dollar became much more expensive, people really got into trouble. Sometimes banks help them out. Sometimes debtors ask for a lower repayment rate per month, which gives them more time to pay back a loan. Instead of paying 200 dollars per month, they pay 100 dollars, but then they [have to] pay not for one year but for two.

Apparently, it rarely happened that someone really tried to completely escape his debts. But if it did happen, credit agents had to make a decision. In 2016, Zviad described two possible scenarios: "In some cases, in the case when you know this person and you can trust him... or when something really bad has happened, the credit expert can lend more money to rebuild the business. In other cases, you would ask the client to sell his property to pay back his debt. But if they are close to the client, credit experts avoid such situations." Zviad could recall a case in which a client was forced to pay what he owed. The debtor had left Tbilisi to flee his responsibility. The people who had introduced him were clients of the agency, and BIG put pressure on them. Finally, the guarantors went to the village, found the man, and forced him to sell his property to meet his obligations. The mechanism of social control—when it was exercised—worked very well.

In 2018, Zviad mentioned that credit experts themselves actively tried to get the money back. One method to do so was to send several representatives of BIG to the debtor. These representatives would not leave the house until the money was handed over. They would simply sit on a sofa and stare at the walls until someone came up with the cash. They would put psychological pressure on the debtor, talk to his neighbors, and harm his reputation within his community. Physical violence, at least, is not an option today, but it was different in the 1990s. One of BIG's top managers, who at that time worked for a different credit agency and whom Zviad knew well, told his employees that he had been involved in kidnapping relatives of nonpayers to enforce repayment back then.

BIG's practices are much more subtle, but they still don't meet internationally recognized standards. When an Italian team came to evaluate BIG, employees were instructed not to tell these people about what was happening on the ground. The Italians saw the reports, which looked good, and witnessed procedures that were less dubious than those described above.

Vakho, who in 2018 worked for another company, described more formalized procedures for collecting debts than those described by Zviad:

> First, you ask about the reasons, why they cannot pay back the loan. You try to help them to get a loan from another credit agency or a bank. Then, if this does not work, you talk to the guarantors. There are usually two of them. They have to take responsibility. Then you ask the debtor to sell his apartment. Finally, there is an official warning letter. If there has been no reaction fifteen days after the letter was received, the case might be turned over to a lawyer. Out of a debt volume of 30 million lari, 3 million are problematic cases. Half of these cases go to court. If the debt is still not paid back, all debtor's assets are frozen. The police get involved. If after 120 days, there is still no repayment, the credit expert loses his bonus.

The credit experts who were employed by BIG were recruited on the same basis as the clients. Zviad, as mentioned above, was introduced by a friend. Because of this friend, Zviad immediately got a higher position, that of "credit expert," while newcomers who had formal education in economics but lacked insider friends had to go through the formal process, submit their CVs, start in a lower position, and then slowly climb up the internal hierarchy.[7] With a smile, Zviad summarized his qualifications: "I got the position because I am a great guy."

BIG employed about 200 credit experts, plus other staff like lawyers and an auditor. The salary of each expert depended on the number of his

[7] The hierarchy within the organization is as follows: owners, regional directors (since the organization has offices in different Georgian cities), credit experts, and—Zviad is not sure about the correct term—"micro experts."

clients. Thus, every expert had to drum up his own clients to get enough commissions. When I asked Zviad about the average number of clients per expert, he replied that there was no such thing as an "average number." Some experts had only a few clients, while one of Zviad's friends had about eighty. But according to Zviad, "many of these clients run very small businesses. Some of them just sell a few nuts. Only a few clients run big businesses and are millionaires."

When I inquired about the millionaire clients, Zviad admitted that there were few of them. However, some traders could be perceived as millionaires in the sense that they owned merchandise worth a million lari. "But," Zviad said, "this is stock and not money. These people might need a loan as well, because they might need a lot of cash within a very short period." Dato is an example of such a client. When I visited him in his shop in Lilo Bazroba, he told me, as mentioned in the previous chapter, about his new business idea, which consisted in introducing a new type of beehive.[8] Dato was about to meet with his Turkish business partner, with whom he wanted to discuss the issue. He was sure that his Turkish "friend" would like the idea and would have the technical capacity to produce the necessary plastic components. However, Dato needed some start-up money for this endeavor, and even though he owned a flourishing business, he wanted to get the money as a loan from BIG.

Irma is another example of a BIG client. According to all credit experts I talked to, women are perceived as more reliable debtors than men. "They pay back their debts more often." Irma's business, at least as far as I understood it, is a very vulnerable one. Her profit margin is extremely small, and whenever any problems occur (with customs or with finding clients), she risks ending up in the red. So she obviously needed loans from time to time to keep her business going. So far, this obviously had worked—and the credit expert who introduced us to her was extremely positive about her, calling her an open, active, and very reliable person, which was his impression from their interaction in the context of arranging a loan.

In sum, the data shows how representatives of private microfinance institutions establish personal contacts with debtors and how they use all kinds of techniques based on personal interaction to get loans repaid.

[8] Facebook "Flow Hive": https://www.facebook.com/verge/videos/vb.193742123995472/1169756166394058/?type=2&theater.

The relationships between institutions like BIG and their clients are regulated by official (external and internal) rules. Paperwork must be done according to the rules. At the same time, these rules are manipulated for the sake of potential profit—which, first, is a risk for the credit expert. The whole strategy of a company like BIG is based on relationships of dependence between BIG's employees (so-called credit experts) and debtors. Formal procedures are at least partly replaced by very time-intensive checks, personal trust, individual assessment, and social pressure.

Microfinance and the Banking Sector

There are many microcredit institutions in Georgia. "As of March 2019," according to a study of the European Investment Bank.

> there were 61 microfinance institutions. In total, they employ more than 4 000 people. They have close to 400 branches spread out throughout the country. They make up 4% of the financial sector's assets. In 2018, total assets of the sector amounted to GEL 1.5 million, a decrease of 4% from the same period in the previous year. The average capital hovers around 30%. 70% of total assets were loans. The sectoral distribution of the microfinance loan portfolio was split between loans issued to individuals (92%) and loans issued to legal entities (2%). In the loans to individuals category, custom loans represented 31%, pawnshop loans 27% and trade and services 17% of the total amount. (Conde & Gattini, 2019: 14)

Some of these institutions use very offensive methods. In 2016 I constantly got advertising messages from different international lenders on my cell phone. A friend of mine called it fraud: "Their interest rate is very high. Sometimes they take 200%, which is almost impossible to pay back." I wondered why anyone would agree to such conditions,[9] and Zviad suspected that the reason was probably that "this is a very fast and easy way to get money. They ask for almost no documents. Perhaps because people do not know the conditions."[10]

[9] Such conditions have since become illegal; a new law forbids interest rates exceeding the benchmark set by the National Bank of Georgia.

[10] Giorgi Lomsadze, "Georgia's Predatory Lenders Are Punishing the Poor," Eurasianet, 15/8/2018: https://eurasianet.org/georgias-predatory-lenders-are-punishing-the-poor.

When I asked Mikheil, a lawyer working with traders, what his clients' main legal problems were, he promptly replied that they were usually linked to tax or loan payments:

Mikheil: People take out loans, but they do not read the contracts, and sometimes the people selling the loans tell them lies.
Zviad: It's more like a *formalnij obman* ["formal fraud", формальний обман].
Mikheil: Yes. For example, they say that the interest rate is 15%, but they do not tell you that after a year or a few years, the rate changes... and that it gets very high.
Zviad: They tell you the truth, but not the whole truth.
Mikheil And then people sign, and if they pay on time, there might be no problem. But the problem comes up if they do not pay back on time. And once they have signed, you cannot do anything anymore.
Zviad: No.
Mikheil: If they want to take your house, for example, you can stop this process for a while.

As a result of easy access to loans, exorbitant interest rates,[11] and an unstable job market low-income households in Georgia are becoming saddled with heavy debt. (Khalvashi, 2015; Khalvashi & Gilbreath, 2013) "[S]tories abound of households selling their homes and belongings because of one family member's ill-advised borrowing"; "according to the IMF Georgian households, collectively speaking, are paying 13.6% of their income to cover debts—both the service fees and principal payments."[12]

Indebtedness has long been a political topic and was discussed in pre-election debates in 2018 (Eradze, 2021). The National Bank finally "brought the previously autonomous 'microfinance' industry under its regulatory purview" by setting a cap on effective interest rates.[13] "The bank also defined requirements for personal-loan eligibility, tying it to the borrower's income and the value of secured property. ... The second round of measures came this year. ... The cap on effective interest rates

[11] For interest rates, see "Data: Lending Interest Rate Georgia": https://data.worldbank.org/indicator/FR.INR.LEND?locations=GE&view=chart.

[12] Lomsadze, "Georgia's Predatory Lenders."

[13] 100% for both bank and non-bank loans. Previously, some loan sharks had been lending at up to a 4,000% effective interest rate (Eurasianet).

was lowered again, to 50 percent",[14] This was widely discussed among my interlocutors in summer 2018.[15] Many microfinance lenders, especially smaller ones, shut down because of these measures. As discussed in *The Financial*,[16] they were not able to cover their costs:

> [Since] microfinance organizations give out smaller loans, their interest rates must be higher to cover the simple costs of loan management. A $2K real estate loan at 3% per month only generates $60 of income for the microfinance company. ... Even though microfinance organizations typically operate more efficiently than banks, there is still [a] direct, flat cost associated with loan management. $25 per month for loan servicing costs is [a] not uncommon internal charge, leaving the company with only $35 from which to cover their cost of capital, just to break even.

Traders were ready to accept the high interest rates charged by sometimes predatory private lenders, because they simply did not meet banks' official requirements. For instance, they might not have the required documentation or sufficient collateral. Many traders turned to credit agencies because they already "had problems with the bank," had negative credit records, and had been blacklisted (cf. Pelkmans & Umetbaeva, 2018). Microfinance institutions, even large ones like BIG that followed the law on paper, provided more informal space and loopholes.

A last resort for traders, if neither banks nor credit agencies were willing to lend, was to borrow money from individual lenders. These moneylenders, like other entrepreneurs, cashed in on the increasingly monetized context of the post-Soviet transition to capitalism and "the resulting demand for financial services" (Pelkmans & Umetbaeva, 2018 [preprint]: 6). They charged high interest rates and, again, had their own methods to guarantee their money, which were similar in Georgia to those

[14] Lomsadze, "Georgia's Predatory Lenders."

[15] The National Bank of Georgia (NBG) regulates the microfinance sector, issuing lenders licenses and auditing them. Microfinance lenders "can offer up to GEL 50 000 in microcredit to a single client. Minimum paid share capital must be over GEL 250 000. Recently, the registration processes and rules for liquidation with NBG have been made more transparent. As of December 2018, capital adequacy and liquidity ratios were introduced" (Conde & Gattini, 2019: 14).

[16] "Why is Microfinance Growing so Quickly in Georgia?" *The Financial*, 06.10.2013: https://www.finchannel.com/opinion/36003.

in Kyrgyzstan published by Pelkmans and Umetbaeva (2018). Moneylenders (worldwide) often combine their business with other entrepreneurial (trade) activity. They lend to people they already know and use their networks, personal knowledge, and moral and social pressure (cf. Durst, 2015; Guérin, 2014; James, 2014; Water 2018). The threat of force might be a last option, although I never personally heard of such measures being taken. But even in this informal niche, moneylenders usually back their deals with a notarized contract. In such contracts, the loan is defined as a fixed amount that must be paid back by a fixed date.

Blacklisting, the reason many traders turn to private credit agencies and moneylenders, is managed by creditinfo.ge, a private company founded after the Georgian-Russian war of 2008, according to Vakho. As a result of the war, many businesses got into financial trouble because of lack of access to Russian markets, and they did not recover until 2010, by which time they had found new niches and markets. To get through the difficult postwar period, many businesspeople had to take out not only one, but many loans, borrowing from different institutions to hide the actual extent of their indebtedness. As there was no flow of information between banks and/or microfinance institutions, there was no way to get an overview of a client's financial situation. Lenders now all send information on their clients to creditinfo.ge, which makes it available for a monthly charge of about U.S.$1.50, I was told. In addition, credit expert and bank employees rely on their personal contacts with experts working in other institutions. I was really surprised how often the people I talked to in the financial sector had changed jobs. Some had undergone real relays through many different financial institutions and had friends in each of their former workplaces. Irakli knew people from BIG and Basis Bank and his friend Vakho, who had worked for BIG and Basis Bank but now worked for another credit company, knew people who worked for ProCredit and Credo Bank, and so forth. Such personal networks were used to exchange information about clients simply in a phone call between two friends.

In encounters with clients, bank employees, unlike credit experts, do not engage in personal negotiations, which is not part of their job. Even when small amounts of money are involved, they follow formal, standardized procedures, with written contracts and legal proceedings. Personal interaction, which is time-intensive (and therefore cost-intensive), is kept to a minimum, and banks do not give loans to dubious candidates.

Traders affirm that they feel more responsible towards "real people" than to banks, which seems logical to many citizens, given banks' bad reputation. This became most obvious when BIG was sold to Credo Bank in 2018. Why BIG was sold is not clear. Zviad once heard his boss saying that "every company has its ups and downs, and you have to get out when you're on top." Perhaps this was a motivation. A small circle of BIG managers founded a new credit company, but most of the credit experts who worked for BIG were fired when BIG was taken over. According to Zviad and his friends, this was a big mistake by Credo Bank, because when these experts were fired, the personal relationship between debtor and creditor was severed. The debtor, who felt a personal obligation towards his credit expert, now regarded himself as released from his contract, framed as a personal agreement between two individuals. Although the relationship between lenders and borrowers is ambiguous, it is framed as a kind of "friendship," according to Vakho, and friendship is always linked to trust and, more important, to honor in Georgia (Fehlings, 2022). The debtors did not recognize Credo Bank as a legitimate successor of their contract partners, and Credo Bank did not have the tool of social pressure to make its new BIG clients pay up. Debtors did not care about their debts to Credo Bank, which thus lost a lot of money.

Many Georgian banks nonetheless specialize in microfinance and seem to profit from it. Branches of such banks can be seen all around Lilo Bazroba, where they have popped up like mushrooms in recent years. KfW (Kreditanstalt für Wiederaufbau), a development bank owned by German government that was formed in 1948 under the Marshall Plan after World War II, was one of the first banks to establish a microfinance program in Georgia. KfW's development program is termed financial cooperation,[17] and its agenda included SME promotion, a traditional focus of German financial cooperation.[18] In Georgia, KfW founded ProCredit Bank (PCB)

[17] KfW's financial cooperation began in 1958 with several separate financing operations scattered around the world. Most of these were projects that the German Federal Government saw as politically expedient and commissioned KfW to implement. In the early 1960s, these separate international tasks were superseded by "capital assistance to developing countries," a major new business area, which was enshrined in the law concerning KfW in 1961 (see KfW Development Bank "Financial Cooperation": https://www.kfw.de/KfW-Group/About-KfW/Identit%C3%A4t/Geschichte-der-KfW/Finanzielle-Zusammenarbeit/).

[18] It represents 40% of the total financial-sector portfolio in financial cooperation and so plays by far the greatest role, ahead of microfinancing and energy and environmental

in 1999.[19] Like other international financial institutions (e.g., the ILO and World Bank),[20] it assigned a major role to SMEs in the transformation from a planned to a market economy (see Chapter 3) and identified the difficulty of obtaining formal loans as a major obstacle to the successful development of the SME sector in the Caucasus. ProCredit Bank, at least at the beginning, was the first microfinance bank in the region to aim explicitly at providing inexpensive loans to micro-, small, and medium entrepreneurs.[21]

Georgian SMEs represented a risk group, and at least according to KfW's report, many of them got access to formal loans for the first time through ProCredit Bank. The bank sought to become the most customer-friendly bank in Georgia, as demonstrated by its variety of services and comparatively easy and fast procedures. So-called express loans, for example, could be made in a single day, and loans of up to U.S.$10,000 within two days, but reviews of potential clients were nevertheless intensive and careful. On average, one out of five loans was rejected, because the client could not prove creditworthiness or had a negative credit record. A third of all loans clients applied for were not approved for the full amount, because the collateral was insufficient for the requested amount or because the conditions were assessed to be risky. For loans exceeding U.S.$10,000, clients had to pledge houses, apartments, and land, and they had to register all their property as back-up security and provide two guarantors who would stand surety with their own property. The majority of loans were 200% collateralized, which, as the bank's report put it, "is indispensable [German: ***unabdingbar***] for

financing (27% and 18% of the total portfolio respectively). KfW Development Bank "Materials on Development Financing", 02 February 2017: https://www.kfw-entwicklungsbank.de/PDF/Download-Center/Materialien/2017_Nr.2_KMU_EN.pdf.

[19] ProCredit Bank was founded as a closed stock company under Georgian law. Its registered capital was 5 million GEL, raised to 10 million in 2001. Partners included the German-Georgian Foundation (GGF) founded by KfW, the Nederlandse Financierings-Maatschappij voor Ontwikkelingslanden NV (FMO), the International Finance Corporation (IFC), International Micro Investment (IMI), and four Georgian banks (KfW-Entwicklungsbank, 2005).

[20] The World Bank "Enterprise Surveys": http://www.enterprisesurveys.org/data/exploretopics/finance.

[21] KfW Development Bank "Georgien": https://www.kfw-entwicklungsbank.de/International-financing/KfW-Development-Bank/Local-presence/Europe/Georgia/.

establishing a long-term and sustainable credit relationship in the complicated Georgian environment" (KfW-Entwicklungsbank, 2005: 4). Small loans of up to U.S.$10,000 were more flexible, however, and granted on much more moderate terms. In general, according to the bank's report:

> ProCredit Bank monitors the loan portfolios carefully. Payment arrears can be retrieved in the management information system on a daily basis. The loan-loss provisions created for the purpose of risk management are in line with international regulations. Debt rescheduling and loan restructurings are undertaken by the respective credit committee[s]. Bad loans are pursued in court. However, on average, it takes 2–3 years for these procedures to finish. Thus, to save time and court costs, ProCredit Bank strives for out-of-court settlements with borrowers if loans cannot be paid back. (KfW-Entwicklungsbank, 2005: 4)

In 2005 ProCredit Bank was the third-largest bank in Georgia. It had 85 branches, and until 2016, it was very visible in the cityscape. Since then, it has given up microfinance (and many of its branches). When I tried to talk to a representative of KfW, I was rudely told that KfW has changed its agenda and that the representatives of KfW in charge of the microfinance program were no longer available. The bank's procedures, as described in KfW's 2005 report, have nonetheless become a model for many Georgian banks. As I was told by Irakli and some of his friends, people who had previously worked for ProCredit could find jobs easily in the Georgian banking sector and ask for a good starting salary. With microfinance becoming a rewarding business, banks received them with open arms.

Traders as Clients

In the post-Soviet region as elsewhere, microloans were seen a few years ago as a kind of "miracle cure" for poverty. "Microfinance became one of the world's most high-profile and generously funded development interventions. Everyone, it seemed, was talking about how small loans could unlock endless opportunities for the world's poorest people."[22]

[22] "The Rise and Fall of Microfinance," *The Guardian*, 21 November 2012: https://www.theguardian.com/global-development/poverty-matters/2012/nov/21/rise-fall-microfinance.

Georgia has been a testing ground, not only for KfW's financial cooperation, but also for international fund-raising organizations like KIVA[23] and EthicCapital, which provide microloans for start-ups.[24] It is difficult to assess the importance of microloans in the Caucasian SME sector, especially in the niche of my target group of bazaar traders. KfW's evaluations talk about positive results, which means that their clients reported back that they were able to grow their businesses with the help of a loan and applied for new, larger loans. But KfW's clients, even though they were classified as SMEs by the bank, did not necessarily correspond to the group of traders who are the focus of this book—and who do not need loans of up to 10,000 lari, but of 300 or 500 lari.

On the global level, enthusiasm for microfinance projects has faded. Critical studies discuss the limitations of microloans, assess their effects on borrowers' well-being as negative, or deconstruct them as a new form of power and control (Augsburg et al., 2014; Bateman, 2014; Bateman et al., 2019; Bateman & Chang, 2012; Guérin, 2014; Lont & Hospes, 2004; Peebles, 2010). In Georgia, microfinance has become a lucrative business and is considered responsible for the indebtedness of many Georgian citizens (cf. Khalvashi, 2015; Khalvashi & Gilbreath, 2013). "[A] vast and growing number of Georgians are trapped by debt," according to an article published in *Eurasianet* in 2018. "Prime Minister Mamuka Bakhtadze said in June (2018) that 630,000 Georgians have a debt they are unable to pay off—about 30% of what Bakhtadze called the 'economically active population'".[25]

My qualitative data and the data from our survey suggest that microfinance institutions are nonetheless important for traders to keep their businesses operating. Traders try to get loans from banks, and if this does not work, they supplement or replace microloans from banks with loans from other financial sources. Many of these loans are perhaps never paid back, but still, Lilo Bazroba's management seem to have invested in a successful concept when they founded Lilo Capital, which initially

[23] Kiva "Home": https://www.kiva.org/.

[24] The number of such loans was and is very low, however, perhaps almost negligible. When I checked KIVA's webpage in 2016, its Georgian projects involved starting a trading business in clothes and a taxi service company. In 2018, most of the loans were projected to finance businesses in the tourist sector.

[25] Lomsadze, "Georgia's Predatory Lenders."

concentrated on providing microloans to Lilo's traders and is now planning to expand. Giving credit to a Lilo trader is judged particularly risky. When Vakho worked for BIG, he had a portfolio of 150 clients, most of them Lilo traders, with a total credit volume of around 800,000 lari. Individual traders from Lilo Bazroba usually took out loans starting at 500 lari (in other bazaars the amount was even smaller, starting at 300 lari), and the maximum amount was about 10,000 lari. Vakho explained that "it is taking a big risk to give them [the traders] big money. You give them a loan, and the next day they simply disappear." Reliable clients given small loans for one or two years up to eight times were, however, a profitable source of income for BIG.

The owners of Lilo Bazroba, in contrast to individual traders, are seen as big players in Georgia's world of finance. Bigger even in Georgia than big-box retailers like Carrefour. Irakli, who had worked for BIG a few years earlier, introduced us to a friend of his who was a manager at Basis Bank. "Everyone wants to cooperate with them [Lilo Bazroba's owners and administrators]," this man said, citing as examples the Bank of Georgia and TBC. Like these banks, Basis Bank was a leading Georgian bank,[26] he noted, whose clients are mostly "profitable organisations with huge collateral." A few years earlier there had been a secret meeting between Lilo's owners and the managers of Basis Bank, he told us with a conspiratorial expression on his face. The bank had wanted to buy information about Lilo Bazroba's traders (or at least get a list of traders), which the market's management offered to sell for 200,000 lari. This was too much for Basis Bank at that time, and the deal did not work out. When I asked why this information would be important, given that Lilo traders are small, risky clients, the manager said that even though big clients are easy and reliable, SMEs (taking out loans of less than 200,000 lari) account for 9 to 19% of the bank's profits, because they get loans with a higher interest rate. Even large banks thus apparently still have an interest in the SME sector.

ProCredit, Basis Bank, Credo Bank, Lilo Capital, and BIG are just examples or case studies of different institutions providing microfinancing, but these examples (and some other alternatives mentioned in

[26] It was founded by Georgians in 1993 and taken over by the Chinese Hualing Group in 2012. Since the takeover, the bank's capital has grown from 90 to 900 million lari, because Hualing made a large investment. Now, the board is Chinese, but the management is still Georgian. Only the deputy director is Chinese.

this section) give insight into the environment for and constraints on acquiring money within the formal-informal framework and the possible choices traders can make within this dynamic system. Both banks and credit agencies are legal entities and follow similar guidelines, but while banks function through standardized procedures, credit agencies, because they base some of their mechanisms on personal relationships between lenders and borrowers, were more flexible and easier to access for traders—especially because these methods corresponded to the traders' usual business practices.

This said, it is worth mentioning that big banks' procedures do not completely exclude informality either. For example, employees hired as experts rotate through different institutions and thereby establish networks including former colleagues, who can give (personal) access to information on clients. At the same time, the formal procedures applied with small clients are not necessarily applied in all dealings within the banking system. Again, there are different levels—corresponding to different levels of networks and contacts. When we (Irakli, Zviad, and another of Irakli's banker friends, whom we met randomly) were standing in front of the main branch of Basis Bank, I asked Irakli why someone—like many of his and Zviad's friends—would prefer to work for a private credit agency rather than for a bank. Irakli and the banker laughed:

Irakli: Because it is difficult to make a career in a bank.
Susanne: Why?
Irakli: Because of Georgians.
(Everyone laughs.)
Irakli: This explains everything.
The banker: True, it explains everything.
Irakli: Ha-ha, yes, you need connections to people on the top.

Thus even institutions that are considered formal and represent formal procedures, as almost everywhere worldwide, incorporate informal aspects and mechanisms on some levels within their architecture.

Bureaucracy

While taking out loans from formal institutions, traders had to adjust to certain formal rules. They thus indirectly interacted with the state, which provided the legal framework. Encounters with the state usually happen in the context of bureaucracy. While on the one hand this means that traders have to cope with formal requirements and a lot of paperwork, this also includes face-to-face interaction with state officials, who contribute their own readings of legal texts and bureaucratic procedures (Fuller & Bénéi, 2001; Fuller & Harriss, 2001; Gupta, 1995, 2012).[27]

Several studies exist that focus on state-people encounters in the Caucasus and in Georgia, in particular—either directly or indirectly. Such studies are often concerned with citizenship, state representation and nation-building, privatization, conflict, repression, protest movements, and border issues (e.g., Aivazishvili-Gehne, 2015; Grant & Yalçın-Heckmann, 2007; Khutsishvili, 2016; Mühlfried, 2007, 2010; Pelkmans, 2013; Yalçın-Heckmann, 2012, 2016). One of the earliest ethnographic studies concerned with problems of citizenship and people-state interfaces in Georgia is that of Dragadze (2016) on rural families in Soviet Georgia. More recent studies are those by Mühlfried (2014) on the relationship of shepherds to the state and state borders, by Christophe (2005), Voell (2015), and Voell and Kaliszewska (2015) on legal practice and bureaucracy, and my own work on the relationship between private, public, and state-controlled space (Fehlings, 2014).

In studies of economic activity and trade, the state and the relationship to formal state institutions is a constant topic. Some researchers dealing with Central Asia, the Caucasus, and other post-Soviet countries show how states regulate traders' access to space (e.g., Rekhviashvili, 2015; Taalaibekova & Melkumyan, 2018); others mention the state, state boundaries, and conflicts between states as obstacles to business (Khutsishvili, 2017); and yet others focus on the state's restrictive aspects and its failure to create a business-friendly environment (Rekhviashvili, 2015; Stefes, 2006, 2008). The absence of states, their weakness, their inability to establish order, and corruption have also produced a vast literature (see e.g., Iskandaryan, 2014; Kandiyoti, 2003; Rasanayagam, 2011), filling the pages of the *Caucasus Analytical Digest*, for example.

[27] According to Fuller and Harris (2001), the role of the state has often been neglected in anthropology. It has been perceived as an entity apart, something separate from society and social values (cf. Bouchard, 2011). Fuller and Harris point out that although states impact the everyday lives of their citizens, there is a line that separates them, even if a fuzzy one. Gupta (1995, 2012) talks about such blurred boundaries and the mediating function of state officials. In ethnography on Soviet and post-Soviet societies, the state is never missing. As the Soviet state was omnipresent and undeniably sustainably influenced and organized—not to say manipulated—people's everyday lives, it has been a constant concern for researchers. The same is true of post-Soviet states and regimes.

During my research, encounters with the state and bureaucracy were most tangible at border crossings and in confrontations with the tax system. The state materializes at checkpoints and in consular offices, clearance zones, custom terminals, and, finally, computers. It is here that changes can be observed in the state practice framing many of the economic activities of small, medium, and large entrepreneurs—and again, in these contexts, one can see that the bureaucracy consists of people.

Many studies[28] show, for example, that borders are not demarcated solely by state institutions, but are negotiated for social and economic reasons and challenged by "pre-existing networks of kinship, clanship, and business partnership... seldom eliminated by the imposition of political boundaries," which, however, "does not mean that state power is absent in gatekeeping or that national borders do not exist anymore... in most instances, their presence is visible and clear" (Ngo & Hung, 2018: 185–187). As I have shown in the previous chapters, they determine the traders' pathways and according to Cantens, Ireland and Raballand (2015), cited in Ngo and Hung (2018: 188), regulate the global flows of wealth.

Customs Clearance

In shuttle and long-distance trade, people and goods cross borders. People need passports, visas, and permits, and goods must pass customs clearance. Consequently, the topic of customs came up quite frequently during my fieldwork. Ramaz, for example, was very angry about the fact that he was supposed to pay fees. In his opinion, the state was not helping him with his business, and he did not see why he should share his profits with any state institution.

Tricking customs officers is common. Especially if the amount of goods is small, traders claim that the goods in their luggage are for their own use. Even though this is an easily recognized lie, customs officials may be accommodating. Irma told me, for example, that she had negotiated with an officer at the airport when he saw that she had about ten or more cocktail and evening dresses in her bag. After a while, he let her go without demanding a fee, but he told her that he would remember her

[28] See Balibar (2002), Baud and Van Schendel (1997), Herzog (1990), Newman and Paasi (1998) and Reeves (2014). For an overview see Ngo and Hung (2018).

face and stop her the next time she tried to cheat in this way. Another way to get merchandise across borders,[29] as mentioned earlier, is to split it among fellow travellers so as not to exceed the allowed quantity per person. As I witnessed many times, shuttle traders try to persuade their fellow travellers to do this, and although the latter are sometimes not inclined to participate in this kind of maneuver, they often feel unable to refuse.[30]

If it is a matter of large quantities, however, such tricks do not work. Levan said he paid at least a large percentage of the required customs charges, for example. He told me that customs work quite well in Georgia today, because since the Rose Revolution, bribery has been severely prosecuted and the level of corruption has been significantly reduced (see Di Puppo, 2013). Transparency has become a leading principle, made visible, among other things, by the architecture of new official buildings, in which glass has become the most important building material (Darieva, Kaschuba & Krebs, 2011: 18).

Still, Levan declared only half his goods. As mentioned earlier, his Georgian middlemen working at the cargo terminal in Beijing helped him to fake his documents by not mentioning the weight but only the size of the merchandise packages and by putting only half the actual number of items on the invoice. Small traders, as Irakli confirmed, are rarely checked intensively, and even if they are, it is still worth the risk, because if it happens once in a dozen times, it is still profitable.

In September 2016, Zviad and I visited Tbilisi's customs clearance zone, one of four such zones in Georgia, the other three being at the Tbilisi airport, in Poti, and in Batumi (plus five subdivisions, one in Tbilisi for goods transported by rail and the others in Telavi, Akhaltsikhe, Kutaisi, and Rustavi, as well as privately operated terminals like the one set up by the Hualing Group, discussed below).[31] The customs terminal in Tbilisi is located in a nondescript area along the highway between Lilo Bazroba and the Tbilisi airport. On one side of the road, there is the customs zone;

[29] This practice has been described by many authors who deal with post-Soviet shuttle trade. See, e.g., Humphrey (2018a) and Holzlehner (2014).

[30] There are numerous ethnographic accounts of such practices from all over post-Soviet Eurasia. See, e.g., Holzlehner (2014) or Aivasishvili and the literature on post-Soviet shuttle trade cited earlier.

[31] Revenue Service "What to Know about the Clearance of Goods": http://www.rs.ge/en/5380.

on the other side, there is a Socar[32] post consisting of a shop with a small canteen and two petrol stations, with a large parking area. There is also a hotel, which advertises its proximity to the clearance zone and to Lilo and the Rustavi car market. The customs clearance zone itself consists of two main buildings: "Customs Clearance Zone Tbilisi–1" and "Customs Clearance Zone Tbilisi–2."

The architecture of these boxy concrete buildings is simple. The first building consists of a huge open hall, with nothing but an information desk in the center of it. Behind the desk hang large photographs of all Georgian border crossings, illustrating the new taste for transparency. At these crossings, which had been unimpressive a few years ago, new construction had appeared within the space of only a few months. I remember how I stood staring as if I were seeing a mirage when I saw the steel-and-glass construction at the Sadakhlo border crossing for the first time. A few months earlier, there had been nothing more than dust, stones, a barrier, and a small border post there. The terminal in Tbilisi, however, was almost austere. In each wing, to the right and left, there were small workstations. There were seats for waiting clients, and although the building was almost empty, traders were required to take a number that determined their place in line displayed on a screen when their turn came up. The second building was a smaller copy of the first one. It was used for the declaration of high-value goods imported by individuals for personal use.

Behind the buildings there was a huge parking area with trucks. There was nothing chaotic about it. It was not very busy that day, and the few trucks I saw were parked in orderly lines. A female security guard told me that it was not allowed to go there and take pictures. Zviad and I asked the woman at the information desk whether there was something like a map of the area. She said no. Walking around, we saw a fence and another security guard, who protected the parking and the loading zone. Trucks had to enter the area through a control post. Numerous Georgian Post Office minivans and small trucks, which transported traders' shipments from the terminal to Lilo Bazroba, were parked outside the closed-off area. The atmosphere of the place was official, sober, well-organized, and pragmatic—just the reverse of a bazaar.

[32] Socar is an Azerbaijani company.

The official website of the Georgian Revenue Service states that goods are to be declared within thirty days of importation, but that the Revenue Service is authorized to extend this deadline by sixty days, and in case of goods stored in the customs warehouse, to up to five calendar years. Declarations must be filled out by the shipper, a representative, or the tax authorities. The required documents include an invoice certifying the purchase of the goods and "waybills" such as a consignment note, a railroad bill of lading, an air waybill, or "CMR or TIR documents" (for road transportation). Documents must include:

> the general description of the cargo, the quantity, gross and net weight, the goods' code, the number of containers, and information on the carrier, the shipper of goods, and place of loading the goods, as well as the destination and information about the consignee of the goods. If non-tariff measures apply to the goods, or they are subject to additional customs control, a relevant license, a permit, a certificate, and other necessary documents shall also be submitted.[33]

A proper invoice includes "The date of issuance of the document and the number thereof; particulars of the seller; particulars of the buyer; description of each type of goods [e.g., a men cotton coat or a men wool coat], quantity of each item (pieces, kilograms, etc.)," "price of each type of goods," and "terms of delivery." "The document shall certify the fact of actual selling and buying (the document must be attested to by a seal, if any, or by other means of attestation)." This was easy for the Chinese business partners who worked with Georgian traders in Beijing. Under the Georgian tax code then in effect, import duty was set at 0, 5, or 12% of the value of the goods and VAT at 18%. Import duties and fees were to be paid within five days of the clearance of goods, or within fifteen days in the event of prior declaration.[34]

Irakli told me that despite my first impression, the clearance zone was a busy place. In 2016, he worked for the Vengo Group, which is a Georgian cargo company. Two years later, he had become the manager

[33] Revenue Service "What to Know about the Clearance of Goods": http://www.rs.ge/en/5380 (in Georgian).

[34] As laws and regulations change quite often, this information might be outdated by the time it is published in this book. But even so, the quoted information shows the language used by the official institutions that traders have to deal with. This language does not change.

of a privately run customs terminal next to the newly built Tbilisi See Plaza and Hualing City. The terminal was built by the Chinese Hualing Investment Group, and run by the group and a German cargo company called Barth + Co Spedition GmbH & Co. KG. Consequently, Irakli knew a great deal about the clearance process. As I learned, the privately owned customs and storage terminals, which were run according to Georgian law, were regularly inspected by government officials. According to Irakli, there were about ten such terminals in Georgia. These places had to adhere to many regulations and had to fulfil security standards; for example, "there has to be a fence, cameras, security guards, etc." Videos and procedures had to be shown to officials. In spring 2018, Irakli showed us the already-functioning terminal, its monitoring and security system, and its warehouses. Again, the area was almost empty, and the three or four people working there, including Irakli, were quite relaxed (all in all, there were 16 employees, including 5 security guards).

Irakli took us to have a look inside the warehouses, where many goods were stored before re-export. "'Temporary importation' allows for bringing goods of foreign origin temporarily into the customs territory of Georgia (as a rule, the period shall not exceed 3 years)."[35] As Irakli explained to me in summer 2018, Georgian law did not prohibit rebranding (except for medication), which meant that many goods that, because of sanctions, were not allowed to be imported from Russia to the United States or Europe—or the other way around—could do so after having gone through Georgian customs and rebranding. Rebranding meant that goods coming from Turkey, for example, got new packaging and new documents (including sanitary/veterinary certificates) certifying that the goods had been made or repackaged in Georgia, and as Irakli pointed out: "As the documents and stamps are written in Georgian, foreign customs, for example, in Russia, cannot read what is written there in any case."

When we visited the warehouse in spring 2018, the floor was still covered with old packages. With a special trading license, according to Irakli, one was even allowed to re-export goods for less than the declared price paid for them. A way to get such a license was to register a business in one of Georgia's free economic zones. Thus goods were brought to Georgia and received new, legal documents that estimated their value

[35] Georgian Revenue Service, "Temporary Admission": http://www.rs.ge/en/5273 (in Georgian).

at less than the value declared when they entered the country. Then the goods could be declared for this lower price at the Russian border, and Russian customs never saw the original bill. For this reason, some companies used Georgia as a "broker" or point of entry for importing goods into Russia. Armenia was another such entry point, as Armenia had special agreements with Russia. So sometimes, in order to make use of all these juridical loopholes, goods came from Turkey to Georgia, went from there to Armenia (or Kazakhstan), and then went from there to Russia. Another common practice was legally to bring brand-name goods from China to Georgia, mix/hide these brand-name goods in among other goods in one truck in order to obtain Georgian documents that only mention the number of items legally, and then illegally to import the brand-name goods to Ukraine. Georgia thus had legal means to facilitate and to conceal imports that were illegal in the receiving countries. The crime thus did not occur in Georgia, but on foreign territory.

Irakli showed me many interesting procedures, which were sometimes quite complicated. Another warehouse was full of bottles of mineral water, and the next one was for consolidation, meaning that several individuals or firms put their merchandise together to fill a container and share transportation costs. Furthermore, as I have mentioned, it was also possible to store goods until one was able to pay clearance fees, which sometimes was done little by little. Thus some of the building units were simply used for storage.

Already in 2016, Irakli had explained that there were different procedures when goods crossed the border. According to his explanation:

> When trucks cross the border, they must pay 300 lari if there are more than 17,000 tons of cargo. If there is less, you pay a little less. But this is not for clearance. This is simply for crossing the border and entering Georgia. Then you go to the clearance zone and do all the paperwork there. You show all the documents, which you should fill out correctly beforehand.

The young woman at the information desk of "Customs Clearance Zone Tbilisi-1" gave Zviad and me a similar account. She told us that trucks got permission at the border to come to the clearance zone in Tbilisi. Only from the clearance zone did they have the right to continue to their actual destinations. However, as she added, "some go directly to their storage. It is a question of negotiation." In some exceptional cases and for goods up to the value of 10,000 GEL, this was a legal procedure. These goods could be cleared at the border customs crossing points.[36]

Irakli further explained how goods were classified by customs officials and passed on to the green, yellow, or red line, with the following consequences:

> If you are in the green line, this means that everything is fine. If you are in the yellow line, there is a problem. For example, the computer tells you that some of the same goods have been declared for another amount a few days or a month earlier. All these checks are done by computers, which gather all the information about prices, commodities, taxes, laws, etc. Then someone from the revenue service has to check it. A real person does this. Usually, this happens quite fast, and it doesn't take too much time. If you end up in the red line, this means that there are real problems. Then it takes much more time.

It was not only the documents that were checked, but the goods themselves, which might not correspond to the goods declared in the documents. According to Irakli, when it came to serious inspections, Georgian customs officials cooperated with their partners from abroad, for example with their Chinese counterparts. "For example, if you want to know the real price of specific merchandise, you call an official in China, who will check with the factory. This is easy. We have a good relationship." This information was confirmed by Lasha, who was responsible for clearing the goods imported by Hualing Group (see chapter 5).

Many of the procedures described (filling out documents, crossing borders, talking to custom officials) were not performed by traders (or companies) themselves, but outsourced to cargo companies, which took over the task of dealing with all the requirements and potential problems. Traders thus did not talk much about these procedures. Cargo/logistic companies not only deal with local Georgian regulations, but do so on an international level. They even adjust their transport routes to these legal conditions. As an example, I was told by the managing partner of the Vengo Group cargo company that "it is not allowed to transport pork meat through Turkey. In this case, one has to go through Russia." Cargo companies and their partners deal with many such constraints on

[36] Revenue Service "What to Know about the Clearance of Goods": http://www.rs.ge/en/5380.

behalf of their clients, who, for their part, simply have to sign a contract and a few documents while they wait for delivery. Levan and Ramaz, as described in the previous chapter, for example, entrusted their goods to a cargo company that organized their smooth transfer from China through Central Asia to Georgia. Even though Levan and Ramaz had visited their cooperation partners along the transport route, they did not have full control over them and had to trust them and their expertise when it came to border crossings along the journey.

Customs regulation is a very complex matter: First, it is necessary to read and understand the regulations cited above (which is not as easy as it might appear), and second, these regulations change all the time. What I have concluded from the materials I gathered during my fieldwork is that there were many loopholes in the system, which were used by shuttle traders as well as by large companies to reduce costs. Simultaneously, the representatives of the system were known for generally adhering to Georgian laws. Thus there was a very thin line between informal and formal practices, right and wrong behavior.

Most loopholes did not include an obvious and active violation of Georgian regulations on Georgian territory. Take the example of rebranding. Even though it was illegal under Russian or Ukrainian law to import certain goods, for example, their export and the procedures enabling their export were legal in Georgia—although it was clear that the methods used had no other purpose than to bypass Russian, Ukrainian, or other countries' controls. Ignoring what happens beyond their borders enabled Georgian officials to have a clean slate. Georgian traders who tricked Georgian customs faked their bills in China, since in Georgia this would be much more difficult—almost impossible, Levan and Ramaz said. Thus the actual "crime" happened in China, and Georgian officials had the choice of whether to trust or not trust the documents. They did not actively participate in the process of fraud, but simply turned a blind eye to it, and they did not profit from this behavior. By contrast, as soon as an obvious violation of the law occurred, the bureaucratic machine moved into gear.

This could even rise to the level of absurdity, as one of Irakli's stories demonstrated. Irakli got into serious trouble for a trifle: a Georgian trader who was trading in goods from Germany got a present from the German company, a freebie of five little protein cakes, which measured not more than 10 cm each. Because these five protein cakes were given as a present, the trader did not have a veterinary certificate for them and could not declare them properly. He therefore left them at customs. According to Georgian law, such goods that are not declared must be destroyed after a few days. When the state officials came to Irakli's terminal to supervise the process of destruction, one of the five cakes was missing. The officials gave Irakli an ultimatum of a few more days to solve the problem. Irakli went without sleep from then on. He was considering travelling to Germany to buy such a cake so as to replace the missing item. Luckily, after the employees had turned all the warehouses upside down, they found the cake under some packages. This saved Irakli from a high fine and, above all, enabled him to sleep. Formal rules, as such incidents show, had to be respected in some contexts, and in these contexts, there was no way to escape them. In major cases of intentional fraud, people went to jail.

Digitalization

Digitalization, which has been implemented by state bodies within their institutions[37]—and which has constantly been adapted and improved, as the e-court system shows[38]—has had a major impact on all bureaucratic procedures in Georgia.

The aim of digitalization, it was argued, was to provide transparency and to minimize "operational" and "human deficiencies."[39] In the context of clearance, for example, as mentioned, computers were fed information on goods and prices, which were then compared automatically. If there was a large discrepancy, alarm bells rang, and the documents and goods were checked. It was often thus the computer that discovered mistakes and fraud.

Computers are unbiased, and the Georgian state counts on them. Citizens can pay their taxes and their electricity, water, gas, and telephone bills and buy public transport tickets at electronic terminals that can be found on every corner in Tbilisi. From these terminals, which are run by banks or private companies, citizens can also transfer money to bank accounts. Customers feed the machine with cash and simply enter the number of

[37] Civil Service Bureau of Georgia "Report": http://csb.gov.ge/en (in Georgian; document no longer available).

[38] Civil Service Bureau of Georgia: http://csb.gov.ge/uploads/news_pdf_2/sabiujeto_dawesebulebebSi_saqmiswarmoebis_avtomatizirebuli_sistemis_standarti.pdf?fbclid=IwAR0YHKOXGApt_l0gaAHQSFcTurxHOxqkGIBp9lPmt8zA8th7ffvwfRXN1Z0.

[39] Community Center "Online Consultation": https://sda.gov.ge/?lang=en.

the recipient, which can be that of the official revenue service or a private person. Traders thus only need an official ID, and not necessarily a bank account, to transfer money (including taxes), explaining the paucity of bank accounts in Georgia mentioned in the Introduction of this chapter. Zviad told me that BIG's loans were paid back by clients monthly in cash through these machines, for example.

Many digital procedures have significantly simplified interactions with government institutions. Having experienced paying my electricity bill at a bank counter and garbage-collection and elevator fees at the local post office around the corner each month in Yerevan, I admit that it can be much more pleasant to deal with a machine than with real people, which here means a furious mob fighting for the first place in line and a grim official looking like a guardian of purgatory. In front of the electronic terminal in Tbilisi, at least, one fights only one's own limitations. Trying to understand these machines, I was made desperate by the fact that the computer did not negotiate. Computers are relentless. And, if we adopt Max Weber's (1985 [1921]) definition of bureaucracy as a neutral and proficient form of organization, we can, in my opinion, say that it is perfectly incarnated in computer systems, and that computers are perfect bureaucrats.

Businesspeople (including traders) use several digital services, some of which are optional, while others are mandatory. Importers of goods, for example, can theoretically, if they wish, make a preliminary online declaration of their goods before the goods reach Georgia. Using special software, they can upload all their documents to the website of the Georgian Revenue Service. The documents are then reviewed, and the declaration forms are prepared and returned to the importers. Based on the submitted documents, the risk corridor/line is determined beforehand, which means that the traders know whether the goods will end up in the red, yellow, or green line. If the goods go to the green line, the traders can take them directly from the border to their warehouses or shops. If traders choose this preliminary declaration option, service fees, according to the official website, significantly decrease.[40] But neither Levan nor Ramaz used this service. Irakli explained that you need a very "qualified person" to handle it. You need an account with the customs program, and only large companies hire someone to deal with it.

[40] Revenue Service "Types of Services Offered in the Customs Clearance Zone": http://www.rs.ge/Default.aspx?sec_id=5378&lang=2.

According to Irakli, "If you make a mistake, you will have to pay a fine of 4,000 lari, which is a huge risk." This risk, obviously, is too high for individual traders and taking it does not pay off.

The online registration of businesses at the revenue service, on the other hand, is easy and obligatory. According to the law, "It is necessary to be registered as an entrepreneur–legal person to start a business (an entrepreneurial activity)."[41] In the spirit of the reforms mentioned earlier, which aimed to provide easy, favorable business conditions, the revenue service's website declares, "Georgia introduced simple procedures for registration as an entrepreneur–legal person and it takes only one day for this."[42] As I learned from Ketevan's husband, who had registered a public-relations and advertising company at the Georgian House of Justice a few days before I talked to him, this was true. Within a day, the task was completed.

To register a business, it is important to choose among various forms of entrepreneurs as legal persons, which differ in their nature, obligations, and responsibilities. Most of Lilo Bazroba's traders are registered as limited liability companies (LTD). The National Agency of Public Registry at the Ministry of Justice of Georgia carries out the registration, issuing an identification number. Entrepreneurs may then also register online at the "taxpayer e-page,"[43] which "allows the taxpayer to manage his/her business remotely from home or/and without leaving the office" and enables him or her to "submit various applications; send email and track the evaluation processes of registered applications, as well as post his/her data or that of trustees; file tax returns and calculations; electronically issue invoices; electronically issue bills of lading; view his/her personal registration card at any given time [...]; make electronic payments; [and] receive information and messages pertaining to various issues."[44] The official revenues of an enterprise and the amount of taxes it must pay can be seen on this platform.

[41] Revenue Service "Registration of a Business": http://www.rs.ge/Default.aspx?sec_id=5356&lang=2.

[42] Revenue Service "Registration of a Business": http://www.rs.ge/Default.aspx?sec_id=5356&lang=2.

[43] Revenue Service "Registration": https://eservices.rs.ge/Registration.aspx.

[44] Revenue Service "The Taxpayer's Page": https://www.rs.ge/Default.aspx?sec_id=5362&lang=2.

There are several ways to handle accounting for official purposes. One way is to use a so-called cash register, a small machine that issues sales receipts and sends all necessary information to the revenue service. If a trader sells an item, he/she types in the price, and that is it. Another way is to organize all transfers through a bank account linked to the revenue service. This method makes less sense for small entrepreneurs, since they deal with very small sums. It is also possible to mix the two methods. Not organizing revenue issues through a bank account does not necessarily mean traders do not need a bank account for other purposes. Traders may use a "cash register" to do their accounting and use a bank account for managing their loans or private transfers.

BIG, which worked with personal sureties, guarantors, and obligations and interdependencies within creditor and expert networks, also used the revenue service's digital tools to check on its clients. It asked for a borrower's personal ID so as to access his/her account and have a look at the official numbers, which are supposed to be confidential. Similar official electronic databases, such as those recording the registration of citizens at a specific address (voters.cec.gov.ge, through which you can find out who lives with whom) and court records (napr.gov.ge) are also used (and misused) by private interest groups like credit agencies.

But the officially registered information does not always tell the whole truth. Many traders keep two sets of books, for example, and do not use the "cash register" to record all transactions, asking clients whether a deal can be done "without a receipt," avoiding its electronic registration. Undercover tax officials check, however, to see whether traders are using the "cash register" correctly. The penalty for not using the machine was between 200 and 500 lari, but it was nonetheless worth it to try. As noted in Chapter 2, most purchases abroad were paid for in cash anyway, which enabled traders to manipulate the records.

Although there are many ways to circumvent taxes and to trick state officials, successful traders like Levan met many of the official requirements. One reason for this was that it had become more difficult to escape state control, because of the formalization and digitalization of bureaucracy. The second reason was that since Saakashvili's reforms, Georgian government officials "had become clever" and "quite good at their jobs." Based on statistics, corruption was impressively low. Officials checked traders' documents frequently, Giorgi said, and those who did not follow the rules ran the risk of having to pay fines. Tax officials sometimes even came to the bazaar and went from stall to stall to conduct inspections and to check whether the amount of merchandise in the stalls corresponded to the records. When Mikheil, who worked as a lawyer, told a story about some Turkish who had tried to launder money, Irakli was more than astonished, saying: "No one can trick the state that way anymore!" The Turks had in fact been arrested. Having to pay fines arouses indignation, which may lead to turmoil, as happened in Batumi at the time of our joint business trip to China, but apparently the government usually wins out.

Legislation

Entrepreneurs do not necessarily always evade taxes and legal regulations on purpose. Some procedures, like the preliminary declaration of goods at customs, are, as mentioned, very complicated and need a great deal of expertise, which small traders simply do not have. Another major problem seems to be that many traders, especially those at the lower end of petty trade and street vending, are often unaware of current law. This is not very surprising, because laws in Georgia change all the time. During my research, tax regulations, laws on interest rates for loans, trading agreements, and so on, were introduced, adjusted, and changed. I was really confused by all these modifications, and I am afraid that the official rules and regulations cited in this chapter might be out of date by the time the book is published. Still, despite the confusion created by changes, trading is done within a framework created by local and international legislation. The challenges of the system that manifest themselves in everyday life are also those that shape the business sphere. Traders must adapt to rules or find other ways to cope with state regulations and government agencies, or they will have to face the consequences. This is most obvious a) in cases when traders come into conflict with legislation and are penalized, and b) when new laws or modifications of the legal code on the local and international level impact trading conditions and opportunities.

The official website of the Georgian Revenue Service gives very detailed information on types and rates of taxes, how to register a business, how to manage clearance, and other formal procedures in relation to business. It links this information to the related legislation, which can be checked online on a government webpage that even provides a hotline.[45] This transparency and accessibility has been one of the results

[45] Legislative Herald of Georgia: https://matsne.gov.ge/en; Supreme Court of Georgia "Legislation": http://www.supremecourt.ge/legislation/.

of Saakashvili's reforms and—if one believes reports about the previous Shevardnadze system—has turned Georgia upside down. After considering developments since the 1990s, I therefore turn below to the effects and limitations of Saakashvili's reforms and, finally, report on the attitudes of traders and of Georgians in general to the legal system, which determine their behavior. To understand Georgians' assessments of the current legal system and bureaucracy, it is important to contextualize these historically, because it is comparison with the past that influences perceptions today.

From Shevardnadze to the Rose Revolution

In Shevardnadze's time, according to Christophe (2005, cf. Zuev & Habeck, 2019), Di Puppo (2004), and my Georgian friends, complying with tax regulations was an almost impossible task: The state bureaucracy was a machine purposely producing contradiction and uncertainty and forcing citizens into corruption, bribery, and informal agreements with tax officers. As noted by Christophe, the Georgian tax code has been corrected and supplemented a 100-fold since its implementation in 1997. Just one paragraph of a few lines has been changed twenty-three times. This obsession with details clashed with a reality in which tax revenue was consistently less than 10% of GNP (according to Christophe) or 14% (according to Di Puppo), the lowest level of all CIS countries (Di Puppo, 2004). Christophe reports that most registered taxpayers had never filed any tax declaration, and that the rules concerning VAT (value-added tax), which accounted for 40% of total tax revenue, were particularly contradictory and confusing. Christophe and Di Puppo both agree that this was a consciously maintained system, aimed at producing space for interpretation, bribery, clientelism, and the exercise of power in general (Christophe, 2005: 45; Di Puppo, 2004):

> The drafting of opaque und unrealistic regulations in several areas of legislation constitutes a means of extracting resources through bribery and of potential state control of all economic activities. In this sense, corruption as an informal institution of governance does not appear to undermine the state's capacity to secure compliance and may in fact actually help to enhance it. Hence in some circumstances, corruption may fall under the compliance strategies developed by the state. Laws and regulations are

> designed in such a way that their violation is encouraged. (Di Puppo, 2004: 50)

A small entrepreneur questioned by Christophe put the mechanism of this system in a nutshell by explaining that, while the state created uncertainty in regard to the governing legal system and forced individuals into informal agreements, the side effect of all this was that this forced involvement in the corrupt system prevented everyone from opposing state institutions, which would then have used the law to persecute the accusers (Christophe, 2005: 43).

Corruption thus became normal and simply mirrored the actions of the political leadership. Di Puppo reasons that individuals with a criminal background led the 1992 coup that brought Shevardnadze to power. These individuals and their allies "developed an interest in a formal restoration of law and order, hoping to stabilize their criminal accumulation and redistribution of resources by means of a semblance of order" (Di Puppo, 2004: 49), which in fact was a system of extortion. It was to this system and the associated practice of blackmail that Saakashvili's reforms aimed to put an end (Di Puppo, 2004; Light, 2014).

Saakashvili's reforms, in general, have been assessed positively, not least by the World Bank (2012). Between 2004 and 2007 Georgia adapted its reforms to the demands of the World Bank's "Ease of Doing Business Index," and it has since been labelled a "world's top reformer" (Di Puppo, 2013). In 2017, the Georgian economy was ranked fourth on the list. According to this assessment, starting a business was easier only in New Zealand, Canada, and Hong Kong.[46] Di Puppo described Georgia's quick and visible reforms as an encompassing agenda:

> The government has framed the fight against corruption both into a state-building project and the promotion of economic liberalism. Anti-corruption reforms are closely associated with the country's ambition to strengthen its statehood and introduce a new mentality in the public administration through a new generation of non-corrupt young officials. Furthermore, a reform agenda that has been described by observers as being inspired by an economic libertarian ideology drives reforms that aim at downsizing the state administration through the abolition of

[46] The World Bank "Doing Business": http://www.doingbusiness.org/rankings.

> non-efficient agencies instead of their restructuring. (Di Puppo, 2013: 111)

As a rule, I would say, Georgians are proud of the changes that have taken place and—compared to other post-Soviet countries (or China)—perceive themselves and their governmental elites as modern, Western, and legally democratic. Even after Saakashvili left office, his reforms and the ideas attached to them persist. My Armenian friends (before the Velvet Revolution) usually looked at Georgia with admiration and a little envy, complaining that Armenia had not been able to implement similar reforms and still struggles with a high level of corruption.

However, not all segments of Georgian society took full advantage of the reforms' benefits, for example, the measures and the simplification of the tax code described above. Some new laws were perceived as restrictive, and others as (still) too complicated. Because the rules were (still) too difficult to understand and follow (and changing all the time), Lilo Bazroba's administration provided traders with assistance from experts to improve their accounting practices. Knowledge about legal rules was still often transmitted by word of mouth, which sometimes seemed to be more gossip than information. Thus, for example, there was a heated debate during my fieldwork concerning a new law (Order 73) that declared that the taxes on an item should remain the same, even though the value of the item might change over time. The traders discussed what this would mean, and uncertainty about formal rules in general, rooted in mistrust of the state and irritation at having to adapt to an imposed framework, immediately led to a search for loopholes.

Law Versus Alternatives

Mikheil—who was, as has been noted, a lawyer—had just founded a company offering "legal assistance to whoever needs it," and over coffee with Zviad and Irakli, he spoke to us of his plans, which were linked to Lilo Bazroba. Up to then, he had dealt mostly with divorce cases, but what he really wanted to do was to pursue a new business idea, providing legal insurance in Georgia. Insurance was not very popular in Georgia, he said, so he needed first of all to convince people of its desirability. Our conversation sheds light on the attitude of many Georgians to the law. Mikheil said:

I will offer legal insurance for 30 lari per month. This is really cheap. If an incident suddenly comes up, and if people then need a lawyer, it is much more expensive. But people in Georgia do not want to pay for something that is not a problem at the moment, right now. I tell them that it is going to be very expensive once there is a problem. But they say, "Why should I pay if there is no problem?" People do not understand.

To develop his business ideas, Mikheil used examples from the United States and Germany. As a first step, he wanted to approach traders from Lilo Bazroba. When I asked him how he planned to do so, he told me that he would first distribute flyers and then discuss the details of legal insurance with anyone who expressed an interest. Mikheil had also come up with a strategy that reminded me the methods of the credit agency BIG. He was planning to enter into contracts with about five people who would work for him: "This is not going to be very time-consuming or regular work. Their job is going to be to find clients—through their own networks, but also by advertising or something like that. If they can find a client, they will get the first monthly payment." The client would thereafter be expected to pay the monthly premium to Mikheil.

Much Georgian legislation, according to Mikheil, has been taken from U.S. legislation, and other parts from the German law code. One problem, he said, however, was that Georgian law changed very frequently:

Mikheil: Every government does what is good for it, and they do whatever they like.

Susanne: How can you get to know about these changes?

Mikheil: You can check them online. They have a webpage. They also print books. Many, many books and very often. But they do not change the whole law. Just short paragraphs.

Susanne: And what happens if a trader does not know about the changes, for example, and does something wrong?

Mikheil: The first time, the officials will just give him a warning. They will give him a chance to fix the problem within a certain number of days. Of course, if someone does something wrong for years and then says that he did not know, that is too late. They won't believe him.

Susanne: How do they check whether traders act according to the law? Do they send the police?

Mikheil: No, it's mostly about taxes. The tax police are notified and check.

The changes in the legal code were indeed a problem. Every time I went to Georgia, I was told about such changes, which sometimes had positive effects, like the reduction in taxes for businesses with an annual sales volume of less than 100,000 lari, but often caused perplexity, like the announcement that all businesses soon had to be re-registered, which was simply impossible, because the lines for registration were too long and not everyone could make it by the deadline.

Even if people tried to adapt to new laws, they were not always sure what was expected of them. A law concerning the display of cigarettes in public, for example, caused many arguments in shops. While some parties held that the law said that cigarettes should not be visible from outside the shop, others believed cigarettes had to be hidden completely, so some shopkeepers covered them with mats or tablecloths. This may seem odd, but it reflects a sense of helplessness and the conviction that the state can push through "any stupid order."

Lawyers can function as middlemen between citizens and the state, explaining the rules and providing clear guidance. When I asked how someone could check a lawyer's quality, Mikheil answered that he could check the lawyer's education or CV and see how many cases he had won. Zviad was not convinced. Like many Georgians I talked to, he did not trust the Georgian government and legal system—not even after the Rose Revolution and the reforms that followed.

There were, in fact, several scandals during my fieldwork, one of which occurred during the campaigning for Georgia's parliamentary elections in October 2013. It concerned abuses in Georgian prisons. Videos of beatings and torture of prisoners, circulated on social media, leading to public protests and the electoral victory of the opposition party, the Georgian Dream coalition, led by the billionaire Bidzina Ivanishvili (Light, 2014). My roommate Natia was interested in a similar scandalous story about a young woman who had been accused of murder, while the real murderer had the protection of a rich and influential family. The young woman spent several years in prison and had been released only recently. This young woman was planning to become a lawyer to put an end to such misinterpretations and manipulations of the law, Natia told me. "The Georgian Dream's victory" in 2013, according to Light, "reflected widespread resentment of authoritarian features of Saakashvili's rule, including perceived official impunity, politicization of law enforcement and criminal justice, extra-judicial punishment and coercion, and draconian sentencing policies that arguably amount to "governing through crime (Light, 2014: preprint)".

Common practices of manipulating court decisions in the Caucasus, as I witnessed myself, traditionally include private agreements among the parties in conflict, mediation by community members, the performance of rituals, and the exchange of gifts and different kinds of payments. When a car hit the younger brother of an Armenian friend of mine in Yerevan, the driver slaughtered an animal for the family of the victim, and negotiations about how much the driver should pay in order not to be taken to court commenced with acceptance of this gift. There were similar stories in Georgia. When a young man was killed by a drunk driver, the latter's family offered the family of the victim a flat as compensation, for example, and the case was shelved, the two families thereafter living side by side.

In a classic anthropological study of legal pluralism, in the tradition of Gluckman (1955, 1965) and Bohannan (1957), Stéphane Voell (2015) reports on other such cases involving traditional law and informal agreements. Even in Svan communities, which are famous for their traditional legal practices, including blood feuds and oaths (Grigolia, 1939), these do not replace official law enforcement:

> Since 2004 the government of President Mikheil Saakashvili [has] made important changes, especially in law enforcement and the juridical systems. The police are in control in Kvemo Kartli and infractions of the law are generally pursued according to official rules. At this local level, corruption is not possible and the local population accepts the police and its work. (Voell, 2015: 100)

In 2018, my friend and colleague Ketevan asked me to accompany her to the courthouse, where she had to sign a document confirming her role as a witness in a trial. When I agreed to come with her, I had already accepted the fact that this affair would keep us busy for the rest of the day. But Ketevan signed the document and got an ID with which she could register online to follow the stages of the trial and to check whether her documents had been forwarded, and we left after twenty minutes. Ketevan, who had guessed what I was thinking, joked that this was a test of friendship, confirming that dealing with bureaucracy is usually associated with long lines and unpleasant procedures. Even she seemed surprised about the smoothness of the procedure in this case. On the way back to the city center, her husband, who came with us, proudly asked me whether justice worked as well in Germany. Ketevan and her husband opined that on "this level, justice really works well and provides good services to Georgian citizens."

However, this does not mean "that any formal trial in court results in the full 'resolution' of a problem" (Voell, 2015). According to Voell, especially in the context of homicide, the formal legal framework is respected, but not "considered sufficient from a moral point of view" (109). Especially in a small community, where people have to continue living side by side, out-of-court arrangements are necessary for the sake of peace and order: "In the end, some form of reconciliation will have to take place. The parties have to be brought together again and maybe they will even seal their reconciliation with god-parenthood. An oath on the icon and a large banquet ... will probably take place to conclude [the matter]" (Voell, 2015: 108).

In other cases, traditional law and informal legal practices are used in Georgia to mark identity and to claim access to land and property (Voell et al., 2014). Such incidents, which challenge the official code of law, as well as the scandals mentioned above, are discussed in the media and cause many conflicts and a great deal of indignation. Many citizens, I deduced from my conversations, feel that their rights are being threatened or that there is a lack, not of legislation, but of rights. The state, no matter whether headed by Shevardnadze, Saakashvili, or Ivanishvili, is perceived as playing an ambiguous role. It is alternately accused of incompetence, corruption, and despotism, which is why it seems preferable to resolve problems oneself.

During our conversation with Mikheil, Zviad expressed his doubts about whether going to court makes sense, stating, "I know that most of the cases in Georgia are won by prosecutors." As a lawyer, Mikheil did not agree with Zviad. He agreed that Zviad's claim was true for criminal law, but he was sure that things are "different with civil law," giving traders a chance to win. This fits with Voell's (2015) finding that official law is usually accepted, and that it is usually only questioned—or perceived as insufficient—in situations of "moral breakdown," meaning situations that threaten the social order, peaceful coexistence within the community, and basic sociocultural values. Homicide is the ultimate example of this. One way to deal with legal problems in Georgia is to hire someone like Mikheil, but whereas such lawyers act as intermediaries between individuals and the state, respected elders or other socially high-ranking individuals commonly mediate extra-legal arrangements between community members.

Law's Impact on Trade

Legislation on both the local and national levels obviously shapes trading. Vendors and traders have been driven from the streets, marketplaces have been closed or replaced because they did not meet legal standards, and visa issues and transnational trading agreements restrict the mobility of traders and their business opportunities. New legislation immediately affects businesses and economic practices (see, e.g., Ngo & Hung, 2018). Such changes had a very visible effect on the Rustavi car market, which can serve here as a case study shedding light on the broader impact of legislation on small-scale trade.

The Rustavi car market (*rustavis avṭobazroba*, რუსთავის ავტობაზრობა) had started to function just a few years earlier, towards the end of the Saakashvili era, Tamta, who lived nearby, told me. Before that there had been an auto racetrack there, which, Tamta concluded, had led to the development of everything related to cars: the car market, a car registration center, and a driving school. My Armenian colleague Hamlet Melkumyan had bought his car in Rustavi right at the very start of all this, from a person who "was not a professional trader but just someone who wanted to get rid of his old car and make some money." Hamlet did all the paperwork in the official registration building, which even then was located next to the informal or semi-formal marketplace.

The first things one sees when entering Rustavi today are Soviet housing blocks and the car market area, located on the gently sloping terrain of the barren landscape on the outskirts of the city. The market area is huge. It is structured by different terrace levels and service buildings, all of which are overlooked by the official car registration building, where one can register a car, pay the transfer taxes, get license plates, take driving lessons, get a driver's license, and go through all the formal processes linked to buying, selling, and driving cars. In one location, motor and serial numbers and so on are checked after every completed deal. Many of the formal procedures are done online and do not require much face-to-face interaction. Inside the official building at the upper end of the market, there are computer terminals where customers can type in the model year and engine volume of any car. The transfer fee is then automatically calculated by the computer. I entered a few numbers to check the system, and it seemed quite simple. A car buyer can also choose a license plate number, then pay for the plates at a bank counter a few steps further on, and finally pick up the license plates at one of the service windows. Although the car business involves many informal practices, the formal requirements are strict.

Rustavi is the largest second-hand car market in the Caucasus. The cars that are sold here usually originate in Europe, Japan, or the United States. During the week the market is usually almost empty. The main business takes place on weekends. But the car business had slowed down, because of new regulations recently introduced in many countries in the region. Formerly, many of the Rustavi car market's customers had come from countries like Azerbaijan, Armenia, and Iran, even from Central Asia, I was told. Laws restricting the sale of second-hand and old cars in all these countries naturally affected the Rustavi marketplace. Several years ago, the father of one of Zviad's friends brought cars from Germany regularly. He stopped doing so because it was not profitable anymore. According to this trader, the reason was a law passed in Azerbaijan that prohibited the buying and driving of cars produced before 2005.[47] As a result, demand dropped significantly.

At the time of my research trip in 2017, the introduction of similar laws was also planned in Georgia, which, of course, initiated a major debate that took place in every taxi and marketplace. A law had already been launched earlier that restricted the use of right-side steering wheels in the taxi business. As usual, many of my interlocutors alleged that the state was not worried about the safety of its citizens but had other reasons for introducing new regulations. "The government argued that the number of cars in Tbilisi should be reduced," according to Zviad, who suspected that there were economic and political reasons for the decision, like trading agreements with Germany or Europe. Right or wrong, these conjectures reflected the general attitude and lack of trust in the government. At the same time, people said, "things are not as bad as they seem." Enforcement of the new regulations was not strict. "Everyone in Tbilisi knows this law, but no one cares," a friend said. "The police do nothing. The government

[47] I heard about this law for the first time through a radio broadcast in a cab in Bishkek in 2013. I had a short conversation about it with the taxi driver, who commented that it would lead to a lot of changes. Apparently, he was right.

said that it is allowed to drive Japanese cars that were bought before the law was passed. But people still buy Japanese cars and drive them. Even now, after the law was passed. Nobody cares, not even the police."

Still, regulations are not entirely ignored. Government agencies enforce most of them, and the level of corruption among officials is low compared to that in other post-Soviet countries. Lilo, on the face of it, seems a chaotic, informal bazaar, but comparing its administration and the practices of its businessmen with administrative structures and practices in Central Asian bazaars like Dordoj, however, one notes a huge difference. The same is true if we compare the border practices of traders shuttling between China and Russia (Holzlehner, 2014; Humphrey, 2018a) or within Central Asia (Turaeva, 2014) with the practices of the group of traders I travelled with. The picture was different before the Rose Revolution, of course, when Caucasians in general, and Caucasian businessmen in particular, were associated with mafia-like structures, which flourished in the early 1990s (see Chapter 3). But those chaotic times are over.

Today, national and international laws frame the whole trading system. On the one hand, laws restrict traders' mobility and the import and export of specific goods, as the example of the used-car business shows; on the other hand, other laws promote specific trading niches, for example in the framework of the free trade agreement between China and Georgia, established in 2018. Laws, regulations, and agreements create interdependencies, markets, demands, possibilities, cooperation, and competition, to which traders must adapt. Thus, to some degree, very much as Polanyi would predict, the state creates—or shapes—the market.

Assessments of the State

In every section of this book, whenever I am talking about personal relationships, the topic of trust and mistrust is implicitly addressed. In this section, by contrast, I am going to talk about the traders' attitudes, their trust and mistrust, of the state as a formal institution. How do traders assess the state and its role in the context of business? How does this assessment impact traders' behavior? And what is the relationship between the target group's sociocultural values, described in previous chapters, business, and state institutions?

In her introduction to *Trust and Mistrust in the Economy of the China-Russia Borderlands*, Humphrey (2018a) points to a corpus of writings that discuss the relationship between trust and political forms. Usually, this literature focuses on democracy, good governance, perceived political freedom, public safety, and economic performance. According to Humphrey:

> many authors see general public trust as a consequence, understood as the outcome of either a civic culture with high levels of shared customs, values, and beliefs that promote institutional and interpersonal trust (Hosking, 2010; Putnam, 1993), promotion by voluntary associations (Putnam, 2000), or the public expectation that democratic institutions will function effectively (see discussion in Mishler & Rose, 2005) (2018a: 11).

Conventional arguments about democracy, according to Rosanvallon (2008), furthermore, "conflate questions of legitimacy" with "questions of trust," while "people's distrust gives rise to positive attempts to impose controls on the political processes carried out in their name" (Humphrey, 2018a: 11). However, a general lack of trust is perceived as a problem, the reason for or the outcome of crisis (Corsín Jiménez, 2011). As for Simmel (1992) and Giddens (1990), for Habermas (1981) a general atmosphere of trust is the basis of the functioning of society—of societal understanding and consensus, which Habermas took as prerequisites for modernity (see Mühlfried, 2019: 10–11). It is a widespread assumption, which mirrors in Fukuyama's (1995) conclusion that while so-called high-trust societies are characterized by political and economic stability, "low-trust societies" are not.

In the context of the economy, Humphrey refers to Dasgupta (1988), saying that here "trust rests on the existence of a background agency, usually the state, that reliably enforces contracts and provides credible and impartial punishment for errant behaviour" (Humphrey, 2018a: 11). If the state fails to create this trust, according to this analysis, forms of interpersonal trust like those that I have described earlier replace it.

This short summary points to a much more complicated and general debate on the possible relationships (a) between the economy and state institutions and regulations and (b) between formal and informal institutions and practices. Here, I will simply address the topics of trust and mistrust in and the assessment of state institutions. As mentioned earlier, post-Soviet societies, and Caucasian societies in particular, are usually characterized as societies with low levels of "social trust." This is also true of China. Thus there seems to be a cross-local particularity, one that is sometimes explained by the historical experience of having had to deal with an authoritarian regime:

> In both China and Russia, a consequence of decades of Party grandiloquence that is clearly contradicted by the evidence of one's eyes has been not only popular cynicism and lack of trust in the government, but also indeed the desire to attempt to penetrate to other people's true thoughts, to "tear off the masks" (Fitzpatrick, 2005). (Humphrey, 2018a: 15)

In China, according to Steinmüller (2016), people invoke the expression *biao li bu yi* (the outside and the inside are not the same), while in Armenia and Georgia, I came across phrases like "people will never tell you what is going on in their kitchen" and "you should close the curtains, because everyone is going to watch you" (see Fehlings, 2010).

In Armenia and Georgia, locals explained such suggestions to me in terms of the experience of Soviet surveillance, which was feared and had left marks, but also in terms of a cultural attitude rooted in social constellations that are based on and produce social control over the members of one's kinship group, neighborhood, and community (Fehlings, 2010, 2014, 2015). The two explanations both suggest that before, during, and since Soviet times, mistrust has been perceived as a positive, logical, and necessary strategie, the best way to get along in the region's economic, sociopolitical, and sociocultural contexts (cf. Mühlfried, 2019; Tikhomirov, 2017). Thus there is good reason to believe that, as Humphrey says, "discourses of truth and sincerity of course predated the opacity of the socialist and post-socialist governments," and that "they can be seen as age old cultural-philosophical resources for reflection" (2018a: 15).

The Soviet state was clearly not trusted, and its breakdown caused even more mistrust in state institutions. Post-Soviet citizens witnessed the complete decay, not only of the political and economic system, but also of ideals, hopes, moral norms, and the physical environment, which literally fell to pieces.[48] The existence of different and competing value systems and state ideologies in parallel described in Chapter 3 is a result of this turbulent history and both causes and reflects friction within

[48] The ruins of Soviet factories and infrastructure, which are part of the post-Soviet landscape, are ever-present symbols of the negative development of urban space and industries.

society. Meanwhile, social goods that had been supplied by the state for decades, such as free housing, heating, electricity, healthcare, and education, have been turned over to the private sector since the breakup of the Soviet Union. Although privatization turned inhabitants into homeowners, it also entailed the state's withdrawal from many responsibilities. Some citizens, used to the Soviet system, felt abandoned (Fehlings, 2014; Mandel & Humphrey, 2002).

Since 2008 I have listened to the same discussions again and again in the Caucasus (Fehlings, 2012, 2014): On the one hand, (a) many citizens complain about the current lack of state support, contrasted with the Soviet system (see Fehlings, 2012, 2014, 2016), as is nicely summarized by Humphrey, who notes: "the evaporation of high socialist ideals—which, it is generally thought, earlier generations believed in—was followed by a dominant discourse of decline, in which people situate themselves, one way or another, in an unprincipled world" (2018a: 15). This "unprincipled world" is sometimes referred to as ***dikij kapitalizm*** ("wild capitalism", дикий капитализм). My Armenian colleague Harutyun Marutyan, who, as he made clear in conversations with me, does not approve of the latest social and economic developments in his country, defines (wild) capitalism as "an insatiable desire for the accumulation of money and property at any cost... through malpractice (bribery, embezzlement of state property under the protection of high officials or criminal cartels) or in the context of—in the broadest sense—trade" (2007: 13).[49] Wild capitalism was described to me as ruthless and brutal and "mistrust, and the difficulty of trusting or being trustworthy, are part of this" (Humphrey, 2018a: 15).

However, (b) there seems no doubt that Soviet rule was felt as an occupation. Post-Soviet nationalism is widespread and openly demonstrated in all three South Caucasian republics. In Tbilisi, the Historical Museum has an exhibition on "Soviet Occupation," and all three republics celebrate their independence with many national holidays, which offer an opportunity to express pride in national history (excluding the Soviet part) and identity and to dance national dances, wear national costumes, sing national songs, and remember national traditions (Fehlings, 2017). Especially in the context of the current ethnic conflicts and wars, national

[49] Translation from Russian by the author.

belonging is a major theme, linked to language, religion, and other spheres that are part of everyone's everyday life.

However, opinions on how the nation should be ruled differ, and are reflected in (c) debates about possible models of political leadership. Some people apparently want a strong, prominent leader—a philosopher king of sorts who treats his people justly and enjoys their trust—but the younger generation especially would prefer Western-style democracy and want to get rid of the old guard and eliminate corrupt elites and cliques. This tendency has been obvious in many demonstrations that have taken place in Yerevan and Tbilisi in recent years, seeking to negotiate the role of the state and its rulers. This was the case during the Georgian Rose Revolution in 2003, the Velvet Revolution in Armenia in 2018, and the protests against corrupt leadership in Tbilisi in 2019. The burning questions are always whether citizens' expectations are being met, and whether government regulations and individual freedom are in balance.

Traders seem to adopt a pragmatic stance. Most told us that they got no or little support from state institutions in the sense of financial benefits. However, the Georgian government had in fact implemented several significant reforms aimed at turning Georgia into an attractive place for business in general. These reforms included a reduction of state intervention in business affairs and simplification of bureaucratic processes. Traders have no doubt benefited from these changes, but those I talked to were critical of the government, feeling that it should focus more than it does currently on keeping order and maintaining infrastructure, creating a framework within which capitalism can develop to best advantage.

Traders like Ramaz and Giorgi were convinced that they could do very well without any state structure. Paying taxes or customs charges was perceived as an imposition. Why, Ramaz argued, should the state have any right to profit from a deal negotiated between two individuals? Business is a face-to-face affair! Levan, Ramaz, and Giorgi all praised the Chinese government, which, according to them, did not interfere in personal matters. States produce conflicts, embargos, and laws restricting trade, Lena said. This attitude is comprehensible if one considers that the traders' activity creates its own business culture. Traders working in a transnational environment must comply with certain regulations like customs laws, visa regimes, and border procedures. But trading is based on personal relationships, business networks, codes of honor, and trust in individuals, and not on some "background agency, usually the state, that reliably enforces contracts and provides credible and impartial punishment for errant behaviour" (Dasgupta, 1988; Humphrey, 2018b).

This fits with the conclusion reached by Mars and Altman, who argue the opposite proposition, contradicting many explanations of why social networks are important in post-Soviet spaces and in Georgia in particular. Instead of saying that the absence of state institutions is compensated for by personal networks, they say that social networks leave no room for state interference:

> In this kind of "honour and shame" society where peer approval is so important hierarchical official relations are resented and resisted and are the source of perpetual conflict. The individual Georgian sees honour accruing to families and sees families linked by common honour. In such a context there is little role for the state or for any centrally-organized hierarchy. Relationships need always to be personalized and abstraction has no place. (1983: 549)

This may explain why interaction with state agencies is avoided and personal ties are stressed, transferring the values applied to family to relationships in the context of business (cf. e.g., Chapters 2 and 3 on male bonding and relationships between traders, and this chapter on the relationship between traders and credit experts).

The problematic aspect of the state is that it is perceived as alien—no matter whether it is represented by corrupt or less corrupt elites or an impersonal bureaucracy. "Anyhow, you do not know the truth," Lena said. "When I was a child, I was told that Stalin was the best person on earth, and today, they tell you that he was bad." In *Custom and Justice in the Caucasus: The Georgian Highlanders* (1939), Alexander Grigolia describes the legal codes of the Svans and other ethnic groups in the Caucasus, observing that:

> Theft committed outside the group was regarded as neither a crime nor a delict, but on the contrary was viewed as an accomplishment of courage and bravery, elevating the culprit in social prestige and creating even gradations in distinction, according to the danger involved and the success of the accomplishment, the procedure resembling in some ways the coups of the American Indians. Among Georgians of Megrelia, in time past, a young man had difficulties in getting a wife if he had not stolen at least one horse. There were various and numerous tales of gallant and cunning

> thieves who outwitted their pursuers and escaped safely with their spoil, and who had the admiration of the people. (Grigolia, 1939: 153)

Although it might be argued that Grigolia is reporting historical evidence and/or reproducing Pushkin's, Lermontov's, and Tolstoy's romantic clichés[50] about the savage margins of the Russian empire, the essence of this account still has some relevance and truth. In the Caucasus, values apply only to one's own community or network (Fehlings, 2010, 2014, 2015) and cease to be relevant in interactions with strangers.

Such moral relativism has been described by many anthropologists, including Evans-Pritchard with reference to the Azande (Evans-Pritchard, 1937). "Moral judgements have normative force relative to a particular group of persons or epistemic circumstances" (Miller, 2016: 84). If honesty, mutual support, and trust have moral importance *within* a community, the opposite may still be acceptable or even honorable in interactions with strangers—and since Soviet times, the state has been perceived as a stranger, an entity outside of the community, characterized by interpersonal relationships. Thus, not paying taxes or not meeting obligations to formal institutions like banks, is generally not perceived as immoral. On the contrary, as noted in Chapter 2 and Chapter 3, "being a 'močaliče' (მოჩალიჩე) (an 'apt, cunning and resilient' person, who 'is able to find an easy path to success and for acquiring material or other goods while circumventing the formal rules') is highly valued in Georgian society" and "rule-breaking is frequently encouraged as a display of 'courage' or 'manhood'" (Kupatadze, 2009: 12).

Traders who stick to these kinds of values have specific skills with which to navigate the small-scale trade sector. The same values and skills produce a negative attitude to the state. Traders who are good at negotiating and communicating in personal interactions are not necessarily good at handling impersonal bureaucratic procedures. This is why many of the businesses described in this book do not formalize—and grow.

[50] Examples include Pushkin's poem "Captive of the Caucasus" (1820–21), Lermontov's novel "A Hero of Our Time" (1839), and Tolstoy's war stories "The Cossacks" (1862) and "Hadji Murat" (1896–1904).

Conclusion

Formal institutions like banks, credit agencies, customs, tax agencies, and other legal entities play an important role in traders' lives. Since the reforms after the Rose Revolution, these institutions have been shaped by measures fostering formalization, which has been implemented partly through attempts at digitalization. Traders cannot escape these formal structures. However, they have different ways to deal with them and to "navigate" the system. Instead of fully adjusting to the impersonal machine of a Weberian bureaucracy, traders use intermediaries to bridge the gap between their own needs and capacities and formal requirements. This is not an allusion to illegal practices such as bribing state officials or engaging in blackmail. It simply means that there are interim solutions. Thus, for example, if traders find themselves on a bank's blacklist, lacking a good credit record, they turn to credit agencies, which operate according to legal standards but are more flexible because they negotiate with traders, combine legal contracts with personal obligations, and invest more time and patience in building long-term relationships that become the basis for agreements. The most important component of the interaction is face-to-face contact, through which a relationship is established. This relationship, although it is a business contact, is linked to concepts like trust, honor, and friendship, the importance of which in Georgian society has been extensively discussed.

Micro-finance firms like cargo companies and lawyers function like plug adapters for different ports. On one end, they are compatible with the formal state apparatus; on the other, they are compatible with individual traders. On one side, they sign written contracts and fill out forms; on the other side, they negotiate and shake hands (Fig. 4.1).

As a country, Georgia performs a similar plug-adapter function between different foreign countries, transforming illegal or informal exports and imports into unproblematic merchandise by (legally) providing formal documentation. Whether this documentation, which is obviously used to circumvent embargos, is accepted by foreign customs officials depends on their flexibility.

Caucasian traders' attitudes to bureaucracy and state agencies are mirrored by their attitudes to the local legal system. Looking at the development of the legal system and its functioning in practice since the early 1990s reveals huge transformations. Under Shevardnadze it was perceived as corrupt and contradictory, but the post-reform system has provoked

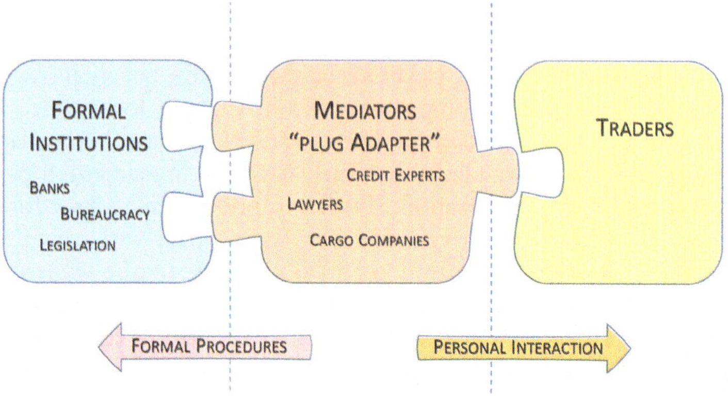

Fig. 4.1 The function of middlemen mediating between formal state institutions and individual traders

many visible changes that are generally described as progress for neutral justice. Especially in the domain of civil law, juridical procedures usually follow the written code and are executed according to transparent rules set out in documents accessible to everyone. However, the problem of mistrust has not been entirely resolved. The state is still suspected of not applying the rules to everyone in the same way. Furthermore, scandals that have shocked the public in recent years have been widely discussed in the media. Consequently, the law and moral justice are not always perceived as on the same level. Sometimes, this means that legal punishment is regarded by citizens as being too hard or too soft—in any case, as unfair. In such situations, individuals seek alternative, additional, and parallel solutions, which often have a pragmatic basis. Again, this includes mediation between state bodies and individuals, between formal procedures and informal agreements, and between different perspectives on what is right and wrong.

As a rule, people—and this is also true of Caucasian traders in particular—expect the state to provide them with good living (and business) conditions. At the same time, their connection to the state, which is an impersonal one, is shaped by caution. It is not perceived as a bilateral relationship of mutual obligations. Especially in the case of international trade, traders operate in spheres where day-to-day business is organized outside of state control and protection. Traders thus experience the state as a disruptive element, because it only becomes tangible in the form of restrictions and obstacles, such as at border posts, or in the form of payments. On the one hand, the state's problem is that it is a formal institution, and traders prefer face-to-face communication. Only face-to-face communication is linked to obligation. On the other hand, face-to-face communication with state officials is condemned, since it is easily associated with corruption. Nobody—at least as far as I understood from my interlocutors—wants to go back to the Shevardnadze system, when a small elite extorted money from the rest. The challenge is to find a balance and the fine line between formality and informality.

Small-scale trade is often under pressure because it evades state regulation. Many small businesses are only practicable and profitable if they do not have to meet certain requirements and do not lose part of their profits to taxes. But they have the same or a worse problem if there is chaos and they are blackmailed and protection bribes are extorted from them. The solutions I have described above can be perceived as a compromise between the nature of the bazaar and petty trade and legal institutions, between informally and formally structured spheres. At least in the contexts I have described, such compromises guarantee some flexibility, while allowing for no major violations of regulations, whether on the side of the traders or that of officialdom.

References

Aivazishvili-Gehne, N. (2015). *Staatsbürgerschaft an der Grenze: Das Beispiel der georgischsprachigen Ingiloer in Aserbaidschan* (PhD). Martin-Luther-Universität Halle-Wittenberg, Halle an der Saale.

Ardener, S., & Burman, S. (Eds.). (1996). *Money-Go-Rounds: The Importance of Rotating Savings and Credit Associations for Women*. Berg.

Augsburg, B., De Haas, R., Harmgart, H., & Meghir, C. (2014). *The Impacts of Microcredit: Evidence from Bosnia and Herzegovina* (NBER Working Paper, No. 18538).

Balibar, É. (2002). *Politics and the Other Scene*. Verso.

Bateman, M. (2014). The Rise and Fall of Muhammad Yunus and the Microcredit Model. *International Development Studies Working Paper Series, 1.*

Bateman, M., Blankenburg, S., & Kozul-Wright, R. (Eds.). (2019). *The Rise and Fall of Global Microcredit: Development*. Routledge.

Bateman, M., & Chang, H.-J. (2012). Microfinance and the Illusion of Development: From Hubris to Nemesis in Thirty Years. *World Social and Economic Review, 1.*

Baud, M., & Schendel, W. v. (1997). Toward a Comparative History of Borderlands. *Journal of World History*, *8*(2), 211–242.

Beyer, J. (2016). *The Force of Custom. Law and the Ordering of Everyday Life in Kyrgyzstan*. University of Pittsburgh Press.

Bohannon, P. (1957). Justice and Judgment among the Tiv. Routledge.

Bouchard, M. (2011). The State of the Study of the State of Anthropology. *Reviews in Anthropology, 40*, 183–209.

Breman, J. (2009). Myth of the Global Safety Net. *New Left Review, 59*.

Christophe, B. (2005). Kultur der Korruption? Anmerkungen zur politischen Ordnung in Georgien. In B. Schröder (Ed.), *Georgien: Gesellschaft und Religion an der Schwelle Europas* (pp. 33–46). Röhrig Universitätsverlag.

Conde, J., & Gattini, L. (2019). Financing in Georgia: Small and Medium Enterprises and the Private Sector. *Economics—Regional Studies*: European Investment Bank.

Corsín Jiménez, A. (2011). Trust in Anthropology. *Anthropological Theory, 11*(2), 177–196.

Dasgupta, P. (1988). Trust as a Commodity. In D. Gambetta (Ed.), *Trust: Making and Breaking Cooperative Relations* (pp. 49–73). Wiley-Blackwell.

Di Puppo, L. (2004). Corruption as an Instrument of State Control in Georgia. *Berliner Osteuropa-Info, 21*, 47–54.

Di Puppo, L. (2013). The Construction of Success in Anticorruption Activity in Georgia. *East European Politics, 30*, 105–122.

Dragadze, T. (2016). *Rural Families in Soviet Georgia: A Case Study in Ratcha Province*. London & New York: Routledge.

Durst, J. (2015). Juggling with Debts, Moneylenders and Local Petty Monarchs: Banking the Unbanked in 'Shanty-Villages' in Hungary. *Review of Sociology, 25*(4), 30–57.

Eradze, I. (2021). Imbalanced Foreign Trade, Debt, and Investment in Developing Countries: The Case of Georgia. *E-paper of the Heinrich Böll Stiftung*. https://eu.boell.org/en/2021/06/16/imbalanced-foreign-trade-debt-and-investment-developing-countries-case-georgia

Evans-Pritchard, E. E. (1937). *Witchcraft, Oracles And Magic Among The Azande*. Oxford University Press.

Fehlings, S. (2010). The Private and the Public Spheres in Yerevan, as observed from an Anthropologist from abroad. In Armenian Academy of Sciences (Ed.), *Armenian Popular Culture: Tradition and Modernity in Armenian Culture* (Vol. XV, pp. 108–118). Gitutyun pub.

Fehlings, S. (2012). Auf der Suche nach der verlorenen Zeit. In W. Kaschuba, M. Krebs, & M. Pilz (Eds.), *Die Postsowjetische Stadt: Aushandlungsprozesse im Südkaukasus* (pp. 150–167). Panama Verlag.

Fehlings, S. (2014). *Jerewan: Urbanes Chaos und soziale Ordnung*. LIT-Verlag.

Fehlings, S. (2015). Intimacy and Exposure: Yerevan's Private and Public Space. *International Journal of Sociology and Social Policy, 35*(7/8), 513–532.

Fehlings, S. (2017). Armenian History in Urban Everyday Life. *Habitus: Studies in Anthropology and Archaeology, 2*, 10–41.

Fehlings, S., & Karrar, H. (2016). Informal Markets and Trade in the Caucasus and Central Asia: A Preliminary Framework for Field Research, *Informal Markets and Trade Working Paper Series, 1.*

Fitzpatrick, S. (2005). *Tear Off the Mask! Identity and Imposture in Twentieth Century Russia*. Princeton University Press.

Freeland, C. (2000). *Sale of the Century: Russia's Wild Ride from Communism to Capitalism*. Doubleday Canada.

Fukuyama, F. (1995). Trust: The Social Virtues and the Creation of Prosperity. Free Press Paperbacks.

Fuller, C., & Harriss, J. (2001). For an Anthropology of the Modern Indian State. In C. Fuller & V. Bénéi (Eds.), *The Everyday State and Society in Modern India* (pp. 1–30). Social Science Press.

Fuller, C. J., & Bénéi, V. (2001). *The Everyday State and Society in Modern India*. Hurst & Co.

James, D. (2014). 'Deeper into a Hole?' Borrowing and Lending in South Africa. *Current Anthropology, 55*(9), 17–29. https://doi.org/10.1086/676123

Giddens, A. (1990). *The Consequences of Modernity*. Polity Press.

Gluckman, M. (1955). *The Judicial Process among the Barotse of Northern Rhodesia*. Manchester University Press.

Gluckman, M. (1965). *The Ideas in Barotse Jurisprudence*. Yale University Press.

Gonzàlez de la Rocha, M. (2007). The Construction of the Myth of Survival. *Development and Change, 38*(1), 45–66.

Graeber. (2011). *Dept: The First 5.000 Years*. Melville House Publishing.

Grant, B., & Yalçın-Heckmann, L. (Eds.). (2007). *Caucasus Paradigms: Anthropologies, Histories and the Making of a World Area*. LIT-Verlag.

Gregory, C. (2012). On Money, Debt and Morality: Some Reflections on the Contribution of Economic Anthropology. *Social Anthropology, 20*(4), 380–396.

Grigolia, A. (1939). *Custom and Justice in the Caucasus: The Georgian Highlanders*. AMS Press.

Gröner, A.-M. (2010). "*Meine Versicherung?—Meine Familie!*" *Sicherheit durch Pflege sozialer Obligationen: Aus dem Alltag aserbaischanischer Familien* (Magisterarbeit). Eberhard Karls Universität Tübingen, Tübingen.

Guérin, I. (2014). Juggling with Debt, Social Ties, and Values The Everyday Use of Microcredit in Rural South India. *Current Anthropology, 55*(9), 40–50.

Gupta, A. (1995). Blurred Boundaries: The Discourse of Corruption, the Culture of Politics, and the Imagined State. *American Ethnologist, 22*(2), 375–402. https://doi.org/10.2307/646708

Gupta, A. (2012). *Red Tape: Bureaucracy, Structural Violence, and Poverty in India*. Duke University Press.
Guzei, I. (2015). The "Russian" Market in the Center of Beijing. In V. Dyatlov & K. Grigorichev (Eds.), *Ethnic Markets in Russia: Space of Bargaining and Place of Meeting* (pp. 159–170). Publishing House of ISU.
Habermas, J. (1981). *Theorie des kommunikativen Handelns* (Vol. II). Suhrkamp Verlag.
Herzog, L. (1990). *Where North Meets South: Cities, Space, and Politics on the U.S.-Mexico Border*. Austin: Center for Mexican American Studies.
Holzlehner, T. (2014). *Shadow Networks: Border Economics, Informal Markets and Organized Crime in the Russian Far East*. LIT-Verlag.
Hosking, G. (2010). *Trust: Money, Markets and Society*. Seagull Books.
Humphrey, C. (2002). *The Unmaking of Soviet Life: Everyday Economics after Socialism*. Cornell University Press.
Humphrey, C. (2018a). Introduction: Trusting and Mistrusting Across Borders. In C. Humphrey (Ed.), *Trust and Mistrust in the Economy of the China-Russia Borderlands* (pp. 9–35). Amsterdam University Press.
Humphrey, C. (Ed.). (2018b). *Trust and Mistrust in the Economy of the China-Russia Borderlands*. Amsterdam University Press.
Iskandaryan, A. (2014). Formalization of the Informal: Statebuilding in Armenia. In C. Giordano & N. Hayoz (Eds.), *Informality in Eastern Europe: Structures, Political Cultures and Social Practices* (pp. 451–484). Peter Lang.
Kandiyoti, D. (2003). The Cry for Land: Agrarian Reform, Gender and Land Rights in Uzbekistan. *Journal of Agrarian Change, 3*(1–2), 225–256.
KfW-Entwicklungsbank. (2005). *Georgien: Microfinance Bank of Georgia-Procredit Bank (Schlussprüfung)*. KfW.
Khalvashi, T. (2015). Peripheral Affects: Shame, Publics, and Performance on the Margins of the Republic of Georgia. (PhD). University of Copenhagen, Copenhagen.
Khalvashi, T., & Gilbreath, D. (2013). Georgia: Hard Money, Hard Times. *Eurasianet*. https://www.academia.edu/4433935/Hard_Money_Hard_Times
Khutsishvili, K. (2016). Across the Enguri Border: Lives Connected and Separated by the Borderland Between Georgia and Abkhazia. In T. Bringa & H. Toje (Eds.), *Eurasian Borderlands: Spatializing Borders in the Aftermath of State Collapse* (pp. 107–131). Palgrave Macmillan.
Khutsishvili, K. (2017). Suddenly a Border: Hazelnut Trade across the De Facto Border between Abkhazia and the Zugdidi Municipal Region of Georgia. *Caucasus Analytical Digest, 96*, 9–12.
Krebs, M. (2011). *Zwischen Handwerkstradition und globalem Markt Kunsthandwerker in Usbekistan und Kirgistan*. Klaus Schwarz Verlag.

Kuehnast, K., & Dudwick, N. (2004). *Better a Hundred Friends than a Hundred Rubles? Social Networks in Transition—The Kyrgyz Republic*. The International Bank for Reconstruction and Development. Washington D.C.

Kupatadze, A. (2009). Georgia's Fight against Organized Crime: Success or Failure? *Caucasus Analytical Digest, 19*, 9–12.

Ledeneva, A. (1998). *Russia's Economy of Favours: Blat, Networking and Informal Exchange*. Cambridge University Press.

Light, M. (2014). Police Reforms in the Republic of Georgia: The Convergence of Domestic and Foreign Policy in an Anti-Corruption Drive. *An International Journal of Research and Policy, 24*(3), 318–345.

Lont, H., & Hospes, O. (Eds.). (2004). *Livelihood and Microfinance: Anthropological and Sociological Perspectives on Savings and Debt*. Eburon Academic Press.

Low, A. (1999). *A Bibliographical Survey of Rotating Savings and Credit Associations*. Oxfam and CCCRW.

Mars, G., & Altman, Y. (1983). The Cultural Bases of Soviet Georgia's Second Economy. *Soviet Studies, XXXV, 4*, 546–560.

Marutyan, H. (2007). Armenia-Diaspora: Meeting in the Yerevan Center. *Handes Amsorya, 2007*, 363–428.

Miller, R. B. (2016). *Friends and Other Strangers: Studies in Religion, Ethics, and Culture*. Columbia University Press.

Mishler, W., & Rose, R. (2005). What are the Political Consequences of Trust? A Test of Cultural and Institutional Theories in Russia. *Comparative Political Studies, 38*(9), 1050–1078.

Mühlfried, F. (2007). Celebrating Identities in Post-Soviet Georgia. In T. Darieva & W. Kaschuba (Eds.), *Representations on the Margins of Europe: Politics and Identities in the Baltic and South Caucasus States* (pp. 283–300). Campus Verlag.

Mühlfried, F. (2010). Citizenship at War: Passports and Nationality in the 2008 Russian-Georgian Conflict. *Anthropology Today, 26*(2), 8–13.

Mühlfried, F. (2019). *Misstrauen: Vom Wert eines Unwertes*. Philipp Reclam jun. Verlag GmbH.

Mühlfried, F. (2014b). *Being a State and States of Being in Highland Georgia*. Berghahn Books.

Ngo, T.-W., & Hung, E. P. W. (2018). The Political Economy of Border Checkpoints in Shadow Exchanges. *Journal of Contemporary Asia, 49*(2), 1–15. https://doi.org/10.1080/00472336.2018.1555273

Peebles, G. (2010). The Anthropology of Credit and Debt. *Annual Review of Anthropology, 39*, 225–240.

Pelkmans, M. (2013). Powerful Documents: Passports, Passages, and Dilemmas of Identification on the Gorgian-Turkish Border. In J. Lauth Bacas & W.

Kavanagh (Eds.), *Border Encounters: Assumetry and Proximity at Europes Frontiers* (pp. 90–107). Berghahn.

Pelkmans, M., & Umetbaeva, D. (2018). Moneylending and Moral Reasoning on the Capitalist Frontier in Kyrgyzstan. *Anthropological Quarterly, 91*(3), 1044–1069.

Putnam, R. (1993). *Making Democracy Work*. Princeton University Press.

Putnam, R. (2000). *Bowling Alone: The Collapse and Revival of American Community*. Simon and Schuster.

Rasanayagam, J. (2011). Informal Economy, Informal State: The Case of Uzbekistan. *International Journal of Sociology and Social Policy, 31*(11/12), 681–696. https://doi.org/10.1108/01443331111177878

Reeves, M. (2014). *Border Works: Spatial Lifes of the State in Rural Central Asia*. Cornell University Press.

Rekhviashvili, L. (2015). Marketization and the Public-Private Divide: Contestations Between the State and Petty Traders over the Access to Public Space in Tbilisi. *International Journal of Sociology and Social Policy, 35*(7/8), 478–496.

Rosanvallon, P. (2008). *Counter-Democracy: Politics in an Age of Distrust*. Cambridge University Press.

Rudaz, P. (2018). Informal Entrepreneurship or "Survivalship"? Results of an Empirical Study of Self Employment, Micro-, and Small Businesses in Georgia. *Anthropological Researches, IV*, 79–89.

Rudaz, P. (2019). Trading in the Bazaars of Dordoi and Lilo at the Frontier of Formality, Entrepreneurship and Globalization. *Central Asian Survey, 39*(1), 11–32.

Sayfutdinova, L. (2018). Taps. In A. Ledeneva & P. Zusi (Eds.), *The Global Encyclopaedia of Informality: Understanding Social and Cultural Complexity* (Vol. 1, pp. 82–85). UCL Press.

Schrader, H. (2006). *Spar- und Kreditvereine als Mittel zur Armutsbekämpfung in Entwicklungsländern* (p. 39). Otto-von-Guericke-Universität Magdeburg.

Simmel, G. (1992 [1908]). *Soziologie: Untersuchungen über die Formen der Vergesellschaftung*. Suhrkamp.

Stefes, C. H. (2006). *Understanding Post-Soviet Transitions: Corruption, Collusion and Clientelism*. Palgrave Macmillan.

Stefes, C. H. (2008). Governance, the State and Systematic Corruption: Armenia and Georgia in Comparison. *Caucasian Review of International Affairs, 2*(2), 73–83.

Steinmüller, H. (2016). Introduction. In H. Steinmüller & S. Brandtstädter (Eds.), *Irony, Cynicism and the Chinese State* (pp. 3–13). Routledge.

Taalaibekova, G., & Melkumyan, H. (2018). Public Space Comercialised and Comodified: A Case Study od the Vernissage in Yerevan. *Anthropological Researches, IV*, 48–64.

Tikhomirov, A. (2017). The Grammar of Trust and Distrust under State Socialism after Stalin: An Introduction. *Journal of Modern European History, 15*(3), 313–329.

Turaeva, R. (2014). Mobile Entrepreneurs in Post-Soviet Central Asia: Micro-Orders of Tirikchilik. *Communist and Post-Communist Studies, 47*(1), 105–114. https://doi.org/10.1016/j.postcomstud.2014.02.001

Voell, S. (2015). Moral Breakdown among the Georgian Svans: A Car Accident Mediated between Traditional and State Law. In S. Voell & I. Kaliszewska (Eds.), *State and Legal Practice in the Caucasus: Anthropological Perspectives on Law and Politics*. Ashgate [unofficial maniscript].

Voell, S., Jalabadze, N., Janiashvili, L., & Kamm, E. (2014). Identity and Traditional Law: Local Legal Conceptions in Svan Villages (Georgia). *Anthropological Journal of European Cultures, 23*, 98–118.

Voell, S., & Kaliszewska, I. (2015). *State and Legal Practice in the Caucasus: Anthropological Perspectives on Law and Politics*. Routledge.

Water, H. A. (2018). The Financialization of Help: Moneylenders as Economic Translators in the Debt-Based Economy. *Central Asian Survey, 37*(3), 403–418. https://doi.org/10.1080/02634937.2018.1442317

Weber, M. ([1921] 1985). *Wirtschaft und Gesellschaft: Grundriss der verstehenden Soziologie*. LCB Mohr.

Werner, C. (1998). Household Networks and the Security of Mutual Indeptedness in Rural Kazakhstan. *Central Asian Survey, 17*(4), 597–612.

World Bank. (2012). *Fighting Corruption in Public Services: Chronicling Georgia's Reforms*. World Bank.

Yalçın-Heckmann, L. (2012). Re-thinking Citizenship in the South Caucasus. *Europe Asia Studies, 64*(9), 1724–1738.

Yalçın-Heckmann, L. (2014). Informal Economy Writ Large and Small: From Azerbaijani Herb Traders to Moscow Shop Owners. In J. Morris & A. Polese (Eds.), *The Informal Post-Socialist Economy: Embedded Practices and Liveliyhoods* (pp. 165–186). Routledge.

Zuev, D., & Habeck, J. O. (2019). Implications of Infrastructure and Technological Change for Lifestyles in Siberia. In J. O. Habeck (Ed.), *Lifestyle in Siberia and the Russian North*. OpenBooks Publishers.

CHAPTER 5

Chinelebi: Chinese Entrepreneurs in the Caucasus

> It must have been in the brain of a merchant that the first peaceful thought arose—the idea that a milder approach might be useful. You see, the inspiration was that peaceful methods could yield greater advantage than violent ones.
>
> —Berthold Brecht, *The Business Affairs of Mr Julius Caesar*

The Chinese entrepreneurs who have in recent years been setting up shops in Georgia—counterparts to the Georgian long-distance traders who travel to China and the Russian market in Beijing—have their own ways of making contacts, using both formal and informal methods, and negotiating government regulations. Coming from a different cultural background, the Chinese (*činelebi*, ჩინელები) adopt different approaches, but their practices are nonetheless compatible with local conduct. They face problems similar to those of the Georgian traders of my target group, and to deal with these, they employ Georgian middlemen. In this chapter, I look at how the Chinese do business in the Caucasus, adapting surprisingly easily to local constrains.

I first became aware of the Chinese presence in Georgia in 2014. Individual Chinese had come to the Caucasus earlier, but they had only then become visible as an ethnic minority in Tbilisi. After my lectures at the Ivane Javakhishvili University, I regularly went to a Chinese restaurant next to the university building on Chavchavadze Street, one of a

S. Fehlings, *Traders, Informal Trade and Markets between the Caucasus and China*, Politics and History in Central Asia,
https://doi.org/10.1007/978-981-19-5205-0_5

few of its kind, which started to appear after 2003.[1] The staff spoke neither Georgian nor Russian, and the next time I came to Tbilisi in 2016, the restaurant had disappeared. But even though there were still only few Chinese there, their presence in Tbilisi had become, so to speak, "normal."

In October 2015, the Georgian and Chinese governments had jointly organized the Tbilisi Silk Road Forum, co-funded by the Chinese government, one of the first of its kind outside the People's Republic of China (PRC), conceived as a platform for discussing the future role of Georgia, "at the heart of the Eurasian continent" (Pantucci & Lain, 2016), in China's new strategic foreign policy "One Belt, One Road" (OBOR) initiative.

In September 2016, there were many rumors about Chinese people and investors who had become active in Georgia. However, few locals had thus far paid much attention to the huge buildings being erected on the shore of Tbilisi Lake by the Hualing (ჰუალინგი) investment group, the biggest Chinese investor in Georgia. When I visited the Hualing construction site for the first time, I wondered how this new complex, including a huge marketplace, could have been built only a few kilometers from the center of the capital and remained virtually unnoticed by the local population.

Only a few months later, however, large-scale Chinese projects like Hualing's were being widely discussed by the Georgian media in the context of OBOR, and everyone was talking about Georgia—which had signed the Deep and Comprehensive Free Trade Agreement (DCFTA) with the European Union in 2014 and has overland links with Turkey—potentially becoming "a logistics hub linking China to the EU and beyond" (Pantucci & Lain, 2016). A bilateral free trade agreement between Georgia and China was signed in May 2017.

According to Pieke et al., "the new Chinese globalization has opened up a range of transnational social spaces that combine 'transnationalism from above' and 'transnationalism from below' of a variety and scale that are unprecedented" (2004: 12). I tried to assemble what I could grasp of this on the ground. Much of it was difficult to contextualize

[1] The economic migrants who opened restaurants and small shops in Georgia after 2003 were from Fujian and Zhejiang in southeastern China, both provinces "well-known for their residents' propensity to go overseas" (Zhou, 2012: 9).

and make sense of. In September 2016, however, I discovered the "Chinese market," which is a hidden commercial area loosely linked to the main corpus of Lilo Bazroba. In the same year, I went to see the "2016 Georgia-China (Jiangxi) Featured Commodities Exhibition" hosted by the Georgian Chamber of Commerce and Industry. Like Xinjiang, the home region of Hualing Group, Jiangxi, the Chinese province from which the exhibitors came, is one of the "region-to-region partners",[2] with which Georgia has embarked on an intensive relationship. Finally, I explored Hualing City, which was still under construction in 2016.

Because of the language barrier, I was not myself able to speak much with the Chinese traders or entrepreneurs I met in the different places, where Chinese play a dominant role. At best, some of them spoke some very poor Russian. I had one long interview with a Chinese employee working for a Chinese construction company. This man (later referred to as John), who was fluent in English, gave me valuable insights, but was my only Chinese interlocutor. I hope to be able to get access to and to follow up research with Chinese in the future.[3] For now, most of the information I have got on the Chinese is second-hand information from Georgian citizens, who work with or for them. This chapter is less based on participation than on oral accounts, rumors, and a description of how the macro-economic and macro-political sphere is implemented and interpreted on the microlevel. Consequently, serves more to provide some insight into Georgian perceptions of Chinese and their economic behaviour than it describes their actual activity, which is somewhat mysterious from the point of view of my Georgian interlocutors.

There are many opinions about Chinese ambitions in the Caucasus. While some Georgians and Armenians admire Chinese businessmen for their economic diligence and ability to adapt to the local environment, others are afraid of their power and hidden motivations. "'Rising China'—the nation, the notion, and the buzzword—sparks dreams and triggers fears" (Zhang & Saxer, 2017b: 11).

[2] One point emerging from discussion during the Tbilisi Silk Road Forum was that, "from a country-to-country perspective, opportunities for co-operation do not just exist at a national level, but also at the province-to-province and region-to-region levels" (Pantucci & Lain, 2016: 10).

[3] Meanwhile, I have started to learn Chinese. With the help of my colleagues and a translator I hope to start a new project, for which the Volkswagen Foundation already has promised funding.

Chinese in Georgia stress face-to-face collaboration with local partners at all levels of interaction. I shall thus focus on the relationship between Chinese entrepreneurs and representatives of the Georgian and Armenian governments, Chinese entrepreneurs and their Georgian partners, Chinese entrepreneurs and Georgian businessmen (traders), and Chinese entrepreneurs and the local public. A key word describing the nature of many of these relationships is "informality."

I shall try to situate these materials into the context of the current literature on Chinese business ambitions in other parts of the world and the One Belt, One Road Initiative. I will start with the description of the Chinese market section at Lilo Bazroba and with a report on the activity of Hualing Group. I will then turn to the macro-economic and macro-political framework of the Georgian-Chinese relationship, which is the basis of face-to-face encounters on the ground. The final section will focus on these face-to-face encounters, which I analyze and try to explain, inasmuch as they are formative and crucial for business behaviour and economic exchange. To my knowledge, apart from Jiayi Zhou's very well researched 2012 European Centre for Minority Issues (ECMI) paper "Chinese in Georgia," which offers a Chinese perspective on the subject, this ethnographic study is the first of its kind, because the Chinese presence in the Caucasus has been given little attention in scholarship so far. My descriptions will provide materials for comparison with the activity of local traders described in the previous chapters, but will also add to the broader picture of the multi-dimensional Caucasian business environment and its dynamics.

The Chinese Market at Lilo Bazroba

The Chinese market next to Lilo Bazroba is one of two Chinese shopping centers opened in Tbilisi in 2006, the Chinese market at Lilo and the so-called Chinese Commodity Center, both of which served to facilitate Chinese chain migration, mainly from the Zhejiang and Fujian provinces in southeastern China. The Chinese Commodity Center closed in 2007. Lilo's Chinese bazaar was established by a group of Chinese that partnered with a Georgian woman who owned the property. The market area was divided into small parcels, which were leased to Chinese shopkeepers, most of whom came and still come from the Zhejiang province, more precisely from Qingtang County. These people usually share a background in poverty and speak their own dialect. In 2007, some two hundred

Chinese from Zhejiang lived in Georgia, and that year, they funded a Zhejiang fellow villagers' association, but since the economic crisis in 2008, the size of their community has declined (Zhou, 2012: 9–10).

To get from Lilo Bazroba to the Chinese market, one crosses a tiny, overcrowded metal bridge that spans the highway, followed by a ten-minute walk through a desolate area. The marketplace itself is stuck among the remains of an abandoned Soviet industrial zone. Approaching it, one sees Chinese characters on a building, and a few meters further on, there is a Chinese-style gate (Fig. 5.1), the entrance to the small bazaar. There is a travel agency at the front of the market advertising a Chinese airline, but the rest of the building from the first to the third floor is empty. On the door of one of the few shops in another building, a sign in Russian and Georgian states that merchandise cannot be returned, and that a salesperson is wanted. Perhaps, this will one day turn into a shopping mall, but for the present, it is dim and unattractive.

Ana Ramazashvili, one of the project's PhD students, introduced me to this Chinese market. The contact who showed her the place, a Georgian woman, who, according to Ana, was called "the Chinese woman (činel-a) because of her "Chinese" eyes, regularly bought merchandise there to sell in the city center.

Fig. 5.1 The Chinese Market at Lilo Bazroba, 2016

The atmosphere of the Chinese market section differed from the ambiance of other local marketplaces, not only because of the Chinese characters on buildings, packaging, and merchandise, or the many Chinese around, but because of the smells, sounds, and look of the place. The first time Ana, Zviad, and I visited the area together was on a so-called wholesale day. It was about lunchtime, and some Chinese men set up a table and brought Chinese food, which looked particularly delicious. Fried shrimp, which are not part of the local Georgian cuisine,[4] seemed a special luxury contradicting the poverty[5] of the shabby shops, one-story shanty buildings, narrow, muddy streets, and cheap goods for sale. The Chinese traders paid no attention to us. I was allowed to take a few pictures, and they continued to have lunch.

The market was not crowded. There were only two alleys for shops, one of which was abandoned. Between these two alleys, there was a hall with storage space. The storage compartments were closed, and even though nobody asked us to leave, I felt that we should not stroll around. The Chinese families who worked in the market section lived partly in their shops. Behind the counter desks, I could see beds, and in the back rooms, people were cooking in small kitchens equipped with big refrigerators. Some people also cooked on fireplaces in front of their shops or played with their children, who were running outside. Apart from a few Georgian clients, everyone spoke Chinese. In each shop, there were a Chinese and a Georgian seller. Chinese vendors and shopkeepers were usually sitting at the counter desk. They did not seem interested in starting any kind of conversation. It was the Georgian employees (mostly women), who talked to us or to potential buyers.

One week later, I noticed high-tech surveillance cameras all over the place. They were not yet plugged in but made me wonder what kind of valuables might be hidden behind the Chinese market's miserable façade. Zviad and I had come back, because Natia, my roommate, had heard

[4] According to Zhou (2012: 12), the Georgian diet and the lack Chinese food is perceived as a major problem by Chinese migrants living in Georgia.

[5] My colleague Agnieszka Joniak-Lüthi warned me not to interpret the poor appearance of the market as a sign of poverty. According to her, their strict focus on business prevents Chinese from caring about aesthetics. However, I believe, that in comparison to established Georgian traders in Lilo Bazroba and Chinese big investors, the traders in the Chinese Lilo section were still relatively poor. At least, from the Georgian point of view, their living standard would be classified as such. Furthermore, the fact that they originate from Zhejiang or Fujian supports this assumption.

rumors about a Chinese village that had supposedly sprung up next to the marketplace. Natia, who was toying with the idea of shooting a documentary on Chinese in Georgia, was convinced that there was an illegal settlement, because "clever Chinese people silently establish themselves and [then] take over the area." It turned out that this was not true, at least as far as I could tell. Aside from three or four wooden houses alongside the market, in front of which the Chinese occupants raised vegetables on small plots of ground, the market itself supplied housing in units the size of an average garage. We explored the whole area on foot, and behind some Soviet factory ruins, we came across other small garden lots hidden between trash and debris. The place would have made a great set for a secret mafia meeting in a gangster film, and it seemed like such a setting, in fact, when a man appeared out of nowhere and knocked on the door of one of the partly demolished factory houses, and, incredibly in this wasteland, someone inside opened it.

Obviously, the Chinese traders working in Lilo's Chinese market section weren't getting rich and didn't constitute an economic threat to Georgian bazaar traders. According to Zhou (2012), who interviewed some representatives of this group, Chinese small-scale entrepreneurs had to keep their prices extremely low to be able to compete with local vendors of similar merchandise. Still, their presence was perceived with suspicion and resulted in a lot of rumors and false information (like the story of the mythical Chinese village mentioned above and rumors about Chinese men paying Georgian women to marry them so as to get Georgian citizenship).[6]

The situation of Chinese traders in Georgia seemed comparable to that of the Chinese migrants in eastern Europe described by Nyíri (2011), for example. Aside from a few exceptions, the Chinese traders in Lilo and similar places, were obviously not well integrated. They couldn't speak Georgian and apparently had no long-term plans to establish themselves in the Caucasus. They stuck to their community, maintaining strong links to their homeland, Zhou says.

[6] Compare Zhou (2012: 14).

Hualing City and Sea Plaza

The Chinese market at Lilo Bazroba is, however, only one facet of Chinese economic engagement in the region. The most visible representative of Chinese business in Georgia is the Hualing Group, funded in Ürümqi in 1988, which started to invest in Georgia in 2007. Aside from the Hualing industrial zone in Kutaisi[7] and the Olympic Village and Hualing New City[8] near Tbilisi Lake, the so-called Hualing Tbilisi Sea Plaza (*Hualingi Tbilisis Zǧvis Plaza*, ჰუალინგი თბილისის ზღვის პლაზა), intended to be the largest trading center in the Caucasus and an important wholesale, retail, and distribution center in Eurasia as a whole, was under construction on a site covering 150,000 square meters.[9] I wondered what this would mean for Lilo Bazroba and its traders.

In September 2016, Zviad and I visited Hualing's development for the first time. From the Varketili metro stop, we took an almost empty *maršuṭka* there, getting off at a small bus station in front of the main gate. What is called Hualing New City is built more or less in the middle of nowhere. Hualing has bought most of the land in the vicinity adjacent to Tbilisi Lake, flanked on the city side by a typical Soviet housing complex and a Yazidi temple, and by steppe on the other side. Just an empty little fenced enclave there was still owned by the Georgian Orthodox Church.

What we got to see was fascinating. Only few people I had talked to in Tbilisi at the time knew what was going on at Hualing New City, which had largely escaped public notice, and I was surprised to find multi-story blocks there with cars parked in front of them, flowers and laundry on balconies, and trees, grass, fountains, and artificial streams. There was even a playground with children in it. Hasan and Rune, who visited the place two years later (in 2018) told me that the buildings resembled prototypes in the Xinjiang Uygur Autonomous Region in northwestern China and Chinese cities elsewhere. Irakli was convinced, though, that the Chinese had tried to adapt the architecture of the buildings to "Georgian style." In addition to the residential blocks and green areas, the new suburb included a smart hotel, a sports complex, and a concert hall. A

[7] Hualing "Free Industrial Zone": http://hualing.ge/language/en/hualing-free-industrial-zone/.

[8] Agenda.ge, 20 July 2015: http://agenda.ge/news/39419/eng.

[9] Hualing "Tbilisi Sea Plaza": http://hualing.ge/language/en/tbilisi-sea-plaza/.

wall surrounded the complex, but the guard at the gate, who was half asleep, did not seem bothered by visitors.

Manana, who had visited Hualing New City with her father on a weekend trip, told me that she had heard that some of the houses had been built for refugees from Abkhazia,[10] which, as I later discovered, was true. She interpreted this as evidence of an agreement between the Hualing Group and the Georgian government. Many government meetings and events took place in the aforementioned hotel, she said, interpreting this as further proof of the close relationship between Georgian and Chinese officials. Salome, a friend of Natia's working for a television channel, reported that she had participated in the annual government-sponsored "Georgian Manufacturing Day"[11] at a big hall (probably the concert hall) in Hualing New City. Salome had been impressed by the giant crystal chandelier that illuminated the hall, but when she saw the lavatories, she was shocked and understood that this was "Chinese quality," she said: "They just want to show off, but then, the toilets are really bad." She had heard that the apartments were small and narrow: "The Chinese built it, and they built it for Chinese people. Not for people like us." Such stories, typical of the first contacts between Chinese and Georgians, reflect prejudice among the latter about what they call "Chinese quality."

Apartments in Hualing New City were apparently expensive even in 2016, going for between U.S.$640 and U.S.$680 a square meter, whereas a square meter in Tbilisi itself cost about U.S.$600. Irakli got an apartment there because of his status of a displaced person (IDP) from Abkhazia. But, according to him, "even though some particular houses were dedicated to IDPs, you had to have connections with someone in the Ministry to get a place." Irakli's friend Lasha, who was not a refugee, had got an apartment there at a special price because he worked for the Hualing Group. Irakli told me that when he tried to buy an additional apartment in his Hualing neighborhood, he was told that there were only six left. All the other apartments had been sold. Lasha said he was very happy with his apartment, because it was comparatively cheap and the Hualing Group took care of everything, including heating and repairs. Hualing supplied such services in the old Soviet way, but Georgia and

[10] As a result of the 2008 Georgian-Russian (Abkhazian) war.

[11] A fair at which goods produced in Georgia are presented and awarded prizes.

other post-Soviet countries have privatized them, and they are a source of constant complaints. “There are many regulations, and for security reasons, you are not even allowed to do repairs yourself,” Lasha said. “When you call the service, they will fix everything for a payment of 50 lari a month.” He added that since there had been problems with people fighting with security staff, a wall had been built around the complex, and after September 15, 2017, no one would be able to pass the security checkpoint without permission. Anyone who did not own an apartment there would have to park in the parking lot outside and enter on foot. Hualing New City thus became a gated community, something relatively new in the Caucasus, usually reserved for the very rich.[12]

The Chinese investors had brought everything from China to build Hualing New City, not only building materials, but workers and vehicles too. Whenever I walked around there, Chinese trucks passed by. Obviously, the project was/is far from being completed. Most of the area was still undeveloped in 2016, and the infrastructure was under construction. Zviad and I took a taxi to cross the empty land that separated Hualing New City's housing area from the other end of the complex, where we saw the enormous new “Tbilisi Sea Plaza” shopping mall. Back then, it was still being built and closed, but the entrance was already demarcated by two statues of five rearing horses, symbolizing the gateway to Hualing's territory and prosperity, which had been specially imported from China.

The commercial part of the territory, as one can read on Hualing's website, includes, in addition to the Plaza, a market zone, a processing zone, a custom bond zone (Irakli's workplace), warehouses, commercial pedestrian streets and many other businesses.[13] The marketplace next to the mall consists of long streets lined with low, flat-roofed buildings, which are grouped into four clusters (A, B, C, D), and rows of trees (1, 2, 3) (Fig. 5.2).

In September 2016, all this looked like a ghost city. At the street corners, we met few Chinese workers and some Georgian guards, but aside from them, the streets were totally empty. A map and signs written in English, Georgian, and Chinese told where to find which merchandise.

[12] Agnieszka Joniak-Lüthi said this corresponded to the *danwei* in the PRC, in which so-called work units (mostly state-owned enterprises) provide housing and other services for employees.

[13] Hualing “Tbilisi Sea Plaza”: http://hualing.ge/language/en/tbilisi-sea-plaza/.

Fig. 5.2 Tbilisi Sea Plaza and market place, 2016

Posters advertised various products and depicted Hualing construction projects in Georgia. One showed a photo-shopped version of what Hualing New City would look like in the future. In addition to the Tbilisi Sea Plaza mall and housing area, noted above, it showed small suburban houses and another concert hall, planned to be built along the shore of Tbilisi Lake. A huge Spanish Armada–style sailing ship portrayed in the background provided a mystical touch.

To our surprise, one of the shops was open. It was full of things for sale, and Zviad and I went in. Apparently, the shop served as a display and storage area at the same time. Boxes with Chinese markings were stacked all over the place, and the shelves held samples of simply designed tea sets and plates. There were two salespeople, a Chinese man and a Georgian woman, who pointed to the door of another shop, saying we would find handicrafts there. This other shop was huge and nicely designed. Chinese calligraphy, lamps, and pictures created a very "Asiatic" ambience. There was a display of porcelain ware for sale at many different prices, depending on quality and size. In another section, there were suitcases, good winter clothes, expensive tea, building materials, and many other imports from China, reflecting the whole spectrum of Chinese goods.[14] Two very young, friendly women, one Chinese and one Georgian, awaited customers at a desk at the entrance to the shop. They seemed happy to see us, and since no one else was there, they gave us a tour. The Chinese woman knew a bit of Russian, but it was Nino, the Georgian saleswoman, who took the lead in the conversation, speaking highly of her Chinese bosses.

Apparently, Nino is fluent in Chinese. After university, she wanted to work in China. Her parents were against this, but Nino nevertheless headed for the People's Republic. It is not unusual for young Caucasian (Georgian and Armenian) women to go to China to work as housemaids or teachers, which guarantees a good salary. In recent years, this has become a popular option. Nino first worked as a waitress. Then, a family, who liked her, asked her to work for them and to look after their children. This family took her to Guangzhou, where she was introduced to a representative of the Hualing Group. In all, she had lived a year and a half in China at that point. The fact that she was Georgian had interested the Hualing representative, and she had subsequently become a dependable local employee of the company in Georgia. She helped her Chinese superiors with everything, she said, showing them around, taking them to tourist sites, and accompanying them to meetings, where she translated for them. A few days earlier, for example, she had assisted at a meeting of the Hualing bosses with the local minister of provincial transport (Zviad told me later that he had seen film of this on TV).

Hualing in return treated Nino well, providing her with a free apartment in Hualing New City and a permanent job with a good salary. It was obvious that Nino was satisfied and proud of her Chinese superiors. She showed me a picture in the shop's lobby of a college in the Chinese countryside built by Hualing for Georgian students, who were sent there by the company to learn Chinese. These students got their studies paid for and were guaranteed a job at the Hualing branch in Georgia afterward. Nino told us that there were forty-five Georgian students in this program at that time, one of whom was a close friend of hers. Next to the picture there were a Georgian flag and some texts talking about Chinese-Georgian friendship. Nino was sure that both sides, Chinese and Georgians, profited from cooperation. Referring to her own experience, she described the Chinese entrepreneurs as fair partners. She had observed

[14] Most of the prices were indicated in both renminbi and lari.

her superiors' interest in local Caucasian culture and was sure that they would not only profit from the sale of Chinese goods in Georgia, but would support the Georgian economy by buying Georgian wine and traditional clothing.[15]

After this instructive conversation with Nino, Zviad and I decided to go to the market's Chinese restaurant nearby. Again, we were the only guests in the huge canteen. It was a strange experience. Even in Simferopol's graveyards, where I had been done fieldwork before, there had been more people to talk to. The servers were Georgians, but the cook was Chinese. We ordered a very spicy noodle dish and talked about the marketplace. Zviad told me that a friend of his had bought a motorcycle there. A hospital built by Hualing next to the market had opened and had a good reputation, but the market did not seem to have come to life yet in 2016. "Apparently, few Georgians know that it's already functioning," Zviad said.

The Tbilisi Sea Plaza mall and the marketplace officially opened on September 30, 2017. I was in Germany at the time, but local media described the opening ceremony. When I came back in spring 2018 for a short visit, however, the place was still empty. "Merchants from China, Turkey, and Dubai (UAE) have signed agreements to [participate in the] Hualing International Trade Center and have already started operating,"[16] a website proclaimed, but the mall was only minimally functioning. Bacho, who sold his father's merchandise (shoes from China) in the mall complained that there was nothing going on. Business had been quite good right after the official opening, he said, but fell off once the euphoria was over. The person working in his neighboring shop had not shown up for a while, he observed. "That's bad," he said. "If half of the shops are closed, nobody comes." He blamed the Chinese, who were bad

[15] Indeed, according to official media, the PRC has become Georgia's fourth largest trading partner (the turnover reached 717 million USD in 2016) and second largest exporting market for Georgian wine (see GT Georgia Today "China-Georgia Friendship Celebrates the 25th Anniversary of Diplomatic Relations", 13 June 2017: http://georgiatoday.ge/news/6781/China-Georgia-Friendship-Celebrates-the-25th-Anniversary-of-Diplomatic-Relations). Georgian exports to China increased from 6 million USD in 2009 to 170 million USD in 2016. Chinese exports to Georgia, in the same period, increased from 175 million USD to 548 USD. Currently, Georgian exports to China mainly consist in minerals, including copper ores and concentrates (Larsen, 2017).

[16] Hualing "Tbilisi Sea Plaza": http://hualing.ge/language/en/tbilisi-sea-plaza/.

managers, he said, and did not advertise enough to promote business. Bacho's young wife told me that they would have to leave soon.

My colleague Rune Steenberg, who had come with to the Caucasus for one of our project's workshops, and who had conducted research in Xinjiang, was not surprised about the emptiness of the site. Empty Chinese-built shopping malls are a phenomenon that is often described in literature on Chinese investments in China's neighboring countries in Asia. Rune talked to a Chinese shopkeeper who had a different explanation of why clients failed to come to the shopping mall. This man argued that it had nothing to do with the state or the mall's management, but that the Georgian economy was simply not growing fast enough, and that people thus did not have money to go shopping. Be that as it may, Bacho's outlet in the Hualing Plaza was obviously a failure and had to be shut down in 2018. Meanwhile, his father's business in Lilo Bazroba grew and expanded.

The Tbilisi Sea Plaza's management did not give up, however. Mariam, a young sales manager responsible for a whole floor of the Plaza, whom I got to know in summer 2018, explained:

> When the Plaza was built, the idea of the Hualing people was to transfer Lilo Bazroba to the Plaza. The Chinese wanted to rent the place to Georgian traders and companies. But this did not work. They wanted to change Georgian customers' behavior. There was a private meeting between the Chinese and the Lilo owners,[17] but they did not agree on a deal. It is not easy to communicate with Chinese business people. They have so many requirements. ... Hualing's goal was initially to run the biggest shopping center in the Caucasus. Something like Saba, but not just for furniture. They wanted an expensive shopping mall.

But, according to Mariam, prices were too high and Georgian customers "don't come just like this on their own." There was no advertising, and this, in Mariam's opinion, was a problem. However, she said, "Chinese are not worried and have new plans. The government plans to close Eliava Market. They will try to transfer Eliava to the Plaza."

Located in the center of Tbilisi, Eliava Market is a chaotic bazaar specializing in spare car parts and building material. In the media it was often discussed as a problematic place, where poverty was on display.

[17] Lilo's managers, to whom I talked later, denied that such a meeting had taken place.

Everyone I talked to was surprised to hear of plans to transfer it to Hualing's territory. The only rational explanation my interlocutors could think of was: "Probably a government deal!"

The Chinese Presence in Georgia

How does all this fit into the broader picture of Chinese politics, international trading relations, and Georgian-Chinese economic cooperation and exchange in particular? And what effect has Chinese investment had on Georgian businesses?

There is no long history of Chinese migration to the Caucasus, where they are perceived as aliens. A man named Liu Junzhou, who settled in Chakvi in 1890, where he introduced and cultivated tea plants, is one of the very few examples of an early Chinese presence in this part of the world. Liu left in 1924, when the new Soviet regime started to put pressure on him. His family is quite famous in Georgia, however, and maintained connections with the country (Zhou, 2012), symbolizing the positive side of cultural exchange between Asia, Russia, and the Caucasus to this day.

It was only after the collapse of the Soviet Union that Chinese really started to discover Georgia. The first pioneers were sent and financed by the People's Republic. Unlike other post-Soviet countries that attracted Chinese migrants in the late 1980s and early 1990s (Nyíri, 2011),[18] Georgia was not then a favored destination for Chinese entrepreneurs: "it is likely that without any initial network of Chinese, the country and its market were less accessible. It is also possible that Georgia was still too obscure and unknown, even for enterprising Chinese. Georgia was not yet a destination in itself, but it was briefly used as a stepping stone for Chinese migrants seeking entry into Europe proper" (Zhou, 2012: 4).

Contacts between Chinese and Georgian locals remain limited. Many Chinese, like those working in the Chinese market at Lilo, do not integrate into Georgian society. In Russia, where the situation was similar, Chinese markets that sprang up in cities like Irkutsk "were regarded by municipal authorities as 'crime-promoting spaces' and by the townsfolk

[18] Between 1989 and 1992, "economic and political anxiety in China" and "the collapse of state socialist regimes in Eastern Europe created economic and political conditions for Chinese immigration: a brief window of liberal immigration policies" (Nyíri, 2011: 145), which led to a mass migration.

as useful but alien closed enclaves," from which Chinese traders rarely ventured out "for fear of xenophobic attacks" (Humphrey, 2018: 23). Because of the Chinese traders' "legal vulnerability to expulsion, they were inclined to take on economic roles or methods seen as deviant (such as usury). This led to an increased identification of the entire group with a particular business and the cementing of a view of it as an economic—as well as a moral and a sanitary—threat" (Nyíri, 2011: 147). The atmosphere, although it is less tense in Georgia than in Russia, is comparable.

Research has identified different outcomes of ethnic competition: if competition is high, ethnic migrant groups concentrate in a limited range of industries, and if competition is very high, "a group may be forced out of more lucrative activities, and either squeezed into interstitial lines or pushed out of business altogether" (Aldrich & Waldinger, 1990: 118). On the other hand, if there is a lack of interethnic competition, migrant groups may enter a number of industries or function as middlemen. Chinese who settled in Lima, Peru, and New York in the early twentieth century, for example, encountered different host environments after immigration. The level of discrimination was relatively high in the United States and even reflected in legislation like the U.S. Chinese Exclusion Act of 1881 (which was not repealed until 1943), but Peru was open to Chinese immigration. New York Chinese, as a consequence of repression, concentrated in a few industries in the city's Chinatown, and economic exclusion strengthened their group cohesion. The Chinese in Peru, albeit from the same province in China as those in New York, formed a loose community and got involved in a wide range of businesses (Aldrich & Waldinger, 1990). It is difficult to apply these findings to the situation in Georgia, where Chinese constitute an almost invisible minority and fall into two or three separate groups, or social classes, even aside from hierarchies within these (see Fehlings, 2019).

The first social group, the class of traders described in the section above on the Chinese Lilo Market section, is indeed very vulnerable to discrimination and, apparently, limits itself to petty trade and lives in an ethnic enclave (linked to the Chinese section of Lilo Bazroba). This group seems to have little interaction with the local population.

The second group, the class of big investors and their employees (like the people working for Hualing), may experience similar everyday face-to-face discrimination, but, on the official level, they are supported by local (state) institutions and thus gain a completely different status within the host society. Instead of competition, cooperation is emphasized—not only officially, but also on the personal level of everyday business interactions. It is noteworthy that this group consists of Chinese Muslims. The funder of Hualing Group, Mi Enhua, is a Hui from Shandong province, who, at the age of four, moved to Xinjiang with his family (Zhang & Alon, 2009: 119–120), and his employees are mostly Uyghurs.

For political reasons, companies at the forefront of many Silk Road projects have been from the Xinjiang Uygur region of China, whose capital, Ürümqi, markets itself as the "gateway to Eurasia" (Pantucci & Lain, 2016: 10). As "a tiny ethno religious minority living side by side with the polytheistic or atheist majority, Chinese Muslims [especially Hui people] have traditionally engaged in ethnic entrepreneurship as a strategy of survival and resistance" (Wang, 2018: 133) and "historically have played the role of a middleman minority" (153). Since the 1980s, China's Muslims have gained new importance in the context of China's policy of opening up to the world and took advantage of globalization. According to Yuting Wang, Chinese Muslims "have earned the reputation of trustworthy trading agents in Guangzhou and Yiwu, the epicenter of China's manufacturing and commodity distribution grid" and "have evolved from a middleman minority that exists on the margin to cultural brokers who are increasingly central in China's Belt and Road Initiative" (134). Wang talks of Hui Chinese in Dubai as cultural ambassadors, a term that can also be applied to the representatives of the Hualing group, who mediate between Georgia and China and help to initiate business deals between the two countries.

Finally, there is a third group of Chinese, not hitherto mentioned. These are the representatives of Chinese construction companies, usually closely linked to Chinese state institutions and associated with China's One Road One Belt (*yi dai, yi lu*) initiative (OBOR). These companies, I was told, mainly recruit Han Chinese from the different parts of China, who dissociate themselves from traders and businesspeople from China's south and west. Most of the employees of construction companies live in camps close to the construction sites, which they usually do not leave.[19] My Chinese informant, who worked in a construction company's head office in Tbilisi, was an exception. He was not too happy to have been sent to Georgia and would have preferred to live in a "more developed

[19] For working conditions of these Chinese workers see Zhou (2012).

country." On the other hand, he admitted, that circumstances were not too bad, because "there is no discrimination," and "I could have been sent to Africa."

Apparently, there are few contacts between the different groups of Chinese living in Georgia. Individuals might meet at embassy events such as major celebrations like the spring festival, but the social hierarchies between different groups of diverse social backgrounds seem to limit interaction. Still, from a Georgian perspective, Chinese are Chinese. They are perceived as one group and associated with official Chinese policy, which in the Caucasus is related primarily to OBOR.

Globalization with a Chinese Face

In recent years, Beijing's "outgoing" policy and the ambitions of Chinese enterprises and entrepreneurs in various parts of the so-called Third World have become a much-discussed topic in academia. Chinese investment and entrepreneurship in Africa is an especially well-studied field. Research has explored the Chinese role in the African mining and construction sector (Lee, 2014), African health systems, and African business and trade (Kim, 2017; Röschenthaler & Socpa, 2017). The Frankfurt-based Afrikas Asiatische Optionen (AFRASO)[20] and the International Institute for Asian Studies' (IIAS) "Africa-Asia: A New Axis of Knowledge" collective[21] have contributed much to this field. Researchers have also paid special attention to the role of borderlands in Chinese ventures in Asia. Interesting studies have emerged from the Asian Borderlands Research Network[22] and research projects like "Remoteness & Connectivity: Highland Asia in the World," funded by the European Research Council.[23] Stimulating contributions, have, for example, been published by Nyíri (2012, 2017), Harris (2013), Billé (2014), Karrar and Mostowlansky

[20] Afrikas Asiatische Optionen (AFRASO): Frankfurter Inter-Zentren-Programm zu neuen afrikanisch-asiatischen Interaktionen (BMBF, 2013–2019); Goethe-Universität Frankfurt "AFRASO": https://www.uni-frankfurt.de/44349588/AFRASO; AFRASO "Home": http://www.afraso.org/.

[21] Africa-Asia: New Axis of Knowledge: https://www.iias.asia/programmes/africa-asia-new-axis-knowledge.

[22] International Institute for Asian Studies "Asian Borderlands Research Network": https://iias.asia/research/asian-borderlands-research-network.

[23] Highland Asia "About": http://www.highlandasia.net/about/.

(2018), Zhang and Saxer (2017b), and Rippa (2018). Another focus of research, which is probably the most suitable for comparison, has been the case of Russia and Central Asia, where much scholarship on markets and trade contributes to a diachronic perspective, given the region's geographical proximity to China and the ethnic links between Chinese and Central Asian minorities (Alff, 2014, 2016; Dyatlov & Grigorichev, 2015; Grigorichev et al., 2019; Holzlehner, 2014; Nyíri, 2007, 2011; Steenberg, 2016).

The Chinese presence has a long history in this latter region.[24] Owing to the hostile relations between the USSR and Maoist China, the Sino-Russian border was closed for some thirty years, from the late 1950s to the late 1980s (Humphrey, 2017, 2018),[25] but relationships, trading links in particular, were re-established immediately when visa regimes eased in the 1980s (see Chapter 3). This development was supported by the Chinese government, which promoted small-scale private trading ventures across its borders, encouraged provincial border administrations to make international agreements, opened border trading posts and invested in infrastructure (Humphrey, 2018; Karrar, 2013; Steenberg, 2016).[26] The first result of these measures was "a sharp economic imbalance, in which the vast majority of goods, especially consumption items, came from China, and the purchasers came from Russia" (Humphrey, 2018: 18; cf. Nyíri, 2007: 77–78).

[24] For an overview over the history of Chinese in Eastern Europe and Russia see Nyíri (2007). His monograph includes chapters on "Early contacts", "Chinese farmers, hunters, workers and merchants in Russia, 1858–1914", Chinese as laborers and soldiers in Russia's war 1914–22", and Chinese in the Soviet Union, 1922–89", and refers to the relevant literature and sources.

[25] During this period trade consisted only in state-to-state transfers (Humphrey, 2018).

[26] Before WW II frontiers and border zones were under fuzzy sovereign rule. The attitude changed in the 1990s and China, asserting its borders, got involved in several border disputes and armed conflicts. China's closure was one consequence of this situation, which only changed after the end of the Cold War. In 1992, border issues were resolved with Vietnam, and in 2004, with Russia. China became a member in different international groups like the SCO (Zhang & Saxer, 2017a: 23). China sought to connect its western periphery to its east coast economic hub with the *xibu da kaifa* ("Open up the West," or "Great Western Development") campaign proclaimed in 1999, supporting infrastructural development, urbanization, industrialization, and education in the PRC's west. This and the adoption of wages were meant to decrease social and ethnic tensions. Opening up to neighboring states like Kazakhstan and Kyrgyzstan was fostered at the same time (Alff, 2014: 4). Xinjiang in particular has since developed into a prospering trading and infrastructural hub (Alff, 2014, 2016).

The Russian state was worried about this development, and because of its long "historical obsession with sovereignty and its fear of an influx of Chinese population and influence," it "neglected local economic prosperity in favor of the paramount importance of border security" (Humphrey, 2018: 18). Nevertheless, in the late 1980s and early 1990s, numerous Chinese shuttle traders and Chinese ethnic markets started to establish themselves in Russia's Far East,[27] in Moscow, and other Russian and eastern European cities (Dyatlov & Grigorichev, 2015; Nyíri, 2007, 2011; Григоричев et al., 2019). When I studied in Moscow in 2005, the Izmailovo Market there had a huge Chinese section, run by Chinese. Chinese students also formed a closed but visible community at the Lomonosov University. Most of them were studying at the Institute of Asian and African Studies. I remember that some of them ran a fast-food delivery service in the university's dormitory. Since then, Russia has tried to gain control over Chinese "migration" and Chinese entrepreneurs. After 2007, "'foreign' citizens were debarred from the right to trade in Russian marketplaces" Humphrey (2018: 18–19); numerous border crossings were closed around 2010, and Chinese migration was subsequently restricted (Namsaraeva, 2018). Still, this has not stopped the flow of Chinese goods, which easily enter Russia through Kazakhstan and are traded with the help of Central Asian middlemen (Humphrey, 2018).

As noted, the Chinese presence in the Caucasus is still a relatively new phenomenon in comparison to that in Africa (Röschenthaler & Socpa, 2017) and Russia. Migration to Georgia has become relatively easy for Chinese citizens. Since March 2009, migrants have had to register with the Ministry of Justice's Civil Registry Agency to obtain an identification card, which is also a kind of work permission. Registration allows an initial one-year residency, which can be extended twice, for another two and then for another three years. After six years, migrants have to apply for permanent residence (Zhou, 2012: 14–15). In July 2011, only 974 Chinese nationals were registered in Georgia.[28] Yet, as in Central Asia, China's OBOR initiative made many headlines in Georgia even before it went global. Large-scale construction projects in Georgia were awarded to Chinese contractors, and the Chinese embassy in Georgia has made a

[27] In November 1985, the PRC adopted a new entry-and-exit law that liberalized travel abroad and enabled border crossings between the Soviet Union and China waiving visa requirements in 1988 (Nyíri, 2007: 51).

[28] I could not find more recent statistics.

great effort to establish good relationships in and with the country. The Chinese presence is now no longer associated only with small-scale trade, but also with official Chinese policy and state investment.

OBOR was first proposed by Xi Jinping in a talk at Nazarbaev University in Astana, Kazakhstan, on 7 September 2013.[29] It is a flexible concept, initially aimed at enhancing security in China's Xinjiang border region (Clarke, 2008), but aligned with four of the PRC's key aims: (1) pacifying the country's periphery, (2) sustaining high economic growth, (3) maintaining internal order, and (4) cementing the PRC's international status (Larsen, 2017). Meanwhile, much has been written about OBOR, BRI and "the New Silk Road" and its effects in different parts of the world.[30] Some texts, at least partly, use anthropological methods and explore OBOR from a grassroots perspective. Such studies focus, for example, on the implementation of the China-Pakistan Economic Corridor (CPEC), which is one of OBOR's flagship projects (Akhter, 2018; Karrar, 2019; Karrar & Mostowlansky, 2018; Rippa, 2018; Shah, 2018), or on Chinese projects in Central Asia (Laruelle, 2018). OBOR signals a shift in Chinese foreign policy from maintaining a low profile to "striving for achievements" (Kaczmarski, 2016). China now seems to seek to assume a leading role in the world system and is actively promoting a modernization and globalization with a "Chinese face" (Alff, 2014; Pieke et al., 2004). By doing so, China presents OBOR as an opportunity for transnational and regional cooperation facilitating economic development and cultural exchange to, as one can read in any Chinese statement, "the benefit of all parties involved". As Xi Jinping put it in a speech in May 2014: "The Chinese people, in their pursuit of the Chinese dream of great national renewal, stand ready to support and help other peoples in Asia to realize their own great dreams. Let us work together for realizing the Asian dream of lasting peace and common development, and make [a]

[29] A Summary of the speech has been published by the Ministry of Foreign Affairs of the People's Republic of China: https://www.fmprc.gov.cn/mfa_eng/topics_665678/xjpfwzysiesgjtfhshzzfh_665686/t1076334.shtml; a video of the whole speech is available on YouTube: https://www.youtube.com/watch?v=dHkNzMjEv0Y. First, there was just the idea of the Silk Road Economic Belt (SREB), a system of land crossing connection. The announcement of a Maritime Silk Road followed soon afterwards. and the two routes became "One Belt One Road" (OBOR). OBOR was then rebranded as BRI (Belt Road Initiative).

[30] For an overview see, e.g. the "Belt & Road Initiative eLibrary" of the International Institute for Asian Studies: https://iias.asia/research/belt-road-initiative-electronic-library.

greater contribution to advancing the noble cause of peace and development of mankind."[31] My Chinese acquaintance summarized the agenda of OBOR in his own way: "The Silk Road is the Chinese Dream. There is the American Dream, and this is the Chinese Dream. You know the ancient Silk Road. This big route for trade. China wants to revitalize this route and become the leaders of the world."

In the Caucasus, the narrative of the Silk Road is quite popular and thus falls on fertile ground. The history of local trade is usually linked to typical Silk Road imaginaries. One learns that trade has flourished since the Bronze Age (Beriashvili, 2016; Dundua & Avdaliani, 2021; Khutsishvili, 2018), and that in medieval times there were many trading centers, which were visited by all the ethnic groups living in the surrounding territories. Armenian traders, who are known to have established trading posts in Europe, the Middle East, Central Asia and even India (Aslanian, 2014; Kalandarova, 2005), are especially associated with this commercial past, as reported the thirteenth-century Armenian historian Kirakos Ganjakec'I, who described the journey of the Armenian king of Cilicia, Hetum I, to the court of Möngke Khan in Karakorum (Kirakos Ganjakec'i, 1961: 364–372) (Conrad, 2021).

Such Silk Road narratives[32] allow states to establish partnerships with other states by alluding to an imagined common history of connectivity, linked to romantic imaginations of camels, caravans, oriental bazaars and rich merchants. Even Japan emphasizes the historical heritage of the Silk Road in introducing Buddhism and Western influences (Dadabaev, 2018).

[31] Summary by the Chinese Ministry of Foreign Affairs: https://www.fmprc.gov.cn/mfa_eng/topics_665,678/yzxhxzyxrcshydscfh/t1162057.shtml.

[32] In 1877, the German geographer Ferdinand von Richthofen coined the term "Silk Road" to link the ancient Han and Roman empires conceptually and thus promote a railway connection between Europe and China (Mertens, 2019; Wu, 2014), but it is nonetheless grounded in historical evidence. In the second half of the fourth century CE, the Roman soldier historian Ammianus Marcellinus speaks about the "longest route" used by traders to reach the "silk people" (ad Seras). In the late second century CE, the Chinese Han emperor Wu had sent an official named Zhang Qian to the West, who crossed the Tarim Basin, the Tian Shan mountains, reached the Ferghana Valley, Bactria, and Parthia, and initiated an exchange that lasted for centuries (Conrad 2021; Hopkirk 1980). Religions, philosophies, ideas, art, technology, languages, and goods traveled this route, along with merchants, pilgrims, diplomats, and adventurers (Conrad, 2021; Frankopan, 2015; Höllmann, 2008; Pourtskhvanidze & Tskhvediani, 2021). The Muslim Hui Chinese trace their ancestors back to Arab and Persian merchants who reached China by it in the mid-seventeenth century, for example (Wang, 2018).

"There are two divergent frames for thinking about Eurasian exchange and mobility: the so-called Silk Road, which has purportedly engendered East-West connectivity for two thousand years, and the contemporary Central Asian [and Caucasian] bazaar, which emerged during the twilight of the Cold War, in the wake of perestroika in the Soviet Union and the reform era in China," Karrar writes (2018: 13, cf. Chin, 2013).

But China, in particular, has made use of the Silk Road narrative to launch its infrastructural program. Negative foreign reactions to OBOR have raised concerns about "unfair competition" and promotion of "despotism" and "human right violations" (see, e.g., Dams & Van der Putten, 2015). OBOR has "come to represent the extension of China's economy initially into Central Asia, and then beyond" (Karrar, 2018: 15). Silk Road images, globalization with a Chinese face, "are part of a conscious construct of a new capitalist space" (Marsden, 2016).

In many locales, including Georgia, OBOR has involved the building of new roads, ports, and special economic zones, so-called economic corridors cutting through the topography connecting pivotal centers, ignoring topographical obstacles (Sternberg et al., 2017) and local structures or aspirations (Karrar, 2019; Rippa, 2018). The agreements at the basis of such projects, however, differ from global partnerships initiated by Western countries in the sense that they are "based on the principle of none-involvement" (Kaczmarski, 2016; Shah, 2018: 380). The PRC's Ministry of Foreign Affairs confirms that OBOR aims to connect a primarily economic "community of interests" for the purpose of "sustainable growth,"[33] backed by both multilateral and state financial institutions,[34] which "has now come to encompass more than sixty countries across Afro-Eurasia" (Karrar, 2018: 15; cf. Kaczmarski, 2016). This is almost two-thirds of the world's population, and one third of global

[33] Ministry of Foreign Affairs of the People's Republic of China President "Xi Jinping Delivers Important Speech and Proposes to Build a Silk Road Economic Belt with Central Asian Countries", 7 September 2013: http://www.fmprc.gov.cn/mfa_eng/topics_665678/xjpfwzysiesgjtfhshzzfh_665686/t1076334.shtml.

[34] The Silk Road Fund, the China Development Bank and the Import Bank of China. Additional financing is provided by the Chinese-led multilateral Asian Infrastructure Investment Bank (based in Beijing) and the New Development Bank (based in Shanghai), and private investors (6%). Total investment in BRI related projects was estimated 401 billion USD in 2016.

GDP (Larsen, 2017). Apart from the maritime routes, OBOR consists of six economic corridors, onshore, spanning Asia, Europe and Africa.[35]

Georgia and Azerbaijan are located on one of these (Larsen, 2017). In what follows, I discuss what this means for Georgia as a country, for the Georgian national economy, and for the Georgian businessmen, small entrepreneurs, and bazaar traders of my target group. As noted, earlier, globalization from above promotes globalization from below (Portes, 1997). OBOR mirrors the benefits individual Georgian and Chinese traders get from trade agreements and new infrastructures. At the same time "globalization from above references a world where mobility transcends borders. In grassroots globalization, mobility is there, but it is a mobility *despite* borders" (Karrar, 2018: 14). The "arrows" symbolizing economic corridors in maps of OBOR thus "represent how China's influence and economic power can reach beyond its borders," but "often show connections where there are none (yet), while hiding others that have been in place [since] well before the launch of the initiative" (Rippa, 2018) (Fig. 5.3).

The Georgia-China Partnership

In October 2015, the Georgian and Chinese governments co-hosted the Tbilisi Silk Road Forum. According to the official report, the event "reflected not only Beijing's desire to engage with Silk Road participating countries directly, but also Georgia's recognition of a need for greater inter-regional engagement in order to identify those ideas or projects which might offer opportunities for greater engagement under the Belt and Road Initiative" (Pantucci & Lain, 2016: 1–2).[36]

[35] For a detailed description of the economic corridors and the existing and emerging infrastructure they build upon, see Inan and Yayolan 2018.

[36] "The event also highlighted Georgia's willingness to be at the forefront of China's outward-facing foreign policy push, and to help shape Eurasian engagement with the Belt and Road project, following on from Tbilisi's hosting of the Asian Infrastructure Investment Bank (AIIB) negotiations in July 2015. The forum addressed ways to enhance transport, energy, trade and people-to-people connectivity across the Eurasian landmass from east to west, from China to Europe, as well as north to south, reconnecting Iran and Afghanistan to their Central and South Asian neighbors—in many cases reviving Silk Road routes that had fallen foul of border disputes, security or more recent cross-border sanctions. Discussions aimed to identify co-operative approaches to improving and increasing cross-border trade... Inevitably a large portion of the forum was also dedicated to discussing and promoting investment opportunities in Georgia itself and understanding

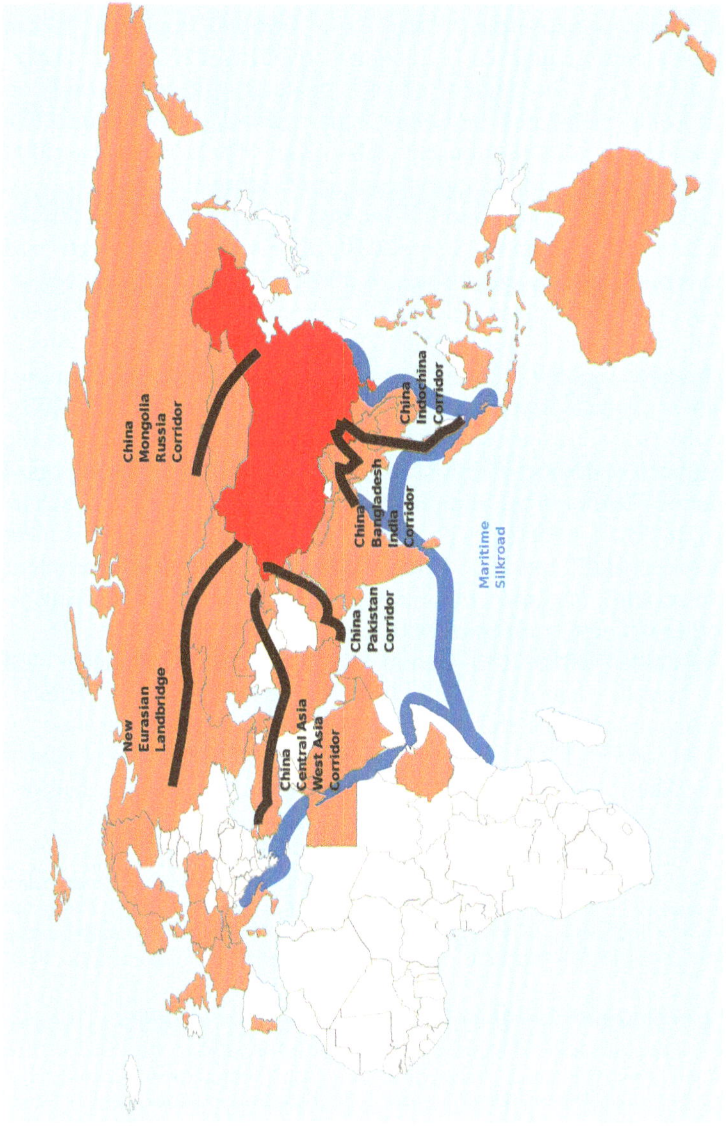

Fig. 5.3 Map of OBOR/BRI emphasizing the "China–Central Asia–West Asia Corridor" (*Source* "One-belt-one-road.svg" by Lommes, used under CC BY-SA 4.0)

China has been reluctant to introduce clear programmatic rules for OBOR, which might limit Beijing's room to maneuver, and the so-called New Silk Road is becoming a "kind of a universal 'umbrella' spread over China's current practice of building-up bilateral relations" (Kaczmarski, 2016: 18). The content of such bilateral relations depends on the relationship negotiated between China and the partner state (26). The Georgian-Chinese relationship dates from 1992, when the PRC recognized the newly independent Republic of Georgia.

Georgian-Chinese cooperation is focused on state-organized foreign direct investment and trade. Since 2010, after Georgia had recovered from the economic crisis and the war of 2008, Chinese, including private entrepreneurs, became more active in the region, and Chinese investment expanded significantly (Larsen, 2017; Zhou, 2012). The largest Chinese foreign investor was the aforementioned Hualing Group. Other important Chinese market players were the ZTE Corporation and HUAWEI Technology Co. (both active in telecommunications), Sichuan Electric Power Import & Export Corporation, the Chinese 20th Metallurgical Construction Corporation, and the Sinohydro Corporation and China Railway 23rd Bureau Group Co., Ltd.[37] The Hualing Group was most active between 2007 and 2015. Statistics show that Chinese investment has more recently declined, and the Georgian government is trying to attract other Chinese companies, with Hualing as mediator.

In September 2016, the Georgian Chamber of Commerce and Industry hosted what was called the "2016 Georgia-China (Jiangxi) Featured Commodities Exhibition" at the Expo Georgia Fairground on Tsereteli Avenue.[38] The event was well organized and had a very formal character. When Ana, Zviad, and I entered the main exhibition hall, we

ways in which Georgia can benefit from, and build on, China's Belt and Road policy and other regional connectivity initiatives. While Georgia aspires to become a transit and logistics hub, it still needs to leverage further economic investment for infrastructure development if it is to fully realize its own economic potential" (Pantucci & Lain, 2016: 1–2).

[37] For a list of Chinese projects in Georgia see (Zabakhidze et al., 2019).

[38] I got informed about it through a Facebook advertisement (Facebook "2016 Georgia-China (Jiangxi) Featured Commodities Exhibition": https://www.facebook.com/FeaturedCommoditiesExhibition2016/). Chinese (and Georgians) make extensive use of social media. There are Facebook groups and there is an online media initiative called Sinomedia (Sinomedia "Home": https://sinomedia.ge/en/) spreading information on China, China-Georgia relations, and Chinese in Georgia.

had to register to get visitor badges and also received a booklet listing all the exhibitors. The Chinese director of the event welcomed us in person. He spoke good English and guided us through the different exhibition stands, apparently taking us for potential Georgian business partners. He told us that Jiangxi province in China had not yet established business contacts in Georgia, and that the exhibition was an opportunity to get together with Georgian partners. The idea was to promote Chinese products and find Georgians to sell them in the Caucasus. The pavilion was not very crowded, and I wondered whether this was going to be a success. But the variety of the featured goods was amazing, including Chinese technology, chemicals, construction materials, pearl jewelry, clothes, preserves, tea, mushrooms and medicinal herbs. I asked a few questions about the merchandise and its price. The Chinese businessmen thought big, setting a price of 20,000 lari on sixty tons of preserves (the equivalent of one container, or a cargo load, the smallest amount offered), for example. Officially organized events like this reflect Chinese business ambitions in Georgia and the attitude of the Georgian government to them, as do cultural events jointly organized by Georgian officials and the Chinese embassy and Chinese donations to local institutions, such as the Tbilisi public library.[39]

Georgia celebrated the Georgia-China Friendship Day and twenty-five years of diplomatic relations between the two countries on 9 June 2017.[40] The Georgian prime minister, Giorgi Kvirikashvili, gave a public speech in which he acknowledged that China was one of the largest trading partners and investors in Georgia and that "traditionally, Georgia and China have a friendly relationship based on the principles of equality, respect and cooperation".[41] "Twenty-five years ago, China was one of the first countries to recognize Georgia's independence after the fall of

[39] Rusudan, the president of the Georgian Library Association, told me that the Chinese government had donated a large sum of money for the national library, which was earmarked for high-tech scanners that had to be bought from a Chinese company. The deal was mediated by the Chinese embassy, where Rusudan had good connections with the Chinese woman in charge, who coordinated many such projects. The embassy also donated Chinese books to the library's Chinese studies section.

[40] The event was sponsored by the PRC's embassy in Georgia and Tbilisi City Hall. See Agenda.ge "Georgian PM: 'Today Georgia-China relations are stronger than ever'", 9 June 2017: http://agenda.ge/news/81087/eng.

[41] Agenda.ge "Georgian PM: 'Today Georgia-China Relations Are Stronger Than Ever'", 9 June 2017: http://agenda.ge/news/81087/eng.

the Soviet Union," a local website reported. "Since then, the two countries have grown ever closer, especially since Chinese President Xi Jinping announced his ambitious $900 billion 'One Belt, One Road' initiative."[42]

The PRC's interest in Georgia is certainly due to Georgia's geographical position and its role as a transportation and trading hub (Ismalov & Papava, 2018).[43] Georgia is located at the crossroads between the Black Sea and the Caspian Sea, a historical transit zone, and has good relationships with its neighbors Armenia and Azerbaijan.[44] It is a participant in the Trans-Caspian International Transport Route (TITR),[45] which was established under Chinese OBOR patronage to connect China to Ukraine and Turkey via Kazakhstan, Azerbaijan and Georgia.[46] Georgia is also a participant in the Transport Corridor Europe-Caucasus-Asia (TRACECA), a regional infrastructure initiative OBOR seeks to build on, and the Batumi Bypass Road Project, financed by the Asian Infrastructure Investment Bank, another on-going project, intended to facilitate access to Turkey (Zbakhidze et al., 2019: 4). The Baku-Tbilisi-Kars (BTK) railway, opened in October 2017, already covers part of the China–Central Asia–West Asia Corridor (Larsen, 2017).[47] "The overland journey between China and Europe via the BTK rail line will take around 15 days, which is more than twice as fast as sea transport at less than half the price of air travel. Trains can depart from a variety of cities in China, cross into Kazakhstan at the Khorgos Gateway, be easily transported by ferry

[42] Jako.fm: http://archive.jako.fm/en/this-friday-china-georgia-friendship-day-celebrates-25-years-of-diplomatic-relations.

[43] Georgia is not the only candidate for this role. "Baku reacted positively to the (OBOR) initiative, hoping that the ambitious project would bring more Chinese investment to the country. Baku realizes the importance of implementing economic diversification strategies before the depletion of its hydrocarbon reserves. Such a tendency has contributed greatly to shaping Azerbaijan's bilateral relations with China, allowing the latter to rise to become one of Azerbaijan's top ten trading partners" (Shahbazov, 2017a). Furthermore, "Azerbaijan is seeking opportunities to increase its role as a regional transit hub" (Shahbazov, 2017c).

[44] For the role of BRI for Armenia and Azerbaijan see Zabakhidze et al. (2019).

[45] See Shahbazov (2017c).

[46] It involves co-operation between port, railway, shipping and logistic companies from Azerbaijan, Kazakhstan, Georgia, and Turkey to build a transport corridor to China. The aim is to reduce transport time along this corridor to fourteen days, which would make it the quickest route from China to Europe (Pantucci & Lain, 2016: 2).

[47] And is planned to be joined by TITR.

across the Caspian Sea to the New Port of Baku, and then be loaded directly onto the BTK and head on to Europe—and vice versa in the opposite direction" (Shahbazov, 2017b).[48] Chinese (usually parastatal) construction companies are involved in all these projects.[49]

Georgia has several Black Sea ports. The biggest, for now, is Poti. But the Anaklia Black Sea Deep Water Port, U.S.-Georgian joint venture, whose completion was originally scheduled for December 2020, but has been delayed, would have much more capacity and be able to process up ten thousand container ships and 100 million tons of cargo annually.[50] It would also include a Free Industrial Zone of about 600 hectares allowing goods to be produced for export under a tax-free regime (Larsen, 2017). "Located on the eastern edge of the Black Sea, Anaklia strategically sits on the shortest route from China to Europe. The route has recently become a focal point for $40 billion in Chinese infrastructure investments under the Silk Road Development Fund and already accounts for 26 percent of Chinese foreign trade volume."[51] The port also has the potential to become a main contact point with Ukraine, an important Chinese trading partner.[52]

China is thus supporting and expanding the existing structures and is building physical, political, and economic bridges between Asia and Europe in the Caucasus. Whether these bridges will really develop their full and predicted potential, of course, is an open question, which is

[48] For more details see Inan and Yayloyan (2018): "In western Turkey, the newly built Yavuz Sultan Selim Bridge in Istanbul, including a railroad, aims to ensure a corridor for a seamless flow of goods and people between Asia and Europe. Furthermore, Azerbaijan and Kazakhstan have recently constructed modern ports on the Caspian Sea, Kuryk and Alat, respectively. At the other end of the Trans-Caspian corridor, Kazakhstan's internal rail network stretching from China to the Caspian Sea is also completed. In Khorgos collaboration with China, Kazakhstan plans to construct a railway from on the Kazakh Chinese border to the Caspian Sea port of Aktau, a promising development adding to the value of the Caspian connection" (36).

[49] For a more detailed overview see Zhou (2012: 6).

[50] The Maritime Executive "Georgia to Build New Silk Road Port", 2 September 2016: https://www.maritime-executive.com/article/georgia-to-build-new-silk-road-port#gs.BhIywYw.

[51] The Maritime Executive "Georgia to Build New Silk Road Port", 2 September 2016: https://www.maritime-executive.com/article/georgia-to-build-new-silk-road-port#gs.BhIywYw.

[52] In 2015, China was the third-largest consumer of all Ukrainian exports, and the biggest share of Ukraine's agricultural exports went to the PRC (Larsen, 2017).

often skeptically discussed. Thusfar, the corridor is still underused. There are several reasons for this: (1) long waiting periods and high costs for crossing the Caspian Sea, (2) deficits of infrastructure, for example, poor rail links between Turkey and the EU, (3) the gauge differences of railway networks along the routes, creating costs and delays, and (4) complicated regulations, tariffs, and border-crossing procedures.[53]

Georgia has free-trade agreements with both the EU and China,[54] however, giving China access to European markets (Pantucci & Lain, 2016: 4; Lambert, 2017).[55] Georgia benefits as a state, at least currently, from this middleman role. Given that Georgia already allowed the importation of Chinese products at very low tariffs, the free-trade agreement with China is probably good for the Georgian economy. The elimination of all tariffs is estimated to be likely to lead to a 1.6–2.2% annual increase in Chinese exports to Georgia, while Georgia would benefit from a 9% increase of exports to the PRC[56] (Larsen, 2017).[57] China has also become an important market for Georgian wine.

At the same time, according to Larsen, there is little risk of Georgia becoming overdependent on China. As discussed by many authors (Dadabaev, 2018; Lee, 2014; Nyíri, 2012), and as I could see for myself, Chinese paternalism and China's postcolonial attitude are much feared—including by Georgians. However, China's influence seems to be limited in the region, because of the Caucasus's geographical distance from Asia and because of Georgia's strong ties with Azerbaijan, the EU, Turkey, and other local players. China has no military presence in the Caucasus and has an economic interest in the region's stability.[58] Georgia might also

[53] For more details, see Inan and Yayloyan (2018).

[54] Since September 2015 Georgian and Chinese politicians were discussing the possibility of establishing a free trade zone between the two countries. A Memorandum on finalizing this free trade agreement was signed in October 2016, and the final agreement on 13th of May 2017.

[55] Michael Lambert, "Is China Building a Bridge or an Outpost in the Caucasus," Macdonald-Laurier Institute, 27 September 2017, https://www.macdonaldlaurier.ca/is-china-building-a-bridge-or-an-outpost-in-the-caucasus-michael-lambert-for-inside-policy.

[56] Larsen refers to the 2015 "Joint Feasibility Study on China-Georgia Possible Free Trade Agreement" of the PMC Research Centre.

[57] Agenda.ge "Georgia, China Sign Historic Free Trade Agreement", 13 May 2017: http://agenda.ge/news/79386/eng.

[58] China's interest in Caspian oil and gas is one of these reasons that has not been mentioned so far. Since 1993, China has become an oil importer, and since 2006, a net

profit from Chinese-Russian bargains. Although China expressly avoided interfering during the Georgian-Russian war in 2008 (Zhou, 2012),[59] the Chinese Foreign Ministry voiced concerns about developments in Abkhazia and South Ossetia (Larsen, 2017),[60] which was regarded as positive in Georgia.

Georgian traders, and Georgians in general, were concerned about the growing economic power of Chinese competitors, but they nevertheless saw profit in the possibilities offered by this new partnership. In face-to-face encounters, Chinese usually treated Georgians respectfully, and they accepted Georgian businesspeople as equal partners. Many of my interlocutors were thus quite positive about future relations with the Chinese.

Chinese-Georgian Encounters on the Ground

Sinophobia is a common phenomenon in post-Soviet Eurasia (Humphrey & Skvirskaja, 2009; Nyíri, 2011), originating Billé (2014) argues, in Russian stereotypes of Asia, which have influenced the perception of Chinese, in neighboring countries. Using evolutionist jargon taken from Marxist theory,[61] such stereotypes treat Asian cultures as backward and savage. Such attitudes frequently surface in the Caucasus, too, with respect, not only to so-called Asians, but to people said to behave "like Asians." Talking about macho behavior, my interlocutors would say things like, "Our men are still Asians!" or say of poor living standards, "It's like in Asia" (Fehlings, 2014: 317–323; 2016).[62] Simultaneously,

gas importer. By 2020, if trends continue, it will have to import 66% of its oil needs. Currently, significant proportions of energy supply come from the Middle East and Africa, along a path through the Strait of Malacca, which is controlled by the U.S. Navy. The Strait of Malacca has thus become a weak spot for China, which is why China seeks to construct overland pipelines. The Caspian oil, in this context, has become a major concern (Smith Stegen & Kusznir, 2015).

[59] Cf. China's stance on the Karabakh conflict (Shahbazov, 2017a).

[60] Kieran Pender, "Abkhazia: Is Chinese Investment a Panacea or a Pipe Dream?" Eurasianet, 20 September 2017, https://eurasianet.org/node/85226.

[61] Marx speaks of the Asian mode of production as the most primitive (1977 [1859]).

[62] This is harmless chatting in comparison to open discrimination of Asian individuals (including Chinese, Central Asians, Koreans etc.) in Russia, which frequently leads to physical attacks. For example the day of Hitler's birthday is particularly dangerous for Asian looking people, as I could witness in Moscow in 2005. On this day my friend from

unlike Central Asia or India, China has often been romanticized in the Caucasus. This was especially true in the 1980s and 1990s, when Chinese martial arts, films, medicine, mystics, and philosophy became very popular among youth, not only in the Caucasus but also in Russia and other parts of the former Soviet Union. Translations of Confucius and pictures of Bruce Lee, common in many late Soviet households (cf. Fehlings, 2019), were still there, when I did my fieldwork thirty years later. Some of my friends were quite interested in Chinese symbolism, and Chinese astrological animals are often cited in New Year's wishes.

China is admired in the Caucasus for its rich, ancient civilization, which is compared to local pasts and cultures, and given the Armenian obsession with history, ancestors, and genealogies, it is no surprise that legends about these invoke connections with the Chinese (and with other peoples).[63] Movses Khorenatsi's *History of Armenia*, allegedly written in the fifth century CE, asserts, for example, that Mamik, one of two brothers, members of General Ma Chao's family, who fled from China during the Three Kingdoms period (220–80 CE), was an ancestor of the Mamikonyan spiritual and military leaders who ruled much Armenian territory between the fourth and eighth centuries CE (Zhou, 2012).[64]

Since few Georgians have had personal contact with Chinese immigrants, however, the attitudes of most "are presumed to be formed based on secondary information" (Chumburidze et al., 2016: 18). Many Georgians take a neutral postion, but generally, Chinese are regarded as "the worst and messiest of tourists," and Armenians and Georgians worry about their demographic and economic power. Locals more than once exclaimed disappointedly to me: "The real Chinese have nothing in common with those in books!".

Georgians and Chinese workers got into a fight at a Georgian village on 4 November 2016. I heard several versions of the story. Tatia said "a Chinese firm had bought a piece of forest in the mountains that separate eastern and western Georgia" and problems arose when the Chinese started to cut down the trees:

Yakutia stayed over night, because she was afraid to leave my place. The television and radio warned about fascist groups and recommended to stay at home.

[63] As I have shown in my previous writings (Fehlings, 2014).

[64] The legends about and the genealogy of the Mamikonyan family is accessible on Wikipedia.

> One issue was that workers were all Chinese, and the local population did not profit from the economic activity started in their neighborhood. Villagers continued to cut down trees on the Chinese land, and the Chinese started to guard the area. One day, there was an incident. A Chinese guard caught a villager in the act. The villager resisted and hit the guard, who went back to his dormitory and mobilized all his Chinese co-workers. Together, they went to the Georgian village to take revenge. The villagers were in the minority, and the Chinese workers won the battle.

Another version of the story said that the fight was between Georgian employees and Chinese employers, and when the firm's Georgian employees helped the villagers move firewood, they were attacked with knifes, truncheons, and batons by the company's Chinese personnel.[65] Physical violence between locals and Chinese is nevertheless rather an exception.[66] According to my colleague Ketevan, the incident caused an uproar in Georgian media, which called for protest against the Chinese and a boycott of Chinese goods."The protests lasted a few weeks, and it was a big issue," she said. "Then everybody forgot about the story. It was as if nothing had happened."

Hualing Group as Employer

Many of the activities of Chinese representatives in Georgia seemed enigmatic and thus suspect to outsiders. During my recent stays in the Caucasus, I heard several stories about Chinese who threaten to "silently take over the country." Manana, who worked with the Ombudsman and was concerned with ethnic and religious minorities, and had previously been working for the Georgian Ministry of Energy and in a parliamentary program on conflict resolution, remembered that a few years before, a lot of Chinese migrants had come to Georgia: "They were everywhere. They had small shops at every street corner of Tbilisi. Then they started

[65] Vestnik Kavkaza "Police Detains Chinese Citizens for Attacking Georgian Workers", 6 November 2016: http://vestnikkavkaza.net/news/Police-detains-Chinese-citizens-for-attacking-Georgian-workers.html.

[66] Unlike in Russia, for example, physical attacks on Chinese are rather an exception in Georgia today. The Chinese Embassy reported several robberies, thefts, and attacks, but pointed out that such incidents equally happened to Westerners and other foreigners. Also, the security situation for foreigners and locals alike has improved since the Rose Revolution and anti-corruption campaign (Zhou, 2012: 16).

to buy land in the villages. I guess people got frightened, and there were cases of racism—and suddenly all these Chinese disappeared. Apparently, they have thought up other ways to establish Chinese business. They are very clever. That's for sure." Manana heard that Chinese migrants of the first wave had got support from the Chinese government to leave their country and settle abroad. This rumor was widespread (cf. Zhou, 2012). Manana was sure that China was seeking to expand to the Caucasus, and that one could "observe this all over the world," for example "in the United States, where Chinese have established Chinatowns." She regarded Chinese ambitions with suspicion, convinced that their interests might "not converge with what is good for Georgia, at least not in the long run."

Manana was also critical of the strategy of the Georgian government for this reason. She was disturbed by the fact that after 2003, to reduce unemployment rates, Georgia had done its best to attract foreign investors to build factories and create jobs because "it is easier to let someone from outside do this." Indeed, the Georgian government advertises the improving business climate and argues that Georgia is "a politically stable, corruption-free investment destination with low business costs,"[67] as proved by statistics and international comparisons like the World Bank's "Ease of Doing Business Index"[68] (Di Puppo, 2013; Zabakhidze et al., 2019; and see also Chapter 4). When Manana worked for the Ministry of Energy, a whole department was assigned to promoting Georgia and attracting investors from abroad to build power plants. John, my Chinese informant, worked for such a foreign investor, a Chinese construction company. For the present, foreign (Chinese) investment might have a positive impact on the Georgian economy, Manana admitted, because the Chinese created jobs. However, she doubted that this was a good solution for the future. Georgia, in her opinion, should have used its own potential to build factories instead of letting foreigners do so: "It may be good for us now, but who knows what [the situation] is going to be in ten years," she said, reflecting a concern of many of my Georgian and Armenian interlocutors.

[67] Invest in Georgia "Home": http://www.investingeorgia.org/en/.

[68] The World Bank "Doing Business": http://www.doingbusiness.org/rankings.

Irakli's and Lasha's Experience

People working with Chinese subscribed to another perspective. As employees of the Hualing Group, Irakli and his friend Lasha regarded Chinese investment very positively. One day in 2017, Lasha, Irakli, Zviad, and I were sitting on a terrace and were eating fish from the restaurant's own fish farm. Lasha, who arranged custom clearance for the Hualing Group, was a great entertainer. After having ordered vodka and lots of food, he started to talk about his job. Since he prepared the documents for all goods that entered Georgia from China, Lasha said, he knew the amount and value of goods that crossed the border. He and Irakli, who oversaw the transportation of goods, ran most of Hualing's import business. According to Lasha, five thousand containers shipped by the Hualing Group had thusfar (in 2017) reached Georgia in five vessels. Goods were sent not only by sea but by truck via the road from China through Kazakhstan and Russia, provided Russia permitted it; or along the Black Sea, if transit through Russia got difficult because of political conflicts. According to Lasha, the Hualing Group had been involved in building these roads, and it had started operating in Georgia by buying a former Soviet factory in Kutaisi[69]:

> There, the company employed about 300 individuals, half of whom were Georgian. Apparently, things were going well and the leadership of Hualing Group became convinced that the conditions for investment in Georgia were good. Hualing started to expand. In 2011, the Georgian government was looking for an investor to help build the Olympic City for the Youth Olympic Games in 2014. Hualing Group agreed to invest in this endeavor and took care of housing construction and the Plaza building, which covered 110,000 square meters. The Hualing Group became a partner of Tbilisi City Hall and the Georgian Government, and the president of the Hualing Group and the president of Georgia became close friends around the same time.

Hualing had brought almost everything—trucks, machinery, and building materials—from China to build Hualing New City, and the Group did not pay tax on any of these things, Lasha said. He seemed fascinated

[69] Forbes "Silk Road Impact: Chinese Company Turns Old Soviet Factory in Kutaisi Into Free Industrial Zone", 30 June 2016 (by Wade Shepard): https://www.forbes.com/sites/wadeshepard/2016/06/30/how-chinas-hualing-group-revived-an-old-soviet-factory-to-help-restore-an-ailing-economy-in-kutaisi-georgia/#6da987c21c80.

by the money and goods invested by the Chinese. According to him, the company had spent U.S.$5 million to build the hospital next to the marketplace; it had already invested a total of U.S.$1 billion in Georgia and planned to invest U.S.$4 billion in all.

Irakli and Lasha both thought that this was good for Georgia. Even though Hualing had brought in high-tech equipment for automatic assembly, it had created jobs for Georgians: "Hualing employs ten thousand workers," Lasha said. "Only 30 percent of them are Chinese. The other 70 percent are supposed to be Georgian."[70] Lasha told me that the Hualing Group had twenty offices in Georgia. He worked in the main office and reported that most of the office workers were Georgians like him.

When I asked how he had got his job, he said that his father had worked for Hualing first. His father was an engineer and responsible for the security measures at the construction site of Hualing New City. One day, he invited some of his Chinese bosses to his home for dinner. During the evening, the Chinese guests told Lasha that they were looking for someone to manage their customs clearances. Lasho said he could do this, and they took him on for a trial period of four months. Then, when they saw that he was "a good guy and doing a good job," they gave him an open-ended contract. "As long as Hualing Group operates in Georgia, this contract will last, too," he said.

Lasha tried to explain the hierarchy within the Hualing Group. Mi Enhua was at the top of the Group's hierarchy, Lasha said, and Wenxian Zhang and Ilan Alon's *Biographical Dictionary of New Chinese Entrepreneurs and Business Leaders* (2009: 119–120) confirms this, stating:

> In 1988 Mi borrowed 30 000 yuan from friends to build a construction materials market named Red October Market in the provincial capital

[70] As in Africa, there are rumors that Chinese companies would import their own labor force instead of hiring locals. Surveys and evidence quoted by Lee suggest that—at least in Africa—Chinese contractors employ only a minority of skilled Chinese supervisors. The majority of workers—about 85–95%—are hired locally (Lee 2014: 46). My own observations in the Caucasus suggest similar proportions. The issue of "local content" in terms of employees and materials was also discussed during the Tbilisi Silk Road Forum in 2015 and mentioned as an important condition for equal partnership (Pantucci & Lain, 2016: 5). PRC parastatals have agreed to a ratio of 70% of Georgian and 30% of Chinese workers. Private investors have individual agreements (Zhou, 2012: 6).

> Ürümqi and founded his new company, Xinjiang Hualing Group. Xinjiang shared a border with what were then Soviet Central Asian republics and political trade barriers were only just beginning to thaw. At first business was slow, but when the Soviet Union collapsed in 1991 Mi was well placed to take advantage of the emerging market in Central Asia. Mi was twice forced to relocate his market at great personal cost, but by the mid-1990s trade between Xinjiang and Kazakhstan and Russia was booming. Mi Enhua's personal wealth grew to the point that in 2003 Asia Money ranked Mi as the 38th wealthiest individual in China with estimated assets of $155 million.

Mi Enhua's fortune thus actually originates in post-Soviet petty and shuttle trade, the same political and economic conditions that have framed the business of Lilo's bazaar traders.

Georgian news mentioned that Mi Enhua had been honored with several titles and awards for his economic achievements, his outstanding charity activities, and his contributions to his homeland.[71] "This man has achieved everything by himself and has a background in a poor family," Lasha said. "He knows what it means to be poor. This is why he does a lot of good. He has 500 children. Four of them are his own offspring. The others are orphans. He pays for their education and gives them jobs in the Hualing Company."

Chichi, one of Mi Enhua's biological sons was a permanent resident of Georgia, Lasha said.[72] He was married to a Chinese woman who had lived in Georgia for a long time and who spoke fluent Georgian. According to Lasha, nothing worked without Chichi. "He has to sign off on everything the Hualing Group does in Georgia. Under him, there is a general director, called the 'Big One,' because he is tall. And there is the 'Little One,' the most active one, who is my boss... Then, there is the executive director, who does not have an international position but is responsible for all construction and permissions in Georgia."

Lasha and his boss apparently had a very good relationship. As a rule, employees of the Hualing had to check in with a card when they came to work and check out when leaving the office. But the "Little One" told Lasha to ignore this rule: "Do your work, and then leave when you have

71 "Who Is Behind Tbilisi Olympic Village?", 20 July 2014, http://agenda.ge/news/39419/eng.

72 He has different names in different languages.

finished," he said. Lasha worked many more than the mandatory working hours, however, he told me. He liked his job, and he liked to work for his Chinese employers.

Irakli and Lasha both expressed surprise at how much Chinese and Georgians have in common. "Even though they are less emotional and do not show their feelings, it is very easy to communicate with them," Irakli said.[73] Lasha and Irakli spoke of the interest of the Chinese in Georgian culture, as Nino had also done earlier. The "Little One" loved Georgian traditions, according to Lasha. A few weeks earlier, one of Lasha's relatives had died. The funeral took place in a rural part of Georgia, and Lasha had invited some of his colleagues. He was overwhelmed when his Chinese boss also attended the ceremony. He said:

> In Georgia, there is a tradition of giving money to the family members of the deceased to support them holding the funeral. My boss even knew this tradition. He came, gave me money, and said, "Lasha take this and write my name in this book." He even knew about that![74] He likes to participate in supras, and even very often does the job of the *tamada*,[75] you know… These Chinese come from Xinjiang, and there are a lot of Muslims there. Many of them are Muslims,[76] but "the Little One" drinks *chacha*[77] and eats pork. He doesn't care. There are even some Christians. Once, I saw a Chinese person who had a problem at the customs. When they did not let him go for days, he showed the cross he wore around his neck. He showed it and said: "Please, help me, I am Christian."

Lasha was not impressed by Chinese drinking capacity, however: "Chinese vodka is not bad, but it is not as strong as vodka," he said. After Lasha had

[73] Communication between Chinese and their Georgian employees takes place in Russian.

[74] There is the Chinese tradition of giving monetary gifts (*lijin*) and keeping gift lists, so-called *lidan*, at funerals (Yan, 1996: 49–50). Such practices at funerals and weddings are widely established throughout Asia and the Caucasus (see, e.g., Brumann, 1998; Yalçın-Heckmann, 2001; Yan, 1996). Thus the Chinese might feel familiar with the Georgian practice even though it might be slightly different.

[75] The (ceremonial) master of the table and the *supra*.

[76] Mi Enhua was born in Tai'an in Shandong province to a family of ethnic Hui Muslims. At the age of four he moved with his family to Xinjiang (Zhang & Alon, 2009: 119–120).

[77] A very strong alcoholic drink, also called "Georgian vodka".

been out drinking with some of his Chinese colleagues, they had terrible headaches. This is regarded as discreditable sign of weakness in Georgia, but both Lasha and Irakli nevertheless appreciated the effort made by the Chinese to drink with them and believed that "common cultural ground" allowed for good personal relationships between Georgians and Chinese. As did Zviad and other traders, Lasha and Irakli said that Georgians and Chinese seem to understand one another because of their post-socialist pasts.

Mariam's Experience

Mariam was equally positive about Hualing Group as an employer. Mariam's biography somewhat resembled Nino's, whose experiences are reported earlier in this chapter. Mariam lived in Xian for two years. After earning her BA, she went to China to work there as an English teacher along with four other young Georgians. She never regretted her decision. She appreciated her freedom, her life as a single, the great job opportunities and the respect with which Chinese people treated her: "It was so good! For foreigners, China is heaven! … Sometimes people, complete strangers, just wanted to take photos with me. I really got the 'superstar syndrome' and it cost me an effort to overcome it back home in Georgia."

Thus, when she was back, she missed China. She continued to order Chinese goods from taobao.com, and as soon as she heard about Hualing, she applied for a job there: "When I heard that there was this Chinese company in Georgia, I was so happy". Because of her language skills and experiences in China, she was immediately invited to a job interview and got the position of a sales manager in the big Hualing-owned "Tbilisi Sea Plaza" shopping center. She left the company for about a year to pursue MA studies in Warsaw. After that, she called her former director, and received a job at the Plaza again, this time, as an operations specialist, and became responsible for the whole first floor of the shopping mall. As she told me, she loved to work for the Hualing Group because of the attitude of her Chinese employers towards their staff: "If you work well, they will love you forever. If they see that you are counting hours, they will hate you. They are much stricter than Georgians. For them, working hard is an important value. I know their mentality, and I felt very respected by them."

The Chinese expected their Georgian employees to work hard, but they paid overtime or allowed them to take time off in compensation. According to Mariam, the salary was very good by Georgian standards, and after a while (five years at latest), one got promoted. The work environment, as Mariam said, was great. She liked her colleagues and even invited some of her age group to visit her at home. Employees were all surprised with presents from the company's management on the 8th of March (International Women's Day) and to celebrate the New Year. "This was just a good feeling," she said. "It is a detail, but it makes you feel appreciated." Apparently, as I understood from her, such a gesture is nothing one could expect from a Georgian employer.

Mariam left the Hualing Group for private reasons. She had a hard time taking this decision, she said, because "the Plaza was my second home." After she left, she kept in touch with her friends there. She herself found someone to replace her, whom she recommended to Hualing: "I found a responsive, hard-working person. After two months, she called me to thank me, because she was also so happy with the job at Hualing."

Like Lasha, Irakli, and Nino, Marjam thus painted a very positive picture of her Chinese employers at Hualing Group and emphasized the good personal face-to-face relationship based on mutual respect and trust. Although Lasha, Irakli, Nino, and Mariam may not represent a huge segment of Georgian society, their cases nevertheless indicate the treatment of locals by Chinese businesspeople, who try to establish good relationships on a personal level, which is well received by their Georgian employees.

Hualing's Encounters with Georgian Formal Institutions

The Hualing Group apparently has long-range plans in Georgia. Lasha was sure that Hualing was not about to stop at this point. "Next year, they intend to build a kindergarten, a school, and a high school next to Tbilisi Lake, and a library, a cinema, and a lot of private houses too," he said. "Profits are not for tomorrow [...]. These are long-term investments. They are not planning for one or two, but for ten or more years. [...] For example, Hualing has bought Basis Bank, and instead of making ten-year loans, as is usual in Georgia, it makes thirty-year loans, which enables people to buy apartments in Hualing New City."

"Hualing intends to invest several hundred million US dollars in Georgia," it was reported in May 2016. Hualing's president, Mi Enhua, and Prime Minister Giorgi Kvirikashvili had met to discuss investments in natural gas storage facilities, educational institutions, hospitals, a new airline, and the Georgian tea and tourist industries. Vice Prime

Minister and Minister of Economy and Sustainable Development Dimitry Kumsishvili told journalists after the meeting that the Chinese investors had the full support of Georgia's government.[78]

In 2018, I heard rumors about plans to transfer Tbilisi's city hall to Hualing New City. Hualing would profit from this, it was argued, because it would put the Hualing Sea Plaza on the mental map of Tbilisi's residents. Another rumored deal with the government involved moving Eliava Market to the Hualing Sea Plaza. Typically, my Georgian interlocutors were convinced that the government was cooperating with the Hualing Group, not just in the interests of the municipality, but to benefit individual government officials personally.

Lasha, Irakli, Mariam, and other people working with the Chinese group did not see this as a threat, however, and hoped to profit as much as possible from Hualing's success. Lasha had definitely found a niche for himself. Dealing with customs clearances for Hualing made him a mediator between Georgian officials and the Chinese. "Georgian customs work really well," he told me. "The process is transparent. One just has to fill out the paperwork the right way. This is really easy." Lasha and Irakli were agreed: "Chinese are very bad at filling out documents. They just don't do it correctly." And Irakli said:

> Goods coming from Europe always have good documents. There are no questions. If the goods come from China, the documents are always very bad. It is very complicated. You have to talk to them, and you have to call to China to ask more questions on the phone. It is hard to believe. But even goods from Iran always have good documents. But China... They declare goods for 50,000 lari and have goods for 100,000. So there is a special customs task force to deal with Chinese imports and determine their real prices. At least it will get easier. Thanks to the free trade agreement, Chinese will only have to pay import tax in the future... and Hualing does not pay VAT or import tax, anyway.

Whereas Chinese businesspeople seem able to adapt to Georgian codes of social conduct, they apparently have difficulty understanding the mix of formality and informality that characterizes the local socioeconomic

[78] Newsday.ge "Hualing Intends to Invest Several Hundred Million US Dollars in Georgia", 10 May 2016: http://newsday.ge/new/index.php/en/component/k2/item/19085-hualing-intends-to-invest-several-hundred-million-us-dollars-in-georgia.

and political environment and the complex context of personal interaction shaped by government agencies, official and private actors, economic exchange, and local values. The Chinese realize, moreover, that they need an insider to help them navigate this system. Lasha explained:

> Chinese think they can get everything for money. In China, this works. You can get everything if you pay for it.[79] When we had some problems with customs clearance, the Chinese came to me and said: "Let's just give U.S.$100 to each customs agent, that should fix it." I told them that if they tried that, they would end up in prison. Until 2003, it was the same in Georgia. Bribery was very common. But this has changed.[80] Now, customs is very efficient. Even after six years, they have the right to check what happens to the goods—and they really do it. Usually, there are no problems with clearance. If the documents are okay and everything is filled in correctly, everything works well. Only once, there was a problem with a ship, because the shipping company had made a mistake. Hualing Group was penalized. But then they talked with the government and explained that it was not their fault but a mistake by the shipping company. Then, everything was fine and they did not have to pay.

John, whom I told about the accusation that Chinese often try to bribe customs, immediately admitted that this was highly probable. Looking at me with astonishment, he explained that "the results of bribery are positive. Bribery is not positive, but the results are. They work." In further discussion with Lasha, Lasha admitted that correctly completed paperwork is not the only reason why clearance usually goes so smoothly:

> There are three customs lines: a green line, which means there is nothing to declare, a yellow line, which means that documents have to be checked, and a red line, where one has to go through a more drastic check. In the beginning, all Hualing Group containers ended up in the red line. I told my boss that he should invite some customs officials—say, ten of them—show them what Hualing Group does and how it works, and give them a Chinese meal. ... It worked. These people came, looked at everything ... and now, if there is some problem with Hualing Group, they make no trouble.

[79] In Kazakstan, however, Chinese traders and officials are evidently perceived as less corrupt than local ones (Alff, 2014).

[80] Lasha is referring to the Rose Revolution in 2003 as a watershed and President Saakashvili's anti-corruption campaign.

After the relationship was established, Lasha made the next move:

> Then I asked if we could clear customs in our storage area. Just bring the goods there and do it with no rush. The red-line supervisor agreed. Then, later, he asked if I could perhaps find a job for his daughter. I recommended to the Hualing Group to employ her, and now she does the clearance under her father's supervision. If her father makes trouble, it means trouble for his daughter. So he looks at it like this [Lasha squints] and says, "Okay," and everything is fine.

Meanwhile (in 2018), because of the new free trade agreement and special arrangements with the Georgian government, Hualing no longer paid custom dues.

This does not mean that Chinese did not have to deal with bureaucracy in their own country. Aside from its own structure and hierarchy, Chinese government regulations seem to have been the main obstacle for the Hualing Group. "Chinese bureaucracy takes a lot of time," Marjam said. "There are many steps—even within Hualing. For the Plaza this means than any small change at the building, for example, must be approved on all levels of the hierarchy, going as far as to China. This makes everything very complicated."

I do not know how Hualing Group dealt with the Chinese state bureaucracy. On the level of direct interaction with local elites, who, at least partly, were above bureaucratic procedures, representatives of Hualing seemed to feel quite confident. "They [the Chinese] are like Georgians but bigger," Marjam said. In the Caucasus, elites represent political, economic, religious and moral power. Lasha offered an example of how this worked: "The bishop of Qazbegi wanted to do some renovations. He asked the president of Georgia how to go about it, and they approached the Hualing Group.[81] Hualing agreed to back this project and brought in materials worth U.S.$300.000 from Turkey, which it simply donated to the church. When there was the flood in Tbilisi in 2015, which destroyed parts of the city (Saburtalo) and the zoo, Hualing donated U.S.$150,000. Hualing even made a gift of some roads, but I forget which ones."

[81] I was never able to confirm this story.

The Chinese know how to impress. According to Lasha, money means nothing to them: "They have so much money. I did the customs clearance for the [Hualing] president's car. When I looked at the documents, I saw it was a Rolls Royce. We paid 11,000 lari just for clearance and another 10,000 lari for registration. If the president [of Hualing] comes, we take the car out of the garage, and when he leaves, we put it in again." There are other stories like these: Lasha had had to steer some extravagant objects through the clearance process, including the sculpture of five rearing horses that marked the entrance to the Hualing Group's Tbilisi Sea Plaza mall, mentioned earlier. The high value of European paintings in the private art collection of Hualing's president, Mi Enhua, had also attracted the attention of customs officers, but Lasha had stressed to them that these works were "for private use only." Mi Enhua, who came to Georgia regularly, had his own private aircraft. During his journeys here, he lived on the ninth floor of the big hotel in Hualing New City. The whole floor, whose marble fittings and expensive furniture Lasha had taken through customs as well, was reserved for him. "When Hualing's president comes, he brings his own personal driver from China," Lasha said. "This man is a kung-fu guy... But we call the police then, too, and they provide protection for him when he goes somewhere." Mi Enhua was thus effectively treated as a guest of the Georgian state and its leaders.

Analysis of Chinese Activities in Georgia

When I asked Lasha and Irakli about their opinion of Georgian citizens' reactions to the Hualing Group, they said that there were some tensions in the beginning: "People were afraid, that only Chinese people would live in Hualing City, for example," Lasha said. "But this did not happen. Instead, Hualing Group helps the Georgian government. They create jobs and bring a lot of investment. Hualing also agreed to find other investors from China for Georgia and already have introduced a Chinese concrete factory." For this reason, according to Irakli and Lasha, most Georgians are likely to be satisfied with Hualing, now.

As mentioned earlier, this did not always correspond with the opinions of my friends and colleagues. Local bazaar traders, however, had an astonishingly positive attitude to the Chinese and took their ambitions with a pinch of salt. Positive experiences with Chinese in Beijing might explain this. Owing to interactions with Chinese partners, local traders in Kazakhstan have, for example, acquired affirmative views of "what has been described... metaphorically as the 'Chinese Dream'" (Alff, 2014: 2), in contrast to widespread anti-Chinese hysteria in that country, and they sometimes question the post-Soviet state's ability to progress. These views and attitudes, as far as I could observe, are—at least to some degree—shared by Georgians doing business locally with Chinese. When I asked whether Chinese competition was a threat to Georgian business, Dato said he was not afraid of competing with the new Tbilisi Sea Plaza. The Hualing Group had offered him a place in it, but he had refused, thinking: "Why should I go there?! I have my shop here, and people come to Lilo." He was convinced that good Georgian-Chinese relationships benefitted both sides, and he was sure in any case that Chinese traders would sell much less than he did, because they lacked contacts.

The empty mall and marketplace I visited in 2018 seemed proof of these convictions. As mentioned earlier, Mariam told me that the Tbilisi Sea Plaza's management had initially hoped that Lilo Bazroba could be transferred there, but this did not work out. Like Dato, almost none of the Georgian traders left Lilo. "We could not fill the place [with Georgian traders]," Marjam explained. "So they went to China in 2016 to find traders in Ürümqi to work in the Plaza. They also found Chinese from Dubai and Kyrgyzstan." Still, some Georgian traders like Levan opened branches in the Tbilisi Sea Plaza so as not to miss out if the Chinese investors succeeded. Georgian traders obviously paid attention to the political developments. They tried to be on good terms with Chinese businesspeople and to get their share of the government's deals with China and the Hualing Group.

According to my Georgian interlocutors, Hualing did everything it could to establish good relationships with these traders. Zviad told me that Hualing had invited all traders/contractors who rented in the Tbilisi Sea Plaza to a huge *supra*. The local traders were quite impressed by this event, I was told. I saw some photographs of it, which were published in the local media, in one of which I identified Levan. They reflect the good, friendly atmosphere established drinking and toasting regardless of ethnicity, religion, and business hierarchies.

Like the Sea Plaza mall, the Hualing-run customs terminal raised questions about the success of Chinese enterprise. Discussing the projected Chinese terminal in 2016, Lasha explained:

> They will have storage facilities there, and if people are not able to pay the whole amount of clearance fees, they can just take a part of their goods,

> pay the clearance for this part, and leave the rest of the goods in the storage hall. Then, at a later point, they can take their goods and do the clearance step by step and little by little. Goods that have to travel further, to Azerbaijan and Armenia, for example, can be stored here and prepared for transit. In that case, the goods are in the customs storage area, and traders do not have to pay for clearance, but just 50 lari for re-export. From next year on, Georgia is going to have a free market [agreement] with China anyway.

In spring 2018, Irakli had become the manager of this terminal and was employed by the holding company running it, which was a joint venture of Hualing and the German Barth+ Co Spedition GmbH & Co. KG. Pointing to the crumbling floors of the storage buildings, Irakli explained that Chinese had invested the equivalent of five million U.S. dollars in building the complex, and that it would cost another five million to renovate it. Georgian workers and companies were now being hired for this purpose. As the manager, Irakli had made some rational choices. For example, he closed an entry to the processing zone and rationalized some of the control procedures: "Chinese even check the roofs of the trucks. We don't need that in Georgia." Like the mall, the terminal was almost empty in spring. In late summer, however, the situation was different. Irakli was very stressed and reported on full storages, many trucks, and a busy schedule. The business was running well, and everyone was in a good mood. The cooperation with Hualing was successful—on the economic as well as on the personal level. Everyone was happy, and one of Hualing's bosses, a representative of the German Barth-Co Spedition, and a Georgian partner were planning to travel to Munich to spend some quality time together at the Oktoberfest, Irakli reported.

What does the Chinese presence mean to Georgians and the Georgian economy? How is this linked to informality and informal globalization? What does this mean for marketplaces like Lilo Bazaar? And what does this signify for the Caucasian traders working at bazaars and travelling abroad (to China in particular) and for their businesses? Some of what is reported above allows for a few preliminary assumptions, but my observations of and information about Chinese business in the Caucasus were too diverse and confusing to provide satisfactory answers. The future role of Chinese in the region will, among other things, depend on the development of interethnic relationships on both the inter-personal and official levels.

"Cultural Brokers" and "Guanxi"

Let me take an analytical look into what has been explained above. As mentioned, my interlocutors in Lilo did not worry too much about Chinese competition. "Trade works through personal relations," Dato said. "If you do not have personal relations, you have no clients... This is why stores like Carrefour and big brands work in big countries like Germany, for example, but not in Georgia. Georgia is small and here everything works though relations." A huge part of running a good business depends on experience with the local legal framework, knowledge about local rules and opportunities, and skills in bargaining and maintaining social relationships. According to Lasha, Chinese businessmen are familiar with informal strategies in general but do not know the local rules of the game. They therefore need local consultants and mediators.

Citing Jezewski and Sotnik (2001) and Michie (2003), Mathews (2015) refers to "cultural brokering," defined as "bridging, linking, or mediating between groups or persons of differing cultural backgrounds for the purpose of reducing conflict or producing change" (Jezewski & Sotnik, 2001: 21). Mathews observes that "in an age of globalization, the role of [the] cultural broker has become important as never before" (Mathews, 2015: 120). In his examples, these cultural brokers are African logistic agents and middlemen, who help African businessmen, having difficulties navigating in Guangzhou. Wang (2018) discusses Chinese Muslims in Dubai who assume this role, mediating between Arabs and Chinese. In Georgia, it is the other way around: it is the Chinese who need such help.

Matthews writes:

> The concept of [the] cultural broker has been only intermittently used in anthropology, but it is... an essential concept for anthropological analysis. In an age of globalization, people are increasingly thrust into parts of the world of which they may know little: It is cultural brokers who provide them [with] an anchor of cultural knowledge. This is particularly true within the world of low-end globalization, where there are few formal institutional structures—everything is based on trust and human relations rather than contracts and laws, and cultural brokers are brokers exactly because they have acquired such trust. (Mathews, 2015: 139–140)

In my view, Nino, Lasha, Irakli and Mariam are such mediators.

"[I]t has always been a long and difficult process for non-Chinese to become Chinese," Mathews notes (123–124). It is probably just as difficult for Chinese to become Georgian. Nevertheless, there seems to be a common understanding between post-Soviet people and Chinese, and between Georgians and Chinese in particular. Some of this understanding is rooted in the nature of business itself, some of it might be explained by their common socialist past, and some, finally, can be understood as the outcome of a similar perception of what social relationship is about. Alff's summary of Kazakh traders' opinion of Chinese mirrors Georgians' assessment of them. "For the Kazakh traders, their Chinese partners' "moral accountability, flexibility and adaptability," demonstrated through personal interaction over an extended period of time, were "conducive to societal improvement and personal entrepreneurial success alike... These positively reflected features of what is often [called] Chinese flexible capitalism (Ong, 1999) are enacted [best through] enduring interpersonal connections... [established] between business partners through close interaction often over the course of years" (Alff, 2014: 8).

As Humphrey points out, "if trust is the outcome of culturally specific performances, it will be doubly problematic in trans-border situations where there are radical differences in social strategies and ideas about what should be revealed and what hidden" (Humphrey, 2018: 13). But what if two sets of culturally specific practices are similar and/or compatible? As the cases described above indicate, it is because Chinese businesspeople understand Georgian values that they are able to find local partners with whom to establish personal relationships and through them get the assistance they need.

People usually conceptualize trust in terms of specific types of relationships, which are sometimes associated with kinship-like closeness and imply a moral economy counterbalancing commercial individualism (cf. Humphrey, 2018). This is not only true of Caucasian traders, but also seems to pertain to Chinese. The Chinese concept of *guanxi* (关系; 關係; relationship or connection), for instance, is very similar to Russian *blat* (блат) (Alff, 2014: 8), but also has commonalities with Armenian *axperowt'yown* and Georgian *ʒmaḳacoba* (see Chapters 2 and 3).

Often described as a tool for getting things done, obtaining a scarce commodity, or taking advantage of an opportunity (Yang, 2018: 75), *guanxi* is not just "a means of entering 'back doors'" (Yan, 1996: 227), however, but a network of relationships associated with good feelings (*renqing*, 人情). It includes the exchange of a vast range of gifts, some in ritual contexts, others in everyday life situations, some for purely social reasons, and some for utilitarian ones. Yunxiang Yan writes:

> To summarize the relationship between the gift on the one hand and *guanxi/renqing* on the other, I suggest that the gift can be seen as a sign or a vehicle, which conveys *renqing* against the social matrix of *guanxi*. Yet the gift is more than a sign, it is also a material object or substance on and of itself, with use value and exchange value. Thus the endless process of gift transaction, including banquets or family ceremonies, constitutes a gift economy in its own right, in this sense, the gift can be regarded as a relationship in a moral economy nevertheless, the meaning of this gift relationship derives from the larger context of *guanxi* and *renqing* in a local moral world. (Yan, 1996: 226)[82]

But Yan's study refers to a rural context. In urban and international settings, *guanxi* is frequently associated with calculation that uses and manipulates the idea of reciprocity and mutual obligations. "Guanxi practices grow out of the traditional Chinese cultural emphasis on social relationships and the interpersonal ethics of obligation and reciprocity. The Confucian classical texts are filled with discussions of the reciprocal duties and obligations of different social roles and relationships, and the ethics and etiquettes of gift-relations and host-guest relations at rituals and banquets" (Yang, 2018: 76). Participating in the Georgian *supra* (სუფრა) was thus probably a rather minor challenge for Chinese businessmen like the "Little One," who was used to the Chinese version called *xi* (feast) or *jiuxi* (liquor feast) (Yan, 1996: 46).

Guanxi, like the related concepts of *blat, axperowt'yown, ʒmaḳacoba,* and *biržа,* "is often used to skirt around the cumbersome bureaucracy" (Yang, 2018: 75). Yang (1994) argues that *guanxi* was born out of Maoist state order. Like *blat,* it was used to get permissions from "gatekeepers" controlling social paths and opportunities. Yang's account correlates with the way Chinese investors approach Georgian elites[83]:

[82] My colleague Agniezka Joniak-Lüthi calls *guanxi* "a violent social institution" that serves to "entangle you in ways you can't control; service is not infrequently thrust on you, and obligations expected for it." This squares with some other accounts.

[83] In Armenia, conversely, according to my colleague Yulia Antonyan, Chinese opened shops and markets but failed to cooperate with the local oligarchs and so were pushed out of the country.

> If one needs the help of an influential person, but there is no prior relationship, then a new guanxi must be initiated and carefully cultivated. Often the help of guanxi intermediaries are necessary to introduce one to the target person who may grant a favour. Once the introduction is made, one needs to cultivate the relationship over some time, with friendly visits or conversation, and gift-giving or a banquet, before a request can be made with decorum. ... The offering of the gift, favour or banquet must be couched in the terms of friendship, rather than naked instrumentalism, so that sociality, affect and utility coexist as key components of guanxi. (Yang, 2018: 76)

Lasha's advice to his Chinese bosses on how to handle Georgian custom officials might thus have sounded familiar to them.

Like the practices of Georgian traders and intermediaries, *guanxi* is not considered criminal. It is not the same as bribery (*xinghui*, 贿赂; Russ.: vzjatka, взятка), because the emphasis is not on the exchange of goods and favors, but on the relationship (cf. Alff, 2014: 8). As noted earlier, it would be wrong to overstate the utilitarian side of *guanxi*, which is primarily a social term according to Yan (1996). *Guanxi* has, however, become transnational: "Not only Chinese capital and businesses expand across the globe, but also Chinese education and cultural networks extend overseas, thus enabling Chinese both inside and outside China to gain new opportunities abroad through transnational guanxi networks, which now may even include non-Chinese" (Yang, 2018: 78). In Chapter 3, I describe how the local concepts of *axperowt'yown*, *ʒmaḳacoba*, and *birža* shape the understanding of relationships and moral codes and how these understandings and codes are transferred to the new sphere of international business. Yang writes similarly of the globalization of *guanxi* (cf. Namsaraeva, 2018).

Such concepts should probably not be overestimated. Their meaning may change over time and in different situations, or they may be replaced by other terms and meanings. My interlocutor John was confused when I asked him about the concept of *guanxi*. For him, it simply meant "relationship." He told me it was a synonym of *renqing*, which means getting involved in mutual obligations. John did not interpret the term as connected to "positive feelings," but as an "exchangeable resource, something that is primarily instrumental and less sentimental or moral" (Yan, 1996: 227). Such exchanges are common, not only in business, but in healthcare and education. "If someone pays for a meal for you, you can count on it that he may expect you to return the favor," John said.

"You can also go further and give more. A teacher might, for instance, tell parents, 'My phone is old', and they will understand from this that they need to give him a new phone if they want their child to get good marks. The same happens in the context of business. Such requests are not made directly, but in the form of a seemingly random remark like 'My wife's car is broken'." John was very critical of this practice and blamed the Chinese mentality for it. He argued that it was also a problem between generations, the older generation persisting in such behavior.

Other sociocultural factors and markers, especially religious affiliation, also, of course, shape the business context I have described. As noted earlier, Georgians' identity is usually tightly linked to Georgian Orthodox religion, whereas Xingjian Uyghurs' religious affiliation is Muslim. Religion was mentioned by my Georgian interlocutors from time to time when they talked about their Chinese/Uyghur employers or business partners. But they generally concluded that religion was unimportant, although acknowledging Muslim Uyghurs' reservations in this regard. "Ninety percent of [the Chinese working for Hualing] are Muslim," Marjam said. "You can't eat pork in the Hualing hotel. But I've never had any conversation about religion there. They just told me that they did not have pork, because they are Muslims, when I started to work there. It never came up again after that." Still, as the basis of values and morality shaping social practice and behavior, religion may have functioned as an invisible matrix. It certainly is no coincidence that interactions between Chinese and Georgians are described as most intensive in ritualized contexts, such as *supra*s or funerals.

This only seems true of the Hualing Group, however, and not of Chinese traders in Lilo Bazroba or the Chinese workers of parastatal Chinese construction companies. As mentioned above, Lilo's Chinese traders live relatively isolated in an ethnic enclave. Workers of construction companies live in camps, which, for security reasons, they are rarely allowed to leave. The workers' lives are uniformly boring, I was told by John. Therefore, they usually long to get home as soon as possible. As a rule, they must stay for the duration of a project phase, which is two or three years.[84] During this time, living conditions are hard. As Zhou notes, and as has been reported from Africa, Chinese workers are very "vulnerable to their employers' whims" (2012: 13). Many Chinese workers have

[84] Workers can rarely afford to go home—at best, they do once a year for the Chinese New Year's celebrations.

been brought to Georgia without signing a formal contract and when their companies got into financial difficulties, they were left unpaid (13). For such workers, it does not matter, whether they are sent to Georgia or Africa. As also seems to be true for Lilo traders, they have no future in the country. There is no need—sometimes not even an opportunity—to establish firm relationships to places or to locals. Although they may work well and hand in hand with Georgian workers on construction sites, Chinese laborers' strategies, like those of Lilo traders, focus on their futures in China (Fehlings, 2019).

"Encompassing Accumulation"

How, generally, to explain Chinese ambitions and activities in the Caucasus? What does the empty marketplace tell us about motivation and success? What is the possible prognosis for the future?

"Hualing is not making plans for this or the next one or two years, but for ten years," Lasha says. China's foreign ventures are often attributed to its rapid economic growth. Overcapacity, falling profits, surplus capital, shrinking demand in traditional export markets, and scarcity of raw materials are the major reasons driving Chinese firms and citizens overseas "in search of new opportunities," according to Lee. "Chinese investment is qualitatively different from conventional foreign investment." Chinese are often looked upon with suspicion and accused of imposing slavery and inhumane working conditions, and Chinese businesspeople are not only perceived as private investors but as representing the PRC's state interests (Lee, 2014: 29, 33). "The generic term 'Chinese investment' masks a hierarchy of capitals of varying status, resourcefulness and connection to the Beijing government. At the top of this pecking order are the central state-owned enterprises and policy banks, below these are provincial-level state owned enterprises, private companies of varying sizes, and at the bottom of the heap, entrepreneurial and family firms," Lee says (2014: 34–35).

These differences are quite difficult to sort out. Projects like Hualing's can be seen as private initiatives for profit. But it is never clear how much the state is involved in (so-called) private ventures. Hualing's activities serve state purposes as well. These purposes cannot be explained purely in terms of financial goals. They create space for "achieving other types of return" (Lee, 2014: 36), like, one could argue, political influence and access to raw materials in the name of the PRC.

Lee calls this logic of accumulation "encompassing" and contrasts it to the profit-maximizing logic of global private capital (36–38). Encompassing accumulation leads strikingly different strategies of cooperation in foreign settings—especially in times of crisis (38). With long-term interests, Chinese managers in Africa thus invest in stable relationships with the local elites, and condone temporary bottlenecks, losses, and throwbacks. Perceiving diplomacy and investment and politics and economics as intertwined, they develop strategies to gain influence. This is a risky game, because it makes Chinese businessmen and companies vulnerable to host-country politics (43), local public opinion, and regional instability (like the Georgian-Russian relationship).

In the Caucasus, during the Tbilisi Silk Road Forum, public-private partnership was highlighted as "essential for the full realisation of the Silk Road's potential by the governor of Xinjiang and the vice governor of Shaanxi provinces, respectively, who spoke at the event and headed large regional delegations who visited the forum. A key objective for Georgia and other countries along the route is to develop multilateral relations with countries and companies, as well as regions, in order to establish relationships that go deeper than just government-to-government contact" (Pantucci & Lain, 2016: 5). OBOR was never mentioned within Hualing, Miriam and Lasha told me, and Hualing's activity was thus never directly linked to the giant Silk Road project of the Chinese government. Still, Hualing's activity somehow takes place in this context.

Conclusion

In this chapter, I have tried to relate the Chinese presence in Georgia, and in the Caucasus more broadly, to the broader context of China's overseas ventures, which, again, are linked to Xi Jianping's leadership and political notions and agendas like the "China dream." Such political programs can partly be interpreted as pure propaganda, according to Kaczmarski (2016). On the other hand, they transform into new ideologies, which manifest in concrete prospects for the future, one of which is turning China into a society of "moderate prosperity." Attempting to achieve this has put China in the vanguard of globalization (Pieke et al., 2004).

Big investments in the Caucasus like those of the Hualing Group can be interpreted as the outcome of top-down strategies fostering a specific version of globalization from above. At the same time, strategies on the ground align with the definition of globalization from below: face-to-face interaction, oral agreements, the establishment of personal relationships based on social norms and values and local concepts of honor, hospitality, kinship, friendship, brotherhood, and a common understanding of social obligations. Chinese interaction with Georgians takes place on different levels. On the level of state agreements, on the level of bureaucracy, on the level of elites, on the level of business partnerships, and on the level of encounters between individuals. Within these encounters, trust is important, especially where public opinion is heated and sinophobia flares up easily.

Chinese and Georgian businesspeople alike use informal practices, but in different ways and on different levels. One Chinese strategy is to establish deep personal relationships with local "cultural brokers," who help their Chinese friends navigate the complicate pathways through bureaucracy, formal and informal practices, and social behavior. Even though many Georgians and Chinese practices seem compatible, there are significant differences, and Chinese are easily recognized aliens on Georgian territory. Chinese more obviously try to cooperate with official bodies, while local traders seem to try to avoid contact with state institutions. This strategy is successful, last but not least because of the prosperity and financial generosity of the Chinese. Following the long-term strategies of China and Chinese private investors in the Caucasus during the next decades will be interesting. Time will show how these strategies will affect the Georgian economy and the business of small local entrepreneurs who work in the local bazaars in Tbilisi, Batumi, Yerevan, Baku, and elsewhere.

References

Akhter, M. (2018). Geopolitics of the Belt and Road: Space, State, and Capital in China and Pakistan. In B. Neilson, N. Rossiter, & R. Samaddar (Eds.), *Logistical Asia: The Labour of Making a World Region* (pp. 221–241). Palgrave Macmillan. https://doi.org/10.1007/978-981-10-8333-4_11

Aldrich, H. E., & Waldinger, R. (1990). Ethnicity and Entrepreneurship. *Annual Review of Sociology, 16*, 111–135.

Alff, H. (2014). Embracing Chinese Modernity? Articulation and Positioning in China-Kazakhstan Trade and Exchange Processes. *Crossroads Asia Working Paper Series, 21.*

Alff, H. (2016). Introduction. *Central Asian Survey, 35*(3), 327–333.

Aslanian, S. (2014). *From the Indian Ocean to the Mediterranean: The Global Trade Networks of Armenian Merchants from New Julfa*. University of California Press.

Beriashvili, L. (2016). Georgia on the "Great Silk Road" Trade Route [in Georgian]. In L. Beriashvili & L. Melikishvili (Eds.), *Georgians: Everything on Georgian Culture and Ethnicity* (pp. 473–479). Palitra L.

Billé, F. (2014). *Sinophobia: Anxiety, Violence, and the Making of Mongolian Identity*. University of Hawaii Press.

Brumann, C. (1998). Geld als Geschenk: Aspekte japanischer Beziehungsarithmetik [Cash as a Gift: Aspects of Japanese Relational Arithmetics]. In A. Ernst & P. Pörtner (Eds.), *Die Rolle des Geldes in Japans Gesellschaft, Wirtschaft und Politik [The Role of Money in Japanese Society, Economy, and Politics]* (pp. 77–79). Institut für Asienkunde.

Chin, T. (2013). The Invention of the Silk Road, 1877. *Critical Inquiry, 40*, 194–219.

Chumburidze, M., Zurabishvili, T., & Zurabishvili, T. (2016). Attitudes Towards Immigrants in Georgia: Myths of Tolerance and Empirical Evidence. *Caucasus Analytical Digest, 85*, 16–18.

Clarke, M. (2008). China's Integration of Xinjiang with Central Asia: Securing a 'Silk Road' to Great Power Status? *China and Eurasia Forum Quarterly, 6*(2), 89–111.

Conrad, H. (2021). A Road as an Empire: Some Remarks about the Most Important Ancient Periods and Powers of and Along the Silk Road. *Working Paper Series on Informal Markets and Trade, 11.*

Dadabaev, T. (2018). Engagement and Contestation: The Entangled Imagery of the Silk Road. *Cambridge Journal of Eurasian Studies, 2* (Q4GIV6), 1–15. https://doi.org/10.22261/CJES.Q4GIV6

Dams, T., & Van der Putten, F. P. (2015). China and Liberal Values in International Relations: Opposing the Promotion of Democracy, Human Rights and Liberal Market Economy. *Clingendael Report*. Clingendael Netherlands Institute of International Relations.

Di Puppo, L. (2013). The Construction of Success in Anticorruption Activity in Georgia. *East European Politics, 30*, 105–122.

Dundua, T., & Avdaliani, E. (2021). Silk, Spices and Oil: "Transcaucasian" Trade Route and Georgia. *Academia Letters, Article 337*. https://doi.org/10.20935/AL337

Dyatlov, V., & Grigorichev, K. (2015). *Ethnic Markets in Russia: Space of Bargaining and Place of Meeting*. Publishing House of ISU.

Fehlings, S. (2014). *Jerewan: Urbanes Chaos und soziale Ordnung*. LIT-Verlag.

Fehlings, S. (2016). The Ignoble Savage in Urban Yerevan. *Central Asian Survey, 35*(2), 195–217. https://doi.org/10.1080/02634937.2015.1134142

Fehlings, S. (2019). Encounters at the Grassroots Level: Chinese-Georgian Interactions in the BRI Era. *Caucasus Analytical Digest, 111*, 14–17. https://doi.org/10.3929/ethz-b-000368298

Frankopan, P. (2015). *The Silk Roads: A New History of the World*. Bloomsbury.

Grigorichev, K., Dyatlov, V., Timoshkin, D., & Bryazgina, D. (Eds.). (2019). *Bazaar and the City: People, Spaces, Images (Базар и город: люди, пространстеа, образы)*. Ottisk.

Harris, T. (2013). Trading Places: New Economic Geographies across Himalayan Borderlands. *Political Geography, 35*, 60–68. https://doi.org/10.1016/j.polgeo.2012.12.002

Höllmann, T. O. (2008). *Die Seidenstraße*. C.H. Beck.

Holzlehner, T. (2014). *Shadow Networks: Border Economics, Informal Markets and Organized Crime in the Russian Far East*. LIT-Verlag.

Hopkirk, P. (1980). *Foreign Devils on the Silk Road: The Search for the Lost Treasures of Central Asia*. John Murray.

Humphrey, C. (2017). Loyalty and Disloyalty along the Russian-Chinese Border. *History and Anthropology, 28*(4), 399–405. https://doi.org/101080/02757206.2017.1351356

Humphrey, C. (2018). Introduction: Trusting and Mistrusting Across Borders. In C. Humphrey (Ed.), *Trust and Mistrust in the Economy of the China-Russia Borderlands* (pp. 9–35). Amsterdam University Press.

Humphrey, C., & Skvirskaja, V. (2009). Trading Places: Post-socialist Container Markets and the City. *Focaal: European Journal of Anthropology, 55*. https://doi.org/10.3167/fcl.2009.550105.

Inan, F., & Yayloyan, D. (2018). *New Economic Corridors in the South Caucasus and the Chinese One Belt One Road* (Policy Paper, pp. 1–89). The Economic Policy Research Foundation of Turkey (TEPAV).

Ismalov, E., & Papava, V. (2018). Caucasian Tandem and the Belt and Road Initiative. *Journal of Social and Political Studies, Central Asia and South Caucasus, 19*(2), 7–16.

Jezewski, M. A., & Sotnik, P. (2001). *The Rehabilitation Service Provider as Cultural Broker: Providing Culturally Competent Services to Foreign-Born Persons*. Center for International Rehabilitation Research Education and Exchange.

Kaczmarski, M. (2016). *"Silk Globalisation": China's Vision of International Order* (OSW Point of View, 60).

Kalandarova, M. (2005). Indian Merchants in Nineteenth-Century Bukhara: Trade Network and Socio-Cultural Role. In M. Gervers (Ed.), *Traders and Trade Routes of Central and Inner Asia: The "Silk Road", Then and Now* (pp. 93–162). Asian Institute.

Karrar, H. (2013). Merchants, Markets, and the State. *Critical Asian Studies, 45*(3), 459–480. https://doi.org/10.1080/14672715.2013.829315

Karrar, H. (2018). The Silk Road Versus the Central Asian Bazaar: Two Thousand Years or Twenty-Five Years of Exchange and Mobility? *Anthropological Researches, IV*, 13–22.

Karrar, H. (2019). In the Shadow of the Silk Road: Border Regimes and Economic Corridor Development Through an Unremarkable Pakistan-China Border Market. *Comparative Studies of South Asia, Africa and the Middle East, 39*(3), 389–406.

Karrar, H., & Mostowlansky, T. (2018). Assembling Marginality in Northern Pakistan. *Political Geography, 63*, 65–74.

Khutsishvili, K. (2018). Market Infrastructure: Past and Present Transformations. *Anthropological Researches, IV*, 40–47.

Kim, Y.-C. (Ed.). (2017). *China and Africa: A New Paradigm of Global Business*. Palgrave Macmillan.

Kirakos Ganjakec'i. (1961). *Patmut'yun Hayoc' (History of Armenia)*. Xmbagrut'yamb K. Melik'-Ohanˇjanyani (K. Melik-Ohanjanyan, Ed.). Yerevan.

Lambert, M. "Is China Building a Bridge or an Outpost in the Caucasus," Macdonald-Laurier Institute, 27 September 2017, https://www.macdonaldlaurier.ca/ischina-building-a-bridge-or-an-outpost-in-the-caucasus-michael-lambert-for-inside-policy.

Larsen, J. (2017). Georgia-China Relations: The Geopolitics of the Belt and Road. *Policy Paper*. Georgian Institute of Politics. http://gip.ge/wp-content/uploads/2017/10/Chinetipercent20Saqartvelopercent20Eng_Ydit.pdf

Laruelle, M. (Ed.). (2018). *China's Belt and Road Initiative and its Impact in Central Asia*. Washington, DC: The George Washington University, Central Asia Program.

Lee, C. K. (2014). The Spectre of Global China. *New Left Review, 89*, 29–65.

Marsden, M. (2016). *Trading Worlds: Afghan Merchants Across Modern Frontiers*. Hurst & Company.

Marx, K. (1977 [1859]). *A Contribution to the Critique of Political Economy*. Progress Publishers.

Mathews, G. (2015). African Logistics Agents and Middlemen as Cultural Brokers in Guangzhou. *Journal of Current Chinese Affairs, 44*(4), 117–144.

Mertens, M. (2019). Did Richthofen Really Coin "the Silk Road"? *The Silk Road Journal, 17*, 1–9. https://edspace.american.edu/silkroadjournal/wp-content/uploads/sites/984/2020/02/2-Mertens-Did-Richthofen-Really-Coin-the-Silk-Road.pdf

Michie, M. (2003, July 10–12). *The Role of Cultural Brokers in Intercultural Science Education: A Research Proposal*. Paper presented at the 34th Annual Conference of the Australasian Science Education Research Association held in Melbourne. http://members.ozemail.com.au/~mmichie/culture_brokers1.htm

Namsaraeva, S. (2018). Déjà-vu of Distrust in the Sino-Russian Borderlands. In C. Humphrey (Ed.), *Trust and Mistrust in the Economy of the China-Russia Borderlands* (pp. 37–64). Amsterdam University Press.

Nyíri, P. (2007). *Chinese in Eastern Europe: A Middleman Minority in a Transnational Era*. Routledge.

Nyíri, P. (2011). Chinese Entrepreneurs in Poor Countries: A Transnational, "Middleman Minority" and Its Futures. *Inter-Asia Cultural Studies, 12*(1), 145–153.

Nyíri, P. (2012). Enclaves of Improvement: Sovereignity and Developmentalism in the Special Zones of the China-Lao Borderlands. *Comparative Studies in Society and History, 54*(3), 533–562.

Nyíri, P. (2017). Realms of Free Trade, Enclaves of Order. Chinese-built "Instant Cities" in Northern Laos. In M. Saxer & J. Zhang (Eds.), *The Art of Neighbouring: Making Relations Across China's Borders* (pp. 57–72). Amsterdam University Press.

Ong, A. (1999). *Flexible Citizenship: The Cultural Logics of Transnationality*. Duke University Press.

Pantucci, R., & Lain, S. (2016). *Workshop Report: Tbilisi Silk Road Forum: Next Steps for Georgia and the Silk Road*. Royal United Services Institute for Defence and Security Studies.

Pieke, F. N., Nyíri, P., & Thunø, M. (Eds.). (2004). *Transnational Chinese: Fujianese Migrants in Europe*. Stanford University Press.

Portes, A. (1997). *Globalization from Below: The Rise of Transnational Communities*. WPTC-98-1.

Pourtskhvanidze, Z., & Tskhvediani, N. (2021). Cryptolanguage of Georgian Jewish Merchants, *Working Paper Series on Informal Markets and Trade, 10*.

Rippa, A. (2018). *Which Silk Road, and for Whom? Economic Corridors and the End of Proximity at China's Borders* [Unpublished Manuscript].

Röschenthaler, U., & Socpa, A. (2017). The China Challenge: Cameroonians Between Discontent and Popular Admiration. In Y.-C. Kim (Ed.), *China and Africa: A New Paradigm of Global Business* (pp. 155–188). Palgrave Macmillan.

Shah, A. R. (2018). How Does China-Pakistan Economic Corridor Show the Limitations of China's 'One Belt One Road' Model. *Asia & the Pacific Policy Studies, 5*(2), 378–385. https://doi.org/10.1002/app5.224

Shahbazov, F. (2017a). Baku-Beijing Relations and China's Growing Interest in the South Caucasus. *Eurasia Daily Monitor, 14*(51), 1–14.

Shahbazov, F. (2017b). *Baku-Tbilisi-Kars Railway to Become Central Asia's Gateway to Europe*. CACI Analyst, Central Asia–Caucasus Institute. http://cacianalyst.org/publications/analytical-articles/item/13486-baku-tbilisi-kats-railway-to-become-central-asias-gateway-to-europe.html

Shahbazov, F. (2017c). The South-West Transport Corridor Project and the Geopolitical Reshaping of the South Caucasus. *Eurasia Daily Monitor, 14*. https://www.refworld.org/docid/5971d0ed4.html

Smith Stegen, K., & Kusznir, J. (2015). Outcomes and Strategies in the "New Great Game": China and the Caspian States Emerge as Winners. *Journal of Eurasian Studies, XXX, 1–16*. https://doi.org/10.1016/j.euras.2015.03.002

Steenberg, R. (2016). Embedded Rubber Sandals: Trade and Gifts Across the Sino-Kyrgyz Border. *Central Asian Survey, 35*(3), 405–420.

Sternberg, T., Ahearn, A., & McConnell, F. (2017). Central Asian "Characteristics" on China's New Silk Road: The Role of Landscape and the Politics of Infrastructure. *Land, 6*(55). https://doi.org/10.3390/land6030055

Wang, Y. (2018). The Making of China's "Good Muslims": From Middleman Minority to Cultural Ambassadors. *The China Review, 18*(4), 131–154.

Wu, S. (2014). The Search for Coal in the Age of Empires: Ferdinand von Richthofen's Odyssey in China, 1860–1920. *The American Historical Review, 119*(2), 339–363.

Yalçın-Heckmann, L. (2001). The Political Economy of an Azeri Wedding, *Max Planck Institute for Social Anthropology Working Papers, 28*. Max Planck Institute for Social Anthropology.

Yan, Y. (1996). *The Flow of Gifts: Reciprocity and Social Networks in a Chinese Village*. Stanford University Press.

Yang, M. (1994). *Gifts, Favors, and Banquets: The Art of Social Relationship in China*. Cornell University Press.

Yang, M. (2018). Guanxi (China). In A. Ledeneva (Ed.), *The Global Encyclopedia of Informality* (Vol. 1, pp. 75–79). UCL Press.

Zabakhidze, M., Gabriadze, I., Beradze, R., & Khishtovani, G. (2019). Connectivity, Trade and Financial Integration of the South Caucasus Via the Belt and Road Initiative (BRI). *Caucasus Analytical Digest, 111*, 3–9. https://doi.org/10.3929/ethz-b-000368298

Zhang, J., & Saxer, M. (2017a). Introduction: Neighbouring in the Borderworlds Along China's Frontiers. In J. Zhang & M. Saxer (Eds.), *The Art of Neighbouring: Making Relations Across China's Borders* (pp. 11–29). Amsterdam University Press.

Zhang, J., & Saxer, M. (Eds.). (2017b). *The Art of Neighbouring: Making Relations Across China's Borders*. Amsterdam University Press.

Zhang, W., & Alon, I. (Eds.). (2009). *Biographical Dictionary of New Chinese Entrepreneurs and Business Leaders*. Edward Elgar Publishing.

Zhou, J. (2012). Chinese in Georgia, *ECMI Working Paper, 54*.

Григоричев, К. В., Дятлов, В. И., Тимошкин, Д. О., & Брязгина, Д. Е. (Eds.). (2019). *Базар и город: люди, пространства, образы*. Оттиск.

Epilogue

Anthropologists have always tried to understand everyday activities as embedded in broader contexts. Gudeman (2001), Parry and Bloch (1989), and Carsten (1989) offer models of the interdependencies between society, culture, and the economy and between different spheres of economic exchange, mostly in agrarian societies. Money management is usually described as a key element in this process and is sometimes accompanied by complex rituals, as shown in Parry and Bloch's, 1989 edited volume and in studies of gift money, like Brumann's, 1998 discussion of the Japanese case.

In contrast to such models, which describe combinations, entanglements, and imbroglios of (1) markets principles and culture, (2) formality and informality and (3) global and local levels, I argue that every economic practice and almost every kind of exchange taking place in a real setting is double- or multifaceted. I do not perceive communities/societies and trade or markets as separate. I do not even perceive economic exchange as an entanglement of embedded, formal and informal, profit-oriented components and global and local practices. Describing the entanglement of components presumes that one can distinguish them. In my opinion, this is not necessarily the case, although I agree that these categories (profit-oriented/embedded; formal/informal, and global/local) help us see things from different

S. Fehlings, *Traders, Informal Trade and Markets between the Caucasus and China*, Politics and History in Central Asia,
https://doi.org/10.1007/978-981-19-5205-0

perspectives and learn something about them. From my data I have arrived at the following assumptions:

First, Caucasian businesspeople perceived their activity as a coherent entity, not as a combination of embedded and profit-oriented components, formal and informal and global and local practices. However, in some contexts and situations, specific behaviours, practices and strategies were sometimes interpreted and classified in such terms, depending on the perspective of the observer. Second, a) sociocultural concepts and family and community life, b) economy (business), and c) the state create separate spheres and ideologies one has to cope with. Thus, third, like bureaucracy, business itself creates/has its own ideology, its own "culture." Like other parts of everyday life (including family life, bureaucracy, etc.) business adheres to certain rules, norms, and values. Which rules, norms and values become important, depends on the environment and the type of business. Anthropologists look at cultures as a combination of the sociopolitical, economic, and religious spheres. I suggest looking at local "biznes" in the Caucasus and Georgia-China long-distance trade, not only as embedded in culture, but as cultures in their own right, with their own ideologies and rules of behaviour. Fourth, although the ideology of business culture emerges from its practices and the environments in which they take place, the sociocultural background of the traders constitutes a blueprint for many concepts that define and regulate social interactions, rules, and practices, which is transformed, adapted, and reinterpreted in the context of trade. Local ideas about kin and friendship, trust and honor, and relationships in general are thus transferred to a completely new context, where they acquire new meanings and content. Simultaneously, people/traders also refer to Soviet ideology and Western neoliberalism. There are thus influences from many other spheres, which one could link to state powers or the global level. Fifth, in the context of interethnic exchange/business between Georgian and Chinese entrepreneurs, cultural concepts transferred to business seem to be very compatible and thus easily conflate in one business culture, and, sixth, traders use mediators to access and handle the state, because the legal state's logic and bureaucratic apparatus (its ideology) does not always fit with the logic of the business culture of my target group's long-distance and small-scale trading activity. Chinese investors, who do not know how to navigate in the Georgian environment, rely even more on such middlemen. The structure and stability of the state affects the nature of business, however, and in times of political instability, unregulated (informal) exchange increases, whereas strong legal states impose "formal" rules, to which traders have to adapt, as shown by the reforms following the Rose Revolution in Georgia. The role of state regulation in the global context is even more complicated.

Chapter 5 in Fig 1 brings together these six findings, showing the Georgian and Chinese traders' business environments as made up of different influences and interactions. The Georgian and Chinese business cultures are separate cultures but are compatible when they are linked through trade and business (culture) in Yabaolu Market (Chapter 2) or in Georgia (Chapter 5). Both business cultures share a common interest in economic exchange and profit and are equally shaped by the global market, institutional frameworks, international agreements, state policies (e.g., OBOR), and, finally, by concepts originating in their respective local cultures. The latter, again, are shaped by different influences (local, Western, Soviet, or other ideologies). Thus, traders operate in a sphere determined by sociocultural as well as market elements combining competing and refiguring ideologies linked to the local cosmology and social system, to the Soviet past, and to Western-style individualism and capitalism. To deal with their own officials, Georgian traders use intermediaries/middlemen (Chapters 4), who mediate between the traders' business sphere and the formal frameworks, which follow different rules and logics. In China, Georgian traders do not have to deal with the Chinese state. This is done by their Chinese partners. Chinese businesspeople in Georgia, however, especially the big investors, cannot avoid encounters with Georgian state bodies. They use two strategies: First, they establish personal relationships with local elites; second, they employ Georgians as "cultural brokers" to mediate between the Chinese business culture and local (Georgian) official frameworks (Fig. 6.1).

In analyzing economic activity, one has to make use of substantivist and formalist approaches; and pay attention to different contexts on the local, national, international, and global levels. These factors are not separate. Economic behavior frequently has a multiple nature and is simultaneously formal and informal, rational and moral, and global and local, depending on the perspective.

Things change all the time, and the trading activity I have described in this book, which emerged only after the breakdown of the Soviet Union, seems highly sensitive to change, mirroring and adapting to developments. The popping up of bazaars, their proliferation since the early

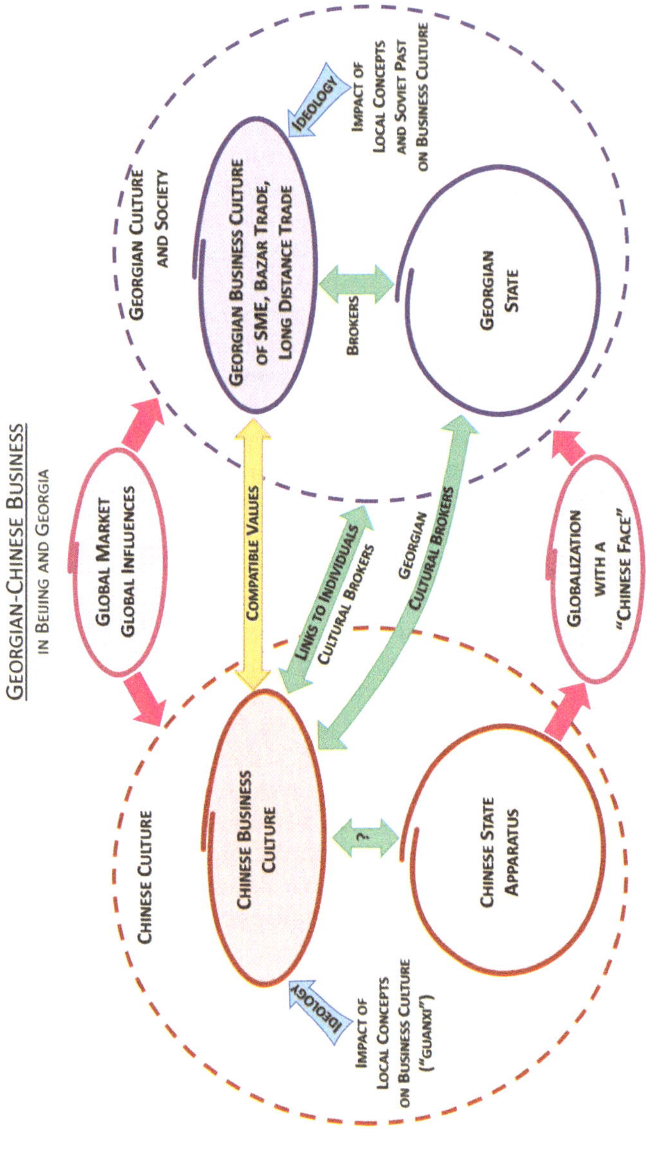

Fig. 6.1 Model representing "business culture"

1990s, the conversion or replacement of some of these bazaars by shopping malls, the transformation of shuttle traders and trade tourists into businesspeople and entrepreneurs, and the massive Chinese investment in the new Silk Road suggest that these changes are immense. This is certainly true. But the unexpected always happens. "We know that things change, we've been told since childhood that things change, we've witnessed things change ourselves many a time, and yet we're still utterly incapable of noticing the moment that change comes—or we search for change in all the wrong places," Arkady Strugatsky writes in his science fiction short story "Roadside Picnic." Georgian entrepreneurs have not become the pioneers of economic change and the driving force for the establishment of a modern, Western-style market economy they were predicted to be; allegedly underdeveloped bazaars have still not been superseded by brand-name stores and shopping malls; and OBOR and other Chinese investment projects remain uncompleted and must still prove their sustainability.

In business everything is about the future: future profit, future challenges, and future plans. Although much of what I have described here talks about change and new developments, however, it builds on the past, or can be seen as a continuation of traditional practices and behaviors shaped by persisting ideas and values. Unfortunately, the forward-looking attitude, which is a comprehensible attitude of stakeholders, state representatives, investors, and traders seeking guidelines for effective action, leads to exaggerated expectations and predictions.

I am surrounded by colleagues who claim to know, and who engage in such expectations and predictions, and I am extremely worried about this. How can we know? Even a little inquiry shows that we do not even fully understand or recognize processes currently happening. We even lack description of many basic activities and circumstances. I have repeatedly been criticized for not being able to give clear answers, and this book is once again full of open questions. I do not perceive this as a weakness. Scientists can develop hypothesis, make assumptions, suggest models, and try to detect and explain causalities, but they should never stop questioning their findings. Although I am constantly told the opposite, a tentative approach cannot be a mistake.

Isaac Asimov, who had much to say about the future, claimed that "the most exciting phrase to hear in science, the one that heralds new discoveries, is not 'Eureka' but 'That's funny,' which both humorously expresses astonishment and suggests new questions. Humor in contemporary anthropology is a rare good. This is a methodological shortcoming, I believe. Although the world might be a sad place, not everything in it is totally serious and to be understood gravely, and not everything need be hewn in stone. One can say serious things by joking, and not every joke must be taken seriously. I learned this from the people I met during fieldwork and from some of my most respected colleagues.

This said, what might the next steps be? I am not sure. I think it would be fun to follow up this study and to observe further developments in the region. There are many phenomena that deserve a closer look, such as entrepreneurship, credit and debt systems, networking, and global interconnectedness.

Personally, I think a study like this one but focusing on Chinese activity in the Caucasus and its sociocultural background (from a Chinese standpoint) would be interesting and useful. It is curious that of all Chinese, it is Muslim Uighurs from the Xinjiang region, who come to Georgia. What are their networks? How does their Turkic Muslim identity influence their practices and relationships? How do they relate to the PRC, other Chinese, and Christian populations in the Caucasus? And what can they teach us about "global China"? A comparative study within and beyond the Caucasus would be a logical next step and might produce new insights, reveal new connections, and raise new questions—or even come up with some answers. Finally, too, I would love to see a broader comparative project that opposes different marketplaces and market environments, not only regionally but globally, using Humboldt's *Naturgemälde* as a model, as I have methodologically outlined in this book.

References

Abrahamian, L. (2001). Afterword: The Artisan: Traditional Figure and Contemporary Functions. In N. Sweezy & L. Abrahamian (Eds.), *Armenian Folk Arts, Culture and Identity* (pp. 261–270). Indiana University Press.

Abrahamian, L. (2007a). Armenia and Armenians Between East and West. *21st Century, 1*, 72–76.

Abrahamian, L. (2007b). *Troubles and Hopes—Armenian Family, Home and Nation*. Campus Verlag.

Acemoglu, D., & Verdier, T. (2000). The Choice between Market Failures and Corruption. *American Economic Review, 90*(1), 194–211.

Adams, D. (1987). *Dirk Gently's Holistic Detective Agency*. William Heinemann.

Aivazishvili-Gehne, N. (2015). *Staatsbürgerschaft an der Grenze: Das Beispiel der georgischsprachigen Ingiloer in Aserbaidschan* (PhD), Martin-Luther-Universität Halle-Wittenberg, Halle an der Saale.

Aivazishvili-Gehne, N. (2018). "Der Staat ist der Präsident". Ingiloer und öffentliche Zeremonien in Aserbaidschan. *Paideuma, 64*, 27–50.

Akhter, M. (2018). Geopolitics of the Belt and Road: Space, State, and Capital in China and Pakistan. In B. Neilson, N. Rossiter & R. Samaddar (Eds.), *Logistical Asia: The Laboiur of Making a World Region* (pp. 221–241). Palgrave Macmillan. https://doi.org/10.1007/978-981-10-8333-4_11

Aldrich, H. E., & Waldinger, R. (1990). Ethnicity and Entrepreneurship. *Annual Review of Sociology, 16*, 111–135.

Alff, H. (2014). Embracing Chinese Modernity? Articulation and Positioning in China-Kazakhstan Trade and Exchange Processes. *Crossroads Asia Working Paper Series, 21*.

S. Fehlings, *Traders, Informal Trade and Markets between the Caucasus and China*, Politics and History in Central Asia,
https://doi.org/10.1007/978-981-19-5205-0

Alff, H. (2015). Profiteers or Moral Entrepreneurs? Bazaars, Traders and Development Discourses in Almaty. *Kazakhstan. International Development Planning Review, 37*(3), 249–267.

Alff, H. (2016a). Introduction. *Central Asian Survey, 35*(3), 327–333.

Alff, H. (2016b). Markt unter Druck: Der Dordoi-Basar in Kirgistan unter dem Einfluss von Eurasischer Wirtschaftsunion und Wirtschaftskrise. *Zentralasien Analysen, 105*, 2–6.

Allix, A. (1922). The Geography of Fairs: Illustrationed by Old-World Examples. *Geographical Review, 12*(4), 532–569.

Amiryan, T., & Kalantaryan, S. (Eds.). (2019). *Firdus: The Memory of a Place*. CSN lab.

Antonyan, Y. (2011). Religiosity and Religious Identity in Armenia: Some Current Models and Developments. *Acta Ethnographica Hungarica, 56*(2), 315–332.

Antonyan, Y. (2016). *Elites and "Elites": Transformations of Social Structures in Post-Soviet Armenia and Georgia*. ASCN.

Antonyan, Y. (2018). Interplay Between the Formal and the Informal: Marketing Religious Festivals in Contemporary Armenia. *Anthropological Researches, IV*, 65–77.

Antonyan, Y. (2020). Markets at Sacred Sites: The Globalized Mobility and Informality of the Armenian Religious Fairs. *Central Asian Survey, electronic preprint*, 1–17.

Appadurai, A. (1996). *Modernity at Large. Cultural Dimensions of Globalization*. University of Minnesota Press.

Applbaum, K. (2005). The Anthropology of Markets. In J. G. Carrier (Ed.), *A Handbook of Economic Anthropology* (pp. 275–289). Edward Elgar.

Ardener, S., & Burman, S. (Eds.). (1996). *Money-Go-Rounds: The Importance of Rotating Savings and Credit Associations for Women*. Berg.

Aslanian, S. (2014). *From the Indian Ocean to the Mediterranean: The Global Trade Networks of Armenian Merchants from New Julfa*. University of California Press.

Aslund, A. (2007). *How Capitalism Was Built: The Transformation of Central and Eastern Europe, Russia, and Central Asia*. Cambridge University Press.

Augé, M. (2008). *Non-Places: An Introduction to Supermodernity*. Verso.

Augsburg, B., De Haas, R., Harmgart, H., & Meghir, C. (2014). *The Impacts of Microcredit: Evidence from Bosnia and Herzegovina* (NBER Working Paper, No. 18538).

Baitas, M. (2017). *Traders of the Central Bazaar in Astana: A Perspective on Motives and Social Networks* (PhD). Nazarbayev University, Astana.

Baitas, M. (2019). The Traders of Central Bazaar, Astana: Motivation and Networks. *Central Asian Survey, electronic preprint*. https://doi.org/10.1080/02634937.2019.1697642

Balibar, É. (2002). *Politics and the Other Scene*. Verso.

Barth, F. (1963). *The Role of the Entrepreneur of Social Changes in Northern Norway*. Universitetsforlaget.

Basu, H. (2013). Ethnologie und die Vervielfältigung von Modernität. In U. Willems, D. Pollack, H. Basu, T. Gutmann & U. Spohn (Eds.), *Moderne und Religion. Kontroversen um Modernität und Säkularisierung* (pp. 379–414). transcript.

Bateman, M. (2014). The Rise and Fall of Muhammad Yunus and the Microcredit Model. *International Development Studies Working Paper Series, 1*.

Bateman, M., Blankenburg, S., & Kozul-Wright, R. (Eds.). (2019). *The Rise and Fall of Global Microcredit: Development*. Routledge.

Bateman, M., & Chang, H.-J. (2012). Microfinance and the Illusion of Development: From Hubris to Nemesis in Thirty Years. *World Social and Economic Review, 1*.

Baud, M., & Schendel, W. v. (1997). Toward a Comparative History of Borderlands. *Journal of World History, 8*(2), 211–242.

Bayadyan, H. (2007). Soviet Armenian Identity and Cultural Representation. In T. Darieva & W. Kaschuba (Eds.), *Representations on the Margins of Europe: Politics and Identities in the Baltic and South Caucasus States* (pp. 205–219). Campus Verlag.

Bechhofer, F., & Elliott, B. (Eds.). (1981). *The Petite Bourgeoisie: Comparative Studies of the Uneasy Stratum*. Macmillan.

Bell, S., & Coleman, S. (Eds.). (1999). *The Anthropology of Friendship*. Berg.

Belshaw, C. S. (1965). *Traditional Exchange and Modern Markets*. Prentice-Hall Inc.

Benet, F. (1957). Explosive Markets: The Berber Highlands. In K. Polanyi, C. M. Arensberg & H. W. Pearson (Eds.), *Trade and Markets in the Early Empires*. Free Press.

Beriashvili, L. (2016). Georgia on the "Great Silk Road" Trade Route [in Georgian]. *Georgians*, 473–479.

Bestor, T. C. (2001). Supply-Side Sushi: Commodity, Market, and the Global City. *American Anthropologist, 103*(1), 76–95. https://doi.org/10.2307/683923

Beyer, J. (2016). *The Force of Custom. Law and the Ordering of Everyday Life in Kyrgyzstan*. University of Pittsburgh Press.

Bhattacharya, B. (2005). Armenian European Relationship in India, 1500–1800: No Armenian Foundation for European Empire? *Journal of the Economic and Social History of the Orient, 48*(2), 277–322.

Bhattacharyya, S., & Hodler, R. (2010). Natural Resources, Democracy and Corruption. *European Economic Review, 54*(4), 608–621.

Black, R. E. (2012). *Porta Palazzo: The Anthropology of an Italian Market*. University of Pennsylvania Press.

Billé, F. (2014). *Sinophobia: Anxiety, Violence, and the Making of Mongolian Identity*. University of Hawaii Press.
Blunch, N.-H., Canagarajah, S., & Raju, D. (2001). *The Informal Sector Revisited: A Synthesis Across Space and Time* (Social Protection Discussion Paper Series). The World Bank.
Bohannan, P., & Dalton, G. (1962). *Markets in Africa*. Northwest University Press.
Bohannan, P. (1957). *Justice and Judgment among the Tiv*. Routledge.
Botoeva, A., & Spector, R. A. (2013). Sewing to Satisfaction: Craft-Based Entrepreneurs in Contemporary Kyrgyzstan. *Central Asian Survey, 32*(4), 487–500.
Bouchard, M. (2011). The State of the Study of the State of Anthropology. *Reviews in Anthropology, 40*, 183–209.
Bourdieu, P. (1977). *The Outline of a Theory of Practice*. Cambridge University Press.
Bourdieu, P. (2001 [1998]). *Masculine Domination*. Stanford University Press.
Boym, S. (2001). *The Future of Nostalgia*. Basic Books.
Bram, C. (2017). Moscow Azerbaijani-Juhuro "Oligarchs" and the Eurasian Trade Networks. *CAucasus Analytical Digest, 96*, 5–8.
Braudel, F. (1979). *Les jeux de l'échange (Vol. 2: Civilisation materielle, économie et capitalisme, XVe–XVIIIe siècle*. Livre Poche.
Brecht, B. (2016). *The Business Affairs of Mr Julius Caesar*. Bloomsbury Methuen Drama.
Brednikova, O., & Pachenkov, O. (1999). Ethnicity of "Ethnic Economy": Economic Immigrants to St. Petersburg. In O. Brednikova, V. Voronkov & E. Chikadze (Eds.), *Ethnicity and Economy: Proceedings of the Seminar Held in St. Petersburg (9—12 September 1999)* (Vol. 8, pp. 108–115). CISR.
Breman, J. (2009). Myth of the Global Safety Net. *New Left Review, 59*.
Broch-Due, V., & Ystanes, M. (Eds.). (2016). *Trusting and Its Tribulations: Interdisciplinary Engagements with Intimacy*. Berghahn Books.
Brumann, C. (1998). Geld als Geschenk: Aspekte japanischer Beziehungsarithmetik [Cash as a Gift: Aspects of Japanese Relational Arithmetics]. In A. Ernst & P. Pörtner (Eds.), *Die Rolle des Geldes in Japans Gesellschaft, Wirtschaft und Politik [The Role of Money in Japanese Society, Economy, and Politics]* (pp. 77–79). Hamburg: Institut für Asienkunde.
Buttimer, A. (2012). Alexander von Humboldt and Planet Earth's Green Mantle. *Cybergeo: European Journal of Geography, Epistémologie, Histoire de la Géographie, Didactique, Document 616*. https://doi.org/10.4000/cybergeo.25478
Cantens, T., Ireland, R., & Raballand, G. (2015). Introduction: Borders, Informality, International Trade and Customs. *Journal of Borderlands Studies, 30*(3), 365–380.

Carey, M. (2017). *Mistrust: An Ethnographic Theory*. HAU Books.
Carlsson, B., Braunerhjelm, P., McKelvey, M., Olofsson, C., Persson, L., & Ylinenpää, H. (2013). The Evolving Domain of Entrepreneurship Research. *Small Business Economics, 41*(4), 913–930.
Carrier, J. G. (1999). People Who Can Be Friends: Selves and Social Relationships. In S. Bell & S. Coleman (Eds.), *The Anthropology of Friendship* (pp. 21–38). Berg.
Carrier, J. G. (2012). *A Handbook of Economic Anthropology*. Edward Elgar.
Carrier, J. G. (2018). Moral Economy: What's in a Name. *Anthropological Theory, 18*(1), 18–35. https://doi.org/10.1177/1463499617735259
Carsten, J. (1989). Cooking Money: Gender and the Symbolic Transformation of Means of Exchange in a Malay Fishing Community. In J. Parry & M. Bloch (Eds.), *Money and the Morality of Exchange* (pp. 117–141). Cambridge University Press.
Carsten, J. (2004). *After Kindship*. Cambridge University Press.
Carsten, J. (Ed.). (2000). *Cultures of Relatedness: New Approaches to the Study of Kinship*. Cambridge University Press.
Carsten, J., & Hugh-Jones, S. (1995). Introduction: About the House—Lévi-Strauss and Beyond. In J. Carsten & S. Hugh-Jones (Eds.), *About the House: Lévi-Strauss and Beyond* (pp. 1–46). Cambridge University Press.
Castells, M., & Portes, A. (1989). World Underneath: The Origins, Dynamics, and Effects of the Informal Economy. In A. Portes, M. Castells, & L. A. Benton (Eds.), *The Informal Economy: Studies in Advanced and Less Developed Countries* (pp. 11–37). Johns Hopkins University Press.
Catania, D., & Rubini, C. (2007). Samarkand: How the Trade Routes Became the Urban Stage of Power. In M. Gervers, U. E. Bulag & G. Long (Eds.), *Traders and Trade Routes of Central and Inner Asia: The "Silk Road", Then and Now*. Asian Institute, University of Toronto.
Charaia, V., & Papava, V. (2017). Belt and Road Initiative: Implications for Georgia and China-Georgia Economic Relations. *China International Studies*, 122 139.
Chayanov, A. V. (1966 [1923]). *The Teory of Peasant Economy*. Richard D. Irwin, Inc.
Chen, M. A. (2007). *Rethinking the Formal Economy: Linkages with the Formal Economy and the Formal Regulatory Environment* (Economic & Social Affairs, DESA Working Paper No. 46).
Chin, T. (2013). The Invention of the Silk Road, 1877. *Critical Inquiry, 40*,, 194–219.
Christophe, B. (2005). Kultur der Korruption? Anmerkungen zur politischen Ordnung in Georgien. In B. Schröder (Ed.), *Georgien: Gesellschaft und Religion an der Schwelle Europas* (pp. 33–46). Röhrig Universitätsverlag.

Chumburidze, M., Zurabishvili, T., & Zurabishvili, T. (2016). Attitudes Towards Immigrants in Georgia: Myths of Tolerance and Empirical Evidence. *Caucasus Analytical Digest, 85*, 16–18.

Cieślewska, A. (2014). From Shuttle Trader to Businesswomen: The Informal Bazaar Econommy in Kyrgyzstan. In J. Morris & A. Polese (Eds.), *The Informal Post-Socialist Economy* (pp. 121–134). Routledge.

Clarke, M. (2008). China's Integration of Xinjiang with Central Asia: Securing a "Silk Road" to Great Power Status? *China and Eurasia Forum Quarterly, 6*(2), 89–111.

Clay, A. T. (2001). Rethinking Moral Economy. *American Political Science Review, 95*, 85–95.

Cohen, A. (2004 [1969]). *Custom and Politics in Urban Africa: A Study of Hausa Migrant in Yoruba Towns*. Routledge.

Conde, J., & Gattini, L. (2019). Financing in Georgia: Small and Medium Enterprises and the Private Sector. *Economics—Regional Studies*: European Investment Bank.

Conrad, H. (2021). *A Road as an Empire: Some Remarks about the Most Important Ancient Periods and Powers of and along the Silk Road* (Working Paper Series on Informal Markets and Trade, 11).

Corsín Jiménez, A. (2011). Trust in Anthropology. *Anthropological Theory, 11*(2), 177–196.

Corso, M. (2011). The Business Climate and Anti-Corruption Measures in Georgia. *Caucasus Analytical Digest, 26*, 10–12.

Cresswell, T. (2006). *On the Move: Mobility in the Modern Western World*. Routledge.

Curro, C. (2015). Davabirzhaot! Conflicting Claims on Public Space in Tbilisi: Between Transparency and Opaqueness. *International Journal of Sociology and Social Policy, 35*(7/8), 497–512. https://doi.org/10.1108/IJSSP-12-2014-0122

Dabaghyan, A., & Gabrielyan, M. (2011). Rural Transcaucasian Trade Before and After National Border. *Acta Ethnographica Hungarica, 56*(2), 333–357.

Dabaghyan, A., & Gabrielyan, M. (2014). On a Village Market at a South Caucasian Border. In A. Bobokhyan, L. Abrahamian & K. Franklin (Eds.), *Market beyond Economy* (pp. 37–53). NAS RA "Gitutyun" Publishing.

Dadabaev, T. (2018). Engagement and Contestation: The Entangled Imagery of the Silk Road. *Cambridge Journal of Eurasian Studies, 2* (Q4GIV6), 1–15. doi: https://doi.org/10.22261/CJES.Q4GIV6

Dalakoglou, D., & Harvey, P. (2012). Roads and Anthropology: Ethnographic Perspectives on Space, Time and (Im)Mobility. *Mobilities, 7*(4), 459–465.

Dams, T., & Van der Putten, F. P. (2015). China and Liberal Values in International Relations: Opposing the Promotion of Democracy, Human Rights and Liberal Market Economy. *Clingendael Report*. Clingendael Netherlands Institute of International Relations.

Dannhaeuser, N. (1989). Marketing in Developing Urban Areas. In S. Plattner (Ed.), *Economic Anthropology* (pp. 222–252). Stanford University Press.

Darieva, T., Kaschuba, W., & Krebs, M. (Eds.). (2011). *Urban Spaces after Socialism: Ethnographies of Public Places in Eurasian Cities*. Campus Verlag.

Darieva, T., Mühlfried, F., & Tuite, K. (Eds.). (2018). *Sacred Places, Emerging Spaces: Religious Pluralism in the Post-Soviet Caucasus*. Berghahn.

Dasgupta, P. (1988). Trust as a Commodity. In D. Gambetta (Ed.), *Trust: Making and Breaking Cooperative Relations* (pp. 49–73). Wiley-Blackwell.

Davis, J. (1977). Economic Anthropology of Mediterranean Societies. In J. Davis (Ed.), *People of the Mediterranean: An Essay in Comparative Social Anthropology* (pp. 17–72). Routledge.

Dermendzhieva, Z. (2011). Emigration from the South Caucasus: Who Goes Abroad and What Are the Economic Implications? *Post-Communist Economies, 23*(3), 377–398. https://doi.org/10.1080/14631377.2011.595135

DeYoung, A. J., Reeves, M., & Valyayeva, G. K. (2006). *Surviving the Transition? Case Studies of Schools and Schooling in the Kyrgyz Republic since Independence*. Information Age.

Di Puppo, L. (2004). Corruption as an Instrument of State Control in Georgia. *Berliner Osteuropa-Info, 21*, 47–54.

Di Puppo, L. (2013). The Construction of Success in Anticorruption Activity in Georgia. *East European Politics, 30*, 105–122.

Dilley, R. (1992). *Contesting Markets: Analyses of Ideology, Discourse and Practice*. Edinburgh Universitiy Press.

Dines, N. (2007). *The Experience of Diversity in an Era of Urban Regeneration: The Case of Queens Market, East London*. Fondazione Eni Enrico Mattei (FEEM).

Dragadze, T. (2016). *Rural Families in Soviet Georgia: A Case Study in Ratcha Province*. Routledge.

Dudwick, N. (2003). No Guests at our Table: Social Fragmentation in Georgia. In N. Dudwick, E. Gomart, A. Marc, & K. Kuehnast (Eds.), *When Things fall apart: Qualitative Studies of Poverty in the Former Soviet Union*. The World Bank.

Dumont, L. (1977). *From Mandeville to Marx: Genesis and Triumph of Economic Ideology*. University of Chicago Press.

Dumont, L. (1980). *Homo Hierarchicus: The Caste System and Its Implications*. University of Chicago Press.

Dundua, T., & Avdaliani. (2021). Silk, Spices and Oil: „Transcaucasian“ Trade Route and Georgia. *Academia Letters, Article 337*. https://doi.org/10.20935/AL337

Durkheim, É. (1969). *The Division of Labor in Society*. Free Press. Originally published as *De la division du travail social: étude sur l'organisation des sociétés supérieures* (Paris: F. Alcan, 1893).
Durst, J. (2015). Juggling with Debts, Moneylenders and Local Petty Monarchs: Banking the Unbanked in 'Shanty-Villages' in Hungary. *Review of Sociology, 25*(4), 30–57.
Dyatlov, V., & Grigorichev, K. (2015). *Ethnic Markets in Russia: Space of Bargaining and Place of Meeting*. Publishing House of ISU.
Eisenstadt, S. (2000). Multiple Modernities. *Daedalus, 129*(1), 1–29.
Endres, K. W. (2018). Markets. In H. Callan (Ed.), *International Encyclopedia of Anthropology*. Wiley Blackwell.
Engels, F. (1975 [1884]). Der Ursprung der Familie, des Privateigentums und des Staats. In K. Marx & F. Engels (Eds.), *Werke* (Vol. 21). Dietz.
Englund, H., & Leach, J. (2000). Ethnography and the Meta-Narrative of Modernity. *Current Anthropology, 41*(2), 225–248.
Eradze, I. (2021). Imbalanced Foreign Trade, Debt, and Investment in Developing Countries: The Case of Georgia. *E-paper of the Heinrich Böll Stiftung*. https://eu.boell.org/en/2021/06/16/imbalanced-foreign-trade-debt-and-investment-developing-countries-case-georgia
Eval, G., Szelenyi, I., & Townsley, E. R. (2000). *Making Capitalism without Capitalists: The New Ruling Elites in Eastern Europe*. Verso.
Evans-Pritchard, E. E. (1937). *Witchcraft, Oracles And Magic Among The Azande*. Oxford University Press.
Fedorova, K. (2012). Transborder Trade on the Russian-Chinese Border: Problems of Interethnic Communication. In B. Bruns & J. Miggelbrink (Eds.), *Subverting Borders: Doing Research on Smuggling and Small-Scale Trade* (pp. 107–128). Verlag für Sozialwissenschaften.
Fehlings, S. (2008). *Ruhestätten in bester Lage: Räumliche Ordnungen sozialer Werte auf Friedhöfen in Simferopol/Krim*. LIT-Verlag.
Fehlings, S. (2010). The Private and the Public Spheres in Yerevan, as observed from an Anthropologist from abroad. In Armenian Academy of Sciences (Ed.), *Armenian Popular Culture: Tradition and Modernity in Armenian Culture* (Vol. XV, pp. 108–118). Gitutyun pub.
Fehlings, S. (2012). Auf der Suche nach der verlorenen Zeit. In W. Kaschuba, M. Krebs, & M. Pilz (Eds.), *Die Postsowjetische Stadt: Aushandlungsprozesse im Südkaukasus* (pp. 150–167). Panama Verlag.
Fehlings, S. (2014). *Jerewan: Urbanes Chaos und soziale Ordnung*. LIT-Verlag.
Fehlings, S. (2015). Intimacy and Exposure: Yerevan's Private and Public Space. *International Journal of Sociology and Social Policy, 35*(7/8), 513–532.
Fehlings, S. (2016). The Ignoble Savage in Urban Yerevan. *Central Asian Survey, 35*(2), 195–217. https://doi.org/10.1080/02634937.2015.1134142

Fehlings, S. (2017). Armenian History in Urban Everyday Life. *Habitus: Studies in Anthropology and Archaeology, 2*, 10–41.
Fehlings, S. (2018). Caucasian "Biznes" (Business): Informality, Cultural Embeddedness, and the Global World. *Anthropological Researches, IV*, 23–39.
Fehlings, S. (2019). Encounters at the Grassroots Level: Chinese-Georgian Interactions in the BRI Era. *Caucasus Analytical Digest, 111*, 14–17. https://doi.org/10.3929/ethz-b-000368298
Fehlings, S. (2020). Doing Business in Yabaolu Market, Beijing: (Inter-)Ethnic Entrepreneurship, Trust and Friendship between Caucasian and Chinese Traders. *Central Asian Survey, Electronic Preprint, 1–21*,. https://doi.org/10.1080/02634937.2019.1696281
Fehlings, S. (2021). „They Are Like Georgians But bigger": The Perception of Chinese Businesspeople in Georgia. *New Diversities, 23*(2), 79–92.
Fehlings, S., & Karrar, H. (2016). Informal Markets and Trade in the Caucasus and Central Asia: A Preliminary Framework for Field Research. *Informal Markets and Trade Working Paper Series, 1*.
Ferry, M. (2013). Female Migration from Georgia: Profiles and Migratory Projects. *Caucasus Analytical Digest, 57*(3), 8–10.
Firth, R. (1939). *Primitive Polynesian Economy*. Routledge.
Firth, R. (1946). *Malay Fisherman: Their Peasant Economy*. Routledge.
Firth, R. (1967). *Themes in Economic Anthropology*. Tavistock Publications.
Fitzpatrick, S. (2005). *Tear Off the Mask! Identity and Imposture in Twentieth Century Russia*. Princeton University Press.
Fontaine, L. (1996). *A History of Pedlars in Europe*. Duke University Press.
Fontaine, L. (2014). *The Moral Economy: Poverty, Credit, and Trust in Early Modern Europe*. Cambridge University Press.
Frankopan, P. (2015). *The Silk Roads: A New History of the World*. Bloomsbury.
Frederiksen, M. D. (2012). Good Hearts or Big Bellies: Dzmakatsoba and Images of Masculinity in the Republic of Georgia. In V. Amit & N. Dyck (Eds.), *Young Men in Uncertain Times* (pp. 165–187). Berghahn Books.
Frederiksen, M. D. (2013). *Young Men, Time, and Boredom in the Republic of Georgia*. Temple University Press.
Freeland, C. (2000). *Sale of the Century: Russia's Wild Ride from Communism to Capitalism*. Doubleday Canada.
Freitag, U., & Oppen, A. v. (2010). Introduction: "Translocality": An Approach to Connection and Transfer in Area Studies. In U. Freitag & A. v. Oppen (Eds.), *Translocality: The Study of Globalising Processes from a Southern Perspective* (pp. 1–24). Brill.
Friedman, M. (2002 [1962]). *Capitalism and Freedom*. University of Chicago Press.
Fukuyama, F. (1992). *Das Ende der Geschichte: Wo stehen wir?* Kindler.

Fukuyama, F. (1995). *Trust: The Social Virtues and the Creation of Prosperity*. Free Press Paperbacks.

Fuller, C., & Harriss, J. (2001). For an Anthropology of the Modern Indian State. In C. Fuller & V. Bénéi (Eds.), *The Everyday State and Society in Modern India* (pp. 1–30). Social Science Press.

Fuller, C. J., & Bénéi, V. (2001). *The Everyday State and Society in Modern India*. Hurst & Co.

Gaonkar, D. P. (2001). *Alternative Modernities*. Duke University Press.

Geertz, C. (1963). *Peddlers and Princes: Social Developments and Economic Change in two Indonesian Towns*. Chicago University Press.

Geertz, C. (1978). The Bazaar Economy: Information and Search in Peasant Marketing. *The American Economic Review, 68*(2), 28–32.

Gell, A. (1982). The Market Wheel: Symbolic Aspects of an Indian Tribal Market. *Man, 17*(3), 470–491. https://doi.org/10.2307/2801710

Gellner, E. (1988). Trust, Cohesion and the Social Order. In D. Gambetta (Ed.), *Trust: Making and Breaking Cooperative Relations* (pp. 143–157). Wiley-Blackwell.

Gereffi, G., Humphrey, J., & Sturgeon, T. (2003). The Governance of Global Value Chains. *Review of International Political Economy, 12*(1), 78–104.

Giddens, A. (1990). *The Consequences of Modernity*. Polity Press.

Giragosian, R. (2009). Networks of Crime and Corruption in the South Caucasus. *Caucasus Analytical Digest, 19*, 2–5.

Gluckman, M. (1955). *The Judicial Process among the Barotse of Northern Rhodesia*. Manchester University Press.

Gluckman, M. (1965). *The Ideas in Barotse Jurisprudence*. Yale University Press.

Glukhovsky, D. (2007). *Sumerki—Dämmerung*. Heyne.

Gonzàlez de la Rocha, M. (2007). The Construction of the Myth of Survival. *Development and Change, 38*(1), 45–66.

Graeber. (2011). *Dept: The First 5.000 Years*. Melville House Publishing.

Grant, B. (1999). The Return of the Repressed: Conversations with Three Russian Entrepreneurs. In G. E. Marcus (Ed.), *Paranoia within Reason: A Casebook on Conspiracy as Explanation* (pp. 241–267). University o Chicago Press.

Grant, B., & Yalçın-Heckmann, L. (Eds.). (2007). *Caucasus Paradigms: Anthropologies, Histories and the Making of a World Area*. LIT.

Gregory, C. (1997). *Savage Money: The Anthropology and Politics of Commodity Exchange*. Harwood Academic Publishers.

Gregory, C. (2009). Whatever Happened to Economic Anthropology? *The Australian Journal of Anthropology, 20*, 285–300.

Gregory, C. (2012). On Money, Debt and Morality: Some Reflections on the Contribution of Economic Anthropology. *Social Anthropology, 20*(4), 380–396.

Grigolia, A. (1939). *Custom and Justice in the Caucasus: The Georgian Highlanders*. AMS Press.
Grigorichev, K., Dyatlov, V., Timoshkin, D., & Bryazgina, D. (Eds.). (2019). *Bazaar and the City: People, Spaces, Images (Базар и город: люди, пространства, образы)*. Ottisk.
Gröner, A.-M. (2010). *"Meine Versicherung?—Meine Familie!" Sicherheit durch Pflege sozialer Obligationen: Aus dem Alltag aserbaischanischer Familien*. (Magisterarbeit), Eberhard Karls Universität Tübingen, Tübingen.
Gudeman, S. F. (2001). *The Anthropology of Economy: Community, Market, and Culture*. Blackwell.
Gudeman, S. F., & Hann, C. (2015). Introduction; Ritual, Economy, and the Institutions of the Base. In S. F. Gudeman & C. Hann (Eds.), *Economy and Ritual: Studies of Postsocialist Transformations* (pp. 1–30). Berghahn.
Guérin, I. (2014). Juggling with Debt, Social Ties, and Values The Everyday Use of Microcredit in Rural South India. *Current Anthropology, 55*(9), 40–50.
Gupta, A. (1995). Blurred Boundaries: The Discourse of Corruption, the Culture of Politics, and the Imagined State. *American Ethnologist, 22*(2), 375–402. https://doi.org/10.2307/646708
Gupta, A. (2012). *Red Tape: Bureaucracy, Structural Violence, and Poverty in India*. Duke University Press.
Gurchiani, K. (2017). How Soviet is the Religious Revival in Georgia: Tactics in Everyday Religiosity. *Europe-Asia Studies, 69*(3), 508–531.
Guzei, I. (2015). The "Russian" Market in the Center of Beijing. In V. Dyatlov & K. Grigorichev (Eds.), *Ethnic Markets in Russia: Space of Bargaining and Place of Meeting* (pp. 159–170). Publishing House of ISU.
Habermas, J. (1981). *Theorie des kommunikativen Handelns* (Vol. II). Suhrkamp Verlag.
Hahn, H. P. (2018). Introduction: Markets as Places: Actors, Structures and Ideologies. In H. P. Hahn & G. Schmitz (Eds.), *Market as Place & Space of Economic Exchange: Perspectives from Archaeology & Anthropology* (pp. 1–18). Oxbow.
Hahn, H. P. (2019). Rural Markets in West Afrika: What Criteria are Required for an Appropriate Description. *Weight and Value, 1*, 367–378.
Hann, C. (2005). Postsocialist Societies. In J. G. Carrier (Ed.), *A Handbook of Economic Anthropology* (pp. 547–557). Edward Elgar.
Hann, C. (2018). Moral(ity and) Economy: Work, Workfare, and Fairness in Provincial Hungary. *European Journal of Sociology/Archives Européennes De Sociologie, 59*(2), 225–254.
Hardenberg, R. (2007). Das "einschließende Haus": Wertehierarchien und das Konzept der "Hausgesellschaft" im interkulturellen Vergleich. *Anthropos, 102*, 157–168.

Hardenberg, R., & Fehlings, S. (2016). *Informality Reviewed: Everyday Experiences and the Study of Transformational Processes in Central Asia and the Caucasus* (Informal Markets and Trade Working Paper Series, 2).

Harris, T. (2013a). *Geographical Diversions: Tibetan Trade, Global Transactions*. Universityof Georgia Press.

Harris, T. (2013b). Trading Places: New Economic Geographies across Himalayan Borderlands. *Political Geography, 35*, 60–68. https://doi.org/10.1016/j.polgeo.2012.12.002

Hart, K. (1970). Small-Scale Entrepreneurs in Ghana and Development Planning. *Journal of Development Studies, 6*(4), 104–120.

Hart, K. (1973). Informal Income Opportunities and Urban Employment in Ghana. *Journal of Modern African Studies, 11*(1), 61–89.

Hart, K. (1986). Heads or Tails? *Two Sides of the Coin. Man, 21*(4), 637–656. https://doi.org/10.2307/2802901

Hart, K. (1988). Kinship, Contract and Trust: The Economic Organization of Migrants in an African City Slum. In D. Gambetta (Ed.), *Trust: Making and Breaking Cooperative Relations* (pp. 176–193). Blackwell.

Hart, K. (1992). Market and State after the Cold War: The Informal Economy Reconsidered. In R. Dilley (Ed.), *Contesting Markets: Analyses of Ideology, Discourse and Practice*. Edinburgh University Press.

Hart, K. (2005). Formal Bureaucracy and the Emergent Forms of the Informal Economy. *Research Paper* (Vol. 2005/011). UNU-WIDER.

Hayoz, N., & Giordano, C. (2013). *Informality in Eastern Europe: Structures, Political Culture, and Social Practices*. Peter Lang.

Hébert, R. F., & Link, A. N. (1989). In Search of the Meaning of Entrepreneurship. *Small Business Economics, 1*(1), 39–49.

Helmke, G., & Levitsky, S. (2004). Informal Institutions and Comparative Politics: A Research Agenda. *Perspectives on Politics, 2*(4), 725–740. https://doi.org/10.2307/3688540

Herskovits, M. J. (1938). *Dahomey*. J.J. Augustin Inc.

Hertz, E. (1998). *The Trading Crowd: An Ethnography of the Shanghai Stock Market*. Cambridge University Press.

Herzfeld, M. (1980). Honour and Shame: Problems in the Comparative Analysis of Moral Systems. *Man, 15*, 339–352.

Herzfeld, M. (1997). *Cultural Intimacy: Social Poetics in the Nation State*. Routledge.

Herzog, L. (1990). *Where North Meets South: Cities, Space, and Politics on the U.S.-Mexico Border*. Center for Mexican American Studies.

Heyat, F. (2002). Women and the Culture of Entrpreneurship in Soviet and Post-Soviet Azerbaijan. In R. Mandel & C. Humphrey (Eds.), *Markets and Moralities: Ethnographies of Postsocialism* (pp. 19–31). Berg.

Höllmann, T. O. (2008). *Die Seidenstraße*. C.H. Beck.

Holzlehner, T. (2014). *Shadow Networks: Border Economics, Informal Markets and Organized Crime in the Russian Far East*. LIT Verlag.

Hopkirk, P. (1980). *Foreign Devils on the Silk Road: The Search for the Lost Treasures of Central Asia*. John Murray.

Hosking, G. (2010). *Trust: Money, Markets and Society*. Seagull Books.

Humboldt, A. v. (1807a). *Essai sur la géographie des plantes, accompagné d'un tableau physique des régions équinoxiales, fondé sur les mesures exécutées, depuis le dixième degré de latitude boréale jusqu'au dixième degré de latitude australe, pendant les années 1799, 1800, 1801, 1802, et 1903 par A. De Humboldt et A. Bonpland*. Fr Schoelle Librairie.

Humboldt, A. v. (1807b). *Ideen zu einer Georgraphie der Pflanzen nebst einem Naturgemälde der Tropenländer: Auf Beobachtungen und Messungen gegründet, welche vom 10ten Grade nördlicher Breite bis zum 10ten Grade südlicher Breite, in den Jahren 1799, 1800, 1801, 1802 und 1803 angestellt worden sind von Al. von Humboldt und A. Bonpland*. Cotta Verlag.

Humboldt, A. v. (1814). *Voyage aux régions équinoxiales du Nouveau Continent fait en 1799, 1800, 1801, 1802, 1803 et 1804, fait par A. De Humboldt et A. Bonpland*. Maze.

Humboldt, A. v. (1845–1862). *Kosmos: Entwurf einer physischen Weltbeschreibung*. Cotta Verlag.

Humboldt, A. v. (1849). *Ansichten der Natur mit wissenschaftlichen Erläuterungen* (3 ed.). J.G. Cotta'scher Verlag.

Humboldt, A. v. (1859). *Views of Nature*. H. G. Bohn.

Humboldt, A. v. (1851). *Personal narrative of travels to the Equinoctial Regions of America during the years 1799–1804*. Routledge.

Humphrey, C. (1983). *Karl Marx Collective: Economy, Society and Religion in a Siberian Collective Farm*. Cambridge University Press.

Humphrey, C. (2002). *The Unmaking of Soviet Life: Everyday Economics after Socialism*. Cornell University Press.

Humphrey, C. (2017). Loyalty and Disloyalty along the Russian-Chinese Border. *History and Anthropology, 28*(4), 399–405. https://doi.org/101080/02757206.2017.1351356

Humphrey, C. (2018a). Introduction: Trusting and Mistrusting Across Borders. In C. Humphrey (Ed.), *Trust and Mistrust in the Economy of the China-Russia Borderlands* (pp. 9–35). Amsterdam University Press.

Humphrey, C. (Ed.). (2018b). *Trust and Mistrust in the Economy of the China-Russia Borderlands*. Amsterdam University Press.

Humphrey, C., & Skvirskaja, V. (2009). Trading Places: Post-socialist Container Markets and the City. *Focaal: European Journal of Anthropology, 55*. https://doi.org/10.3167/fcl.2009.550105

Ibañez-Tirado, D. Marsden, M. (2020). Trade "Outside the Law": Uzbek and Afghan Transnational Merchants between Yiwu and South-Central Asia. *Central Asian Survey, electronic preprint.*

Inan, F., & Yayloyan, D. (2018). New Economic Corridors in the South Caucasus and the Chinese One Belt One Road. *Policy Paper: The Economic Policy Research Foundation of Turkey (TEPAV)*, 1–89.

Iskandaryan, A. (2014). Formalization of the Informal: Statebuilding in Armenia. In C. Giordano & N. Hayoz (Eds.), *Informality in Eastern Europe: Structures, Political Cultures and Social Practices* (pp. 451–484). Peter Lang.

Ismalov, E., & Papava, V. (2018). Caucasian Tandem and the Belt and Road Initiative. *Journal of Social and Political Studies, Central Asia and South Caucasus, 19*(2), 7–16.

James, D. (2014). 'Deeper into a Hole?' Borrowing and Lending in South Africa. *Current Anthropology, 55*(9), 17–29. https://doi.org/10.1086/676123

Jezewski, M. A., & Sotnik, P. (2001). *The Rehabilitation Service Provider as Cultural Broker: Providing Culturally Competent Services to Foreign-Born Persons*. Center for International Rehabilitation Research Education and Exchange.

Kaczmarski, M. (2016). "Silk Globalisation": China's Vision of International Order. *OSW Point of View, 60.*

Kalandarova, M. (2005). Indian Merchants in Nineteenth-Century Bukhara: Trade Network and Socio-Cultural Role. In M. Gervers (Ed.), *Traders and Trade Routes of Central and Inner Asia: The "Silk Road", Then and Now* (pp. 93–162). Asian Institute, University of Toronto.

Kandiyoti, D. (2003). The Cry for Land: Agrarian Reform, Gender and Land Rights in Uzbekistan. *Journal of Agrarian Change, 3*(1–2), 225–256.

Kaneff, D. (2002). The Shame and Pride of Market Activity: Morality, Identity and Trading in Postsocialist Rural Bulgaraia. In R. Mandel & C. Humphrey (Eds.), *Markets and Moralities: Ethnographies of Postsocialism* (pp. 33–51). Berg.

Karrar, H. (2013). Merchants, Markets, and the State. *Critical Asian Studies, 45*(3), 459–480. https://doi.org/10.1080/14672715.2013.829315

Karrar, H. (2017). *Do Bazaars Die? Notes on Failure in the Central Asian Bazaar* (Informal Markets and Trade Working Paper Series, 4).

Karrar, H. (2018). The Silk Road versus the Central Asian Bazaar: Two Thousand Years or Twenty-Five Years of Exchange and Mobility? *Anthropological Researches, IV*, 13–22.

Karrar, H. (2019). In the Shadow of the Silk Road: Border Regimes and Economic Corridor Development through an Unremarkable Pakistan-China Border Market. *Comparative Studies of South Asia, Africa and the Middle East, 39*(3), 389–406.

Karrar, H. (2020). The Bazaar in Ruins: Rent and Fire in the Barakholka, Almaty. *Central Asian Survey, electronic preprint.*

Karrar, H. H., & Rudaz, P. (2022). A Cautionary Tale: Bazaar Trade and Limitations to Growth in Georgia, Kazakhstan and Kyrgyzstan. *Global Networks*. https://doi.org/10.1111/glob.12367

Karrar, H., & Mostowlansky, T. (2018). Assembling Marginality in Northern Pakistan. *Political Geography, 63*, 65–74.

Kaufmann, D., Johnson, S., & Zoido-Lobaton, P. (1989). Regulatory Discretion and the Unofficial Economy. *American Economic Review, 88*(2), 287–392.

Kaufmann, D., Kraay, A., & Mastruzzi, M. (2010). *The Worldwide Governance Indicators: Methodology and Analytical Issues* (World Bank Policy Research Working Paper, 5430).

Kehl-Bodrogi, K. (2008). *"Religion is not so strong here". Muslim Religious Life in Khorezm after Socialism.* Lit-Verlag.

KfW-Entwicklungsbank. (2005). *Georgien: Microfinance Bank of Georgia-Procredit Bank (Schlussprüfung).* KfW.

Khalvashi, T. (2015). Peripheral Affects: Shame, Publics, and Performance on the Margins of the Republic of Georgia. (PhD). University of Copenhagen, Copenhagen.

Khalvashi, T., & Gilbreath, D. (2013). Georgia: Hard Money, Hard Times. Eurasianet. https://www.academia.edu/4433935/Hard_Money_Hard_Times.

Khutsishvili, K. (2006). Bazaar Culture in Georgia: The Case of Tbilisi. *Berliner Blätter, 59*, 41–52.

Khutsishvili, K. (2016). Across the Enguri Border: Lives Connected and Separated by the Borderland Between Georgia and Abkhazia. In T. Bringa & H. Toje (Eds.), *Eurasian Borderlands: Spatializing Borders in the Aftermath of State Collapse* (pp. 107–131). Palgrave Macmillan.

Khutsishvili, K. (2017). Suddenly a Border: Hazelnut Trade across the De Facto Border between Abkhazia and the Zugdidi Municipal Region of Georgia. *Caucasus Analytical Digest, 96*, 9–12.

Khutsishvili, K. (2018). Market Infrastructure: Past and Present Transformations. *Anthropological Researches, IV*, 40–47.

Killick, E., & Desai, A. (2010). Introduction: Valuing Friendship. In E. Killick & A. Desai (Eds.), *The Ways of Friendship: Anthropological Perspectives* (pp. 1–19). Berghahn Books.

Kim, Y.-C. (Ed.). (2107). *China and Africa: A New Paradigm of Global Business*. Palgrave Macmillan.

Kirakos Ganjakec'i. (1961). *Patmut'yun Hayoc' (History of Armenia).* Xmbagrut'yamb K. Melik'-Ohan'janyani (edited by K. Melik-Ohanjanyan). Yerevan.

Kocha, N., & Valiyev, A. (2015). Urban Boosterism in Closed Contexts: Spectacular Urbanization and Second-tier Mega-events in Three Caspian Capitals. *Eurasian Geography and Economics, 56*(5), 575–598.

Koehler, J. (2003). Die Schule der Straße: Georgische Cliquen zwischen Kämpfen um Ehre und organisierter Kriminalität. In U. Luig & J. Seebode (Eds.), *Ethnologie der Jugend: Soziale Praxis, moralische Diskurse und inszenierte Körperlichkeit* (pp. 43–69). Lit Verlag.

Konstantinov, Y. (1996). Patterns of Reinterpretation: Trader-Tourism in the Balkans (Bulgaria) as a Picaresque Metaphorical Enactment of Post-Totalitarianism. *American Ethnologist, 23*(4), 762–782.

Konstantinov, Y., Kressel, G. M., & Thuen, T. (1998). Outclassed by Former Outcasts: Petty Trading in Varna. *American Ethnologist, 25*(4), 729–745.

Körner, A. (2017). Moral Education in Georgian Orthodox Christianity: Striving for a Georgian Modernity. In R. Hardenberg (Ed.), *Approaching Ritual Economy: Socio-Cosmic Fields in Globalised Contexts* (pp. 231–254). RessourcenKulturen Universität Tübingen.

Kotkin, S. (1995). *Magnetic Mountain: Stalinism as a Civilization*. University of California Press.

Krebs, M. (2011). *Zwischen Handwerkstradition und globalem Markt Kunsthandwerker in Usbekistan und Kirgistan*. Klaus Schwarz Verlag.

Kreff, F., Knoll, E.-M., & Gingrich, A. (2011). *Lexikon der Globalisierung*. Transcript Verlag.

Kuehnast, K., & Dudwick, N. (2004). *Better a Hundred Friends than a Hundred Rubles? Social Networks in Transition—The Kyrgyz Republic*. The International Bank for Reconstruction and Development. Washington D.C.

Kupatadze, A. (2009). Georgia's Fight against Organized Crime: Success or Failure? *Caucasus Analytical Digest, 19*, 9–12.

Kupatadze, A. (2011). Similar Events, Different Outcomes: Accounting for Diverging Corruption: Patterns in Post-Revolution Georgia and Ukraine. *Caucasus Analytical Digest, 26*, 2–6.

La Pradelle, M. (2006). *Market Day in Provence*. University of Chicago Press.

Lambert, M, "Is China Building a Bridge or an Outpost in the Caucasus," Macdonald-Laurier Institute, 27 September 2017, https://www.macdonald laurier.ca/ischina-building-a-bridge-or-an-outpost-in-the-caucasus-michael-lambert-for-inside-policy.

Larkin, B. (2013). The Politics and Poetics of Infrastructure. *Annual Review of Anthropology, 42*, 327–343.

Larsen, J. (2017). Georgia-China Relations: The Geopolitics of the Belt and Road. *Policy Paper*. Tbilisi: Georgian Institute of Politics. https://gip.ge/wp-content/uploads/2017/10/Chineti percent20Saqartvelo percent20Eng_Ydit.pdf

Laruelle, M. (Ed.). (2018). *China's Belt and Road Initiative and its Impact in Central Asia*. George Washington University, Central Asia Program.
Ledeneva, A. (1998). *Russia's Economy of Favours: Blat, Networking and Informal Exchange*. Cambridge University Press.
Ledeneva, A. (2006). *How Russia Really Works: The Informal Practices That Shaped Post-Soviet Politics and Business*. Cornell University Press.
Ledeneva, A. (2013). *Can Russia Modernise?: Sistema, Power Networks and Informal Governance*. Cambridge University Press.
Ledeneva, A. (2018). *The Global Encyclopaedia of Informality: Understanding Social and Cultural Complexity* (Vol. 1). UCL Press.
Lee, C. K. (2014). The Spectre of Global China. *New Left Review, 89*, 29–65.
Lehti, M., & Romashov, V. (2021). Suspending the Antagonism: Situated Agonistic Peace in a Border Bazaar. *Third World Quartely*. https://doi.org/10.1080/01436597.2021.1962274
Lévi-Strauss, C. (1963). *Structural Anthropology*. Basic Books.
Lewellen, T. C. (2003). *Political Anthropology*. Praeger.
Lezhava, B., Brekashvili, P., & Melua, I. (2014). Global Entrepreneurship Monitor: Special Topic—Women Entrepreneurship in Georgia. In GEM (Ed.), *GEM* (pp. 1–20). Caucasus University. https://www.gemconsortium.org/index.php/report/women-entrepreneurship-in-georgia
Light, I., & Gold, S. J. (2000). *Ethnic Economies*. Academic Press.
Light, M. (2014). Police Reforms in the Republic of Georgia: The Convergence of Domestic and Foreign Policy in an Anti-Corruption Drive. *An International Journal of Research and Policy, 24*(3), 318–345.
Linß, V. (2014). *Die wichtigsten Wirtschaftsdenker*. maxiverlag.
Lont, H., & Hospes, O. (Eds.). (2004). *Livelihood and Microfinance: Anthropological and Sociological Perspectives on Savings and Debt*. Eburon Academic Press.
Louw, M. E. (2007). *Everyday Islam in Post-Soviet Central Asia*. Routledge.
Low, A. (1999). *A Bibliographical Survey of Rotating Savings and Credit Associations*. Oxfam and CCCRW.
Lundkvist-Houndoumadi, M. (2010). Treading on the Fine Line Between Self-Sacrifice and Immorality: Narratives of Emigrated Georgian Women. *Transcience Journal, 1*(2), 50–71.
Luong, P. J. (2004). *The Transformation of Central Asia: States and Societies from Soviet Rule to Independence*. Cornell University Press.
Ong, A. (1999). *Flexible Citizenship: The Cultural Logics of Transnationality*. Duke University Press.
Maine, H. (1861). *Ancient Law: Its Connection with the Early History of Society, and Its Relation to Modern Ideas*. John Murray.

Mains, D. (2013). Friends and Money: Balancing Affection and Reciprocity among Young Men in Urban Ethopia. *American Anthropologist, 40*(2), 335–346.

Malinowski, B. (1922). *Argonauts of the Western Pacific*. Routledge.

Malinowski, B. (1935). *Coral Gardens and their Magic: A Study of the Methods of Tilling the Soil and of Agricultural Rites in the Trobriand Islands*. G. Allen & Unwin.

Maloney, W. F. (2004). Informality Revisited. *World Development, 32*(7), 1159–1178.

Mandel, R., & Humphrey, C. (2002). *Markets and Moralities: Ethnographies of Postsocialism*. Berg.

Mandeville, B. (1989 [1714]). *The Fable of the Bees*. Penguin Group.

Marat, E. (2009). *Labor Migration in Central Asia: Implications of the Global Economic Crisis (Silk Road Paper)*. Central Asia-Caucasus Institute & Silk Road Studies Program.

Mars, G., & Altman, Y. (1983). The Cultural Bases of Soviet Georgia's Second Economy. *Soviet Studies, XXXV, 4*, 546–560.

Marsden, M. (2016). *Trading Worlds: Afghan Merchants Across Modern Frontiers*. Hurst & Company.

Marsden, M. (2018). Islamic Cosmopolitanism out of Muslim Asia: Hindu-Muslim Business Co-Operation between Odessa and Yiwu. *History and Anthropology, 29*(1), 121–139.

Marushiakova, E., & Popov, V. (2016). *Gypsies in Central Asia and the Caucasus*. Palgrave Macmillan.

Marutyan, H. (2007). Armenia-Diaspora: Meeting in the Yerevan Center. *Handes Amsorya, 2007*, 363–428.

Marx, K. (1977 [1859]). *A Contribution to the Critique of Political Economy*. Progress Publishers.

Mathews, G. (2015). African Logistics Agents and Middlemen as Cultural Brokers in Guangzhou. *Journal of Current Chinese Affairs, 44*(4), 117–144.

Mathews, G., & Alba Vega, C. (2012). Introduction: What is Globalization from Below? In G. Mathews, G. L. Ribeiro & C. Alba Vega (Eds.), *Globalization from Below: The World's Other Economy* (pp. 1–15). Routledge.

Mathews, G., Ribeiro, G. L., & Vega, C. A. (2012). *Globalization From Below: The World's Other Economy*. Routledge.

Mauss, M. (1968). *Die Gabe: Form und Funktion des Austausches in archaischen Gesellschaften*. Suhrkamp Verlag.

Mauss, M. (2015). *Schriften zum Geld* (H. P. Hahn, M. Schmidt, & E. Seitz, Eds.). Suhrkamp Verlag.

Melkumyan, H. (2017). *Informality, Politics and Mutual Support in Flea Markets in Post-Soviet Armenia*.

Melkumyan, H. (2020). From Economic Survival to Lifestyle Choice: Flea Markets in Georgia and Armenia. *Central Asian Survey, electronic preprint*.

Mertens, M. (2019). Did Richthofen Really Coin "the Silk Road"? *The Silk Road Journal, 17*, 1–9. https://edspace.american.edu/silkroadjournal/wp-content/uploads/sites/984/2020/02/2-Mertens-Did-Richthofen-Really-Coin-the-Silk-Road.pdf

Michie, M. (2003, July 10–12). The Role of Cultural Brokers in Intercultural Science Education: A Research Proposal. *Paper presented at the 34th Annual Conference of the Australasian Science Education Research Association held in Melbourne*. http://members.ozemail.com.au/~mmichie/culture_brokers1.htm).

Mikesell, M. W. (1958). The Role of Tribal Markets in Morocco: Examples from the "Northern Zone." *Geographical Review, 48*(4), 494–511.

Miller, R. B. (2016). *Friends and Other Strangers: Studies in Religion, Ethics, and Culture*. Columbia University Press.

Mintz, S. (1961a). *Pratik: Haitian Personal Economic Relations*. Paper presented at the 1961 Annual Spring Meeting of the American Ethnological Society, Seattle & Washington.

Mintz, S. W. (1957). Aspects of the Internal Distribution System in a Caribbean Peasant Economy. *Human Organization, XV, 2*, 18–23.

Mintz, S. W. (1961b). Pratik: Haitian Personal Economic Relationships. *Proceedings of the Annual Spring Meetings, American Ethnological Society*, 54–63.

Mishler, W., & Rose, R. (2005). What are the Political Consequences of Trust? A Test of Cultural and Institutional Theories in Russia. *Comparative Political Studies, 38*(9), 1050–1078.

Miyoshi, M. (1993). A Borderless World? From Colonialism to Transnationalism and the Decline of the Nation-State. *Critical Inquiry, 19*(4), 726–751.

Morris, J., & Polese, A. (2014). *The Informal Post-Socialist Economy: Embedded Practices and Livelihoods*. Routledge.

Mörtenböck, P., & Mooshammer, H. (2008). Spaces of encounter: Informal markets in Europe. *Urbanism, 12*(3/4), 347–358.

Mosashvili, G. (2019). *China's Belt and Road Initiative and Georgia as a Participating Economy*. Paper presented at the 11th GEP-China Conference – Globalization with Chinese Characteristics: The Belt and Road Initiative and International Trade Policies, University of Nottingham, Ningbo, China.

Mühlfried, F. (2006). *Postsowjetische Feiern: Das Georgische Bankett im Wandel*. ibidem-Verlag.

Mühlfried, F. (2007). Celebrating Identities in Post-Soviet Georgia. In T. Darieva & W. Kaschuba (Eds.), *Representations on the Margins of Europe: Politics and Identities in the Baltic and South Caucasus States* (pp. 283–300). Campus Verlag.

Mühlfried, F. (2010). Citizenship at War: Passports and Nationality in the 2008 Russian-Georgian Conflict. *Anthropology Today, 26*(2), 8–13.
Mühlfried, F. (2014a). A Taste of Mistrust. *Ab Imperio, 4*, 63–68.
Mühlfried, F. (2014b). *Being a State and States of Being in Highland Georgia*. Berghahn Books.
Mühlfried, F. (2019). *Misstrauen: Vom Wert eines Unwertes*. Philipp Reclam jun. Verlag GmbH.
Mukhina, I. (2009). New Losses, New Opportunities: (Soviet) Women in the Shuttle Trade, 1987–1998. *Journal of Social History, 43*(2), 341–359.
Nadjmabadi, S. (2014). "Lost in Transit": Ressourcenförderung und Mobilität in der ostiranischen Provinz Khorassan. *Internationales Asienforum, 45*(1–2), 193–221.
Namsaraeva, S. (2018). Déjà-vu of Distrust in the Sino-Russian Borderlands. In C. Humphrey (Ed.), *Trust and Mistrust in the Economy of the China-Russia Borderlands* (pp. 37–64). Amsterdam University Press.
Nasritdinov, E. (2006). *Regional Change in Kyrgyzstan: Bazaars, Open-Air Markets and Social Networks*. Univeristy of Melbourne.
Newman, D., & Paasi, A. (1998). Fences and Neighbors in the Postmodern World: Boundary Narratives in Political Geography. *Progress in Human Geography, 22*(2), 186–207.
Ngo, T.-W. (2015). Asia and the Historicity of the Market Economy. *Verge: Studies in Global Asias, 1* (1), 44–50.
Ngo, T.-W., & Hung, E. P. W. (2018). The Political Economy of Border Checkpoints in Shadow Exchanges. *Journal of Contemporary Asia, 49*(2), 1–15. https://doi.org/10.1080/00472336.2018.1555273
Nikolotov, A. (2019). Volatile Conviviality: Joking Relations in Moscow's Marginal Marketplace. *Modern Asian Studies, 53*(3), 874–903.
Niyozov, S., & Shamatov, D. (2007). Teaching and Trading: Local Voices and Global Issues from Central Asia. *Toronto Studies in Central and Inner Asia, 8*, 281–300.
Nyíri, P. (2007). *Chinese in Eastern Europe: A Middleman Minority in a Transnational Era*. Routledge.
Nyíri, P. (2011). Chinese Entrepreneurs in Poor Countries: A Transnational, "Middleman Minority" and its Futures. *Inter-Asia Cultural Studies, 12*(1), 145–153.
Nyíri, P. (2012). Enclaves of Improvement: Sovereignity and Developmentalism in the Special Zones of the China-Lao Borderlands. *Comparative Studies in Society and History, 54*(3), 533–562.
Nyíri, P. (2017). Realms of Free Trade, Enclaves of Order. Chinese-built "Instant Cities" in Northern Laos. In M. Saxer & J. Zhang (Eds.), *The Art of Neighbouring: Making Relations across China's Borders* (pp. 57–72). Amsterdam University Press.

OECD. (2002). *Measuring the Non-Observed Economy: A Handbook*. OECD Publications Service.

Ohmae, K. (1995). *The End of the Nation State: The Rise of Regional Economies*. Free Press.

Pachenkov, O. (2011). Every City has the Flea Market it Deserves: The Phenomenon of Urban Flea Markets in St. Petersburg. In T. Darieva, W. Kaschuba & M. Krebs (Eds.), *Urban Spaces after Socialism: Ethnographies of Public Spaces in Eurasian Cities* (pp. 181–206). Campus Verlag.

Paine, R. (1969). In Search of Friendship: An Exploratory Analysis in "Middle Class" Culture. *Man, 4*(4), 505–524.

Palomera, J., & Theodora, V. (2016). Moral Economy: Rethinking a Radical Concept. *Anthropological Theory, 16*, 413–432. https://doi.org/10.1177/1463499616678097

Pantucci, R., & Lain, S. (2016). *Workshop Report: Tbilisi Silk Road Forum: Next Steps for Georgia and the Silk Road*. Royal United Services Institute for Defence and Security Studies.

Parry, J., & Bloch, M. (1989). *Money and the Morality of Exchange*. Cambridge University Press.

Paturyan, Y. (2011). (Dis)Trusting People and Political Institutions in Armenia. *Caucasus Analytical Digest, 31*.

Peebles, G. (2010). The Anthropology of Credit and Debt. *Annual Review of Anthropology, 39*, 225–240.

Pelican, M. (Ed.). (2014). *Baohan Street: An African Community in Guangzhou: Documentary Photographs by Li Dong*. Department of Cultural and Social Anthropology, University of Cologne.

Pelican, M., & Dong, L. (2017). Baohan Street: An African Community in Guangzhou. In D. L. Hodgson & J. Byfield (Eds.), *Global Africa*. University of California Press.

Pelkmans, M. (2013). Powerful Documents: Passports, Passages, and Dilemmas of Identification on the Gorgian-Turkish Border. In J. Lauth Bacas & W. Kavanagh (Eds.), *Border Encounters: Assumetry and Proximity at Europes Frontiers* (pp. 90–107). Berghahn.

Pelkmans, M., & Umetbaeva, D. (2018). Moneylending and Moral Reasoning on the Capitalist Frontier in Kyrgyzstan. *Anthropological Quarterly, 91*(3), 1044–1069.

Peoples, J., & Bailey, G. (2011). *Humanity: An Introduction to Cultural Anthropology*. Cengage Learning.

Pfeffer, G. (2016). *Verwandtschaft als Verfassung: Unbürokratische Muster öffentlicher Ordnung*. Nomos Verlagsgesellschaft.

Pfluger-Schindlbeck, I. (2005). *Verwandtschaft, Religion und Geschlecht in Aserbaidschan*. Reichert Verlag.

Pieke, F. N., Nyíri, P., & Thunø, M. (Eds.). (2004). *Transnational Chinese: Fujianese Migrants in Europe*. Stanford University Press.

Plattner, S. (1989). *Economic Anthropology*. Stanford University Press.

Platz, S. (2000). The Shape of National Time: Daily Life, History and Identity during Armenia's Transition to Independence, 1991. In D. Berdahl, M. Bunzl, & M. Lampland (Eds.), *Altering States: Ethnographies of Transition in Eastern Europe and the Former Soviet Union* (pp. 114–138). University of Michigan Press.

Polanyi, K. (1944). *The Great Transformation: The Political and Economic Origins of Our Time*. Beacon Press.

Polese, A. (2012). Who has the Right to Forbid and Who to Trade? Making Sense of Illegality on the Polish-Ukrainian Border. In B. Bruns & J. Miggelbrink (Eds.), *Subverting Borders: Doing Research on Smuggling and Small-Scale Trade* (pp. 21–38). Verlag für Sozialwissenschaften.

Polese, A., Rekhviashvili, L., & Morris, J. (2016). Informal Governance in Urban Spaces: Power, Negotiation and Resistance among Georgian Street Vendors. *Geography Research Forum, 36*, 15–32.

Portes, A. (1997). Globalization from Below: The Rise of Transnational Communities. *WPTC-98-1*.

Pourtskhvanidze, Z., & Tskhvediani, N. (2021). Cryptolanguage of Georgian Jewish Merchants. *Working Paper Series on Informal Markets and Trade, 10*.

Putnam, R. (1993). *Making Democracy Work*. Princeton University Press.

Putnam, R. (2000). *Bowling Alone: The Collapse and Revival of American Community*. Simon and Schuster.

Ram, H. (2014). A Feast for Thoughts. *Ab Imperio, 4*, 85–92. https://doi.org/10.1353/imp.2014.0108

Rasanayagam, J. (2011). Informal Economy, Informal State: The Case of Uzbekistan. *International Journal of Sociology and Social Policy, 31*(11/12), 681–696. https://doi.org/10.1108/01443331111177878

Redfield, R. (1953). *The Primitiv World and its Transformations*. Cornell University Press.

Redfield, R. (1956). *Peasant Society and Culture: An Anthropological Approach to Civilization*. Chicago University Press.

Reeves, M. (2014). *Border Works: Spatial Lifes of the State in Rural Central Asia*. Cornell University Press.

Rekhviashvili, L. (2015). Marketization and the Public-Private Divide: Contestations Between the State and Petty Traders over the Access to Public Space in Tbilisi. *International Journal of Sociology and Social Policy, 35*(7/8), 478–496.

Rippa, A. (2018). *Which Silk Road, and for Whom? Economic Corridors and the End of Proximity at China's Borders* [unpublished manuscript].

Rippa, A. (2019). Cross-Border Trade and "the Market" Between Xinjiang (China) and Pakistan. *Journal of Contemporary Asia, 49*(2), 254–271.

Robbins, J. (2004). *Becoming Sinners: Christianity and Moral Torment in a Papua New Guinea Society*. University of California Press.
Robbins, J. (2007). Between Reproduction and Freedom: Morality, Value, and Radical Cultural Change. *Ethnos, 72*(3), 293–314.
Robbins, J., & Siikala, J. (Eds.) (2014). Dumont, Values, and Contemporary Cultural Change. *Anthropological Theory, 14* (2).
Rosanvallon, P. (2008). *Counter-Democracy: Politics in an Age of Distrust*. Cambridge University Press.
Röschenthaler, U., & Socpa, A. (2017). The China Challenge: Cameroonians Between Discontent and Popular Admiration. In Y.-C. Kim (Ed.), *China and Africa: A New Paradigm of Global Business* (pp. 155–188). Palgrave Mcmillan.
Roth, S. (2013). The Making of Home, the Making of Nation: Cultural Notions of Conflict and Displacement in Post-Soviet Azerbaijan. In S. Voell & K. Khutsishvili (Eds.), *Caucasus Conflict Culture: Anthropological Perspectives on Times of Crisis* (pp. 169–194). Curupira.
Roth, S. (2016). *Making a Home in Baku: Dynamics of Housing, Family and State in Azerbaijan* (PhD). University of Halle, Halle.
Rudaz, P. (2018). Informal Entrepreneurship or "Survivalship"? Results of an Empirical Study of Self Employment, Micro-, and Small Businesses in Georgia. *Anthropological Researches, IV*, 79–89.
Rudaz, P. (2019). Trading in the Bazaars of Dordoi and Lilo at the Frontier of Formality, Entrepreneurship and Globalization. *Central Asian Survey, 39*(1), 11–32.
Rudaz, P. (2020). Trading in the Bazaars of Dordoi and Lilo at the Frontier of Formality, Entrepreneurship and Globalization. *Central Asian Survey, electronic preprint.*
Ryzhova, N. (2008). Informal Economy of Translocations: The Case of the Twin City of Blagoveshensk-Heihe. *Inner Asia, 10*(2), 323–351.
Sahlins, M. (1972). *Stone Age Economies*. Aldine-Atherton Inc.
Sahlins, M. (1999a). Two or Three Things That I Know about Culture. *The Journal of Royal Anthropological Institute, 5*(3), 399–421.
Sahlins, M. (1999b). What is Anthropological Enlightenment? Some Lessons of the Twentieth Century. *Annual Review of Anthropology, 28*, i–xxiii. doi: https://doi.org/10.2307/223385
Salisbury, R. F. (1973). Economic Anthropology. *Annual Review of Anthropology, 2*, 85–94.
Sass, M., Kovacs, O., Jaksa, R. A., & Garbovan, L. (2015). Transfer of Know-how for Small and Mid-size Businesses in Georgia, Moldova and Ukraine: White Paper Moldova. *SSRN Electronic Journal, CASE Network Reports, 122*. https://doi.org/10.2139/ssrn.2637286

Sassen, S. (2001). *Global Cities: New York, London, Tokyo*. Princeton University Press.

Sassen, S. (2006). *Territory, Authority, Rights: From Medieval to Global Assemblages*. Princeton University Press.

Sasunkevich, O. (2014). "Business as Casual": Shuttle Trade on the Belarus-Lithuania Border In J. Morris & A. Polese (Eds.), *The Informal Post-Socialist Economy*. Routledge.

Saul, M. (2018). Markets in West Africa: Karl Polanyi, Or What Sort of Social Formation. In H. P. Hahn & G. Schmitz (Eds.), *Market as Place and Space of Economic Exchange: Perspectives from Archaeology and Anthropology*. Oxbow.

Sayfutdinova, L. (2018). Taps. In A. Ledeneva & P. Zusi (Eds.), *The Global Encyclopaedia of Informality: Understanding Social and Cultural Complexity* (Vol. 1, pp. 82–85). UCL Press.

Schetter, C. (2012). Translocal Lives: Patterns of Migration in Afghanistan. *Crossroads Asia Working Paper Series, 2*, 1–17.

Schneider, J. (1969). Family Patrimonies and Economic Behaviour in Western Sicily. *Anthropological Quarterly, 42*(3), 109–129.

Schrader, H. (2006). *Spar- und Kreditvereine als Mittel zur Armutsbekämpfung in Entwicklungsländern* (p. 39). Otto-von-Guericke-Universität Magdeburg.

Schröder, P. (2020). Business 2.0: Kyrgyz Middlemen in Guangzhou. *Central Asian Survey, electronic preprint*. https://doi.org/10.1080/02634937.2019.1711023

Schröder, P., & Stephan-Emmrich, M. (2016). The Institutionalization of Mobility: Well-being and Social Hierarchies in Central Asian Translocal Livelihoods. *Mobilities, 11*(3), 420–443. https://doi.org/10.1080/17450101.2014.984939

Schumpeter, J. A. (1942). *Capitalism, Socialism and Democracy*. Harper & Brothers.

Scott, J. C. (1977). *The Moral Economy of the Peasant: Rebellion and Subsistence in South East Asia*. Yale University Press.

Serio, J. D., & Razinkin, V. (1995). Thieves Professing the Code: The Traditional Role of Vory v Zakone in Russia's Criminal World and Adaptations to a New Social Reality. *Low Intensity Conflict & Law Enforcement, 4*(1), 72–88.

Shah, A. R. (2018a). How Does China-Pakistan Economic Corridor Show the Limitations of China's 'One Belt One Road' Model. *Asia & the Pacific Policy Studies, 5*(2), 378–385. https://doi.org/10.1002/app5.224

Shah, S. (2018b). Georgia Makes Waves With Anaklia Deep-Sea Port [WWW Document]. https://emergingeurope.com/intelligence/georgia-makes-waves-anaklia-deep-sea-port/

Shahbazov, F. (2017a). Baku-Beijing Relations and China's Growing Interest in the South Caucasus. *Eurasia Daily Monitor*, 14.

Shahbazov, F. (2017b). Baku-Tbilisi-Kars Railway to Become Central Asia's Gateway to Europe. *CACI Analyst, Central Asia–Caucasus Institute*. http://cacianalyst.org/publications/analytical-articles/item/13486-baku-tbilisi-kats-railway-to-become-central-asias-gateway-to-europe.html.

Shahbazov, F. (2017c). The South-West Transport Corridor Project and the Geopolitical Reshaping of the South Caucasus. *Eurasia Daily Monitor, 14*.

Shane, S., & Venkataraman, S. (2000). The Promise of Entrepreneurship as a Field of Research. *Academy of Management Review, 25*, 217–226.

Sik, E., & Wallace, C. (1999). The Development of Open-Air Markets in East-Central Europe. *International Journal of Urban and Regional Research, 23*(4), 697–714.

Simmel, G. (1992 [1908]). *Soziologie: Untersuchungen über die Formen der Vergesellschaftung*. Suhrkamp.

Skvirskaja, V. (2019). New Trade Formations: Precarity, Pragmatic Cosmopolitanism and Long-Distance Trade in the Caucasus. *Global Networks (electronic Preprint)*, 1–17. https://doi.org/10.1111/glob.12267

Slade, G. (2009). The Georgian Mafia.*Caucasus Analytical Digest, 19*, 5–8.

Slade, G. (2012). No Country for Made Men: The Decline of the Mafia in Post-Soviet Georgia. *Law & Society Review, 46*(3), 623–649.

Smith, A. (2002 [1776]). *An Inquiry into the Nature and Causes of the Wealth of Nations*. Chicago University Press.

Smith Stegen, K., & Kusznir, J. (2015). Outcomes and Strategies in the "New Great Game": China and the Caspian States Emerge as Winners. *Journal of Eurasian Studies, XXX*, 1–16. https://doi.org/10.1016/j.euras.2015.03.002

Sombart, W. (2001 [1911]). *Die Juden und das Wirtschaftsleben*. Translated by M. Epstein as *The Jews and Modern Capitalism*. Batoche Books.

Spector, R. A. (2017). *Order at the Bazaar: Power and Trade in Central Asia*. Cornell University Press.

Sprenger, G. (2017). Goods and Ethnicity: Trade and Bazaars in Laos from a Gift Perspective: A Discussion. *Heidelberg Ethnology, 6*, 1–31.

Stammler-Gossman, A. (2011). "Winter-Tyres-for-a-Flower-Bed": Shuttle Trade on the Finish-Russian Border. In B. Bruns & J. Miggelbrink (Eds.), *Subverting Borders: Doing Research on Smuggling and Small-Scale Trade* (pp. 233–256). VS Verlag.

Steenberg, R. (2016a). The Art of Not Seeing Like a State. On the Ideology of "Informality". *Journal of Contemporary Central and Eastern Europe, 24*(3), 293–306.

Steenberg, R. (2016b). Embedded Rubber Sandals: Trade and Gifts Across the Sino-Kyrgyz Border. *Central Asian Survey, 35*(3), 405–420.

Steenberg, R. (2018). Accumulating Trust: Uyghur Traders in the Sino-Kyrgyz Border Trade after 1991. In A. Horstmann, M. Saxer, & A. Rippa (Eds.), *Routledge Handbook of Asian Borderlands* (pp. 294–303). Routledge.

Steenberg, R. (2020). The Formal Side of Informality: Non-State Trading Practices and Local Uyghur Ethnography. *Central Asian Survey, Electronic Preprint*. https://doi.org/10.1080/02634937.2019.1697207

Stefes, C. H. (2006). *Understanding Post-Soviet Transitions: Corruption, Collusion and Clientelism*. Palgrave Macmillan.

Stefes, C. H. (2008). Governance, the State and Systematic Corruption: Armenia and Georgia in Comparison. *Caucasian Review of International Affairs, 2*(2), 73–83.

Steinmüller, H. (2016). Introduction. In H. Steinmüller & S. Brandtstädter (Eds.), *Irony, Cynicism and the Chinese State* (pp. 3–13). Routledge.

Stephan-Emmrich, M., & Mirzoev, A. (2016). The Manufacturing of Islamic Lifestyles in Tajikistan through the Prism of Dushanbe's Bazaars. *Central Asian Survey, 35*(2), 157–177. https://doi.org/10.1080/02634937.2016.1152008

Sternberg, T., Ahearn, A., & McConnell, F. (2017). Central Asian "Characteristics" on China's New Silk Road: The Role of Landscape and the Politics of Infrastructure. *Land, 6* (55). https://doi.org/10.3390/land6030055.

Stewart, M. (1992). Gypsies at the Horse Fair: A Non Market Model of Trade. In R. Dilley (Ed.), *Contesting Markets: An Analysis of Ideology, Discourse and Practice* (pp. 79–96). Edinburgh University Press.

Strathern, A. (2018). The Entrepreneurial Model of Social Change: From Norway to New Guinea. *Ethnology, 11*(4), 368–379.

Strugatzky, A., & Strugatzky, B. (2012 [1972]). *Roadside Picnic*. Chicago Review Press.

Taalaibekova, G. (2018). The Changing Perception of Trade as "Real" Work: The Unmaking of Soviet Workers at the Vernissage in Armenia. *Informal Markets and Trade Working Paper Series, 8*.

Taalaibekova, G., & Melkumyan, H. (2018). Public Space Comercialised and Comodified: A Case Study od the Vernissage in Yerevan. *Anthropological Researches, IV*, 48–64.

Ter Minassian, T. (2007). *Erevan: La construction d'une capitale à l'époque soviétique*. Presses Universitaires de Rennes.

Thompson, E. T. (1971). The Moral Economy of the English Crowd in the Eighteenth Century. *Past & Present, 50*, 76–136. https://doi.org/10.1093/past/50.1.76

Tikhomirov, A. (2017). The Grammar of Trust and Distrust under State Socialism after Stalin: An Introduction. *Journal of Modern European History, 15*(3), 313–329.

Tsing, A. L. (2015). *The Mushroom at the End of the World: On the Possibility of Life in Capitalist Ruins*. Princeton University Press.

Turaeva, R. (2014). Mobile Entrepreneurs in Post-Soviet Central Asia: Micro-Orders of Tirikchilik. *Communist and Post-Communist Studies, 47*(1), 105–114. https://doi.org/10.1016/j.postcomstud.2014.02.001

Van der Laan, L. H. (1992). Migration, Mobility and Settlement of the Lebanese in West Africa. In A. Hourani & N. Shehadi (Eds.), *The Lebanese in the World: A Century of Emigration* (pp. 531–547). Tauris.

Varese, F. (2001). *The Russian Mafia: Private Protection in a New Market Economy*. Oxford University Press.

Varnavskii, P. K. (2010). Nikakikh problem net, yazyk znayu plokho, s dokumentami vse v poryadke': strategii adaptsii migrantov iz Tsentral'noi Azii v Zabaikal'e (na primere goroda Krasnokamensko) ['There Are No Problems at All, I Know the Language Badly, the Documents Are All in Order': Adaption Strategies of Central Asian Migrants in Zabaikalia, the Example of Kransokamensk]. In B. Z. Nanzatov (Ed.), *Transgranichnye migratsii v prostranstve mongol'skogo mira: istoria i sovremenost' [Transborder Migration in the Mongolian World: History and the Present-Day]* (pp. 30–58). BNTs SO RAN.

Venkov, N. A. (2022). Marketplace Decline Heads East: Neoliberal Reform, Socio-Spatial Sorting and Patterns of Decline at Sofia's Public Markets. In C. S. Sezer & R. v. Melik (Eds.), *Marketplaces: Movement, Representations and Practices*. Routledge.

Verdery, K. (1996). *What was Socialism and What Comes Next?* Princeton University Press.

Voell, S. (2015). Moral Breakdown among the Georgian Svans: A Car Accident Mediated between Traditional and State Law. In S. Voell & I. Kaliszewska (Eds.), *State and Legal Practice in the Caucasus: Anthropological Perspectives on Law and Politics*. Ashgate [unofficial maniscript].

Voell, S., Jalabadze, N., Janiashvili, L., & Kamm, E. (2014). Identity and Traditional Law: Local Legal Conceptions in Svan Villages (Georgia). *Anthropological Journal of European Cultures, 23*, 98–118.

Voell, S., & Kaliszewska, I. (2015). *State and Legal Practice in the Caucasus: Anthropological Perspectives on Law and Politics*. Routledge.

Volery, T. (2007). Ethnic Entrepreneurship: A Theoretical Framework. In D. Léo-Paul (Ed.), *Handbook of Research on Ethnic Minority Entrepreneurship: A Co-evolutionary View on Resource Management* (pp. 30–41). Edward Elgar.

Volkov, V. (2012). *Silovoje predprinimatelstvo XXI vek (Violent Entrepreneurship, XXi Century)*. European University Saint Peterburg.

Waldinger, R. (1994). The Making of an Immigrant Niche. *International Migration Review, 28*(1), 3–28.

Wang, Y. (2018). The Making of China's "Good Muslims": From Middleman Minority to Cultural Ambassadors. *The China Review, 18*(4), 131–154.

Water, H. A. (2018). The Financialization of Help: Moneylenders as Economic Translators in the Debt-Based Economy. *Central Asian Survey, 37*(3), 403–418. https://doi.org/10.1080/02634937.2018.1442317

Waterbury, J. (1972). *North for the Trade: The Life and Times of a Berber Merchant*. University of California Press.

Waterbury, J. (1973). Tribalism, Trade and Politics: The Transformation of the Swasa of Marocco. In E. Gellner & C. A. Micaud (Eds.), *Arabs and Berbers: From Tribe to Nation in North Africa* (pp. 231–158). Gerald Duckworth.

Watson, S. (2009). The Magic of the Marketplace: Sociality in a Neglected Public Space. *Urban Studies, 46*, 1577–1597.

Weber, M. ([1921] 1985). *Wirtschaft und Gesellschaft: Grundriss der verstehenden Soziologie*. LCB Mohr.

Weber, M. (1993 [1904). *Die protestantische Ethik und der "Geist" des Kapitalismus*. Frankfurt: Athenäum Hain Hadenstein.

Werner, C. (1998). Household Networks and the Security of Mutual Indeptedness in Rural Kazakhstan. *Central Asian Survey, 17*(4), 597–612.

Werner, C. (2004). Feminizing the New Silk Road: Women Traders in Rural Kazakhstan. In C. Nechemias & K. Kuehnast (Eds.), *Post-Soviet Women Encountering Transition: Nation-Building, Economic Survival, and Civic Activism* (pp. 105–126). Johns Hopkins University Press.

Wielecki, K. M. (2015). *Coping with Uncertainty: Petty Traders in Post-Soviet Russia*. Peter Lang.

Williams, C. C., Nadin, S., & Rodgers, P. (2012). Evaluating Competing Theories of Informal Entrepreneurship: Some Lessons from Ukraine. *International Journal of Entrepreneurial Behaviour & Research, 18*(5), 528–543.

Williams, C. C., & Round, J. (2007). Entrepreneurship and the Informal Economy: A Study of Ukraine's Hidden Enterprise Culture. *Journal of Development Studies, 12* (1).

Williams, C. C., Round, J., & Rodgers, P. (2009). Evaluationg the Motives of Informal Entrepreneurs: Some Lessons from Ukraine. *Journal of Development Studies, 14*(1), 59–71.

Wong, B. (1978). A Comparative Study of the Assimilation of the Chinese in New York City and Lima, Peru. *Comparative Studies in Society and History, 20*(3), 335–358.

Woodburn, J. (1998). "Sharing is not a Form of Exchange": An Analysis of Property-Sharing in Immediate-Return Hunter-Gatherer Societies. In C. M. Hann (Ed.), *Property Relations: Renewingthe Anthropological Tradition*. Cambridge University Press.

World Bank. (2012). *Fighting Corruption in Public Services: Chronicling Georgia's Reforms*. World Bank.

Wu, S. (2014). The Search for Coal in the Age of Empires: Ferdinand von Richthofen's Odyssey in China, 1860–1920. *The American Historical Review, 119*(2), 339–363.

Wulf, A. (2016). *Alexander von Humboldt und die Erfindung der Natur*. C. Bertelsmann.

Yalçın-Heckmann, L. (2001). *The Political Economy of an Azeri Wedding* (Max Planck Institute for Social Anthropology Working Papers, 28).

Yalçın-Heckmann, L. (2012). Re-thinking Citizenship in the South Caucasus. *Europe Asia Studies, 64*(9), 1724–1738.

Yalçın-Heckmann, L. (2014). Informal Economy Writ Large and Small: From Azerbaijani Herb Traders to Moscow Shop Owners. In J. Morris & A. Polese (Eds.), *The Informal Post-Socialist Economy: Embedded Practices and Liveliyhoods* (pp. 165–186). Routledge.

Yalçın-Heckmann, L. (2016). Remembering and Living on the Borderlands in the South Caucasus. In T. Bringa & H. Toje (Eds.), *Eurasian Borderlands: Spatializing Borders in the Aftermath of State Collapse* (pp. 133–158). Palgrave Macmillan.

Yalçın-Heckmann, L., & Aivazishvili, N. (2012). Scales of Trade, Informal Economy and Citizenship at Georgian-Azerbaijani Borderlands. In B. Bruns & J. Miggelbrink (Eds.), *Subverting Borders: Doing Research on Smuggling and Small-scale Trade* (pp. 187–205). VS Verlag für Sozialwissenschaften.

Yan, Y. (1996). *The Flow of Gifts: Reciprocity and Social Networks in a Chinese Village*. Stanford University Press.

Yanagisako, S. J. (2002). *Producing Culture and Capital: Family Firms in Italy*. Princeton University Press.

Yang, M. (1994). *Gifts, Favors, and Banquets: The Art of Social Relationship in China*. Cornell University Press.

Yang, M. (2018). Guanxi (China). In A. Ledeneva (Ed.), *The Global Encyclopedia of Informality* (Vol. 1, pp. 75–79). UCL Press.

Zabakhidze, M., Gabriadze, I., Beradze, R., & Khishtovani, G. (2019). Connectivity, Trade and Financial Integration of the South Caucasus Via the Belt and Road Initiative (BRI). *Caucasus Analytical Digest, 111*, 3–9. https://doi.org/10.3929/ethz-b-000368298

Zabyelina, Y. (2012). Costs and Benefits of Informal Economy: Shuttle Trade and Crime at Cherkizovsky Market. *Global Crime, 13*(2), 95–108.

Zakharova, E. (2017). Black Matsoni: The Pragmatics of the Tbilisi Street Code. *Forum for Anthropology and Culture, 13*, 247–279.

Zakharova, E. (2010). Street Life in Tbilisi as a Factor of Male Socialisation. *Laboratorium, 1*, 350–352.

Zaloom, C. (2006). *Out of the Pits: Traders and Technology from Chicago to London*. University of Chicago Press.

Zhang, J., & Saxer, M. (2017a). Introduction: Neighbouring in the Borderworlds along China's Frontiers. In J. Zhang & M. Saxer (Eds.), *The Art of Neighbouring: Making Relations Across China's Borders* (pp. 11–29). Amsterdam University Press.

Zhang, J., & Saxer, M. (Eds.). (2017b). *The Art of Neighbouring: Making Relations Across China's Borders*. Amsterdam University Press.

Zhang, W., & Alon, I. (Eds.). (2009). *Biographical Dictionary of New Chinese Entrepreneurs and Business Leaders*. Edward Elgar.

Zhou, J. (2012). *Chinese in Georgia* (ECMI Working Paper, 54).

Zimmer, C., & Aldrich, H. E. (1987). Resource Mobilization through Ethnic Networks: Kinship and Friendship ties of Shopkeepers in England. *Sociological Perspectives, 30*(4), 422–445.

Zuev, D., & Habeck, J. O. (2019). Implications of Infrastructure and Technological Change for Lifestyles in Siberia. In J. O. Habeck (Ed.), *Lifestyle in Siberia and the Russian North*. OpenBooks Publishers.

Григоричев, КВ., & Дятлов, В. И. (2017). «Китайские» рынки России: Роль в постсоциалистической трансформации (случай Иркутска). *Вестник Томского Государственного Университета, 419*, 121–132. https://doi.org/10.17223/15617793/419/16

Григоричев, К. В., Дятлов, В. И., Тимошкин, Д. О., & Брязгина, Д. Е. (Eds.). (2019). *Базар и город: люди, пространства, образы*. Иркутск: Оттиск.

Григоричев, КВ., & Тимошкин, ДО. (2019). Базар в движении: Иркутский открытый рынок как точка концентрации мобильностей. *Регионалистика, 6*(1), 26–39. https://doi.org/10.14530/reg.2019.1.26

Гузей, Я. (2015). «Русский» рынок в центре Пекина. In В. И. Дятлов & К. В. Григоричев (Eds.), *Этнические рынки в России: пространство торга и место встречи* (pp. 159–171). Иркутск: Изд-во ИГУ.

Дятлов, В. И., & Григоричев, К. В. (2015). *Этнические рынки в России: пространство торга и место встречи*. Иркутск: Изд-во ИГУ.

Лыкова, М. (1995). Время «челноков» на исходе. *Вечерний Иркутск*.

Сунь, Х. (2002). Китайско-российская народная торговля на примере рынка Ябаолу (The Sino-Russian People's Trade on the Example of theYabaolu Market). *Проблемы Даль-Него Востока, 1*, 92–106.

Захарова, Е. Ю. (2010). Тбилисская улица как среда мужской социализации. *Laboratorium, 2*, 182–204.

Index

S. Fehlings, *Traders, Informal Trade and Markets between the Caucasus and China*, Politics and History in Central Asia,
https://doi.org/10.1007/978-981-19-5205-0

The manufacturer's authorised representative in the EU is Springer Nature Customer Service Centre GmbH, Europaplatz 3, 69115 Heidelberg, Germany. If you have any concerns regarding our products, please contact ProductSafety@springernature.com

Printed and bound by CPI Group (UK) Ltd, Croydon, CR0 4YY

30/09/2026

02225228-0003